Exploring the
APPALACHIAN TRAIL™

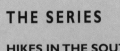

THE SERIES

HIKES IN THE SOUTHERN APPALACHIANS
Georgia ◆ North Carolina ◆ Tennessee

HIKES IN THE VIRGINIAS
Virginia ◆ West Virginia

HIKES IN THE MID-ATLANTIC STATES
Maryland ◆ Pennsylvania ◆ New Jersey ◆ New York

HIKES IN SOUTHERN NEW ENGLAND
Connecticut ◆ Massachusetts ◆ Vermont

HIKES IN NORTHERN NEW ENGLAND
New Hampshire ◆ Maine

Exploring the
APPALACHIAN TRAIL

HIKES in the
SOUTHERN
APPALACHIANS

Georgia North Carolina Tennessee

DORIS GOVE

STACKPOLE BOOKS

Mechanicsburg, Pennsylvania

Exploring the Appalachian Trail™ Series Concept: David Emblidge

Series Editor: David Emblidge

Managing Editor: Katherine Ness

Researcher and Editorial Assistant: Marcy Ross

Volume editor: Dale Evva Gelfand

Book design and cover design: Walter Schwarz, of Figaro, Inc.

Page make-up: Figaro, Inc.

Cartography: Jean Saliter and Lisa Story, of Figaro, Inc. (topo maps); Peter Jensen, of OpenSpace (trail drawing); Kevin Woolley, of WoolleySoft, Ltd. (trail profiles)

Cover photograph: Round Bald, Tenn., Henry Lafleur

Page viii: photograph by David Emblidge

Page xii: photograph of Springer Mt. AT plaque (southern terminus) by Doris Gove

Interior photographs: See credits with each image.

Proofreader: Rodelinde Albrecht

Indexer: Letitia Mutter

©2012 David Emblidge—Book Producer

Trail profiles ©2012 Stackpole Books

EXPLORING THE APPALACHIAN TRAIL™ is a registered trademark of David Emblidge—Book Producer.

Library of Congress Cataloging-in-Publication Data for the first edition
Gove, Doris.
    Hikes in the southern Appalachians / David Emblidge.— 1st ed.
        p. cm.—(Exploring the Appalachian Trail)
        ISBN 0-8117-2668-1
    1. Hiking—Georgia—Guidebooks. 2. Hiking—
North Carolina—Guidebooks. 3. Hiking—Tennessee—Guidebooks.
4. Hiking—Appalachian Trail—Guidebooks. 5. Georgia—
Guidebooks. 6. North Carolina—Guidebooks. 7. Tennessee—
Guidebooks. 8. Appalachian Trail—Guidebooks. I. Title. II. Series.
GV199.42.G46G68   1998
917.504 '43—dc21   97-50085
                                                                          CIP

ISBN 978-0-8117-1063-3

Printed in the United States   **31088100774700**
10 9 8 7 6 5 4 3 2 1

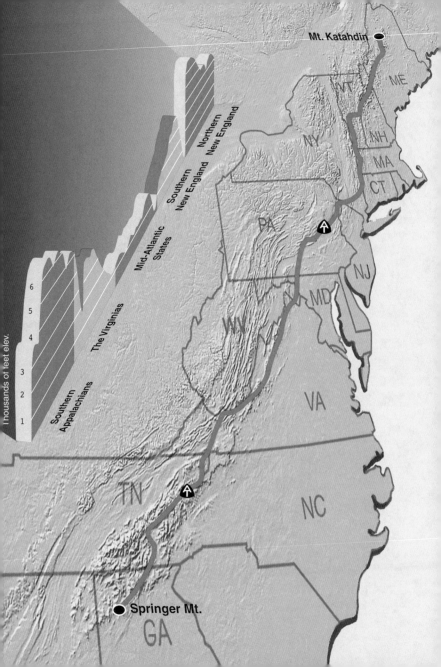

Mt. Katahdin

ME

VT

NY

NH

MA

CT

PA

NJ

MD

WV

VA

NC

TN

GA

Springer Mt.

Northern New England

Southern New England

Mid-Atlantic States

The Virginias

Southern Appalachians

Thousands of feet elev.

6

5

4

3

2

1

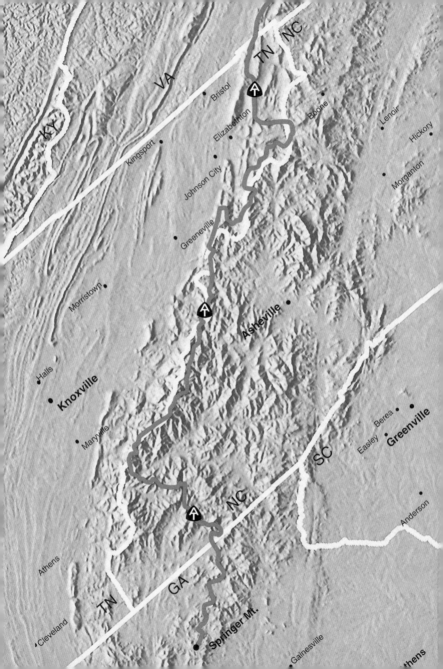

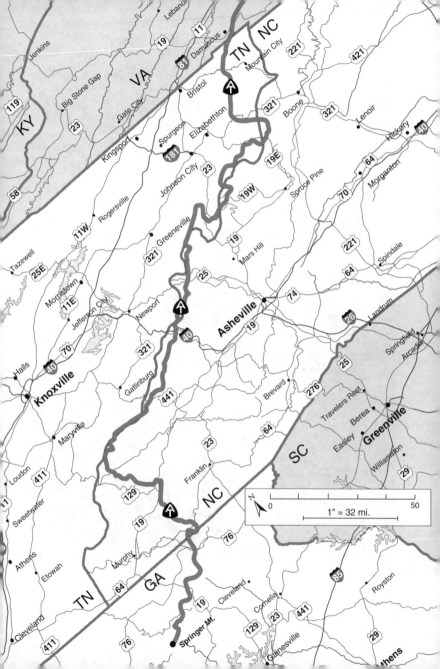

Contents

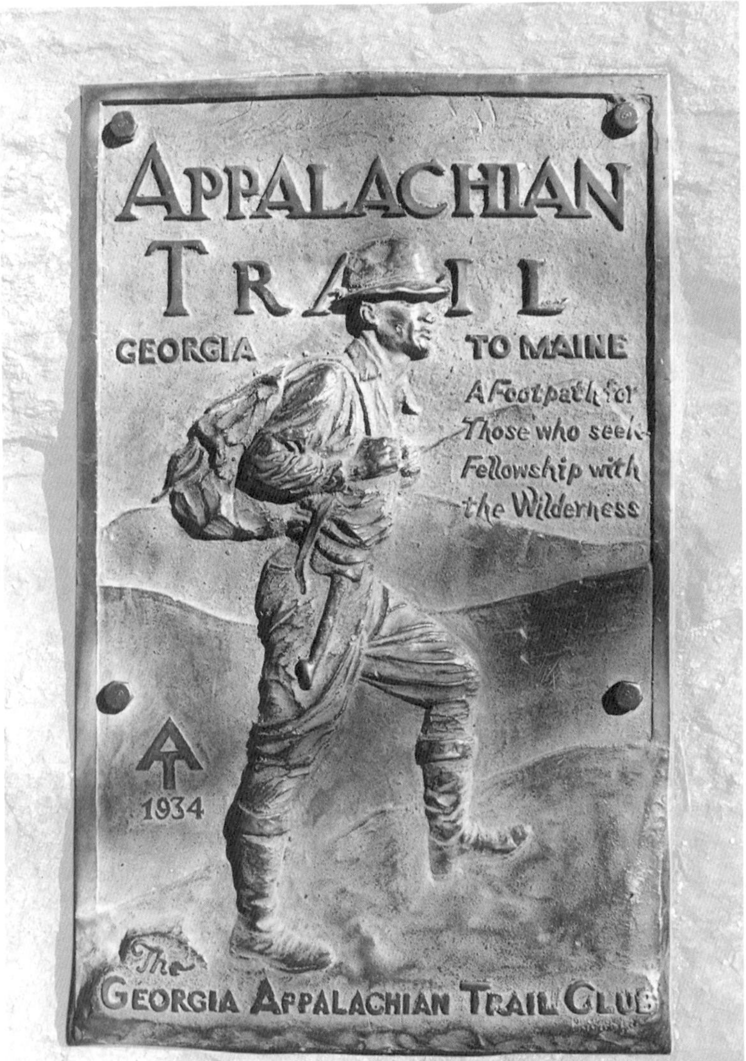
APPALACHIAN
TRAIL
GEORGIA
TO MAINE
A Footpath for
Those who seek
Fellowship with
the Wilderness
AT
1934
The
GEORGIA APPALACHIAN TRAIL CLUB

Introduction

Welcome to *Exploring the Appalachian Trail.* We're glad to have you join us for what promises to be a fine outdoor adventure.

You may not have realized it when you bought or borrowed this book, but if the truth be told, it's all about a long-standing love affair. The authors of the hiking guides in this series have been in love with the Appalachian Trail since before we can remember. And we've come to believe that if you truly love something, you will probably act positively to protect it. So when we invite you to join us in walking on the trail, we're also inviting you to let yourself be seduced, indeed to go ahead and take the leap into a sweet and enduring love affair of your own. But then be sure to act on the responsibility created as a by-product of that love. It's called service and support. In the section below called "Joining Up," you can read more about how each of us can contribute to the health and continuing life of the trail. The Appalachian Trail will give you many gifts. Be sure you give some back.

Unlike other good books about walking the Appalachian Trail, this one will encourage you to slow down, to yield to the many temptations offered up freely by nature and by the social-historical world along the trail. Benton MacKaye, considered by most to be the chief visionary of the early Appalachian Trail, once defined the purpose of hiking on the AT as "to see, and to *see* what you see." MacKaye was something of a romantic, and we know he read Emerson, who instructs us to "Adopt the peace of Nature, her secret is patience." We can't improve on that.

Our intention is to help you plan and carry out a wide variety of hikes on the nation's longest continuously marked footpath, surely one of the most famous walking trails in the world. We'll guide you from point A to point B, to be sure, but as far as this book is concerned, it's what happens for you *between* points A and B that counts the most.

If the goal of hiking on the Appalachian Trail is to come home refreshed in body, rejuvenated in mind, and renewed in spirit, then along with the fun of being outside in the mountains, a little exercise will be required. The most obvious exercise is of the muscular variety. Less obvious but just as rewarding is the mental kind, and it's here that the books in this series will help you the most. The famous world traveler Sven-Olof Lindblad said, "Travel is not about where you've been but what you've gained. True travel is about how you've enriched your life through encounters with beauty, wildness and the seldom-seen."

In these AT hiking books, we'll pause to inspect the rocks underfoot and the mammoth folding and crunching of the entire Appalachian landscape. We'll take time to listen to birds and to look closely at wildflowers. We will deliberately digress into the social history of the area the AT passes through, thinking sometimes about industry, other times about politics, and now and then about a well-known or an obscure but colorful character who happened to live nearby. We'll explore trail towns and comment on trail shelters and campsites (they're not all alike!). And to help make you a savvy hiker (if you aren't already), we will offer up some choice bits of hiker wisdom that just might get you out of a jam or make your load a bit lighter to carry.

This is a participatory book. You will enjoy it and profit from it most if you carry a small notebook and a pen or pencil, and perhaps even a camera and a birding book or a wildflower guide or a guide to some other aspect of the natural world (see the Bibliography for suggestions). Bring a compass and use our maps, or better yet, supplement the maps in this book with the more detailed ones available from the Appalachian Trail Conference and other local sources (see page 10 and the Bibliography).

Chatting with your walking companions is a delightful thing to do some of the time while out on the trail, but the more noise you make, the less wildlife you'll see, and besides, it's hard for anyone to be both in conversation and simultaneously in close observance of the real details of the natural realm. Try hard to make some part of every hike a *silent walk,* during which you open all your senses and your imagination to drink in the marvelous environment of the Appalachian Trail.

The Appalachian Trail in the Southern Appalachians: Landscape and Environment

From Springer Mt. to Damascus, the Appalachian Trail moves northeast through Georgia, swings northwest across North Carolina, and resumes a northeast course along the Smoky Mts. and the Tennessee / North Carolina border—a giant zigzag of mostly ridgetop hiking. After Roan Mt., the AT heads north through Tennessee to the Virginia border and Damascus. The 450 AT miles in this volume are divided into 45 hikes almost completely on land protected by either the U.S. Forest Service or the National Park Service. The highest elevation of this volume (and of the entire AT) is at Clingmans Dome (6643 ft.). The lowest elevation (about 1300 ft.) is at Hot Springs, North Carolina, where the AT crosses the French Broad River. Two areas, the Smokies and Roan Mt., include long stretches above 6000 ft. The next volume in this series covers the AT in Virginia and West Virginia.

Some of the hikes are near towns and are easy to get to; others are deep in national forest and require long drives on gravel roads. Most of the hikes challenge hikers with steep or rocky sections and reward them with views, remoteness, or special features like waterfalls.

Long, slow climate changes of glacial and interglacial periods contributed to the plant and animal diversity of the southern Appalachians. Though no glaciers came this far south, northern species, such as firs, beeches, and spruces, found refuge here during the cold times; tropical species, such as pawpaw and opossums, moved north during warm periods. Like many pioneers, the visiting plants and animals found places where they could survive. The flora and fauna of today reflect this rich history and contribute to complex ecological relationships.

If you have never visited the southern Appalachians, a colorful introduction is *The Smithsonian Guide to Historic America: The Carolinas and the Appalachian States*.

Joining Up
We urge you, our fellow hikers, to honor the thousands of volunteers and paid workers who built and who nowadays maintain the Appalachian

Trail by becoming a volunteer and a financial supporter yourself. Join your local hiking club and join any or all of the following organizations, each of which contributes to the survival of the Appalachian Trail:

Appalachian Trail Conservancy, P.O. Box 807, Harpers Ferry, WV 25425

Appalachian Mountain Club, 5 Joy St., Boston, MA 02108

American Hiking Society, 1422 Fenwick Lane, Silver Spring, MD 20910

Walking Lightly on the Land
On behalf of the hiking community, we urge all hikers to manage their behavior in the woods and mountains so as to have a minimal impact on the land. The old adages are apt: Take only pictures, leave only footprints. Pack out whatever you pack in. Leave no trace. Indeed, be a sport and pack out some other careless hiker's garbage if you find it along the trail. The National Park Service, which maintains a protective corridor along the Appalachian Trail, estimates that between 3 and 4 million people use the trail every year, and the numbers are growing. In many places the ecology of the AT landscape is fragile. But fragile or not, every one of its 2150 miles is subject to abuse, even if unintended. Leave the trail a better place than you found it, and you'll take home better memories.

Soft Paths: How to Enjoy the Wilderness Without Harming It is a good general introduction to the principles of leave-no-trace hiking and camping. See the Bibliography.

We wish you good weather, warm companionship, and a great adventure. The Appalachian Trail belongs to all of us. Treat it as you would something precious of your very own.

Reader Participation

Readers are invited to respond. Please correct our mistakes, offer your perspectives, tell us what else you'd like to see in the next edition. Please also tell us where you bought or borrowed this book. Write to: Editors, Exploring the Appalachian Trail™, Stackpole Books, 5067 Ritter Rd., Mechanicsburg, PA 17055.

Acknowledgments

I am grateful for the editorial help, encouragement, and patience of David Emblidge and Dale Gelfand. Marcy Ross kept drafts, notes, e-mails, and files organized. I thank Bill Cooke for the preliminary book design. Walter Schwarz of Figaro completed the design, di-rected map and trail profile production, designed covers, and directed typesetting. At Figaro I especially thank Jean Saliter and Lisa Story for map work. Also Kevin Woolley, of Woolleysoft Ltd., for digital trail profiles, and Peter Jensen and Kathy Orlando, of OpenSpace Management, for carefully drawing the corrected AT on our maps. Thanks to each photographer, and to proofreader Rodelinde Albrecht and indexer Letitia Mutter, both of whom did a fine job.

Thanks to the following for help with hiking and shuttling: Jean Bangham, Sutton Brown, Murray Evans, Oscar Franzese, Andrew Gove, David Gove, Norwood Gove, Chris Hamilton, Henry the dog, Jamie Herman, Corinna Lain, Mike Lain, Jeff Mellor, Dee Montie, Tommy Small, Arthur Smith, Terry Tollefson, Todd Witcher, Cecilia Zanetta, Smoky Mts. Hiking Club, and Georgia AT Club. Dan "Wingfoot" Bruce, Jack Coriell, Bill Hooks, Marianne Skeen, Morgan Sommerville, and others answered many questions. Thanks to scores of naturalists whose writings and teachings reveal new wonders.

Special thanks to my hiking friend Mike ("Next time let's exchange keys *before* the hike") Lain, to my daughter, Laura ("Jeez, Mom, why don't you just join the *army*?") Mellor, and to my husband, Jeff ("*When* did you say you might be home?") Mellor.

Thanks to Cindy Spangler and Rebekah Bell for help on revision hikes. Thanks to Howard Mac-Donald (Carolina Mt. Club), Don Neal (Nantahala Hiking Club), and Joe DeLoach (Tennessee Eastman Hiking Club) for help with revision details.

A final thanks to the visionaries who designed and built the AT and to the maintainers who keep it safe and beautiful.

USE THIS BOOK as you would the counsel of a wise friend. Absorb the information that seems noteworthy to you; take heed of opinionated statements; consider the logic behind suggested strategies for getting into, and through, the kind of hike you want. But remember that your own personal preferences for length of hike, amount of effort, and things to see along the way will be just as important as—or even more than—any information you may find in these pages. Walking and hiking in the forest and mountains are intensely personal activities. There are few rules to follow, and it's not a competitive game with winners and losers. What works well for Hiker A will be a disappointment for Hiker B. Wallace Stevens gave us a poem called "Sixteen Ways of Looking at a Blackbird." This book should indicate that there are at least that many ways to complete and enjoy a hike on the AT.

How Hike Information Is Displayed Here

INFORMATION BLOCK: The hike's first page, a snapshot of the hike in the form of data and directions. Here you'll find road access information, elevation gain, distance to be walked, names of shelters, and so on. This first section gives an objective overview of the hike.

NARRATIVE: The full story—the hike you're likely to have on this section of the AT. Conditions vary widely depending on season and weather, depending on whether you're a robust twenty-something, a tottering little kid, or a slow-but-steady octogenarian. Our description of the hike aims for a middle-range hiker, in good shape, with modestly ambitious goals but not with an eye on a stopwatch or a pedometer.

Throughout the hike's narrative we cite mileages at the major waypoints and landmarks. Occasionally we indicate the amount of time needed to go from one point to another. Generally, however, we stick to mileage as a reference point because each hiker's pace is different.

The narrative also pauses to describe rocks, plants, animals, vistas, and social history seen along the way. . . and then picks up the hike again with further directions toward its destination.

TRAIL PROFILE: A rendering of the trail's up-and-down travels over the landscape, suggesting graphically how easy or challenging sections may be. The profiles are based on USGS digital elevation maps and were created via cartography software called WoolleySoft developed by Kevin Woolley, of Scotland. The linear scale on the profiles does not match the scale on the hike's topographic map (see below). Instead, the profile gives a cross-section view of the mountains and valleys with the trail running up and down as if on a straight line across the landscape. Trail profiles entail a certain degree of vertical exaggeration to make the rendering meaningful, and they do not show every hill or knob in the path.

TOPOGRAPHIC MAP: Based on USGS 1:100,000 scale maps, the hike topo map also draws on information provided on AT maps published by the Appalachian Trail Conservancy and its member trail clubs. Our scale is usually 1 inch to 1 mile—or as close to that as the page trim size and length of the hike will allow. These maps show actual elevations (read about contour lines on page 8), usually in feet. They also show the compass direction (north) and important waypoints along the trail. See the map legend on page 7. For most day hikes, the maps in this book will serve well. For extended backpacking in the wild backcountry or high mountains, we recommend using Appalachian Trail Conservancy or Appalachian Mountain Club maps.

Note: Some USGS maps have not been updated for several years and may not show recent trail relocations. Follow the dark green line of the AT on the maps in this book. You may see the old AT outlined in gray on the map. In some cases the old path is open and usable, but in many it's not. Check the narrative and consult local trail clubs before hiking on discontinued sections of the AT.

ITINERARY: A summary of the hike in table format, listing important waypoints noted in the narrative and shown on the topo map and/or the trail profile. Both the narrative and the itinerary describe the hike as either a south-to-north (most common) or north-to-south walk. Thus, in a S-N itinerary, directions to turn left (L) or right (R) mean "left when walking northward on the trail" and "right when walking northward on the trail," respectively. On a N-S itinerary, the reverse is true.

Bear in mind that "north" and "south" as used along the AT are not always literally true. The trail is said to run north from Georgia to Maine, but at any given point, even if you're walking "northward toward Maine," the footpath may veer to the west or east, or even briefly southward before resuming its generally northward direction. That's why in the narrative and itinerary we generally use "left" and "right" rather than compass directions. Inexperienced AT hikers simply have to orient themselves correctly at the start of the hike: Make sure you know whether you're following the trail to the north or south, and keep that in mind as you proceed. Then, "left" and "right" in the narrative and itinerary will be easy to follow. In any case, always carry a compass.

Note: In keeping with the tradition of showing north at the top of maps, we structure the itineraries with north always at the top of the table, south at the bottom. Thus, for a S-N hike, you will find the "Start" at the bottom (south) end of the itinerary, and you should read upward. "End" will be at the top (north) end of the table. We give mileage in both directions: the left-hand column goes S-N; the right-hand column goes N-S. Remember that *access trail* mileage must be added to miles walked on the AT itself. We total both mileages for you on the itinerary. Elevations are given in both feet and meters (feet elsewhere in this book). To construct our itineraries, we relied on walking the trail, taking careful notes, and then verifying by reference to other trail guides, especially the Appalachian Trail Conservancy and member club trail guides. Published trail guides, USGS maps, and ATC maps sometimes disagree by as much as a few tenths of a mile (distance) or a few feet (elevation).

SIDEBAR: In some hikes, special topics are discussed in a box set off from the narrative. The sidebars are listed in the table of contents.

Abbreviations
Abbreviations commonly used in this book:

AHS, American Hiking Society
AMC, Appalachian Mountain Club
ATC, Appalachian Trail Conservancy
CCC, Civilian Conservation Cops
USFS, U.S. Forest Service
USGS, U.S. Geological Survey

Geographic Organization
The hikes included in this volume follow the Appalachian Trail from south to north. Most of the hikes are described as south-to-north walks, but many are suitable to walking the opposite way, too. A few hikes are best done from north to south. Pay attention to the suggested direction. We have avoided some wicked climbs by bringing you down, rather than up, certain nasty hills.

Maps: Legends, Skills, Sources

🏃🏃	Start or End of hike
Ⓟ	Trailhead parking
V	Viewpoint
⚠	Camping
▮	Lean-to (a.k.a. Shelter) (anything three-sided)
🏠	Cabin, Lodge, Hut (anything enclosed)
Ⓦ	Water (spring or other source)
Ⓣ	Toilet (outhouse, privy, or better)
El.	Elevation
🍁	Natural History Site
🏛	Historic / Cultural Site

━━━━━━━━━━🔺━━━━━━━━━
Appalachian Trail (solid dark green)

━ ━ ━ ━ ━ ━ ━ ━
Appalachian Trail — before Start and after End of hike

━━━━━━━━━━━━━━━━━━━
Appalachian Trail — planned relocation

• •
Access Trail (to/from AT) or side (spur) trail

SCALE—Unless otherwise noted, approximately 1 inch = 1 mile.

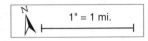

COMPASS DIRECTION AND DEVIATION— The scale bar shows the compass direction North. The north shown on the map is "true" or "grid" north, essentially a straight line to the north pole, whereas the north you see on your compass is "magnetic" north, usually a few degrees different due to the earth's magnetic field. Along the AT, magnetic north deviates from true or grid north by several degrees *west*. The farther north one goes, the greater the deviation. Throughout the southern Appalachians (Georgia–North Carolina), the deviation is a scant 1° west.

CONTOUR INTERVAL—See "Contour Lines" below. Contour intervals on the USGS topographic maps used as the base for the hiking maps in this book are all 50 meters (164.04 ft.)

Reading and planning your hikes with topographic maps can be fun and is certainly useful. Every hiking party should have at least one competent map reader. Often, if there are children aboard, they will be eager to follow the hike's progress on the topographic map. Here are a few pointers for beginning map readers.

CONTOUR LINES—All the hiking maps in this series of guides are based on official topographic maps, which represent the three-dimensional shape of the land with contour lines (CLs). Typically, CLs are drawn at fixed intervals, for example, 20 meters, meaning that between each pair of lines in our example there is a rise or fall of 20 meters in the landscape.

In this example, the CLs are close together, suggesting a steep climb or descent:

In this example, the CLs are farther apart, suggesting a gently sloping or nearly flat landscape:

LINEAR SCALE—To understand CLs fully, they must be related to the *linear scale* of the map. This relationship gives a sense of vertical rise or fall as it spreads out horizontally across the landscape. Thus, if 1 inch = 1 mile and if there are many CLs clustered in, say, a ½-inch section of trail, it's safe to assume that this ½-mile section of the trail will be steep, going up or down, depending on your direction.

MAP SOURCES— All maps in this series are derived from United States Geological Survey topographic maps. Each of our maps is a small slice of a USGS topo map. We have updated relevant AT information (some USGS maps are 10 or more years old; the AT has moved at several points). The original map scale of 1:100,000 is enlarged here generally to about 1:62,000 (around 1 inch = 1 mile) for readability. A 1:100,000-scale map is not practical to carry on the trail. USGS maps scaled at a more convenient 1:62,000 are easy to read as trail maps, but a day's hike may cut across several maps or use only a tiny portion of one large map—an unwieldy affair when hiking.

For short day hikes near main roads, we recommend using the maps in this book. For longer hikes, hikes in remote areas, overnight trips, or serious backpacking, we advise using official AT maps from the Appalachian Trail Conservancy or supplementary maps and guides (see page 10).

Bookstores and outdoor outfitters in towns near the Appalachian Trail usually stock the USGS quadrangles (1:62,500 or 1:24,000) for the local area. USGS maps can also be ordered by telephone (see "Useful Information" and the Bibliography). If you do not know the USGS map name (see the "Useful Information" list for maps used in this book), be sure to indicate (a) the portion of the AT you want to hike by providing nearby cities, towns, rivers, or other landmarks and (b) the scale you prefer. Anything over 1 inch = 1 mile will be impractical for hiking.

The Appalachian Trail Conservancy publishes a set of color-shaded topographic hiking maps for almost the entire length of the trail (excluding the national parks through which the AT passes). The scale is generally 1:38,750. This translates to about 1⅝ inches = 1 mile. In other words, much more detail than on the USGS quadrangles and more than we can show in a book of this size. See your local bookseller or outdoor outfitter, or call the ATC (see "Useful Information"). A catalogue is available. For serious hikers and for any overnight or backcountry hiking on the Appalachian Trail, we strongly recommend these fine maps.

Trails Illustrated (distributed by National Geographic) publishes more than fifty maps of national parks; these include important sections of the Appalachian Trail in Great Smoky Mts. National Park and Shenandoah National Park. These full-color, large-format maps (printed on waterproof, tear-resistant recycled paper) provide detailed topographic information and descriptions of local flora and fauna. A 3-D overview map is an enjoyable bonus. These are metric maps. The scale is 1:100,000, roughly ⅝ inch = 1 mile. A metric conversion chart is provided. See your local bookseller or outdoor outfitter, or contact Trails Illustrated (see "Useful Information" and the Bibliography).

For the AT in the Chattahoochee (Georgia), Pisgah (North Carolina), and Cherokee (Tennessee) national forests, maps and current information are available at ranger stations for each district. The Great Smoky Mts. Association publishes *Hiking Trails of the Smokies* and an inexpensive map of trails, distances, shelters, backcountry campsites, and road accesses. Also useful are *Hiking Trails of the Great Smoky Mountains* by Kenneth Wise and *Wilderness Trails of Tennessee's Cherokee National Forest*, edited by Will Skelton; *Highland Trails* by Kenneth Murray; *The Hiking Trails of North Georgia* by Tim Homan; *North Carolina Hiking Trails* by Alan de Hart; and *The Best of the Great Smoky Mountains National Park* by Russ Manning and Sondra Jamieson. For road access in North Carolina and Tennessee, consider buying the DeLorme Atlas and Gazetteer for each state (DeLorme Mapping, P.O. Box 298, Freeport, Maine, 04032). These books are all updated periodically and are available at bookstores, outdoor outfitters, and at national park visitors centers.

Driving Time to the Trailhead

A factor frequently overlooked when planning a hike is the driving time required to reach the trailhead or to get back to civilization at day's end. When a substantial number of miles must be traveled from a major highway or town to get up into the mountains to the trailhead, we tell you in the information block. You must be sure to leave sufficient time to get to the starting point. Positioning two cars (finish and start) takes even longer.

Remember that many Appalachian Trail access roads are "secondary" at best. Some are decidedly unkind to low-chassis, two-wheel-drive cars. Some are impassable in wet weather and some are closed in winter. Travel to the trailhead can be slow and dicey. Read our instructions carefully. Plan ahead.

Some USFS Trail heads now have parking fees.

Choosing Your Hike / Effort Required

In this book we rate hikes by three levels of "effort required": easy, moderate, and strenuous. Some hikes are a mix of easy, moderate, and strenuous sections.

If little kids or folks with disabilities might find a hike too rugged, we tell you. If there are difficult water crossings, perhaps varying seasonally, we say so.

But remember, our judgments are somewhat subjective.

Easy: gentle ups and downs, fairly smooth path, few obstacles.

Moderate: elevation gain or loss of up to 1000 feet; narrower, rocky path; some obstacles (for example, creek crossings with no bridge).

Strenuous: elevation gain or loss of more than 1000 feet; steep ups and downs; difficult, challenging path;

numerous obstacles; possibly unsuitable for young children or the infirm.

Blazing

A "blaze" (from the Old English *blœse*, meaning "torch") is a bright painted mark (about 6 inches x 2 inches) on a tree, post, or rock indicating the path of a hiking trail. The Appalachian Trail is blazed in white (rather easy to see even in fog, though tough to follow in brightly dappled sunlight), all the way from Georgia to Maine. It's the same in each direction, south–north or north–south.

Side trails maintained as part of the AT (such as trails to springs, shelters, or vistas) are blue-blazed, while other trails (Bartram, Duncan, Benton MacKaye, or any Forest Service trail) have blazes with distinctive colors and shapes as described in the hike narratives. AT blazing policy varies in the three states in this volume. In the Smokies and in designated wilderness areas (especially in Georgia), blazes may be up to 0.2 mi. apart on stretches of trail with no intersections. In places where the trail is hard to see, such as grass balds or the thick spruce woods of Unaka Mt., blazes are placed so that from one blaze you can see the next one.

All trail intersections in the Smokies are marked with mileage signs. All AT trailheads at major road crossings are marked with blazes, an AT mileage sign, an ATC metal "Welcome" sign, or a USFS AT sign. Do not start a hike without seeing one of these signs. If you haven't seen a blaze for several minutes, turn around and look back. If you still don't see one, backtrack to the last blaze to make sure you haven't left the AT. In summer, weeds may grow up and hide the white blazes; take extra care.

Two blazes, one above the other, indicate a turn coming in the trail. In some states, if the upper blaze is positioned to the left, look for a left turn, and vice versa.

Estimating Hiking Times

An average adult hiker's pace is about 2.0 miles per hour on the flat. For every 1000-foot gain in elevation, add 30 minutes of time to your estimate. Thus an 8-mile hike up a 2500-foot mountain might take you 5¼ hours. This formula does not account for rests, mealtimes, or lollygagging to smell the flowers or talk to the bears. With a full backpack, little kids in tow, or slippery conditions, obviously you would add more time.

We recommend that you keep a record of your time and distance and the hiking conditions for a half-dozen hikes, and then compare your averages to ours. You'll soon see whether our numbers match yours and if not, how much time you need to add or subtract from our estimates.

Day Hikes / Overnight Backpacking Hikes

The majority of the hikes in this book can be done as day hikes. Some day hikes can be conveniently strung together to make overnight backpacking trips of 2 or more days' duration. And some hikes are manageable only as overnight backpacking trips.

The general rule: the more wilderness there is to traverse, the less likely it is that you can pop in and out for a day hike only. Read the information block carefully, and look at the hike south or north of the one you're considering to see whether a linkage is feasible.

Avoiding the Crowds

A great debate is raging: Is the AT now overused, too busy to be enjoyable, too tough on the land to be justifiable? Are we approaching, or are we already at, the point where reservations will have to be made for floor space in an AT shelter? (In fact, in some southern sections— Great Smoky Mts. National Park, for example—some space in the shelters is reserved for thru-hikers or other long-distance hikers only.)

We don't mean to equivocate, but the answer seems to be yes and no. Collectively, the authors of this series have hiked thousands of AT miles over several decades. Far more often than not, we have had the trail essentially to ourselves, passing only a few people per day. Inevitably, however, certain sites on the trail (beautifully located shelters, or summits with great views or symbolic significance, for example) attract crowds, especially on weekends and most especially in midsummer or at fall foliage time. The southern section of the AT is busy with hundreds of would-be thru-hikers in early spring. Don't expect to be alone on Springer Mt. in April.

It doesn't require a graduate degree in engineering to figure out a plan to avoid these crowds or to avoid swelling them yourself. The best time to be alone on the trail is midweek. No offense to kids or parents (we love 'em all), but May, before the kids leave school, and August, after they're back in, are great times to find warm-weather solitude on the AT. If you can swing it, why not work on Saturday (or even Sunday) and hike on Sunday and Monday (or better yet Monday and Tuesday). We've tried it with success.

If you can't hike midweek and are headed for peaks or shelters that are likely to be overcrowded, start out early enough to permit you to move on to another site in daylight if your first target has already hung out the "No Vacancy" sign. When the shelter or tent sites are full, accept the bad news and walk on. Carving out an impromptu tent site is generally discouraged except in extremely bad weather. Carry a detailed map. Study it carefully before leaving home to locate the alternative site you may need in a pinch.

Circuit or Loop Hikes / Shuttle Services

Ideally you have a limousine with built-in hot tub and cold drinks awaiting you at the end of the trail. Short of that, you may have to improvise a way to get back to your starting point. Whenever it's convenient and sensible from a hiking viewpoint, we have suggested how to make the hike into a circuit or loop, bringing you back, on foot, to your car or pretty close to it. There are many hikes, however, especially those in wilderness areas, where this is simply not feasible.

It's usually best if you can work out a two-car team for your hike, with one car dropped at the finish line and another driven to the starting trailhead.

Out and back: Most of our hikes are described as linear—from A to B to C. Hikers with only one car available can make many fine hikes, however, by simply going out to a well-chosen point (the mountaintop, the pond) and then reversing direction to the starting point. The mileage indicators in the Itineraries will help you decide on a turnaround point. You may be pleasantly surprised to find that when walked in the opposite direction, the same section of trail yields a very different experience — especially if one direction is steeply up and the other sharply down.

Shuttles: In some areas, and through the auspices of some local hiking clubs, shuttle services are available. For example, the Green Mountain Club in Vermont provides to its members a list of shuttle drivers, although they are few in number and require early notice and modest fees. In this book, when we know there is a reliable shuttle service that is useful on a particular hike, we tell you. If we don't make a shuttle suggestion, it's often worth asking your motel or bed-and-breakfast keeper, or calling the local Chamber of Commerce or even the local taxi company. A hunting-lodge manager helped us one time at a good price. Ask around; make new friends.

Some hikers like to position a bicycle (locked) at the end of a hike so they can ride back to their car at the starting point.

If your hiking group consists of, say, four or more people and two cars, you might swap extra car keys at the beginning of the day and send people, a car, and a key for the other car to each end of the trail. You all meet somewhere in the middle of the hike, trade stories, and perhaps share lunch. And each group finds a car waiting at day's end. Depending on roads and distances to trailheads, this system can shave a good deal of time off the car travel at the start and end of your hiking day. This is especially helpful for very long day hikes and even more so in early spring or late fall when days are short. Besides, meeting friends deep in the forest or on a mountaintop is great fun.

Early Exit Options

Our hikes range from 5 to 15 miles per day. When road crossings and parking facilities permit, we indicate points where you could leave the AT before finishing the entire hike. Sometimes such exits are convenient and safe; sometimes they should be used only for emergencies. Heed our advice. If we do not say good parking is available, don't assume there's a parking lot.

The Early Exit Options can often be used to make a loop hike out of an otherwise longish linear hike. To see your options clearly, study a good local road map.

Camping

Most of the hikes in this volume are on national forest land. Camping is allowed except where posted otherwise, and only a few of the possible campsites are mentioned in this guide. Campfires are allowed, but firewood is not always available, and only dead and down wood can be used. A small camp stove is safer and preferable for the environment. Leave no traces of your campsite, and if an area is too fragile for camping or already damaged by overuse, find another.

Tent camping is not allowed on the AT in the Smokies, and permits are required for shelter space and for tent camping at designated sites on side trails. During the thru-hiker season (March and April, but it seems to get longer each year), overnight backpackers and groups should plan on tent camping to give the thru-hikers space in shelters.

Shelters

The names may vary but the accommodations are much the same: Along the AT, about every 10 to 15 miles, you'll find three-sided lean-tos with minimalist interior decorating. Possibly a picnic table, a fire ring, an outhouse, a water source nearby. Many of these shelters have well-maintained facilities, charming names, and equally charming views. Some you wouldn't let your dog sleep in. We tell you which ones we like. Some shelters have a few tent sites nearby, but avoid sites in overused or bare-earth areas.

Except in the two national parks through which the AT passes (Great Smoky Mts., Shenandoah) and in New Hampshire's White Mt. National Forest, where shelters are reserved for thru-hikers (for a fee), the "reservations policy" is first come, first served. Certain rules apply, however: Maximum stay, 3 nights. If it's raining, squeeze in and make room for late arrivals. Clean up after yourself, and respect others' needs for quiet and privacy.

Trail Registers

At shelters and on Springer Mt., you'll find notebooks where you can, and should, write a few words for posterity and for practicality's sake. Logging in your arrival and departure time will help searchers find you if, unluckily, you get lost or hurt on the trail. But the real fun of the trail registers is adding your own thoughts to the collective wisdom and tomfoolery other hikers have already scribbled in the notebooks. The registers make great reading. A whole new literary genre! Go ahead, wax poetic or philosophical. Surely there's at least one haiku in you to express your joy at the view from the mountaintop or the first time you shook hands with a bear. . . .

Trail registers also sometimes provide helpful warnings about trail conditions (recent mud slides or bridge washouts, for example). If the weather has been wild of late, read back a few days in the register to see what previous hikers may have said about what lies ahead of you.

HIKING: THE BASICS

WHILE IT'S TRUE that we go to the woods and mountains to get away from the trappings of civilization, few of us really want to put our lives in jeopardy. Here are some recommendations every adult hiker (and Boy or Girl Scout–age youngster) should follow.

When the subject is equipment, we suggest you visit your outdoor outfitter to ask for advice or that you read back issues of *Backpacker* magazine, in print or online (see "Useful Information"). *Backpacker's* annual "gear guide" sorts through hundreds of choices and makes useful recommendations. For the truly hiking/camping gizmo-obsessed, there are on-line chat rooms (again, see *Backpacker*) where you and other similarly gadget-crazed friends can compare notes.

Boots / Shoes
Nothing is more important to a hiker than the condition of his or her feet. From this axiom derives an important rule: Wear the right boots or shoes for hiking, or stay home. Some of the easier sections of the AT can be hiked in firm running shoes or high-top basketball sneakers, but most sections require a tougher, waterproof or water-resistant boot providing non-slip soles, toe protection, and firm ankle support. Shop carefully. Go to an outdoor outfitter rather than a regular shoe store. Try on several pairs of boots, with the actual socks you intend to wear (two pair: one thin, one thick). If you buy boots by mail, trace your foot size with those socks on your feet. Save your pennies and buy the best you can afford. Gore-Tex or one of its waterproofing clones is worth the money. Check the hiking magazines' annual gear reviews (in print or on-line) for ratings of comfort, weight, durability, and price. Think of the purchase as a multiyear

investment. Shop long before the hiking season starts, and wear your boots for a good 10 to 20 miles of everyday walking before hitting the trail. Your feet will thank you.

Suggestion for kids: The better discount stores carry boot brands that are quite sufficient for a season of hiking by young people whose feet are still growing. Parents, buy your own boots first and then use your shopper's savvy to find inexpensive boots for the kids.

Clothing

Bring sufficient clothes, appropriate for rain and cold. Layers work best. Gore-Tex and other waterproof fabrics are miraculous, but a $3 emergency poncho will do in a pinch. Think about what you would need to get through a rainy night, even if you're just out for a short, sunny day hike.

A visored hat. The top of your head is the point of major heat loss, whether you're bald or not. Inexpensive hats can be found. Cruise the catalogues.

Sunglasses, in a protective case. (Rhinestone decorative motif not required.)

Cotton socks, sweatshirts, and T-shirts: avoid them. Blue jeans (essentially cotton): avoid them. Cotton is comfortable until it gets wet (from rain or perspiration). Then it's your enemy. It dries slowly and does not wick away perspiration. There are extraordinary synthetic fabrics nowadays for shirts, underwear, and long johns that will keep you warm or

cool and will let the moisture leave your body. Visit your outdoor outfitter for a wardrobe consultation. It'll be money well spent.

Wool is a miracle fabric from nature. Especially good for socks and gloves. Polartec is a miracle fabric from the high-tech world (recycled plastic bottles!). Jackets and pullovers in these miracle fabrics are what you want.

Food

Hiking eats up calories. Cold weather demands body heat, which demands calories. Diet at home. Eat high-energy foods on the trail. Carbohydrates are best. Sweets are less helpful than you might think, though a chocolate or energy bar to help you up the hill is sometimes right. It's better to eat several smaller meals en route than to gorge on a big one, unless you plan for a siesta. Digestion itself takes considerable energy. You'll find it hard to climb and digest at the same time. The hiker's fallback snack plan: (1) "Gorp," a mix of nuts, granola, chocolate chips, dried fruit, and whatever else you like. Mix it yourself at home —much cheaper than the ready-made variety at the store. (2) Peanut butter on anything. (3) Fruit. Heavy to carry but oh so refreshing. The sugar in fruit is fructose, high in energy but it won't put you to sleep.

And remember the miracle food for hikers, the humble banana. Or dried banana chips (crunch them or add water). High in potassium, bananas are your muscles' best friends because the potassium minimizes aches and cramps.

Planning menus and packing food for extended backpacking trips is a subject beyond the scope of this book. Several camping cookbooks are available, and *Backpacker* frequently runs how-to articles. Search their Web site for articles you can download. Advice: Whatever you plan to cook on the trail, try it out first, on the backpacking stove, at home. Make a list of cooking gear and condiments needed, and if the list looks long, simplify the menu. Over time you'll find camp food tricks and tastes to add to your repertoire, such as bagging breakfast granola with powdered milk in self-seal bags (just add water and stir), or choosing tough-skinned veggies like carrots, celery, or snow peas that can be eaten cooked or raw. The ever popular macaroni and cheese (available nowadays in many fancy permutations from Lipton, Kraft, et al.) can be dressed up in countless lightweight, quick-cook ways.

Whatever you plan to eat or cook on the trail, be prepared to clean up spotlessly. Leave no mess—indeed, no trace.

Food Storage

You're not the only hungry critter in the woods. Everyone from the bears to the squirrels and mice would like to breakfast on your granola and snack on your Oreos. Never keep food in your tent overnight. It's an invitation for unwanted company in the dark.

Use a drawstring food sack, wrapped in a plastic garbage bag, which you hang from a sturdy branch on a nearby tree, keeping the sack several feet out on the branch, about 10 feet off the ground and several feet below the branch. Obviously this means you must carry about 50 feet of lightweight cord (useful in emergencies too). Most shelters have cables for hanging food. The population of black bears has been increasing steadily, along with bear-human interaction. Some areas may require bear-proof canisters. Check with the USFS or the park service if you plan to camp.

Don't store your food in your backpack, either, indoors or out. Those cute little chipmunks and their bigger friends will eat a hole right through that expensive high-tech fabric.

Water

Keep drinking a little at a time all day while you hike. Dehydration is the major cause of hiker fatigue. Double or triple your normal daily intake of water.

Sadly, most of the water flowing in streams the AT crosses is polluted to one degree or another, sometimes by industry or agriculture, often by wild animals such as beavers upstream. The most common problem is a nasty protozoan known as *Giardia* from which we get stomach cramps, fever, and the runs. Trust us: you don't want it. The rule is, assume all water must be treated with either iodine tablets or a water filter. Iodine is cheap and lightweight but slow, and it leaves a somewhat unpleasant taste in the treated water (Potable Aqua is an iodine treatment that minimizes the bad taste). Hiker water filters are faster-acting but more cumbersome. They are useful elsewhere, too—on boats, at freshwater beaches, and so forth. A good investment. Look for one that screens out most bacteria, is light-weight, and pumps quickly. The most convenient water bottles are (a) wide-mouth, facilitating refill and filter attachment, and (b) equipped with a drinking tube or nipple, eliminating the need to open the bottle itself. Some hikers use chlorine drops or UV-emitting sterilizers.

When Nature Calls

Every hiker—day only or overnight backpacker—must come prepared to deal appropriately with disposal of human waste in the woods. At most shelters and many campsites along the AT there are moldering privies. Please help to keep them clean. Hikers are encouraged to urinate in the woods, a few hundred feet off the trail. Urine in the privy adds to the bad aroma.

Believe it or not, there's an entire book on the subject of defecating in the woods (see the Bibliography). Good reading on a slow day in camp, perhaps. This much you must know to do: Bring biodegradable white single-ply toilet paper in a plastic bag. Bring a little shovel (a plastic garden trowel will do). Bring a strong self-seal plastic bag to carry out used toilet paper, tampons, etc. If the forest is your toi-

let, get at least 100 feet off the trail and at least 200 feet away from any water. Dig a hole at least 8 inches deep, and cover your waste firmly. A squat is the time-tested position. See "Tennessee Privies" in Hike #26. Most shelters have moldering privies with on-site user manuals.

Weather

Basic precautions include a careful review of weather forecasts and typi-cal conditions in the area you're hik-ing—before you pack your pack or leave home. See "Useful Information" for a weather Web site. If you go ad-venturing outdoors frequently, you'll enjoy and benefit from a lightweight battery-operated weather radio that provides access to several NOAA (National Oceanic and Atmospheric Administration) channels, offering detailed forecasts 24 hours a day, with special recreational forecasts emphasizing conditions at elevations of 3000 feet and above.

Learn to forecast weather yourself by reading the clouds (particularly cumulous clouds with towering thun-derheads) and by noticing changes in animal and plant behavior that may telegraph the advent of a storm. Make it a habit to do a 360-degree sky check every hour or so to see what's coming and from which direction. If trouble is heading your way, plan ahead for emergency shelter. Get off the mountaintop or exposed ridge, where high winds and lightning are most likely to hit. Don't sit under a big rotting tree with branches waiting to clunk you on the head. When lightning is likely, avoid all metal objects (fire towers, tent poles, pack frames, etc.). Do find a dry, wind-protected spot (the downwind side of overhanging boulders is good), and lay a plan to make it your home for a few hours.

Wet weather often brings cool or cold temperatures. Wet clothing or a wet sleeping bag can exacerbate your sense of chill. Hypothermia can set in quickly, especially if you're fatigued or anxious. Even day hikers should carry extra clothing and something, if only a big plastic garbage bag, to cover themselves and their pack. Overnight backpackers, anywhere on the AT, must be ready for the worst. Keep rainwear light and simple so you won't resent carrying it on a sunny day.

See "Unfriendly Weather," in Hike #8.

First Aid

Outfitters such as Campmor and REI (excellent catalogues) offer first-aid kits for everyone from the day hiker to the Mt. Everest climber. Buy from them or patch together your own kit, based on the contents listed in the catalogues. A waterproof container is a must. Be prepared for cuts, scrapes, burns, blisters, sprains, headaches. Include sunscreen if exposure is likely. A lightweight first-aid manual is not a bad idea, either.

One essential is moleskin, a skin-covering adhesive, thicker than a Band-Aid but soft enough to wrap around an unhappy toe. Many a hike has been ruined by blisters. At the first sign (heat, burning, tingling feelings on toes or heels), slap on the moleskin and leave it there until you're back home. Insurance against blisters is cheap: two pairs of (dry!) socks. And break in your new hiking boots *thoroughly* before you hit the trail.

Further insurance: bring a few feet of dental floss. If your teeth don't use it, a sewing job might.

Include a little but loud whistle in your first-aid kit. You might need to call for help.

If first aid is foreign to you, by all means take a course, with CPR (artificial respiration) training, from the local Red Cross. For parents hiking with kids, this is a must. For kids, join the Scouts and earn that First Aid merit badge.

Hiking Alone

There are real pleasures to be had from hiking alone. Generally, however, it's not recommended. Whether you hike alone or in a group, take pains to let someone know your plans (route, estimated times of departure and arrival, what to do if you don't check back in). Often a hiker who wants to walk alone can have that pleasure, letting fellow hikers know that by day's end he or she will rejoin the group.

Hiking in Groups

Keep your group size down to fewer than ten people. Even that many is stretching what the trailside facilities can bear. Large groups tend to overwhelm smaller ones, yet everyone has the same rights to enjoy the space and the quiet on the trail. Don't take a busload of kids on the trail. Find volunteers who will lead sections of a group with at least a mile or 30 minutes between them.

Women Hikers

Statistically, the Appalachian Trail is one of the safest places a woman (or a man) can be in the United States. But there have been some problems with harrassment, and there have been some cases of violence, even a few tragic murders. Play it safe. Don't hike alone. Be sensible—inappropriate clothing may attract the wrong kind of attention. Avoid the rowdy set sometimes found at shelters near road crossings or towns. If you arrive at a shelter and find suspicious people there, move on.

Taking Children on the Trail

By all means, do take the kids. The environment of the Appalachian Trail and the activities of climbing, exploring, and camping will engage the imagination and channel the energies of almost every kid, including those whose regular turf is the city street.

Adult hikers just need to remember that a few things are different about kid hikers. Kids' attention spans are (usually) shorter than grown-ups'. Plan to break your hike into smaller units with something special to do in each part—birds here, lunch there, rock collecting next, photography from the mountaintop, writing messages in the trail registers. Give a kid a

short-term achievable project linked to today's hike (such as collecting as many different-shaped leaves as you can from the ground beneath the trees), and you'll probably have a happy, satisfied kid hiker by evening.

Most kids love hiking and camping gear. Get them involved in planning, shopping, packing for, and executing the hike, especially the camping portion. Let them make breakfast. Teach them to set up the tent; then get out of the way. Take pictures and make a family hiking photo album: it's a memory bank for years to come. Put a map on your children's wall at home and mark the trails they have hiked, the peaks they have climbed. A sense of accomplishment is priceless.

Be realistic, too, about what kids can endure on the hiking trail. Their pain (and boredom) thresholds are lower than most adults'. Don't let blisters happen to kids; check their feet at lunchtime. Bring a book to read, or a miniature chess set if they're old enough to play, in case of rain. Anticipate your own behavior in an emergency situation. If you panic, the kids will. If you're calm, know where to go for help, and know how to keep dry and warm, most kids will rise to the occasion and come home strengthened by the adventure.

Parking

Do not leave a sign on your car saying where you're going or when you'll return. Try not to leave anything (visible) in your car that might interest burglars. Avoid camping at shelters located very close to easily accessible parking lots. Respect the AT's immediate neighbors by not parking on their private property.

Some USFS parking areas charge a small fee.

Hunting

The Smokies is a DMZ (no firearms), but hunting is allowed in national forests. Most of fall is hunting season for something. Keep a blaze orange vest or some brightly colored clothing in your pack and wear it while hiking. Check with the national forest ranger station for current hunting schedules. If you see hunters, ask them what season it is.

PACKING YOUR PACK

Backpacks and Day Packs

It's not quite a science, but it's certainly an art. An incorrectly loaded backpack (badly packed on the inside or poorly fitted or adjusted to your torso and shoulders) can wreck even a sunny day on the world's loveliest trail. Some tips: Fanny packs, worn at hip level, are great for short day hikes as long as you can carry sufficient water, food, clothing, first aid, and map and compass. Less than that and the pack is too small.

Day packs carry proportionately more but without the frame that supports a backpacking pack. For both day packs and true backpacks, similar packing rules apply. Start at the outdoor outfitter. Have a knowledgeable salesperson fit the pack (with realistic dummy weights inside) to your specific torso. Walk around, bend over, squat, and be sure you're comfortable and stable.

At home, make a packing list with items categorized carefully (food, kitchen, first aid, clothes, stove and fuel, etc.). Jettison anything unnecessary. Roll your clothes. Pack one thing inside another (the Chinese box method). Then use the following scheme for stuffing the pack:

Keep weight distributed equally on the horizontal plane, but on the vertical, pack the lightweight items (like a sleeping bag) down low and the heavyweight items (food, water, tent) up high. Keep the heavier items close to your body. But be sure to pad any sharp-edged items so as not to poke you or to rip the pack fabric. Use the pack's outside pockets for a water bottle, fuel bottles, and smelly garbage.

Last, buy a rainproof pack cover, or make one from a heavy-duty plastic garbage bag. Your clothing and sleeping bag will be glad you did.

Pack this book and any electronic devices in ziplock bags.

Flashlight

Even a day hiker should carry a lightweight flashlight, just in case. In winter, early spring, and fall, daylight can disappear quickly, especially if the weather turns bad or you lose time by being temporarily lost. A slim flashlight that's wearable in an elastic headband is a good investment.

Check the batteries before leaving home. Bring an extra bulb.

Matches

Even if you don't intend to camp out and have a campfire, bring a supply of waterproof matches or a cigarette lighter. If you're forced to overnight in the woods, a fire may be good company indeed.

Jackknife

A multipurpose pocketknife will do. It needn't have a built-in chain saw or an eyebrow pencil, but a can opener, a Phillips screwdriver, and tweezers are handy.

Weapons

We strongly discourage hikers from carrying any kind of weapon. Guns are prohibited in the Smokies.

Cellular Phones

People have been hiking safely and contentedly in the woods for several thousand years without the aid or comfort of cellular phones. This is still possible. Many people come to the trail to get away from the electronic web in which we're all increasingly caught up. Here's a way to win friends on the trail: Keep your cell phone, if you bring one, out of sight, beyond earshot, and out of mind for everyone else. Don't use it except for emergencies, and do use it only when you're far away from other hikers. Pizza places don't deliver to most AT shelters anyway. So why even call them?

FINDING YOUR WAY

Map and Compass

Don't go hiking without a map and compass and the skills to use them. In the fog, in the dark, in a storm, even familiar territory can seem like a directionless wilderness. Many hiking clubs offer map and compass ("orienteering") workshops. Map skills are fun to develop and highly useful. Many of the best natural history observations described in this book depend on your ability to locate a spot on the map and to orient yourself once you're there.

At the very least, be sure everyone in your party knows the compass direction of your intended hike, the cars' locations on the map, and the most likely way toward help in an emergency. *Backpacker* has run articles on map and compass skills (check the index on their Web site). The venerable *Boy Scout Handbook* has a good chapter on these skills. Or see Karen Berger's *Hiking & Backpacking: A Complete Guide.*

Being Lost and Getting Found

If you have studied your map before starting the hike, and if you faithfully follow the AT's white blazes or the access trails' blue blazes, the chances of getting lost are just about zero. With a map and compass in hand, there's no good excuse for being lost while you're on the AT itself. Your group should have a leader and a backup leader, and both should know the route. Because hikers sometimes get separated on the trail, everyone should know the direction of the hike, the major landmarks to be passed, the estimated timetable, and how to use the sun and the clock to keep themselves oriented.

But mistakes do happen. Inattention and inadequate planning are the enemies. Sometimes nature conspires against us. Fog (or snow) may obscure the blazes or the cairns above treeline. Autumn leaves or a snowfall may obliterate the well-worn trail that otherwise would guide your eyes as clearly as the blazes themselves.

If you are lost, the first thing to do is to decide that you will not panic. You probably have not been off the trail for long. Stay where you are and think. Keep your group together. Study the map and note the last landmark you're sure you passed.

Get reoriented with the map and compass, and try to go in a straight line back toward the trail. Do not wander. Be especially observant of details until you regain the trail.

If all else fails, let gravity and falling water help you out. Except in the deepest wilderness of Maine or the Smoky Mts., at most places along the AT streams flow eventually to creeks, then to rivers, and where there's a river there will soon enough be a house or even a village. If you have to bushwhack to get out of the woods, and if you're really not sure where you are on the map, follow the water downstream. Patience and a plan will get you out.

Common Sense / Sense of Humor

Taking care of yourself successfully in the woods and on the mountains is not rocket science. It starts with preparedness (physical and mental), appropriate equipment, sufficient food and water. It continues with a realistic plan, guided by a map and compass, a guidebook, a weather report, and a watch. It gets better if you and your companions resolve ahead of time to work together as a team, respecting each other's varying needs, strengths, and talents. And it goes best of all if you pack that one priceless, essential hiker's tool: a ready sense of humor.

AT LEGEND HAS IT that the 2150-mile footpath from Georgia to Maine is an ancient Native American walkway. Not so. In fact, the AT, as a concept, leaped from the imagination of one federal government civil servant who in 1921 had already recognized that Americans were too citified for their own good and needed more convenient opportunities for outdoor recreation.

In 1921, Harvard-educated forester and self-styled philosopher Benton MacKaye, of Shirley, Massachusetts, published an article ("An Appalachian Trail, A Project in Regional Planning") in the journal of the American Institute of Architects. His was a revolutionary idea: a linear park, extending from Georgia to Maine. The concept germinated in a hotbed of idealistic social thinking that called into question many of the assumed values of the capitalist workaday world. Look a little more deeply into MacKaye's thinking and the roots lead directly to the 19th-century romantics and Transcendentalists Thoreau and Emerson. MacKaye had read his John Muir, too.

A whirlwind of self-promoting public-relations energy, MacKaye set the ball rolling to develop the AT. Thousands of volunteers and many legislators helped make it a reality. Two other key players were Judge Arthur Perkins of Hartford, Connecticut, who helped found the Appalachian Trail Conference in 1925, and his successor as president of the conference (1931–1952), Myron Avery, of Maine and Washington, D.C. By 1937, with major assistance from Civilian Conservation Corps workers under President Roosevelt's New Deal Works Progress Administration, the complete trail was essentially in place, though by today's standards much of it was rugged and unblazed.

Thru-hikers are an admirable but increasingly common breed these days. Yet it wasn't until 1948 that anyone walked the entire trail in one season. The first thru-hiker was Earl Shaffer. The first woman to thru-hike in one season was Emma "Grandma" Gatewood, in 1955.

By the mid-1990s the National Park Service was estimating that between 3 and 4 million people per year used the trail. In its first 75 years, from MacKaye's brainstorm to today, the AT has gone from a concept about escaping urban crowding to the point where crowding on the trail itself is a big issue.

In 1968, Congress put the AT under the authority of the National Park Service by passing the National Trails System Act. Overall, the story of the AT is a sweet tale of success. Occasionally there has been a sour note when the government's right of eminent domain has been used to take land required to create a 1000-foot-wide corridor of protection for the trail. By 1995 fewer than 44 miles of the trail remained unprotected by the Park Service corridor.

In the 1990s, environmental impact concerns (wear and tear, sustainability) and hiker management issues (overuse, low-impact camping and hiking, safety) fill the pages of AT magazines and spark many a late-night campfire conversation. While the educational and environmental protection efforts of the Appalachian Trail Conservancy, the Appalachian Mountain Club, and all the regional hiking clubs improve yearly, adding strength to an admirable history, the erosion of financial support from Congress in a budget balancing era threatens to undermine many good efforts at a moment when user demands are growing exponentially. It is a time of fulfillment and challenge for all who use and manage the Appalachian Trail.

Note: A more detailed history can be found in any of the Appalachian Trail Conservancy's hiking guides. The background-reading books mentioned in the Bibliography contain much coloful lore, and the *Appalachian Trail Reader,* edited by David Emblidge, features a diverse collection of writings about the AT.

Appalachian Trail History in the Southern Appalachians

When Benton MacKaye proposed an Appalachian Trail "from Mt. Washington to Mt. Mitchell" in 1921, there were no organized hiking clubs in the South, and most trails went across the mountains instead of along them. But hikers and conservationists met the challenge of MacKaye's vision and became leaders in the business of designing, building, maintaining, and protecting trails. Carolina Mountain Club formed in 1923 as an offshoot of the Appalachian Mountain Club. The Smoky Mts. Hiking Club formed in 1924, and the Georgia Appalachian Trail Club formed in 1930. Crews of men and women scouted routes, carried tools and building materials, cleared brush, published maps and guides, and fought like hornets when anyone proposed roads or private development near their precious trail.

And, of course, they had their own ideas and visions—hence the starting point of Mt. Oglethorpe instead of Mt. Mitchell, and hence the giant zigzag that takes hikers up the eastern rim of the Blue Ridge and then pulls them back across North Carolina to experience the western rim. These folks don't want you to miss anything. Unfortunately, Mt. Oglethorpe had to be abandoned in favor of Springer Mt. in 1958 because parts of the 21-mile section of trail ran through private land, but that loss has been more than offset by protective legislation, designation of wilderness areas, and strong cooperation between land-owning agencies and volunteer hiking clubs. Other clubs

—Nantahala Hiking Club and Tennessee Eastman Hiking and Canoeing Club—sprang up and took responsibility for portions of the AT. The ATC is the umbrella organization: it coordinates club activities, provides support, helps to plan relocations, trains volunteers, and hires skilled crews for big jobs like major rock work or shelter building.

More and more people search out the peace and quiet of the AT, and in some places we are loving it to death —a problem discussed in the 1997 national ATC meeting. During March and April, the AT in Georgia bustles with long-distance and thru-hikers; for the rest of the year, there's plenty of space on trails and in shelters. Benton MacKaye would be amazed to see thousands of hikers migrating north through Georgia mountain fog. But we hope he would be pleased to see that the AT he envisioned still provides the chance "to see, and to see what you see."

The Seven Principles of Leave No Trace

- Plan ahead and prepare.
- Travel and camp on durable surfaces.
- Dispose of waste properly.
- Leave what you find.
- Minimize campfire impacts.
- Respect wildlife.
- Be considerate of other visitors.

Springer Mt. to Hightower Gap

Maps: ATC Chattahoochee Nat'l. Forest

Route: From Springer Mt. to Stover Creek, to Hawk Mt., to Hightower Gap

Recommended direction: S to N

Distance: 9.0 mi. total; 8.1 mi. N on AT

Access trail name & length: AT heading S from USFS 42 parking area, 0.9 mi.

Elevation +/-: 3782 to 2525 to 2854 ft.

Effort: Moderate

Day hike: Yes

Overnight backpacking hike: Optional

Duration: 5 to 6 hr.

Early exit option: Three Forks at USFS 58, at 4.0 mi.

Natural history features: Long Creek Falls; old-growth hemlocks

Social history features: Southern end of AT

Trailhead access: *Start:* There is no road access to the AT trailhead on Springer Mt. USFS 42 crosses the AT 0.9 mi. N of Springer Mt. From GA 60 in Suches, turn S (L) on USFS 42. Pavement ends after about 1.0 mi. Follow well-graded gravel road for 17.1 mi. to parking area (with fee) where the AT crosses USFS 42. (USFS 42 also crosses AT at Gooch Gap, 2.7 mi.; Cooper Gap, 8.8 mi.; and Hightower Gap, 11.7 mi.) A shorter access is from Dahlonega on USFS 80, which meets USFS 42 at Cooper Gap; check with USFS for current road conditions. *End:* High-tower Gap, 11.7 mi. from Suches on USFS 42.

Camping: Springer Mt. Shelter; Stover Creek Shelter; Hawk Mt. Shelter; Three Forks and other campsites; Black Gap Shelter, 1.0 mi. S of Springer Mt. on blue-blazed Approach Trail.

Until 1958, the Appalachian Trail started about 20 mi. southwest of here at Mt. Oglethorpe, Georgia, named to honor the founder of the State of Georgia. (A road leads to the summit and a monument.) However, the land along the trail was private, and the owners built chicken farms. Trail right-of-way problems and the lack of "remote for detachment" quality convinced the trail managers, after long debate, to abandon Mt. Oglethorpe in favor of Springer Mt. Springer is not the highest, most spectacular, or most central Georgia mountain, but it is remote. It is also the point where the east and west rims of the Blue Ridge rejoin after splitting in southern Virginia — and another source of long and heated AT debate in the early years. The

Dale Gelfand

Mountain laurel

Georgia Appalachian Trail Club (GATC) insisted that the route follow the eastern rim, while the Smoky Mts. Hiking Club said they wouldn't help at all if the trail didn't go through the Smokies. Because of a compromise suggested by Horace Kephart (see "Horace Kephart: Honorary Highlander" in Hike #19), the AT uses both rims. The first few hikes head east, and in North Carolina the AT takes a high ridge across to the western rim, which it follows to Virginia. So for most of Georgia, the trail to Maine runs east instead of north.

There are many trails to the top of 3782-ft. Springer Mt. The simplest is described here, but alternatives include the strenuous 8.1-mi. Approach Trail from Amicalola Falls State Park and the 1.5-mi. Benton MacKaye Trail from Big Stamp Gap on USFS 42. The Approach Trail is well blazed and well maintained, and USFS 42 is passable by car. Other road approaches may be rough or require four-wheel drive; check

with the U.S. Forest Service for directions and current road conditions. The hike described here requires two cars, one left at Hightower Gap and the other at Springer Mt. parking on USFS 42. The hike from Springer Mt. to Hightower Gap is relatively easy, with good trail and only a few rocky sections.

Start at the USFS 42 parking lot, facing the U.S. Forest Service map and display board. Turn left, cross USFS 42, and enter the woods on the AT going south. (For a shorter hike — 7.2 mi. to Hightower Gap — but one without Springer Mt., turn right at the display board and look for white blazes heading north at the edge of the parking lot.) It's a 0.9-mi. hike to the top of Springer Mt., where Hike #1 — and the Appalachian Trail itself — officially begin. Our mileage count starts here, as you turn around and head north.

The summit of Springer Mt., a broad dome with thin oak woods and a rock outcrop, has excellent northwest views of the Cohutta Mts. Two bronze plaques mark this as the terminus of the AT. The first plaque was made by the GATC in 1933 and set in the stone here in 1958. The first (or last) white blaze of the AT is painted on the rock a few inches north of the plaque. Behind the second plaque (placed by the USFS and showing the route of the AT) is a metal box with the trail register. Camping is not allowed on the summit.

Thru-Hiking Lab Report

Hiking in the spring is glorious, but there is a substantial risk that you will catch whatever seasonal virus it is that drives people to think they should hike all the way from Georgia to Maine. This insidious disease has a long incubation—so long that you may think you have escaped. However, here are some symptoms that may precede the onset:

- The victims (you or a loved one) start collecting maps and guidebooks.
- They ask everyone they meet about tents, Gore-Tex, and water filters.
- They start introducing themselves by a funny new name.
- They insist on knowing the weight, to the nearest gram, of everything they buy.
- They don't like their 100% cotton underwear and socks anymore.
- They develop an obsessive interest in weather, day length, elevation gains and losses, and how far they can hike in a day.

The most severe form of this syndrome was first described in 1948, but it was rare until the 1960s. Supreme Court Justice William O. Douglas suc-cumbed in 1958. By 1982 there were 1000 cases on record; that number doubled in only 7 years. In the 1990s it became a major epidemic, with thousands coming down with it each year.

The virus respects neither age, sex, physical handicap, nor nationality. An 86-year-old got it in 1975, and a 6-year-old got it just 5 years later. Some people get it several times, and many victims write books about their struggle. Several dogs and at least one cat have also fallen prey to it. More men than women suffer from the disease, but, as with many other conditions, the women are catching up. The causative agent has not been identified; there is some evidence of a tiny parasite that burrows through brain tissue, causing major behavioral changes but minor permanent damage.

No remedy has been found; victims harbor the ailment for the rest of their lives and seem to be highly infectious. However, many victims can lead lives that are surprisingly close to normal if they can acknowledge their affliction and get the hiking done, either all at once or in sections. Many self-help books are available, and support groups exist in some communities.

From the registry box, white blazes indicate the AT, while blue blazes show the Approach Trail from Amicalola Falls. The AT descends along rocky trail sparkling with bits of mica, past flame azalea and blueberry bushes.

At 0.2 mi. two trails enter from the right. First is the 0.2-mi. blue-blazed trail to the Springer Mt. Shelter. Built in 1993, it has a sleeping loft, windows, a large picnic table, and a privy. Like all the shelters on the Georgia AT, it sits well off the trail. A seasonal spring provides water, but it may be dry in summer. There are designated campsites behind the shelter and on a marked side trail.

Just 20 yd. farther on the AT, the Benton MacKaye Trail (BMT) meets the AT. Marked by white diamond blazes, this trail honors Benton MacKaye, who first proposed the AT in 1921. The BMT runs from here through the Cohutta Mts. and the Cherokee National Forest to the western end of the Smokies. It crosses the AT in the Smokies, providing a 250-mi. alternate route for the crowds of hikers who start out every spring for Maine, then runs the length of the Smokies to Davenport Gap, Tennessee, parallel to the overused AT. The BMT provides excellent hikes along the western rim of the southern Blue Ridge Mts. (For maps and information, go to www.BMTA.org.)

The AT continues downhill on good trail, with large boulders on the right sporting rock tripe, a leathery dark lichen. Water from tiny springs seeps across the trail, supporting ferns plus bloodroot and other spring flowers.

At 0.9 mi. cross USFS 42 again, and retrieve anything from your car that you might have forgotten. In March and April, families and friends of thru-hikers gather here to say good-bye and help hoist heavy

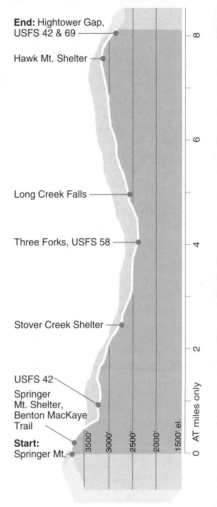

packs up on the trekkers' backs.

A few yards from the USFS sign, enter the woods and cross a grassy roadbed. At 1.2 mi., a blue-blazed trail on the right leads to a spring, and the diamond-blazed BMT merges

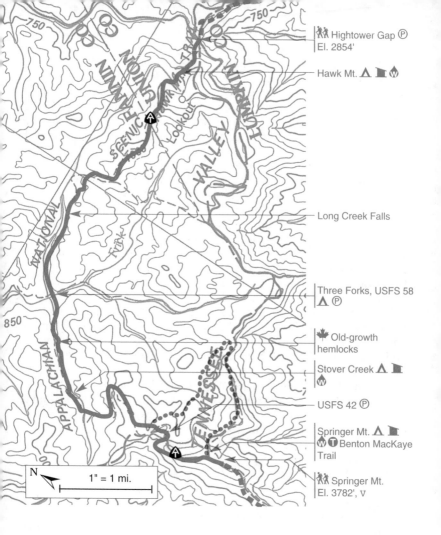

Hightower Gap Ⓟ
El. 2854'

Hawk Mt. ▲ ◼ Ⓦ

Long Creek Falls

Three Forks, USFS 58
▲ Ⓟ

✿ **Old-growth hemlocks**

Stover Creek ▲ ◼
Ⓦ

USFS 42 Ⓟ

Springer Mt. ▲ ◼
Ⓦ ⓣ **Benton MacKaye Trail**

Springer Mt.
El. 3782', V

N

1" = 1 mi.

with the AT. Most of north Georgia was heavily logged earlier in this century, and the trails follow or cross many old logging roads. The AT and the BMT ascend a ridge on the side of Rich Mt.; at 1.8 mi., they split once again. Watch the blazes; the AT goes left (white rectangles) while the BMT (white diamonds) continues straight to go over Rich Mt. At 2.1 mi. descend to a stream and several steps, and turn left on another old road.

A blue-blazed trail leads 0.2 mi. to the new Stover Creek Shelter (built in 2006) and campsites and privy. This shelter sleeps 16, but many more crowd in during thru-hike season.

After traversing a log bridge across a creek, the trail ascends a bit and then descends along a wide, even path through more than a mile of hemlock woods. These old-growth hemlocks were scheduled for Forest Service timber sales, but through actions of the GATC and other groups, the sale was stopped, and now the area is protected as part of the AT corridor. However, the giant trees are being attacked by hemlock woolly adelgid, an aphid-like invasive insect. Stover Creek runs just down the bank on the right, murmuring under a cloak of rosebay rhododendron.

At 3.6 mi. the trail turns right and crosses Stover Creek into mixed deciduous and hemlock woods. The BMT rejoins the AT as both cross Chester Creek on a wide log bridge to enter an area called Three Forks at 4.1 mi. Many campsites are available here, and three large creeks (Stover, Chester, and Long) join to form Noontootla Creek, which flows into the Toccoa River.

After crossing USFS 58 at Three Forks, the AT ascends on an old road. At 5.0 mi. a blue-blazed trail leads left a few hundred feet to Long Creek Falls, a 25-ft.-high waterfall surrounded by hemlocks.

At 5.1 mi. the BMT goes left toward the Tennessee border, while the AT ascends right toward more Georgia mountains and North Carolina. This split also marks the beginning of the Duncan Ridge Trail, a 30-mi.-long trail in Georgia that can be combined with the AT and BMT for backpacking loops.

As the AT climbs the side of a ridge, a gravel logging road at 5.8 mi. leads to the Hickory Flats Cemetery; nearby on the right are picnic tables and a covered pavilion.

Cross a gravel road (USFS 251), ascend on the north side of Hawk Mt. at 7.6 mi., and follow the blue-blazed trail on the left 0.2 mi. to Hawk Mt. Shelter, a shelter with a loft, privy, bear cables, and a nearby spring.

From the shelter side trail, descend to Hightower Gap on a north-facing rocky slope. Hepatica and bloodroot are the earliest spring wildflowers that flourish here in several seeps and tiny springs.

For a one-car alternate hike of about 10 mi., park at Three Forks on USFS 58, 2.6 mi. from USFS 42 at Winding Stair Gap. Take the BMT over Rich Mt., continue on the AT to Springer Mt., and return on the AT to Three Forks.

Miles N	NORTH	Elev. (ft./m)	Miles S
	Total: 9.0 mi. with access trail		
8.1	**End: Hightower Gap,** USFS 42 & 69; park on roadside.	2854/873	0.0
7.6	Trail to **Hawk Mt. Shelter** (0.2 mi.); spring S of shelter.	3250/991	0.5
5.8	Gravel road to **Hickory Flats Cemetery.**		2.3
5.0	Trail to **Long Creek Falls** (0.1 mi.).		3.1
4.1	**Three Forks,** USFS 58; early exit option.	2525/770	4.0
3.6	Trail turns R, across Stover Creek.		4.5
2.5	**Stover Creek Shelter,** old-growth hemlocks along next mile.		5.6
1.2	Blue-blazed trail on R to spring; jct. **Benton MacKaye Trail**		6.9
0.9	Cross **USFS 42,** trailhead parking.	3400/1036	7.2
0.2	Trail to **Springer Mt. Shelter** (0.2 mi.), privy, tent pads, reliable spring; jct. with **Benton MacKaye Trail.**		7.9
0.0	**Start AT miles: Springer Mt.,** views to W. Turn around and head N.	3782/1152	8.1
0.9	Access: USFS 42 parking area. Walk S on AT to reach **Springer Mt.,** the southern terminus of the AT.		0.9

SOUTH

Hightower Gap to Woody Gap

Maps: ATC Chattahoochee Nat'l. Forest
Route: From Hightower Gap to Sassafras Mt., to Devils Kitchen, to Woody Gap
Recommended direction: S to N
Distance: 11.9 mi.
Elevation +/-: 2854 to 2500 to 3150 ft.
Effort: Strenuous
Day hike: Yes
Overnight backpacking hike: Optional
Duration: 7 to 8 hr.
Early exit option: USFS 42 at Cooper Gap, at 3.5 mi.; Gooch Gap, at 8.3 mi.
Natural history features: Rock outcrops
Trailhead access: *Start:* From GA 60 in Suches, turn S on USFS 42. Go 11.7 mi.

on graded gravel to intersection with USFS 69. Watch for white blazes of AT crossing the road and for small USFS route sign. Park on wide area of road. Shorter access from Dahlonega is on USFS 80 to junction with USFS 42 at Cooper Gap; check with USFS for current road conditions. *End:* Woody Gap, 5.6 mi. N of Stone Pile Gap (junction of GA 60 with US 19) and 15 mi. N of Dahlonega. USFS parking on both sides of GA 60.

Camping: Gooch Mountain Shelter; several campsites

I f you're looking for a good introduction to north-Georgia hiking, with several steep climbs and descents, this section of the AT provides it. The trail is good though rocky in spots, and primarily travels through hardwood forests of oak, hickory, and tulip-tree. Most of the good tent sites along this hike are on ridgetops; you will need to carry water. Road access can be long and slow; check with the Forest Service for current conditions. Roadside parking is possible wherever this section comes near USFS 42, so shorter parts of this hike can be arranged.

In October 1995, Hurricane Opal roared up from the Gulf Coast and toppled trees on the AT from Georgia

to upper Tennessee. This section of trail was heavily damaged, especially on ridgetops and through gaps that funneled the strong winds, so say a silent "thank you" to the trail rebuilders as you hike through.

To start, the AT climbs east (back toward Suches) from Hightower Gap (2854 ft.) above USFS 42, passing shagbark hickories on the way up. True to their name, these tall, straight trees have shaggy bark that splits and curls away from the trunk at the ends. Shagbark hickory nuts are delicious but hard to get into. Look for pieces of shell dropped by squirrels that show the intricate design inside the nut.

Toward the top of this first hard

climb of about 0.3 mi., the trail becomes very rocky, and the trees have interesting root twists to anchor themselves. Winter views to the south show a large expanse of the Chattahoochee National Forest with Camp Merrill, an army training camp, nestled around a red-and-white water tower in a valley. Hikers might meet army Rangers on practice maneuvers or hear helicopters overhead. The soldiers may startle hikers, but they have been instructed to be aware of the AT and may help you find your way or deal with an emergency. Near the viewpoint, a small flat area on the right can be used as a tent site.

The AT now descends some treated lumber steps and begins a mile-long series of small ups and downs. USFS 42 may be visible down to the left. Dogwood trees mix with the oaks, and patches of cane, or native bamboo, live at the ridgetops.

During a steep descent into Horse Gap (2673 ft.), you can look across at the next climb to Sassafras Mt., the highest point on this section. At the gap, USFS 42 is visible about 20 yd. to the left. Then comes nearly a mile of steep climbing to the top of Sassafras Mt. (3336 ft., 2.9 mi.). The open, broad summit has a tent site, a large patch of hazelnut bushes, many fallen trees from Hurricane Opal, and a luxurious crop of poison ivy ("leaves of three, let it be"). In spring, poison ivy's tiny new leaves are red and shiny. This plant is common all along the Georgia AT, especially in

areas that have been logged or cleared recently. Poison ivy is native and normally grows at the edges of woods or in open areas; as this forest gets more mature, the amount of poison ivy will decrease. However, don't feel too bad for it; events like Hurricane Opal give it plenty of openings for new growth.

Begin the steep descent (yes, there is a pattern here) on stone steps and small trail relocations around fallen trees. Near the bottom look for beautiful quartz and mica rocks by the trail. Mica is slate that has crystallized as a result of great heat and pressure, and it can be peeled into paper-thin transparent sections.

At 3.5 mi., reach Cooper Gap (2828 ft.) and recross USFS 42 at its junction with USFS 80. This gravel road runs by Camp Merrill and leads to Dahlonega in 14 mi., but it may be rougher than USFS 42. USFS 15 also enters this gap on the far left and goes north to join GA 60 in about 5 mi.

Ascend a steep and rocky trail to the summit of Justus Mt. (3224 ft.). A small rock overhang on the right might make a good rest stop in the rain, and blackberries, hydrangeas, and hollies grow in the openings left by tree fall. Again, stone steps and small detours help hikers through the piles of felled tree trunks. The GATC and the U.S. Forest Service did massive trail work after Hurricane Opal and had the trail reopened in a few weeks. Some now-horizontal yellow poplars still have enough of their roots in the ground to bloom and pro-

I n 1650 the Cherokee Nation spread across most of southern Appalachia. As European settlers moved westward, the Cherokee and other Native Americans lost their land, treaty by treaty and battle by battle. By the 1820s, the Cherokee held only a part of north Georgia — land so hilly and rugged that no one else paid much attention to it — and adopted white culture, government, and farming. Sequoyah, a self-taught Cherokee scholar, developed a Cherokee syllabary, a written language so successful that the entire tribe became literate in one generation. We could use his genius today.

In 1828, the *Cherokee Phoenix* newspaper began publication, and wealthy Cherokees built thriving businesses and large plantation houses. In the same year, a deer hunter named Benjamin Parks discovered gold near Dahlonega. The news brought 10,000 prospectors staking claims and digging into hills and watersheds. White Georgians demanded removal of the Cherokee, and in 1835 a few Cherokees were persuaded to sign the Treaty of New Echota, ceding to the U.S. all land east of the Mississippi for $5 million. But the majority of Cherokees refused the treaty, and the U.S. Supreme Court ruled that Georgia had no claim to their land.

However, President Andrew Jackson ignored the court ruling and sent 7000 U.S. troops, under General Winfield Scott — who has a pretty lake named after him — to round up 15,000 Cherokees and march them to Oklahoma, the infamous Trail of Tears

duce seeds. This may be a chance for a close-up view of their fantastic tulip-shaped flowers colored like lemon, orange, and lime sherbet.

The slope down looks like an abandoned lumberyard, with tree trunks, stumps, stump sprouts, fungi, racing saplings with oversized leaves, and, of course, jubilant poison ivy. This is a good place to look at pit-and-mound ecology. When a large tree falls, the hole where its roots were forms a shallow pit, and the displaced root mass forms a mound as it decays. Both the pit and the mound create microhabitats that are favored by certain plants and animals that have trouble getting established on undisturbed forest floor. On Justus Mt. you can see recent pits and mounds from Opal and older ones from earlier storms that support crowds of wildflowers. The Opal log pile may be a fire hazard in the next few years, and the forest recovery here will be interesting.

After crossing a saddle and another small ridgetop, the AT descends some log steps and crosses a logging road (that leads right about 1 mi. to USFS 42). Descending another 0.5 mi. on good trail, the AT reaches

of 1838–39 (now a National Historic Trail). Cherokee property was looted and burned, and more than 4000 Cherokees died during the march. A few managed to hide out in the mountains and later established the town of Cherokee, North Carolina.

The Dahlonega Courthouse, built in 1838 of bricks with flecks of gold, is now the gold museum, where you can learn about Georgia's gold rush. Gold coins were minted here, and millions of dollars of gold came from the hills. The capitol dome of Georgia is covered with Dahlonega gold. The California gold rush of 1849 drew away most of the prospectors and panners, but gold was mined—using water cannons and huge stamping machines—until the early 1900s. The water cannons stripped away the so-called overburden—trees, soil, and wildflowers—and the stamping machines crushed rock so that the gold could be extracted. Environmental damage from this type of mining destroyed entire mountains and watersheds.

Dahlonega gold is one of the purest golds in the world, but most of it is buried deep in quartz veins under the mountains. Tiny flakes wash out in creeks, and you can still pan for gold and store a few dollars' worth in a vial as a souvenir.

As you walk the AT through Georgia, North Carolina, and Tennessee, there is gold deep beneath your feet, and that is where it should stay. Perhaps if Benjamin Parks hadn't noticed the gold flakes while deer hunting, the Cherokee Nation might still live in north Georgia today.

the lowest point of this hike at Justus Creek (5.5 mi.). Campsites, water, and convenient footbridges mark this low section of 0.8 mi., though the area (called Devil's Kitchen) may be steamy and buggy on summer hikes. Peepers and chorus frogs provide night music in the spring. After the second footbridge crosses Blackwell Creek at 6.2 mi., farm fields appear on the left.

Ascend through a thick laurel tunnel and beside large patches of running ground cedar (a club moss). After crossing another old road, the trail resumes its steep rocky habits as it climbs the side of Horseshoe Ridge, reaching the summit at 6.5 mi. Oaks, sourwoods, and large dogwoods grow here, and piles of rocks at the corners of old fields are reminders of former settlements. The AT curves left and descends to a spring and creek at 8.0 mi., the best water supply while camping at the gap or staying at the upcoming shelter. A blue-blazed side trail leads left to the new Gooch Mountain Shelter, which was built in 2001 and has a privy and a good water source. The AT runs for about a mile to Gooch Gap on a gentle, moist slope with abundant spring wildflowers, including bloodroot in March and trillium in April. Flat tent sites are available in the gap, but overuse has left large bare patches of dirt that may become muddy.

The AT mellows a bit for the last 3.6 mi. of this hike. The uphills are easier, and switchbacks help on the steeper parts. After a climb through hardwoods out of Gooch Gap, the trail descends and enters a healthy patch of mountain laurel, covered with masses of blooms in May. Then it crosses a sunken old road and ascends a north-facing moist slope with plenty of trillium, foamflowers, and violets.

After Grassy Gap (9.5 mi.), the AT enters 2952-ft. Liss Gap (9.8 mi.) with a stand of tall, straight tulip-trees spared by Opal. Ascend along a ridge, switch to its south side, and descend to Jacks Gap (3000 ft., 10.4 mi.). From here to Woody Gap you will be following the divide between the Tennessee Valley, which drains into the Mississippi River, and the Chattahoochee drainage. Climb switchbacks up to the 3200-ft. summit of Ramrock Mt. Here enjoy excellent views to the south of the deep valleys and the mountains fading into the piedmont. Camping is possible along this rocky outcrop, but you must bring water.

Descend to Tritt Gap (3050 ft.) at 10.9 mi., and continue on down to Woody Gap along the southern slope of Black Mt. The plants here—mountain laurel, galax, red oaks, trailing

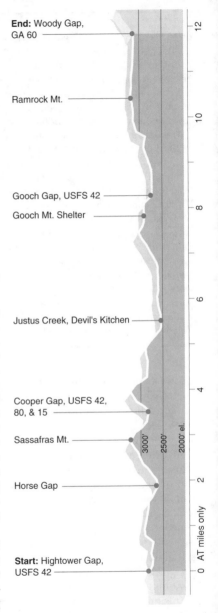

End: Woody Gap, GA 60

Ramrock Mt.

Gooch Gap, USFS 42

Gooch Mt. Shelter

Justus Creek, Devil's Kitchen

Cooper Gap, USFS 42, 80, & 15

Sassafras Mt.

Horse Gap

Start: Hightower Gap, USFS 42

3000' 2500' 2000' el.

AT miles only

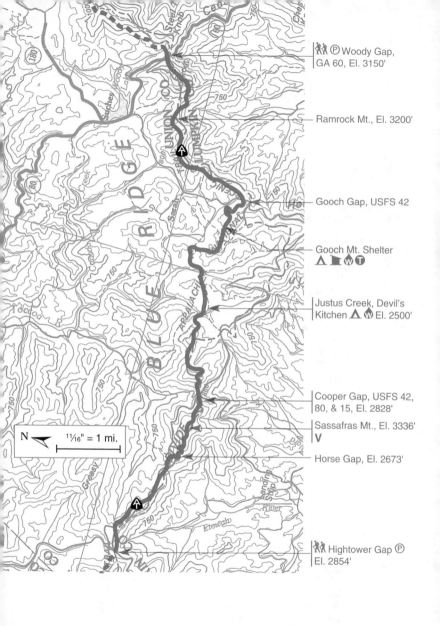

🚶🚶 Ⓟ Woody Gap,
GA 60, El. 3150'

Ramrock Mt., El. 3200'

Gooch Gap, USFS 42

Gooch Mt. Shelter
△ ▰ ⓦ Ⓣ

Justus Creek, Devil's
Kitchen △ ⓦ El. 2500'

Cooper Gap, USFS 42,
80, & 15, El. 2828'

Sassafras Mt., El. 3336'
V

Horse Gap, El. 2673'

🚶🚶 Hightower Gap Ⓟ
El. 2854'

N ➤ ¹¹⁄₁₆" = 1 mi.

Miles N	NORTH	Elev. (ft./m)	Miles S
11.9	**End: Woody Gap,** GA 60; parking, privies, piped spring, and picnic area.	3150/960	0.0
10.5	**Ramrock Mt.,** views to S.	3200/975	1.4
8.3	**Gooch Gap;** jct. USFS 42; early exit option.	2784/849	3.6
7.0	Jct. trail to **Gooch Mt. Shelter,** privy, spring 200 yd. L.		4.4
6.5	Summit **Horseshoe Ridge.**		4.9
5.5	**Justus Creek, Devil's Kitchen;** campsites, water.	2500/762	6.4
3.5	**Cooper Gap,** USFS 42, 80, & 15; early exit option.	2828/862	8.4
2.9	**Sassafras Mt.,** high point.	3336/1017	9.0
1.9	**Horse Gap,** USFS 42 to L.	2673/815	10.0
0.0	**Start: Hightower Gap,** USFS 42; roadside parking.	2854/870	11.9

SOUTH

arbutus—are adapted to dry, exposed areas like this. Also watch for fence lizards and maybe even a garter snake on the rocky outcrops.

Woody Gap was named for "barefoot ranger" Arthur Woody, a Georgian who served as chief ranger of the Blue Ridge District of the Chattahoochee National Forest for more than 30 years. He loved the land, knew it all from boyhood hiking and hunting, and protected his domain, settling fights, dealing carefully with "likker blockaders," and guiding hikers. He is credited with reestablishing the deer population in north Georgia; after overhunting wiped them out, he imported fawns from another state to raise and release. When Woody thought hunters were shooting too many of his deer, he used a gigantic bear paw that he kept in his ranger truck to make tracks around the hunting camps.

Woody Gap Recreation Area, on GA 60, has a large parking area, bathrooms (locked in winter), a piped spring, an information sign, and picnic tables.

Woody Gap to Neels Gap

Maps: ATC Chattahoochee Nat'l. Forest

Route: From Woody Gap to Jarrard Gap, to Slaughter Gap, to Blood Mt., to Neels Gap

Recommended direction: S to N

Distance: 10.7 mi.

Elevation +/-: 3150 to 4461 to 3125 ft.

Effort: Moderate to strenuous

Day Hike: Yes

Overnight backpacking hike: Optional

Duration: 7 to 8 hr.

Early exit option: Jarrard Gap, at 5.3 mi. (to Lake Winfield Scott Recreation Area, 1.0 mi.)

Natural history features: Blood Mt.

Social history features: Battle of Cherokees and Creeks

Trailhead access: *Start:* Woody Gap on GA 60, 15 mi. N of Dahlonega and 1.6 mi. S of Suches, at USFS parking and picnic area. *End:* Neels Gap on US 19/129, 22 mi. N of Dahlonega, 14 mi. S of Blairsville; limited parking at gap, but large parking area 0.5 mi. N at Byron Reece Memorial.

Camping: Blood Mt. Shelter; several tent sites, Byron Reece Memorial

T ake a hike to Blood Mt., the highest peak on the Georgia AT, now usually a quite peaceful place except when invaded by swarms of weekend hikers. Sometime before 1600, however, the aptly named Blood Mt. and its neighbor Slaughter Mt. looked down on another battle between the North (the Cherokee Nation) and the South (the Creek Nation) that made the streams from Slaughter Gap flow red. This war between the Indian nations may have established the boundaries that were found by the European settlers of the following century.

The hike to Blood Mt. crosses between two good highways and has several moderate climbs before the big one to 4461 ft. That climb, how-

ever, is made easier by good trail and switchbacks. Most of the summits and gaps along this AT section have summit campsites, like eagles' aeries —and like eagles' aeries no water, so water must be carried for some of them. However, from Slaughter Gap to Neels Gap, the trail and campsites are heavily used, and the Blood Mt. Shelter may be crowded. Spring wildflowers, excellent views, and forest diversity make this an attractive hike. But be advised that Neels Gap and parts of the AT get very crowded on spring and fall weekends, so hike here on weekdays if possible.

The hike begins north from the U.S. Forest Service picnic area with an easy ascent from Woody Gap (3150 ft.) with GA 60 visible down to the left. Signs indicate that the Blood Mt. Wilderness lies to the left of the AT, and the Chestatoe Wildlife Management Area is to the right. A faint path at 0.2 mi. to the left leads to several quarry pits. There is a winter view to the right of open fields and Woody Lake in Suches, but then the AT turns away from the road into thick woods of oak and sourwood, with flame azalea and blueberries as undergrowth.

At 0.7 mi., descend into Lunsford Gap, where there are a few tent sites but no water supply. Tulip-trees grow tall and straight here, but in October 1995, Hurricane Opal toppled some of them. A few horizontal trees live on, producing leaves and flowers.

The trail ascends steeply toward a high ridge on the right. This area is subject to severe winter ice storms as warm wet air from the Atlantic or the Gulf of Mexico moves up the cold mountains. Inch-thick coats of ice freeze onto branches and twigs, which then snap off in the next wind. A January 1997 ice storm did a major pruning job on the forest, and you may see piles of brush from that or more recent ice storms.

After a switchback and a rocky section, the trail reaches several rocky overlooks near the summit of Big Cedar Mt. (3737 ft.) at 1.3 mi. A good view to the east offers the diminishing hills of the piedmont with occasional sharp bumps of small mountains. Creeks in this valley flow into the Chattahoochee River, which runs through Atlanta and then forms the border between Georgia and Alabama.

At one summit viewpoint, there is a pretty campsite to the left, sheltered from wind and rain by boulders. The AT then turns left for a gentle descent. Look for a small spring left of the trail.

At 1.5 mi. the AT curves left again, while a blue-blazed trail leads 0.1 mi. straight to a rocky overlook and excellent campsites — a good place to wake up to the sunrise. Another spring rises on the left just beyond the curve. The AT continues down on somewhat eroded tread to a level spot with gnarled oak trees and another campsite.

At 2.0 mi., reach Dan Gap and cross an old road, and then ascend to Granny Top Mt. A double white blaze and a flurry of white blazes on several trees indicate a sharp right turn down a pleasant boulevard of May-blooming flame azalea bushes.

At Miller Gap (2980 ft., 2.6 mi.) the Dockery Lake Trail goes right and descends 3.4 mi. through a forested valley along Waters Creek to Dockery Lake Recreation Area. There is an overused campsite near the junction, but no spring.

The next 0.5 mi. is level or downhill and has many sourwood trees. Sourwood bark is deeply furrowed and divided into blocks, and the trunks often angle slightly instead of growing straight up. The midsummer flower clusters look like splayed fingers, each with a single dangling row of tiny white flowers. Some people call it lily-of-the-valley tree. Beekeepers bring their hives into the woods at sourwood blooming time to get sourwood honey, which is dark and distinctive tasting. Sourwood leaves taste—surprise!—sour and turn brilliant red in late summer, especially in dry years. Once you recognize the blocky bark and angled trunks, you'll notice sourwoods all through the woods, especially on dry slopes.

The trail descends onto a south-facing slope lined with white pines and galax, reaching a creek and campsite at 2.9 mi. It then climbs the side of Baker Mt., briefly merges with several old roadbeds, and then crosses a ridge to the moist, sheltered north side. Springs and tiny creeks send water across the trail, and Christmas ferns, large-flowered trilliums, anemones, and foamflowers grow among mossy boulders.

At 3.7 mi., in a thick patch of poison ivy, a clear side trail leads about 700 ft. left to car camping sites (no facilities) at Henry Gap (3100 ft.) and a gravel road that leads about 0.5 mi. to GA 180. The AT continues to climb to Burnett Field Mt. (3478 ft.), passing small tent sites and a series of springs coming out from rock ledges, and then drops to Jarrard Gap at 5.3 mi. A blue-blazed dirt road on the left marks the beginning of the 1.0-mi. trail down to Lake Winfield Scott. A sign here bans fires between Jarrard and Neels gaps because of overuse of the wilderness area.

After a short climb up first Gaddis Mt. (at 5.7. mi.) and then Turkey Stamp

American chestnut leaves

Mt. (at 6.4 mi.), the trail enters Bird Gap at 6.7 mi., notable for a campsite and several toppled trees from Hurricane Opal. The blue-blazed Freeman Trail goes right around the south side of Blood Mt. This bypass should be used if the trail is icy, if thunderstorms are likely, if the fog is too thick for you to see blazes in an open rocky area, or if you want to avoid rocky trail. The bypass is 1.8 mi. and nearly level, whereas the AT over Blood Mt. is 3.0 mi. with a 1000-ft. elevation change.

A second blue-blazed trail leads 0.5 mi. left to Woods Hole Shelter.

The next ascent reaches Slaughter Gap at 7.4 mi. Three blue-blazed trails converge here: the 2.7-mi. Lake Winfield Scott Trail (left); the 30-mi. Duncan Ridge Trail to Three Forks, just north of Springer Mt. (right); and a 200-ft. trail straight ahead to a large flat area with tent pads and a spring. This unreliable spring may be the last water source on Blood Mt.

The AT takes a sharp right at 8.2 mi. and climbs 1.1 mi., past boulders

and tunnels of first rosebay rhododendron, then mountain laurel, then
Catawba rhododendron at the top. At
the summit the trail meets an old
road that passes an outcrop with a
good view north and a U.S. Geological Survey marker, a bronze disk
mounted in the rock to mark an elevation measurement.

The summit of Blood Mt. is covered with flat-topped white oaks and
a cluster of witch hazel growing in
the shelter of a three-story climbable
boulder. This is the highest point on
the Georgia AT (4461 ft.), with views
in all directions. Look for Brasstown
Bald to the northeast, the Nantahala
Mts. beyond, Lake Burton to the east,
and hills leveling out to coastal plain
to the south. Or, enjoy the swirling
fog, all too common because of
humid air moving up from the piedmont and the plains. Blood Mt.
receives many visitors, and the fragile lichens, mosses, and other trailside plants up here have been badly
trampled. Try not to step on the survivors.

Blood Mt. Shelter, a two-room stone
building with a new roof, is right on
the trail. The first room has a rock
floor, and provides space for cooking
and eating. The second room has a
cement floor—and, according to
register comments, a lively mouse
population. However, the shelter is
much appreciated in wind and thunderstorms. This shelter was restored
and repaired in 2012.

The AT descends from the shelter
onto rock outcrops surrounded by

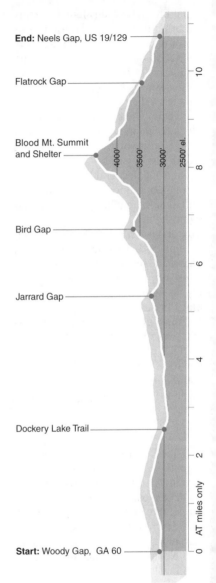

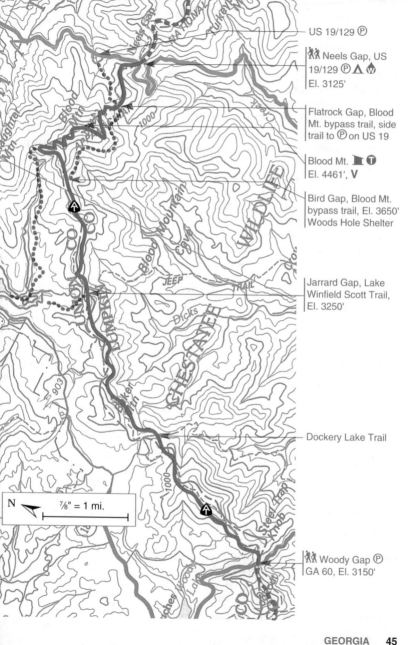

US 19/129 Ⓟ

🚶🚶 Neels Gap, US 19/129 Ⓟ ⛺ Ⓦ El. 3125'

Flatrock Gap, Blood Mt. bypass trail, side trail to Ⓟ on US 19

Blood Mt. 🔭 Ⓣ El. 4461', **V**

Bird Gap, Blood Mt. bypass trail, El. 3650' Woods Hole Shelter

Jarrard Gap, Lake Winfield Scott Trail, El. 3250'

Dockery Lake Trail

🚶🚶 Woody Gap Ⓟ GA 60, El. 3150'

N   ⁷⁄₈" = 1 mi.

rhododendron and white oak. If the blazes are hard to spot, stay generally left on the open, rocky area until you see the trail entering woods.

The white oaks here are ancient, but short. From the summit, their tops look evenly mowed. The trunks grow sideways, in corkscrew shapes, or crooked to avoid pushing branches any higher into the punishing wind. As you descend, you will see successively straighter and taller oak trunks, with their crowns at the same level as the trees on higher ground.

The AT continues down the south side of Blood Mt. on excellent rock steps. Use extra caution if it is wet or icy. Swing right onto a rocky overlook and then left to start a series of switchbacks down. In some spots the trail surface is wet ledges that could be an ice hazard. The GATC has completed a trail relocation with massive rock steps. Since this is the section of AT in Georgia that receives the most use, the GATC and the Konnarok work crew designed the relocated trail to discourage hikers from cutting across switchbacks, which causes erosion and trail degradation.

The AT reaches 3452-ft. Flatrock Gap at 9.7 mi. after a drop of 1000 ft. in 1.4 mi. The blue-blazed Blood Mt. bypass trail comes in from the right, and the AT treadway becomes a well-graded dirt path, a relief to the knees. Another blue-blazed trail leads 0.5 mi. left to the Georgia poet Byron Reece Memorial, parking, and a camping area. Look for the balanced rock on the right just beyond the gap,

a cabin-sized chunk of erosion-resistant Precambrian sandstone perched on raised bedrock. Tread carefully; the State of Georgia will fine you if you topple it.

Swing left from the rock and descend through oak woods on overused trail. Soon US 19/129 in Neels Gap appears below you to the left. You will hear it before you see it, especially since it's a favorite curvy road of motorcyclists. Go down log steps and cross to the Walasi-Yi Inn, built in the 1930s of American chestnut and local rock. Here you can buy boots, tents, or gorp, outdoor books, jewelry, and pottery, and get your pack weighed and its contents evaluated for efficiency and safety (make an appointment in spring). Caution: This is also probably the only place in rural north Georgia where you can get a parking ticket; long-term parking is available 0.5 mi. north at the Byron Reece Memorial parking area.

As an alternate hike to Blood Mt., park at Lake Winfield Scott (for a small fee). Hike to Slaughter Gap, up to Blood Mt., back (south) on the AT to Jarrard Gap, and then back down to the lake. This loop is 8.0 mi., with an elevation gain of about 2000 ft.

Other hikes could be arranged from Vogel State Park and the Dockery Lake Recreation Area. Check U.S. Forest Service maps for details.

Miles N	NORTH	Elev. (ft./m)	Miles S
10.7	**End: Neels Gap,** US 19/129; to **Byron Reece Memorial** (0.5 mi.), parking, camping, water.	3125/952	0.0
9.7	**Flatrock Gap;** jct. blue-blazed **Blood Mt.** bypass trail and side trail to hiker parking on US 19/129 (0.5 mi.).	3452/1052	1.0
8.3	**Blood Mt. Summit and Shelter,** 360° views; highest point on Georgia AT.	4461/1360	2.4
7.4	**Slaughter Gap;** campsite, jct. **Duncan Ridge Trail, Lake Winfield Scott Trail.**		3.3
6.7	**Bird Gap,** campsite; jct. **Blood Mt.** bypass trail (**Freeman Trail**), **Woods Hole Shelter.**	3650/1113	4.0
5.3	**Jarrard Gap,** jct. **Lake Winfield Scott Trail;** early exit option.	3250/991	5.4
3.7	Side trail to **Henry Gap;** car camping.		6.5
2.6	**Miller Gap;** jct. **Dockery Lake Trail,** R 3 mi. to lake.		8.1
1.3	**Big Cedar Mt. Summit,** views to SE.	3157/1333	9.4
0.0	**Start: Woody Gap,** GA 60; parking, picnic area.	3150/960	10.7

SOUTH

Neels Gap to Hogpen Gap

Maps: ATC Chattahoochee Nat'l. Forest

Route: From Neels Gap to Levelland Mt., to Tesnatee Gap, to Hogpen Gap

Recommended direction: S to N

Distance: 6.4 mi.

Elevation +/-: 3125 to 3942 to 3450 ft.

Effort: Moderate

Day hike: Yes

Overnight backpacking hike: Optional

Duration: 4 to 5 hr.

Early exit option: Tesnatee Gap, at 5.5 mi.

Natural history feature: Raven Cliffs Wilderness Area

Social history feature: Walasi-Yi Inn

Trailhead access: *Start:* Neels Gap on US 19/129, 22 mi. N of Dahlonega, 14 mi. S of Blairsville; limited parking at gap; hiker parking area 0.5 mi. N of gap at Byron Reece Memorial. *End:* Hogpen Gap on GA 348. From Helen, cross the Chattahoochee River on GA 75, go 2.5 mi., and turn R onto Richard B. Russell Scenic Highway (GA 348) for 7.1 mi. to parking area at Hogpen Gap. From Neels Gap, drive N past Vogel State Park, turn R on GA 180, and after 1.0 mi., turn R on GA 348. Reach Tesnatee Gap at about 5.0 mi., and 0.7 mi. farther is Hogpen Gap.

Camping: Whitley Gap Shelter; a few camping sites

Open ridgetops with excellent views, spring and fall wildflower displays, and well-graded trail make this a pleasant hike, and the proximity to Neels Gap makes it popular. This short AT section between two paved roads has one hard climb, out of Tesnatee Gap, which can be bypassed in bad weather. Camping is possible at ridgetops and gaps, and water is available within half a mile of most campsites. The Whitley Gap Shelter is 1.2 mi. from the AT, mostly down, on a side trail with good views. If you do take the time and effort to go to this shelter, you will find it either empty and private or full of Boy Scouts.

This hike actually begins within the Walasi-Yi Inn in Neels Gap—0.5 mi. from the parking area—the only time in its entire length that the AT goes *through* a building. The inn was built in the 1930s of American chestnut and local rock by the Civilian Conservation Corps and is on the National Register of Historic Sites. It belongs to the State Department of Natural Resources, and the managers are helpful friends of hikers. Food, water, shelter (only for long-distance hikers), phone, information, picnic tables, and bathrooms are available here at a well-stocked hiking outfitter store.

From the inn's blazed breezeway,

the trail is sandy and dry as it ascends away from the road. Rocky switchbacks lead through a tangle of small trees and grapevines. Back to the right is a view of Blood Mt., looming big from here.

The trail becomes straighter and smoother as it enters better forest and the Raven Cliffs Wilderness Area. The AT in Georgia, Tennessee, and North Carolina goes through several federally designated wilderness areas, which protect the trail corridor from building, timber harvest, and road construction. Power tools are prohibited in wilderness areas, and trail clearing must be done by hand. Georgia Appalachian Trail Club (GATC) members have developed expertise with axes and two-person saws to remove fallen trees. Look for their handiwork along this section of the AT and on other trails.

At 1.1 mi. the trail reaches Bull Gap (3644 ft.), with winter views as well as a large camping area with a spring to the left. A rocky climb from the gap leads to 3942-ft. Levelland Mt. at 1.5 mi., with views right (south) of the Georgia piedmont. March-blooming bloodroot grows along the trail, and the oaks here are twisted and gnarled, as most anyone would be after standing in strong wind for a few hundred years.

Descend on a rocky trail through first mountain laurel and then rhododendron for about 0.2 mi. to a small gap and campsite. In moist areas, look for other early bloomers: toothwort, anemones, and toadshade, this last a type of trillium with mottled leaves and yellow or maroon flowers that sit directly on the leaves with no flower stalk. Most toadshade along here have the maroon flowers, which have an unpleasant smell — at least to people — but it must smell good to the ant and insect pollinators.

A blue blaze at about 1.9 mi. indicates a good spring to the left. Shortly after the spring is a pretty campsite surrounded by flame azalea and oilnut bushes. Another grassy campsite appears at 2.1 mi. in Swaim Gap (3450 ft.). At 2.8 mi., passing a luxurious stand of poison ivy, a side trail leads 50 yd. right to an overlook and excellent grassy campsite. Another short climb brings the AT to Wolf Laurel Top at 3.4 mi., with more twisted white oaks. It then descends past large rock outcrops with lichens to Baggs Creek Gap at 4.2 mi., a level spot with many fallen trees and another spring and campsite.

Ascend to Cowrock Mt. (4.7 mi., 3842 ft.), with a view of Cowrock Ridge extending south above two deep creek valleys. Descend along open rock to a double blaze on a cairn, and turn left to a series of switchbacks and uneven trail.

At 5.1 mi., the AT leaves the Raven Cliffs Wilderness and descends the rest of the way to Tesnatee Gap at almost the same elevation as Neels Gap. Then the trail crosses a large gravel parking lot on the Richard B. Russell Scenic Highway and enters the woods and the wilderness area again to start the climb up Wildcat

Mt. (To bypass the climb up Wildcat Mt., which may be necessary in thunderstorms or icy conditions, turn right from the Tesnatee Gap parking lot and hike 0.7 mi. up to the Hogpen Gap parking lot.)

The trail makes a rocky, steep climb of about 500 ft. in 0.6 mi. Take a breather and look for bloodroot in spring and white wood asters in summer. Another plant to look for on this climb is southern harebell, with wispy stems, narrow leaves, and delicate bell-shaped blue flowers. With a hand lens, you can see how neatly the ends of the petals curl away from the long "style," the stalk that conducts pollen to the ovary of the flower. It blooms from late June until the first frost. Reach the rocky crest of Wildcat Mt. at 6.1 mi. and enjoy the good views. You may get to look down on soaring ravens or hear their hoarse *grok-grok* call. (They only say "nevermore" when it's too foggy to hike.) Odd-shaped Yonah Mt., with trees on top but straight rocky sides, lies to the south, and the Cowrock Ridge stretches southwest above a deep creek valley.

Just beyond the crest, a blue-blazed trail descends 1.2 mi. right along a narrow ridge of mountain laurel and down to the Whitley Gap Shelter. This remote shelter has room for five or six hikers, and its spring is 0.3 mi. farther down on a blue-blazed trail. At the intersection with the Whitley Gap side trail, the AT turns left and descends 0.3 mi. to Hogpen Gap in long, easy switchbacks on well-graded trail. Hogpen Gap is the highest point on the scenic highway, and several signs and a GATC hiker plaque in the large parking lot make the AT easy to find even in the all-too-common fog.

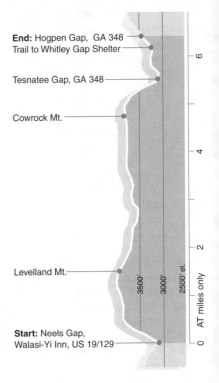

End: Hogpen Gap, GA 348
Trail to Whitley Gap Shelter

Tesnatee Gap, GA 348

Cowrock Mt.

Levelland Mt.

Start: Neels Gap,
Walasi-Yi Inn, US 19/129

AT miles only

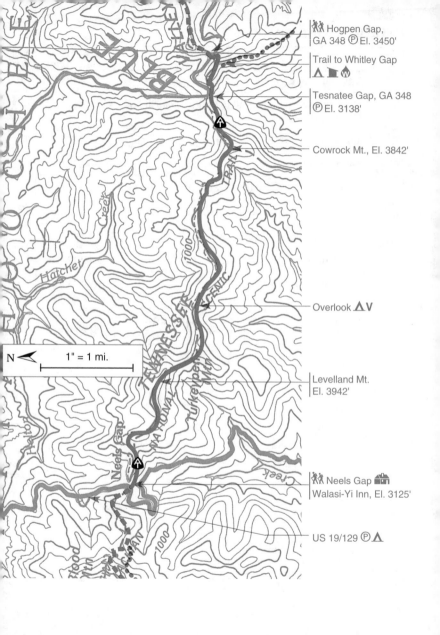

Hogpen Gap,
GA 348 Ⓟ El. 3450'

Trail to Whitley Gap
▲ ⛺ ♨

Tesnatee Gap, GA 348
Ⓟ El. 3138'

Cowrock Mt., El. 3842'

Overlook ▲V

Levelland Mt.
El. 3942'

Neels Gap 🏠
Walasi-Yi Inn, El. 3125'

US 19/129 Ⓟ ▲

N ◄ 1" = 1 mi.

HIKE #4   Itinerary

Miles N	NORTH	Elev. (ft./m)	Miles S
6.4	**End: Hogpen Gap,** GA 348, parking area.	3450/1052	0.0
6.2	Steep blue-blazed side trail to **Whitley Gap Shelter** (1.2 mi.); spring 0.3 mi. farther.		0.2
5.5	**Tesnatee Gap,** GA 348, parking; early exit option.	3138/956	0.9
4.7	**Cowrock Mt.,** campsite and views SE.	3842/1171	1.7
4.2	**Baggs Creek Gap,** spring and campsite.		2.2
2.8	Side trail (50 yd.) to overlook, excellent campsite.		3.6
1.9	Blue-blazed trail L to good spring.		4.0
1.5	**Levelland Mt.,** rocky summit with views S.	3942/1201	4.9
1.1	**Bull Gap,** winter views.	3644/1110	5.3
0.0	**Start: Neels Gap, Walasi-Yi Inn,** US 19/129; hike through the building; toilets, water, food, phone, picnic tables, information.	3125/953	6.4

SOUTH

Hogpen Gap to Unicoi Gap

Maps: ATC Chattahoochee Nat'l. Forest

Route: From Hogpen Gap to Chattahoochee Gap, to Blue Mt., to Unicoi Gap

Recommended direction: S to N

Distance: 13.6 mi.

Elevation +/-: 3450 to 4025 to 2949 ft.

Effort: Strenuous

Day hike: Optional

Overnight backpacking hike: Yes

Duration: 8 to 10 hr.

Early exit option: None

Natural history features: Whiteoak Stamp; boulder fields

Social history feature: Cherokee Nation boundary

Trailhead access: *Start:* Hogpen Gap on GA 348. From Helen, cross the Chattahoochee River on GA 75, go 2.5 mi., and turn R onto Richard B. Russell Scenic Highway (GA 348) for 7.1 mi. to well-marked parking area at Hogpen Gap. Or, from Neels Gap, drive N past Vogel State Park; turn R on GA 180 for 1.0 mi., and turn R on GA 348. At about 5.0 mi., reach Tesnatee Gap. Hogpen Gap is 0.7 mi. farther. *End:* Unicoi Gap on GA 75, 10 mi. N of Helen and 14 mi. S of Hiawassee.

Camping: Low Gap Shelter; Blue Mt. Shelter; several campsites

I magine an ant hiking to see the scenery of a stuffed living room chair. To cross the gently undulating seat cushion, the ant climbs up and over one arm, crosses the cushion, and then climbs over the other arm to get back down to the floor. That about characterizes getting to and from 4 mi. of the easiest AT hiking in Georgia, which comprises the middle of this hike. The AT here makes four short, steep climbs before settling out at 3500 ft. for a stroll along an old forest road. Then it climbs gradually to the summit of Blue Mt. before dropping sharply 1000 ft. in half a mile to Unicoi Gap. The trail goes north for 9 mi. and

then curves southeast around the headwaters of the Chattahoochee River. In two places, hikers travel south on their way north toward Maine.

There are fine views to be had here, but even in a dense, cool February fog it can be exciting. I heard barred owls hooting at midday, watched eight or ten turkeys hurtle through the woods and wondered how they avoided hitting trees, and startled a ruffed grouse, who returned the favor with its explosive whir.

From Hogpen Gap (3450 ft.), the AT leaves the north end of the parking area, about 200 ft. from its southern entry point into the gap. It climbs a ramp into thin woods, then moves away from the road. After a ridge crest, the trail descends gradually past Wolfpen Stamp and then goes through Whiteoak Stamp at 0.8 mi. "Stamps" are open, formerly grassy areas, usually exposed ridgetops or gaps, that probably got the name from being points where livestock were gathered together after summers of grazing in the forest. The forest is returning to stamps now, as it is to the high-elevation grassy "balds" in North Carolina and Tennessee. When the U.S. Forest Service first took over this land, it allowed grazing for many years. In some places cattle still graze on Forest Service land, but you won't see cows in the shelters as hikers did here in the 1940s.

The AT continues up and down along the ridgetop that divides the Chattahoochee River drainage from the Tennessee River drainage. Both drainages flow into the Gulf of Mexico, but water on the Tennessee side first cuts through the western Blue Ridge, then visits Alabama, Tennessee, Kentucky, Mississippi, and Louisiana.

At 1.6 mi. the trail passes Sapling Gap (3450 ft.), ascends to the summit of Poor Mt. (3650 ft.), then follows a narrow ridge down to Wide Gap (3150 ft.) at 2.3 mi. Winter views from the ridge and the gap below reveal the Chattahoochee River Valley in the east and Blood and Slaughter mts. in the west. This divide was also the eastern boundary of remaining Cherokee lands before the tribe was forcibly removed in 1838. When DeSoto arrived in 1540, the Cherokee Nation included what is now Kentucky, most of Tennessee and western North Carolina, and parts of Virginia and West Virginia. The tribal nation was systematically reduced by disastrous treaties, smallpox epidemics, and battles until it occupied just a small part of north Georgia.

After Wide Gap (3150 ft., 2.3 mi.) the AT climbs Sheep Rock Top (3575 ft.), then drops down to 3050 ft. at Low Gap. At 4.2 mi. a side trail leads right 0.1 mi. to the Low Gap Shelter, which has a creek and a spring nearby. In summer, this may be the best water source for camping farther along the trail. The shelter sits on a slope; the front is up on stilts with big logs to climb up to the sleeping platform.

From Low Gap the AT ascends gently on a good, wide trail to Poplar Stamp Gap, with several campsites. Water is seasonally available at a stream about 600 ft. down an old fire road to the right; in dry weather, it may be a longer walk down before reaching running water.

The AT then follows the fire road 0.5 mi. along the east side of Horsetrough Mt. Before 1950 the AT went up Horsetrough Mt. to follow the ridge crest. However, it was steep and hard to maintain, so the Georgia AT Club (GATC) chose the lower route, as many hikers had already done informally. There are many springs and campsites along the road, which goes through mature hardwood forest of white oak, sourwood, hickory, and a few dogwoods. Where streams cross the road, clusters of golden ragwort and other spring wildflowers grow. In summer, white wood asters and bee balm, or wild bergamot, bloom here. Bee balm is in the mint family and has fragrant leaves and flowers. The more common species here has greenish, spherical flowers with ragged petals that stick out like Albert Einstein's hair. Pinch one gently to get a refreshing minty smell on your fingers; you don't have to damage or pick the flower.

On the drier sandy parts of the road, look for pipsissewa, or spotted wintergreen, though it's neither spotted nor aromatic. Only 6 to 8 in. tall, this plant is classified as a shrub because it has some woody tissue in its stem. Each of its narrow pointed leaves has a dark-green margin with paler markings along the central vein and its branches. Another way pipsissewa defies classification is that its few leaves are opposite, whorled (several circled around the same spot on the stem), or scattered. But once you know it, you will always recognize it, and it lives in every state the AT crosses. In July several white flowers hang from the curved stem apex like streetlights for ants. After seed formation, the stems straighten, perhaps to scatter seeds farther from the capsule.

Downy woodpecker

At 8.0 mi. reach Cold Springs Gap (3450 ft.), which has no spring, but there *is* a flat grassy campsite.

The AT leaves the fire road and ascends a bit before turning down a narrow ridgetop to another campsite. After a left turn at 8.5 mi., the trail climbs the opposite ridge, goes over the crest, and enters 3500-ft. Chattahoochee Gap at 9.2 mi. Blue-blazed Jack's Knob National Recreation Trail goes straight, crosses GA 180, and climbs 4.5 mi. to Brasstown Bald. The AT angles right from the top of the ridge, and another blue-blazed trail leads right about 600 ft. to a spring said to be the source of the Chattahoochee River, which provides water for Atlanta and many other Georgia and Alabama communities as it flows south on the border of these two states. In 1932 a party of GATC hikers determined that this spring fed the "highest and most northerly stream source of the Chattahoochee." In 1877 Georgia poet Sydney Lanier wrote "Song of the Chattahoochee," describing the river's path through Georgia. Of course, many springs contribute to the Chattahoochee, and each provides sparkling, clean water purified by percolation through mountain soil and rock, one of the many ecosystem services that forests provide. Even so, treat *all* drinking water in case of surface contamination.

From Chattahoochee Gap, the AT goes down the south side of the ridge to Red Clay Gap (3450 ft.) and then rises to cross over to the left (north) side of Rocky Knob (4014 ft.) at 10.9 mi. There's no longer a shelter here, but the ridgetop makes a good campsite.

From here to Unicoi Gap the trail stays mostly on the north-facing slope and north of the Tennessee Valley Divide. North-facing slopes receive less direct sunlight and thus retain more moisture in the soil. This allows more plants to grow, contributing more leaves for humus. Plants are adapted to each habitat: rhododendrons, tulip-trees, Jack-in-the-pulpits, ferns, and mosses usually thrive on north-facing slopes, while mountain laurel, pines, trailing arbutus, and lichens do better on drier, south-facing slopes. The spring wildflower display is excellent on the rest of this trail, especially near the many springs and seeps.

Some north-facing southern Appa-

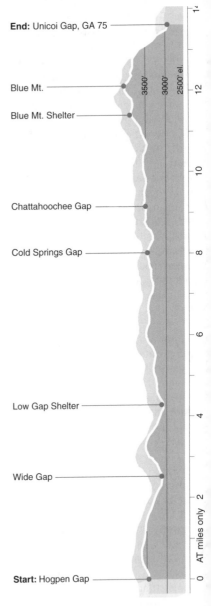

End: Unicoi Gap, GA 75

Blue Mt.

Blue Mt. Shelter

3500'

3000'

2500' el.

Chattahoochee Gap

Cold Springs Gap

Low Gap Shelter

Wide Gap

Start: Hogpen Gap

AT miles only →

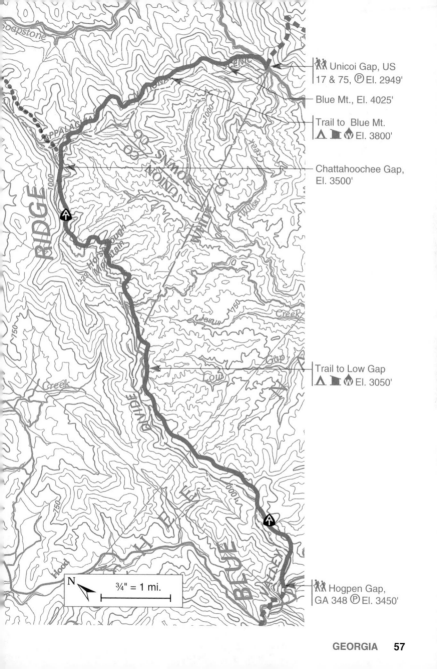

🚶🚶 Unicoi Gap, US
17 & 75, Ⓟ El. 2949'

Blue Mt., El. 4025'

Trail to Blue Mt.
▲ ▉ Ⓦ El. 3800'

Chattahoochee Gap,
El. 3500'

Trail to Low Gap
▲ ▉ Ⓦ El. 3050'

Hogpen Gap,
GA 348 Ⓟ El. 3450'

N
¾" = 1 mi.

lachian slopes have boulder fields, and you will see many between Red Clay Gap and the slope down from Blue Mt. Though no glaciers covered these southern mountains, lots of frigid air flowed south along the Appalachian chain. During glacial periods, water that had seeped down into rock fissures during summer froze in winter and expanded, pushing boulders out of the ground and in some cases sending them tumbling down the mountain. Some of the boulder fields here look like boulder rivers. Ferns and mosses cover the rocks, and some of the boulders have rooftop gardens of trillium, foamflower, and Solomon's-seal.

At 11.0 mi. the AT reaches Henson Gap (3550 ft.), passes a good spring on the left at 11.3 mi., and at 11.4 mi. it meets the blue-blazed side trail to the Blue Mt. Shelter. This relatively new concrete shelter looks like a bus stop up on posts, and it is so open that the wind will blow rain in to clean up after sloppy campers. It faces east; no one will sleep late here. A registry note on a cold, raw February day from Dan and his dog Abby: "God bless the Gore family and their fine fabrics (2/26/97)."

Back on the main trail, the AT keeps to the narrow ridgetop along the wooded and fern-covered Blue Mt. summit for about 0.4 mi. and then drops down left through boulder fields and traverses rocky trail with many switchbacks. And it keeps going down, losing 1000 ft. of elevation in 1.2 mi. Finally it bottoms out at the busy parking area of Unicoi Gap at 2949 ft.

HIKE #5   Itinerary

Miles N	NORTH	Elev. (ft./m)	Miles S
13.6	**End: Unicoi Gap,** GA 75; parking area.	2949/899	0.0
12.2	**Blue Mt.,** wooded summit.	4025/1227	1.4
11.4	Side trail to **Blue Mt. Shelter,** (0.2 mi.).; spring 0.1 mi. back (S) on AT.	3800/1158	2.2
10.9	**Rocky Knob,** campsite.	4014/1223	2.7
9.2	**Chattahoochee Gap;** jct. blue-blazed **Jack's Knob Trail** to **Brasstown Bald** (4.5 mi.).	3500/1067	4.4
8.0	**Cold Springs Gap,** campsite.	3450/1051	5.6
4.2	Trail to **Low Gap Shelter** (0.1mi.); spring and creek.	3050/930	9.4
2.3	**Wide Gap,** winter views.	3150/960	11.3
1.6	**Sapling Gap.**	3450/1051	12.9
0.0	**Start: Hogpen Gap,** parking area.	3450/1051	13.6

SOUTH

HIKE #6
Unicoi Gap to Tray Gap

Maps: ATC Chattahoochee Nat'l. Forest
Route: From Unicoi Gap to Rocky Mt., to Indian Grave Gap, to Tray Gap
Recommended direction: S to N
Distance: 4.4 mi. (6.2 with out and back to Tray Mt.; see Hike #7)
Elevation +/-: 2949 to 4017 to 3847 ft. (4430 ft. with Tray Mt.)
Effort: Strenuous
Day hike: Yes
Overnight backpacking hike: No
Duration: 4 to 5 hr., including Tray Mt. out and back
Early exit option: Indian Grave Gap, at 2.7mi.

Natural history feature: Boulder field
Social history feature: Cheese factory site
Trailhead access: *Start:* Unicoi Gap on GA 75, 10 mi. N of Helen and 14 mi. S of Hiawassee. *End:* Tray Gap, junction of USFS 79 and USFS 698 (Corbin Creek Rd.). Drive 4.5 mi. N on GA 348, R onto gravel USFS 698 for about 9 mi. to junction with USFS 79 at Tray Gap. *Caution:* USFS 698 is steep in spots; check with USFS Brasstown Ranger District (706-745-6928) for current conditions.
Camping: Several campsites

O n a cold day, this hike is guaranteed to warm you up with two climbs of about 1000 ft. plus another 500-ft. climb if you choose to include Tray Mt. (see Hike #7) Southern views from both Tray Mt. and Rocky Mt. show the expanse of diminishing hills toward the coastal plains. Campsites and water are plentiful along this trail; in fact, a two- or three-day backpack combining this hike with Hike #7 is recommended as a beautiful hike of 15.3 mi. with easy access at both ends. Hikes #6 and #7 are described separately because they can be done as day hikes, and loop hikes are possible with Hike #6.

These two challenging hikes run along the extreme southeastern rim

of the Georgia Blue Ridge and offer high ridges, deep gaps, and no comparable mountains to the south. In some parts of the AT, once you reach a high elevation, you stay there for a few miles, but not in Georgia. While the continental collision with Africa that formed the Appalachian chain pushed great, even ridges to the north of here, in Georgia the rock layers slipped and tumbled. Imagine a huge bulldozer moving a solid mass of mountains west across the landscape; you are now hiking up and down the rubble that falls off the left side of the blade.

The climb out of Unicoi Gap is steep and unrelenting for 0.5 mi.; switchbacks help. Look for the fragile white blossoms of bloodroot and the reddish-brown toadshade trillium in spring, and the rattlesnake plantain flowers in July. The evergreen leaves of this small orchid have white veins patterned like snake scales. The leaves lie on the ground in a rosette, while the tiny white flowers grow up on a stalk 10 to 15 in. tall.

Take a rest and look back across Unicoi Gap to the equally steep climb to Blue Mt. After a small seep (a place where spring water flows across the trail surface), the trail continues to climb through a boulder field with many fallen chestnut logs. Though no glaciers reached this far south, the cold winters of the glacial periods formed boulder fields, especially on north-facing slopes. Water that seeped into rock fissures during summer froze in winter and expanded, pushing broken rocks up through the soil—Pleistocene frost heaves. Mosses, rock ferns, and rock tripe live on the boulders. A lichen, rock tripe grows in roundish green and black flakes, from cornflake size to Frisbee size. The Cherokee call it blood leather and used it as bandages over bleeding wounds.

The AT runs parallel to a creek on the left, then turns left and crosses it at 0.6 mi. At 0.9 mi., a blue-blazed trail leads left to Indian Grave Gap. This trail parallels the AT (and is about the same distance) and can be used for a loop or to bypass the summit of Rocky Mt. in stormy or icy weather. There is a pretty ridgetop campsite here at the trail junction also, but you must bring water.

The AT turns right onto the ridge crest and climbs gently to the grassy summit of Rocky Mt. at 4017 ft. and 1.3 mi. There are good winter views to the west, and then the AT swings around for open views to the south. The odd-looking mountain with rock-slab sides is Yonah, visited by John Muir on September 22, 1867. John Muir averaged more than 25 mi. each day on his thousand-mile walk from Kentucky to the Gulf of Mexico— with no Gore-Tex—and he still had plenty of time and energy to socialize in the evening!

Descend the bare rock south face of Rocky Mt., which supports lichens, blueberry bushes, and wind-whipped ancient white oaks. Bluets and mountain mint grow in soil pockets on the rock, while black moss grows in wet spots. If you examine this plant with a hand lens (do this at the moss's level instead of picking it), you will see a bright green spire coming out of each tiny black moss plant.

The trail moves to the middle of the ridge and then back to the southern edge. The trail builders did some excellent rock work to help you down the steepest part, but ice or water may make it slippery.

At 2.7 mi. the AT reaches Indian Grave Gap (3113 ft.) and crosses gravel USFS 283. This road goes left to GA 348 in about 7 mi. but may require high-clearance vehicles. To the right, it joins USFS 79 to Tray Gap. The blue-blazed bypass trail from Rocky Mt. rejoins the AT here, and another blue-blazed trail goes 2.0 mi.

right to the U.S. Forest Service Andrews Cove campground.

The AT ascends steps lined with mountain laurel on the left and rhododendron on the right, their intermingled branches forming a tunnel overhead. Round galax leaves cover the ground, sending up a flower spike in late May or June. The laurel takes over both sides of the trail and then gives way to open forest of sourwoods, maples, and — Georgia's specialty — gnarled and twisted oaks. The trail descends and crosses USFS 79 at 3.4 mi., then repeats the same pattern: up steps, laurel left, rhododendron right. But this time, after the woods there are several open, grassy campsites. A wide grassy gap marks the site of an 1840s cheese factory. Major Edward Williams, a New Englander, came to Nacoochee Valley in 1828. Twenty years later he set up a remote mountain dairy farm for butter and cheese, the only one in Georgia. The cattle thrived in the wilderness, and the cheese factory did quite well for many years. But now the only signs of it are clearings and old roads. A blue-blazed trail left crosses USFS 79 to a creek for water about 100 yd. from the AT.

Cross the clearing and climb, turn left, and climb again to an excellent campsite at about 4.2 mi. surrounded by white oaks and with an eastern view from a rock outcrop. At a double white blaze, turn right through a blackberry patch to Tray Gap. The AT runs beside USFS 79 & 698 and then crosses it at a large parking area. For

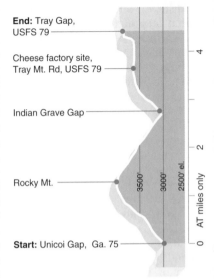

End: Tray Gap, USFS 79

Cheese factory site, Tray Mt. Rd, USFS 79

Indian Grave Gap

Rocky Mt.

Start: Unicoi Gap, Ga. 75

a description of the climb to Tray Mt., see Hike #7.

Alternative hikes could be made with the Andrews Cove Trail and the Rocky Mt. bypass. One possibility would be to park one car at Andrews Cove and a second at Unicoi Gap (avoiding the long gravel-road drive). Andrews Cove is a south-facing warm valley with a good show of wildflowers along a creek. Hike from Unicoi Gap to Tray Mt., back along the AT to Indian Grave Gap, and then down to Andrews Cove (2080 ft.). Total hike distance: 9.5 mi.; elevation changes: 2949 to 4430 to 2080 ft. — enough to impress your friends from New Hampshire.

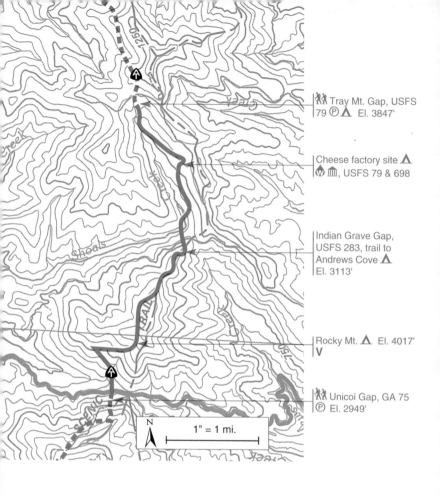

🚶🚶 Tray Mt. Gap, USFS 79 Ⓟ 🔺 El. 3847'

Cheese factory site 🔺 Ⓦ 🏛, USFS 79 & 698

Indian Grave Gap, USFS 283, trail to Andrews Cove 🔺 El. 3113'

Rocky Mt. 🔺 El. 4017' V

🚶🚶 Unicoi Gap, GA 75 Ⓟ El. 2949'

N
1" = 1 mi.

Miles N	NORTH	Elev. (ft./m)	Miles S
4.4	**End: Tray Gap,** USFS 79 & 698; parking and grassy campsites.	3847/1173	0.0
3.6	Cheese factory site, open area in sight of USFS 79; creek 100 yd. from AT.		0.8
3.4	Cross Tray Mt. Rd., USFS 79; limited parking on road.		1.0
2.7	**Indian Grave Gap,** cross USFS 283; jct. blue-blazed **Andrews Cove Trail** to USFS campground (2.0 mi.); early exit option.	3113/949	1.7
1.3	**Rocky Mt.,** exposed rocks with excellent views.	4017/1224	3.1
0.9	Blue-blazed trail L to **Indian Grave Gap,** Rocky Mt. bypass trail; ridgetop campsite.		3.5
0.0	**Start: Unicoi Gap,** GA 75; parking.	2949/899	4.4

SOUTH

Tray Gap to Dicks Creek Gap

Maps: ATC Chattahoochee Nat'l. Forest

Route: From Tray Gap to Tray Mt., to Swag of the Blue Ridge, to Kelly Knob, to Dicks Creek Gap

Recommended direction: S to N

Distance: 11.7 mi.

Elevation +/-: 3847 to 4430 to 2675 ft.

Effort: Very strenuous

Day hike: Yes

Overnight backpacking hike: Optional

Duration: 8 to 10 hr.

Early exit option: None

Natural history features: Tray Mt. Wilderness; Swag of the Blue Ridge

Trailhead access: *Start:* From Unicoi Gap, head 4.5 mi. N on GA 348. Turn R onto gravel USFS 698 (Corbin Creek Rd.) for about 9 mi. to junction with USFS 79 at Tray Gap. *Caution:* USFS 698 is steep in spots; check with USFS Brasstown Ranger District (706-745-6928) for current conditions. *End:* Dicks Creek Gap on US 76, 11 mi. E of Hiawassee and 18 mi. W of Clayton. From Unicoi Gap, drive N on GA 75 for about 7 mi. Turn R (E) on US 76 for about 7 more mi. to well-marked Dicks Creek Gap.

Camping: Deep Gap Shelter; Tray Mt. Shelter; many campsites

If an aerobic challenge gets your heart pumping in more ways than one, this hike will be to your liking —and it's worth every penny of oxygen debt. It starts off at the second highest mountain on the Georgia AT and ends at the lowest trailhead gap. (Want an even greater aerobic challenge? Do it from north to south.) The route includes remote, roadless areas of the Tray Mt. Wilderness, views in all directions, and masses of rhododendron, mountain laurel, and flame azalea. In 1961 the U.S. Congress voted to extend the Blue Ridge Parkway along this route. The Georgia Appalachian Trail Club (GATC) and the U.S. Forest Service had to build and maintain an alternate AT route for almost two decades while controversies over the Blue Ridge extension raged. In the end, the extension was not built. The Wilderness Bill of 1964, the National Scenic Trails Act of 1968, and the publication of this original route into the Federal Register now offer triple protection for this beautiful wild land that the GATC and other groups fought long and hard to protect.

From Tray Gap, enter the woods and pass a Tray Mt. Wilderness sign. A Wilderness designation means no roads or buildings, but it also means no power tools. Look for signs that the volunteer trail maintainers have been there with axes and handsaws

Dogwood

to clear fallen trees from the trail. Climb rocky, narrow trail with switchbacks around huge rock slabs. Bloodroot, toothwort, and star chickweed bloom in moist spots in early spring. A last switchback before the Tray Mt. summit leads into dense mountain laurel and Catawba rhododendron. Usually growing on summits and having shorter, rounder leaves than the more common rosebay rhododendron, Catawba rhododendron has pink to lavender blooms in June.

At 0.8 mi. reach the 4430-ft. summit of Tray Mt., a rock outcrop with 360-degree views. Mt. Yonah is prominent to the south, and Georgia's two highest peaks—Brasstown Bald (4784 ft.) and Rabun Bald (4696 ft.)—are to the northwest and northeast. Between them lie the more distant but higher Nantahalas in North Carolina. Chatuge Lake in Hiawassee is visible just west of Brasstown Bald. An earlier name for this mountain was Trail Mt. because the Cherokee could see from up here if anyone was approaching on the trails of the region.

Listen for the calls of ravens (an eerie *grok, grok*), juncos (a metallic high trill), and towhees (*drink-your-tea* or *charee*). These three birds can be seen and heard on most open Blue Ridge mountaintops. The towhees specialize in real estate, making a racket in dry underbrush as they scratch for insects; the juncos check to make sure you didn't leave any sandwich crumbs; and the ravens use the thermals—warm air masses rising from the valleys—to soar overhead.

Descend past more mountain laurel to a campsite at 1.0 mi. on the right and then to well-graded trail on a broad ridgetop. At a double blaze at 1.0 mi., the white-blazed AT goes right, while a blue-blazed path goes 0.2 mi. left to Tray Mt. Shelter (called Montray on some maps). This shelter, renovated in 2006, is a good place to lunch, rest, or sleep. It has storage shelves under the eaves, more storage shelves and pack hooks inside, a pleasant grassy area in front, a spring, and a privy.

The AT continues steeply down the south slope of Tray Mt., crosses a seep, and descends stone steps to a saddle—a dip in the ridge crest—with especially warty oaks. The descent becomes gentle and easy. At 2.3 mi., the AT reaches Wolfpen Gap (3760 ft.) though open oak woods and some patches of cane, or bamboo, the only native woody grass. Then comes Steeltrap Gap at 2.8 mi.,

Hiking in Fog

No views, cold and damp, too foggy. Might as well stay home, right? Wrong! Foggy hiking is fun and full of surprises.

1. Tastes and smells are more intense in wet weather. To test this, smell or chew any of the following that you can identify with accuracy: sassafras twigs, pine or hemlock needles (the hemlock tree is not the hemlock that poisoned Socrates), bee balm and other mints, wintergreen leaves or berries, rock tripe, sourwood leaves, wood sorrel. Also, take a small piece of candy, perhaps a kind that you gobble after a hard climb, and dissolve it slowly on your tongue.

2. Talk to owls. Barred owls and great-horned owls often call during overcast or foggy days. If you hear a call, especially the *who-cooks-for-you* call of the barred owl, answer it. Cup your hands and call toward the sound. Not loudly—you may offend the owls and other hikers, and you might even get mobbed by crows. Just get a gentle dialogue going.

3. In dense fog on level trail, try an optical illusion. Walk quickly but carefully forward for 50 or 100 paces, focusing on a tree trunk or branch farther ahead. Pine trees or other dark shapes work best. Then stop suddenly (warn fellow hikers beforehand), focusing on the same spot. The trees in your peripheral vision may appear to keep moving in the fog. If it doesn't work, relax and try again later. For me, this works only in dense fog and quiet woods. The effect is enhanced on foggy winter days, when snow increases the contrast in the woods.

4. If you are warm and dry, sit beside a spring or lean back on a mossy boulder and listen, smell, and feel. Taste a raindrop that rolls down your face.

5. In summer, use a flashlight to examine wet rocks, decaying logs, or leaf litter for salamanders, snails, worms, millipedes, daddy longlegs, and other animals that know good weather when they feel it.

---

with a campsite and a blue-blazed trail on the right for water.

The next ascent is also easy. Look for purple-veined hawkweed leaves on the trail bank. The bright-yellow flowers appear from May to July. With a hand lens, you can see that the leaves have a dense coat of hair. While you're down on your knees looking at hawkweed, also look for pussytoes, another flower in the aster family. The flower looks like furry pussy's toes, but a hand lens reveals that each "toe" is a cluster of creamy, delicate flowers.

The trail rises toward a ridge crest and a grassy, even campsite at 3.3 mi. The oaks here reach a new level of wartiness, with warts upon warts and burls like bustles and elephant seal snouts. Some of the larger burls have sprouted anew; some support other plants whose seeds have landed on them. The AT goes along the almost level ridgetop and then down smooth, easy trail to the Swag of the Blue Ridge (3400 ft., 4.5 mi.). This gentle depression in the midst of steep rocky mountains (like the swag, or hanging fold, in a velvet theater curtain) was a rallying point for the GATC and the coalition of conservation groups that worked for so many years to save this high ridgeline trail from road builders. When Earl Shaffer, the first recorded Georgia-to-Maine thru-hiker, came through the swag in 1948, cows, pigs, horses, and sheep grazed in the woods. He found many of the shelters on this trail occupied by cows.

Ascend through a mountain laurel thicket to 3964-ft. Round Top at 5.2 mi., one of the peaks of Dismal Mt., and then descend to Sassafras Gap at 5.6 mi. Another easy descent leads to Addis Gap (3304 ft.) at 6.4 mi., where there are campsites as well as old roads. The Addis family lived in this remote spot until 1942; imagine how surprised they would be today to see hundreds of hikers trudging past their home on the way to Maine. Water and another campsite can be found 0.5 mi. down an old road to the right. The Tray Mt. Wilderness ends here.

The swag part of this hike is over; the climb out of Addis Gap is a steep up, a short rest, then another steep up 600 ft. in less than 0.5 mi. to the side of Kelly Knob. The AT swings around

Continued on p. 70

Kelly Knob (4276 ft., 7.5 mi.), giving a view of Chatuge Lake to the west.

Descend on rocky but good trail to Deep Gap (3550 ft.), where a blue-blazed trail at 8.4 mi. leads 0.3 mi. right, past a good spring to the Deep Gap Shelter. The shelter was built in 1991 by the GATC, the Forest Service, and a local business, Loft Designs. Appropriately, it has two sleeping

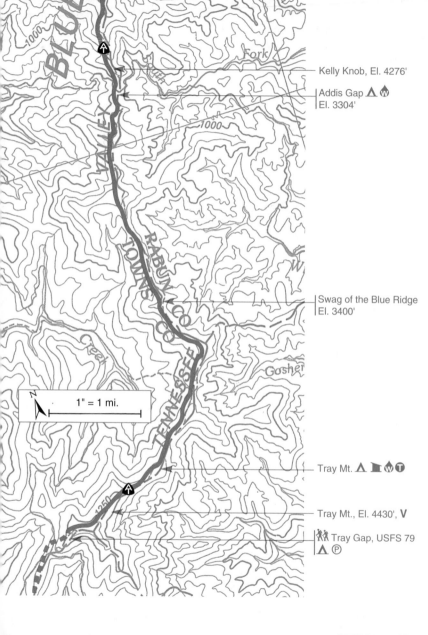

Kelly Knob, El. 4276'

Addis Gap △ ⓦ
El. 3304'

Swag of the Blue Ridge
El. 3400'

Tray Mt. △ ◼ⓦ❶

Tray Mt., El. 4430', **V**

👫 Tray Gap, USFS 79
△ ⓟ

1" = 1 mi.

lofts, a large veranda for cooking and eating, windows, a deck, bear cables, a privy, and plenty of grassy area around for camping.

Leaving Deep Gap, the AT starts another steep climb — but only half as high as the last one. A piped spring near the top of the ridge provides water to hikers and to a large patch of jewelweed, or touch-me-not. This plant grows waist high by midsummer and produces yellow or orange flowers that dangle from threadlike stalks. "Jewelweed" refers to the way water beads on its leaves, and "touch-me-not" refers to its explosive green seedpods that disperse seed with the help of passing hikers to set them off. If you are hiking in late summer or fall, find a ripe seedpod and cup your hand around it to capture the seeds as it explodes. Examine the rough brown coat of the seed with a hand lens. This surface may help the seed stick where it lands and not go rolling downhill to a dry place. Peel the brown skin off the seed to reveal the sky-blue undercoat. Then eat the seeds in your hand. They taste like the meat of black walnuts — and are much easier to get to.

Cross the ridgetop and descend past Whiteoak Stamp (a stamp is an open grassy area where livestock were assembled) and Wolf Stake Knob. At 9.1 mi. a blue-blazed side trail leads right to a small private campsite and a southeastern vista with blueberry bushes surrounding a rock outcrop.

In 0.2 mi. past the side trail, the AT

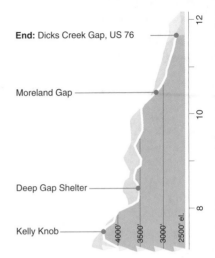

reaches McClure Gap, a notch in the ridgetop that must have caught a blast from Hurricane Opal in 1995; many trees are down here.

Ascend a bit and then descend through a mountain laurel thicket to Moreland Gap and campsite at 10.5 mi. with a spring on the right. The AT turns right and, after a short climb through hollies, tulip-trees, and dogwoods, starts down again. A high ridgeline looms to the left, and seeps and tiny creeks cross the trail. After another mountain laurel tunnel and a small bridged creek, the AT joins an old road and descends steeply through rhododendron with a noisy creek on the left. A double blaze indicates a left turn into a tangle of mountain laurel, and then the trail reaches Dicks Creek Gap and US 76 at 11.7 mi., this hike's end.

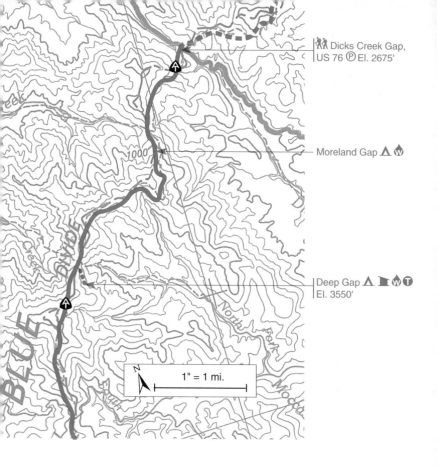

Dicks Creek Gap,
US 76 Ⓟ El. 2675'

Moreland Gap ▲ Ⓦ

Deep Gap ▲ ◼ Ⓦ Ⓣ
El. 3550'

1000

BLUE DIVIDE

North Fork

N
1" = 1 mi.

Miles N	NORTH	Elev. (ft./m)	Miles S
11.7	**End: Dicks Creek Gap,** US 76; parking and picnic area.	2675/815	0.0
10.5	**Moreland Gap,** campsite and spring.	3050/929	1.2
8.4	Trail to **Deep Gap Shelter** (0.3 mi.), good spring, privy.	3550/1082	3.3
7.5	**Kelly Knob,** steep hike up with a R turn on top; views.	4276/1303	4.2
6.4	**Addis Gap,** campsites; water 0.5 mi. to R on old road.	3304/1007	5.3
5.6	**Sassafras Gap.**	3500/1067	6.1
4.5	**Blue Ridge Swag.**	3400/1036	7.2
2.3	**Wolfpen Gap.**	3760/1146	9.4
1.1	Jct. blue-blazed trail to **Tray Mt. Shelter** (0.2mi.), spring and privy; views from rocky summit.		10.6
0.8	**Tray Mt.,** excellent views.	4430/1350	10.9
0.0	**Start: Tray Gap,** USFS 79; parking and campsites.	3847/1173	11.7

SOUTH

Dicks Creek Gap to Deep Gap (NC)

Maps: ATC Nantahala Nat'l. Forest and Chattahoochee Nat'l. Forest

Route: From Dicks Creek Gap to Plumorchard Gap, to Bly Gap, to Muskrat Creek, to Deep Gap

Recommended direction: S to N

Distance: 15.6 mi.

Elevation +/-: 2675 to 4800 to 4341 ft.

Effort: Strenuous

Day hike: No

Overnight backpacking hike: Yes

Duration: 11 to 12 hr.

Early exit option: None

Natural history feature: Southern Nantahala Wilderness Area

Trailhead access: *Start:* From Hiawassee, drive 11 mi. E on US 76 to Dicks Creek Gap. From Clayton, Drive 18 mi. W on US 76. From Unicoi Gap, head N on GA 75 for about 7 mi. Turn R (E) on US 76 for about 7 mi. to well-marked Dicks Creek Gap parking area just W of the gap crest. *End:* From Winding Stair Gap on US 64, head W for 5 mi. Go L onto USFS 71 for 6 mi. to Deep Gap at end of road. USFS 71 is closed in winter.

Camping: Plumorchard Gap Shelter; Muskrat Creek Shelter; several campsites

In May and June, rhododendron, flame azalea, and mountain laurel bloom on the ridgetops of this trail section, while in fall and winter, hikers can enjoy the good views. At any time of year, this hike is a good length for an overnight trip, but it does have some steep and rocky sections. Since the driving distance between Dicks Creek and Deep Gap is long, you may want to hike in to Bly Gap (which has no road access) from either end and backtrack (see the Itinerary). Much of the trail goes through the Southern Nantahala Wilderness Area, designated by Congress in 1984 for its remoteness and beauty. Though the two shelters on this section receive a lot of use in the spring, at other times

of the year they are ideal overnight spots. Two campsites, at 1.2 mi. and 6.6 mi., lie well off the trail and provide quiet and privacy. A side trail to Ravenrock Cliff (1.2 mi. round-trip) near Muskrat Creek Shelter is worth the extra effort, especially if you camp in that area.

To start, look for the white blazes beyond the picnic tables of Dicks Creek Gap. Ascend along a creek to a ridge crest, cross it, and descend into a small gap. Climb the side of the next ridge (Little Bald Knob) on dry, rocky trail to the crest at 1.1 mi. A sign indicates a campsite about 0.1 mi. to the right. Water for camping is available 0.1 mi. farther ahead on the AT. Ascend a little beyond the sign

Christmas fern

and then start down steep trail with switchbacks. At the bottom is Cowart Gap (1.8 mi.) with old roadbeds and tall white pines, probably planted after logging.

The trail climbs, levels briefly, then climbs some more along a narrow ridge crest. It skirts to the right of Buzzard Knob at 3.0 mi., with winter views of Standing Indian Mt. to the northeast and the Nantahala Mts. beyond. Descend to Bull Gap and climb out again, through thickets of mountain laurel.

After a descent of about 0.5 mi., the AT levels out at 4.3 mi. in Plumorchard Gap (3090 ft.), which may have had plum trees at one time but now has white pines and hardwoods. A faint trail leads left to a spring, and a signed blue-blazed trail leads 0.2 mi. right to the Plumorchard Gap

Shelter, the only three-story shelter I have seen. The building sits on concrete supports, and ladders give access to two sleeping lofts above the basic sleeping platform. It was built by the Georgia Appalachian Trail Club (GATC), the U.S. Forest Service, and the Army 5th Ranger Training Battalion. The upper loft even has windows. Hanging pegs for packs, shelves, a picnic table, a grill, a sheltered area for cooking and eating, hooks outside for wet gear, and a privy make this shelter more than comfortable.

The trail crosses a creek where there is a water pipe. (Note: the pipe just serves to make it easier to fill water containers; this water still needs to be treated.) Then comes another climb over As Knob and an easy descent into Blue Ridge Gap (5.6 mi., 3020 ft.) through mountain laurel tunnels. A road (USFS 72 from US 76) crosses the gap, but it usually requires four-wheel-drive vehicles.

The trail climbs steeply out of Blue Ridge Gap through tall white pines and enters the Southern Nantahala Wilderness area, shared by Georgia and North Carolina. After some more climbing, a welcome level stretch appears at 6.6 mi. A side trail to the left leads past two small springs to a campsite on a pretty knoll. From there the AT curves around a sheltered cove between Wheeler Knob and Rocky Knob, with a ridge crest on the right and a wonderful view down into the tops of bushes and trees on the left. You might hear the laughlike call of a

Unfriendly Weather

act one: It will happen. *Rule one:* Be prepared. Get the best weather report you can in the 24 hours prior to your hike. If wet, windy, or cold weather is due, plan for worse in the mountains and woods. Even on day hikes, carry a clothing change in a plastic bag in your pack. If you or others get soaked in a downpour, watch for signs of hypothermia (shivering, disorientation, anxiety, weakness). Wet and cold bring it on; fatigue, despair, and fear exacerbate it. Take preventive steps (shelter, dry clothes, warm liquids, wrap in sleeping bag, reassurance).

Slipping or falling is another danger in wet weather. Stay together, lend a hand, focus on the path beneath your feet. Many hikers find a walking stick helpful. Keep your backpack load reasonable and well balanced (see "Packing Your Pack," page 20).

If a storm approaches (watch the sky for thunderheads or general darkening, listen to the wind or distant thunder), get off mountaintops, exposed ridges, or ledges. Avoid balds and other open areas. Deep forest is safest, but stay away from large dead trees. If you are close to the end of the hike when a storm arrives, keep moving toward your car unless there are exposed spaces to cross.

Overnight hikes are especially prone to weather surprises. If the weather threatens, take the following steps:

- If there is a shelter nearby in either direction, go there to wait out the storm or to decide what to do next.
- If an official campsite is near, get there; set up and take shelter. If not, find a level, well-drained place and set up your tent. Position the door away from the approaching storm.
- Once inside your tent, take inventory. Know where dry clothes, food, light, toiletries, and your first-aid kit are. If you have wet feet or hair, dry off the best you can. Keep your sleeping pad and sleeping bag dry.
- Make a plan: What can you eat without cooking over a stove? If your tent has a vestibule, you may be able to use a stove (with a windshield) at its outer perimeter, but never light a stove inside your tent.
- Before dark, decide how you will handle a run to the privy or pit toilet and how you will hang your food bag outdoors out of the reach of bears (see "Food Storage," page 17).

After you have made these preparations, the fun begins. Indulge in a long nap. Write in your journal. Read, if there's enough daylight. Play word games, sing songs, tell tall tales, or just listen to the music of the storm.

Study your trail guide. Look for alternative early exit routes. If you are the leader, keep your own counsel and do not spread anger or anxiety. Patience, calm, good humor, and a plan will see you through most any bad weather. And it'll make a great story when you get back home.

—David Emblidge

pileated woodpecker from deep in the cove, and in spring and fall, migrating warblers will be active in the treetops. Rocky springs along the trail support mosses, ferns, and wild-flowers, and if the exposed steep ridges of this hike have been too hot, you will feel cooler here.

At the end of this easy section is the moist and fern-filled Rich Cove Gap at 6.8 mi., followed by a short climb, and then some ridgetop ups and downs along the divide. There are winter views and occasional summer glimpses of Hightower Bald on the left and Standing Indian Mt. looming ahead to the right.

The trail leaves the ridge crest and slips to the left. At 8.6 mi. look for a piece of pipe nailed to an oak tree that marks the border between Georgia and North Carolina. About 0.1 mi. after the border, the trail swings right to a hollow with a spring and an overused camping area where tents and campfires have killed most of the groundcover. A short steep climb to the left up an eroded old road brings you to Bly Gap at 8.8 mi., marked by a strange gnarled oak — it looks as if it got wrestled to the ground in its youth but kept growing anyway, and it's a good place to take a picture to celebrate the border crossing.

Bly Gap has sloping grassy areas for camping, and water is available 0.1 mi. south on the AT at the spring beside the lower campsite. The open gap provides good views on both sides, with the Tusquitee Mts. on the left, but it is often windy and cold.

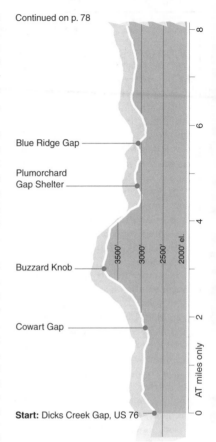

Continued on p. 78

Blue Ridge Gap

Plumorchard
Gap Shelter

Buzzard Knob

Cowart Gap

AT miles only

Start: Dicks Creek Gap, US 76

3500' 3000' 2500' 2000' el.

Camping impact has been heavy at the gap also. Try not to add to the damage. One way to reduce tent impact is to carefully remove sticks and stones rather than kicking them out of the way. When you break camp, scatter them back over the site.

The AT continues on a steep, rocky climb without the benefit of switch-backs, just a few detours around piles

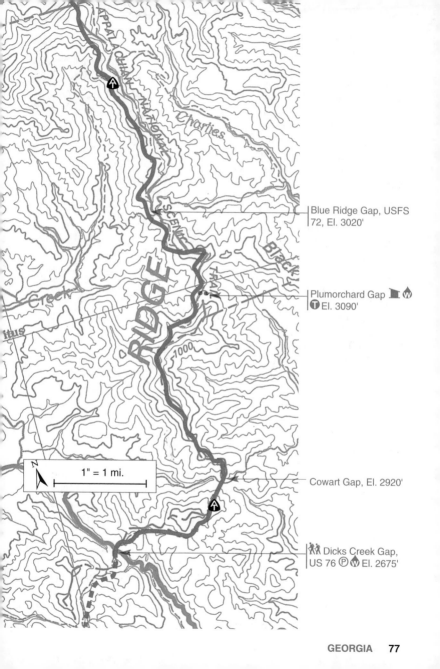

Blue Ridge Gap, USFS
72, El. 3020'

Plumorchard Gap
El. 3090'

Cowart Gap, El. 2920'

Dicks Creek Gap,
US 76 El. 2675'

1" = 1 mi.

of fallen trees from Hurricane Opal in 1995. Grapevines, blackberries, and greenbrier crowd the open areas and may clog the trail between maintenance trips. And just as you think you've reached the top of this aerobic exercise, the trail goes over Sharp Top, dips twice, and climbs even rockier terrain, this time with a couple of switchbacks but big rocks to scramble over, too. Finally, it slips into something more comfortable: two switchbacks in a rhododendron tunnel and then the top of Courthouse Bald (10.0 mi.). This area may have been used for summer livestock grazing and, like many former balds, is now covered with trees.

After an easy descent to 4300-ft. Sassafras Gap at 10.7 mi., and a tiny creek crossing, the trail climbs again for about 0.5 mi. A knoll on the left is a rock ledge campsite (not for sleepwalkers) with a view of Shooting Creek Valley, Chatuge Lake, farm fields, and the Tusquitee and Snowbird mts. A more sheltered (and better cushioned) campsite lies to the right of the trail. A rock outcrop on the left about 0.1 mi. past the two campsites has the same view and would be a good rest stop. Ravenrock Cliff can be seen on the right edge of the view.

Just over the crest of the climb (11.6 mi.), the AT meets a blue-blazed trail that leads 0.6 mi. left to Ravenrock Cliff. The cliff towers over Shooting Creek valley like a flying buttress of the main ridge that the AT follows. This side trail twists through

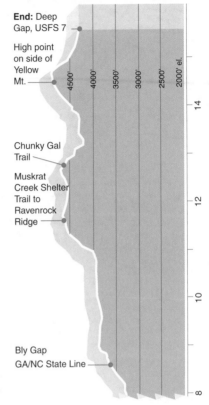

tangles of mountain laurel, highbush blueberries, and flame azaleas to a ridgetop. Watch the blue blazes carefully because the trail can be somewhat overgrown and confusing. A small plane crashed here in the 1970s, and the pieces scattered in a straight line for about 100 yd. Hikers have carried pieces of fuselage back to the shelter for display. The side trail descends left and comes out on top of sheer cliffs. Mountain laurel

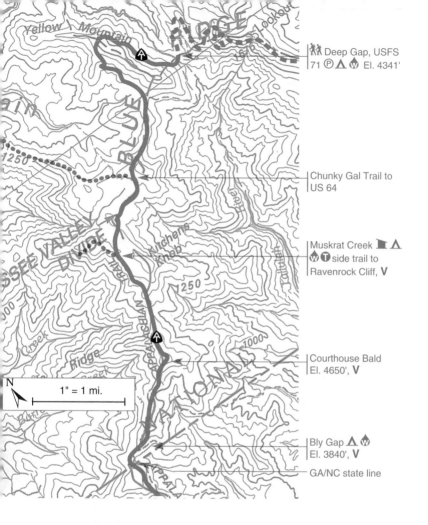

Deep Gap, USFS
71 Ⓟ ▲ Ⓦ El. 4341'

Chunky Gal Trail to
US 64

Muskrat Creek 🍴 ▲
Ⓦ ⓣ side trail to
Ravenrock Cliff, V

Courthouse Bald
El. 4650', V

N
1" = 1 mi.

Bly Gap ▲ Ⓦ
El. 3840', V
GA/NC state line

and Catawba rhododendron bloom profusely here in June, and there are blueberries to eat in August. Billows of reindeer moss (actually a lichen) fill the rock crevices. These rocks get few visitors and look the way the tops of Blood Mt., Standing Indian Mt., and Albert Mt. did before they got popular and trampled. From the cliffs you can hear the voices of northbound AT hikers when they are still nearly a mile away.

Just past the Ravenrock Cliff trail junction, the AT crosses Muskrat Creek on stepping stones, and the Muskrat Creek Shelter appears about 100 ft. up to the right. This Nantahala design shelter, like many North Carolina shelters, has a large covered veranda for cooking and eating, tables, benches, a metal fire ring, gravel to reduce mud, a privy, bear cables, chunks of airplane fuselage, and impressive plank-and-beam construction. Witch hazel bushes grow between the shelter and the creek, and a cold winter's hike may be made cheerful by their wispy yellow blooms. Witch hazels employ insect pollinators and bloom during late fall or winter warm spells. The few insects that venture out in the cold find some nectar and do their jobs. Collect water here if you plan to camp at Whiteoak Stamp.

From the shelter, the AT climbs a bit and then provides an easy stroll along a ridgetop, alternating oak woods with rhododendron tunnels. At 12.4 mi. enter Whiteoak Stamp, a large grassy area and campsite, with old roads and thick rhododendron all around. Water may be available down to the right, but Muskrat Creek is the best source. Linguistic note: This is the last "stamp" for AT northbound hikers.

Next the AT enters oak woods and goes through a large patch of running ground cedar, an evergreen club moss. A big patch like this may actually be just a few plants with underground stems sending up hundreds of scaled fronds that look like bonsai juniper bushes. Botanists call club mosses "fern allies" because they don't fit into any other classification. Before the appearance of flowering plants, ferns and their allies ruled the plant world and fed herbivorous dinosaurs.

At 12.6 mi. the AT enters a signed junction. The Chunky Gal Trail goes 5.5 mi. right to US 64. A group in nearby Hayeville has reworked this 30-mile trail over Chunky Gal and the Tusquittee mountains; this trail provides truly remote and beautiful hiking as it crosses US 64 and heads northwest. The AT turns right at the junction and descends along the side of a ridge to Wateroak Gap. Then it makes the last climb of this section along the north side of Yellow Mt. Foamflower, blue cohosh, and three colors of violets line the trail, and water is abundant.

The AT continues along the side of the ridge. Many rotting American chestnut logs lie in the open woods to the right. They died in the 1930s when the chestnut blight reached these woods. The chestnut heartwood may be soft and spongy, but the outer wood, looking like strings on giant celery stalks, still resists the decomposers.

The AT turns right around the end of the ridge at 15 mi. and descends on switchbacks and some muddy or rocky spots around fallen tree roots. Look for some especially fine stone steps in steep places. Then the trail becomes an easy descent across boulder fields, tiny creeks, and abundant wildflower displays typical of north-facing slopes. Tooth-

Miles N	NORTH	Elev. (ft./m)	Miles S
15.6	**End: Deep Gap,** USFS 71, parking and camping.	4341/1323	0.0
14.5	Open area on side of Yellow Mt. with views N.	4800/1463	1.1
12.6	Jct. **Chunky Gal Trail,** 5.5 mi. blue-blazed side trail to US 64.		3.0
11.6	**Muskrat Creek Shelter,** privy, stream, and nearby campsites; blue-blazed side trail to **Ravenrock Cliff** (0.6 mi.), views SW.		4.0
10.7	**Sassafras Gap;** small creek.	4300/1310	4.7
10.0	**Courthouse Bald.**	4640/1414	5.6
8.8	**Bly Gap,** high, windy gap with campsites; water 0.1 mi. S on AT.	3840/1170	6.8
8.6	GA/NC state line.	3600/1097	7.0
6.6	Side trail to springs, campsite.		9.0
5.6	**Blue Ridge Gap;** jct. US 72, rough road from US 76.	3020/920	10.0
4.3	Blue-blazed trail to **Plumorchard Gap Shelter** (0.2 mi.); picnic table, privy, creek with water pipe.	3090/942	11.3
3.0	**Buzzard Knob,** winter views.	3760/1146	12.6
1.8	**Cowart Gap.**	2920/890	13.8
1.1	**Little Bald Knob;** campsite 0.1 mi. R, water 0.1 mi. N.	3440/1048	14.9
0.0	**Start: Dicks Creek Gap,** US 76; parking and picnic area.	2675/815	15.6

SOUTH

wort, hepatica, and bloodroot bloom here in early spring, followed by foamflower, trillium, and Jack-in-the-pulpit in April. After a few rocky areas, the trail arrives at Deep Gap at 15.6 mi., with parking and camping areas.

Deep Gap to Timber Ridge Trail

Maps: ATC Nantahala Nat'l. Forest

Route: From Deep Gap to Standing Indian Mt., to Timber Ridge Trail, to USFS 67

Recommended direction: S to N

Distance: 10.4 mi. total; 8.1 mi. on AT

Access trail name & length: Timber Ridge Trail, 2.3 mi.

Elevation +/-: 4341 to 5498 to 4700 ft.

Effort: Moderate

Day hike: Yes; ambitious

Overnight backpacking hike: Yes

Duration: 9 to 10 hr.

Early exit option: None

Natural history feature: Flame azalea on Standing Indian Mt.

Trailhead access: *Start:* From Franklin, drive W on US 64 for 14 mi. Turn L onto gravel USFS 71, just past the Macon/Clay county line, for 6.0 mi. to Deep Gap. *End:* From Franklin, drive W on US 64 for 9 mi., then L onto Old US 64 for 2 mi. at sign for Standing Indian Campground. At Wallace Gap turn R onto USFS 67 for about 1 mi. to fork. Take L fork to Backcountry Parking (R fork goes to campground). From Backcountry Parking, drive 4.4 mi. to Timber Ridge Trailhead on R. USFS 71 and 67 are closed in winter.

At 5498 ft., Standing Indian Mt. is the highest point south of the Smokies and the southernmost mile-high peak on the AT. However, the trail climbs gradually with switchbacks, giving this hike a "moderate" rating. The AT follows the Tennessee Valley Divide as it swings north of the Tallulah River valley and then south of the Nantahala River basin. For most of Hike #9, the northbound AT actually goes south. The entire basin is well developed for hiking and camping, and the hikes described here are just some of the possibilities. Maps and current trail conditions can be obtained from the U.S. Forest Service (see "Useful Information"). The 6.0-mi. gravel road to Deep Gap is rough but usually passable by all vehicles; check with the Forest Service about current conditions.

Deep Gap has a large parking area, and the blue-blazed Kimsey Creek Trail goes left down to Standing Indian Campground in 3.7 mi. Another blue-blazed trail leads to a spring near the camping area.

From Deep Gap, the AT ascends the side of a ridge on well-graded trail and enters the 24,000-acre Southern Nantahala Wilderness Area, with a sign-in board and a gray entrance sign a little farther on. ("Nantahala" is a Cherokee word meaning "land of midday sun" because of the steep-sided valleys.) Wilderness areas are protected by federal legislation: No roads, buildings, or power tools are allowed, and the number of people in a hiking group is limited to ten.

The AT swings first right, then left to cross a creek on a plank bridge, then crosses the ridge crest and turns right. The trail continues to climb through oak and beech woods. The trail swings right again, and a creek with campsites comes into view at about 0.6 mi. down to the left. Many of these areas are overused. Here as everywhere, if you camp, be sure to practice no-trace camping.

As you walk, look for chestnut stumps and logs of giant trees that died in the 1930s. A few young American chestnut trees live along this trail, but the chestnut blight fungus will attack them as soon as they get big enough to have cracks in their bark. The fungus lives on other trees, especially oaks, and is transported by birds or wind through the forest. Also look for bits of mica sparkling in the trail. This silicate mineral formed from metamorphic sandstones. As you climb Standing Indian Mt., you will find larger and larger pieces of mica, which you can peel into transparent, flexible sheets.

A woods road comes in from the right; cross it and continue climbing. At 0.8 mi. Standing Indian Shelter appears on the right at the ridge crest (4700 ft.); pass the shelter and then loop back on a blue-blazed trail to reach it. It has the "Nantahala design" —an extended overhang for cooking and eating in the rain—a large covered picnic table with benches, a fire ring, chestnut logs for sitting on, and a composting privy. (The trail maintainers have carried gravel in to reduce mud around the picnic table.) This shelter receives heavy use, and camping away from the shelter will have less harmful impact than pitching a tent on the packed dirt near it.

The AT continues up on an old roadbed to a double white blaze on a yellow birch, where the trail swings right to avoid a pile of blowdowns. (In many cases, especially in wilderness areas where they can't use chain saws, trail maintainers make detours

Doris Gove

Spotted salamander

Salamanders Rule

In a truly democratic Appalachian forest, where votes depended on weight (biomass) and ecological importance, salamanders would rule. Salamanders? Yes, those shy, slippery little critters that come out only when there's more water in the air than air and otherwise stay under rocks.

Salamanders eat insects, insect larvae (especially mosquitoes and gnats), worms, spiders, and other goodies, and, in turn, feed snakes, birds, fish, mammals, bigger spiders, frogs, and other predators. Most salamanders taste pretty good to predators such as water snakes, snapping turtles, many fish, and many birds and mammals. They escape (or delay) predation by fleeing or hiding. A few unsporting types, such as the red-spotted newt, have poisonous skin with warning colors and hike boldly along the trails like little orange dinosaurs. Look for other salamanders under rocks or logs, sunning in the spray zones of waterfalls, or dancing in forest ponds before the ice has even melted. (They can't sing like frogs, so they dance to attract mates.)

Salamanders exploit both water and dry-land habitats-an advantage of the amphibious lifestyle. They are active when there are plenty of insects and sleep when there are not. More kinds of salamanders live in the Appalachians than anywhere else in the world because these ancient mountains provide so many forested habitats and an abundance of water and food. Many salamanders are lungless and get oxygen through their skins and by pumping air into their mouths. Studies of salamanders provide information on forest health, evolution of species, regeneration, embryological development, animal behavior, and the workings of vertebrate nervous systems, including our own.

We humans, who use so much energy to maintain a constant body temperature, think of warm-bloodedness as an advanced condition. However, salamanders, who were here long before we arrived, outweigh us in the ecosystem, do not pollute or build strip malls, and will probably outlast us, if we don't destroy their habitats along with our own.

around fallen trees instead of tackling them head-on.) The AT rejoins the road less than 100 yd. farther on.

This long climb up Standing Indian Mt. has level spots and switchbacks to make it quite easy, and the trail is packed dirt with few rocks. A viewpoint to the right at about 1.5 mi. shows the forested valley of the Tallulah River, which swings east, gets caught in many man-made lakes, and runs through a deep gorge near Clayton, Georgia. The trail moves through a boulevard of flame azalea bushes that produce a spectacular flower show in May and June. The blooms, which open before the leaves get big, come in all shades of yellow, orange, and red. A little higher, the trail enters a tunnel of mountain laurel, which blooms a bit later. These two shrubs are both in the heath family, but flame azalea is deciduous whereas mountain laurel is evergreen.

The AT rises via switchbacks, enters oak and yellow-birch woods, goes through dark rhododendron tunnels, and comes out on a windy ridgetop with grass and rocks. The trail then slips to the left of the ridge and at 2.4 mi. meets a faint trail on the left that leads to a spring. Beyond this trail comes the steep, blue-blazed Lower Ridge Trail to the left, which leads 4.2 mi. to Standing Indian Campground. To the right, another steep blue-blazed trail leads 0.1 mi. to the 5498-ft. summit of Standing Indian Mt. on a rocky, sunken road. While resting on this side trail, look for quartz and flakes or chunks of mica.

At the top, a south-facing rock outcrop gives excellent views back to Georgia, with Brasstown Bald, Blood Mt., and Rabun Bald marching from southwest to southeast. Look for the USGS benchmark, a bronze marker about as big around as a soup can lid, set in the rock in 1934.

In Cherokee mythology a great hornet, the Ulagu, swooped down and carried off children to eat them. In James Mooney's version of this tale, collected in the 1880s, the people finally tracked the Ulagu to its lair — perhaps on the side of this mountain — and killed it with smoke. However, lots of little Ulagus escaped, and so we have hornets today. Another version of the story tells of a brave warrior who went up to fight the Ulagu, and his bravery was so impressive that the Great Spirit helped with a violent thunderstorm. The lightning turned the warrior to stone and the mountaintop to rubble, hence the name "Standing Indian."

Catawba rhododendron, mountain laurel, small red spruces, blueberry bushes, and bush honeysuckle surround the outcrop. Viburnum, another high-elevation plant, also grows here. Its heart-shaped opposite leaves turn brilliant red in the fall.

The AT starts down after the trail sign, passing a small campsite on the left. Look for mica flakes and chips in pits to the right of the trail. Someone dug here to see if the mica was worth mining, as it was in other places in North Carolina, for use in furnace windows; thin layers of mica are presently used in some electronic circuits because of its lack of conductivity.

The trail continues down a ridge crest, and rocky, open spaces alternate with mountain laurel thickets. Rock cairns and blazes mark the way in fog, and the ridge widens to a broad heath bald. Shrubs in the heath family (mountain laurel, rhododendron, azalea, sand myrtle, blueberry) can grow in exposed places like this, where the soil can't support big trees or retain much water. From a distance, the collection of tightly packed heath plants looks as solid as a head of broccoli, and they are called heath balds or laurel slicks.

However, walking *through* a laurel slick is rough going; then it is called a laurel hell.

After the heath bald, the trail enters woods of white oak clipped short by the wind. Farther down, the white oaks can stretch taller to reach the same wind barrier. Switchbacks at about 3.0 mi. ease the descent on the south slope, and then the trail crosses the ridge to the rich woods of the north slope, with spring wildflowers, ferns, and great patches of flame azalea. Fall and winter views show the soft, rounded shapes of the mountains that form a half basin around the source of the Nantahala River.

After about 2 mi. of easy descent on well-graded trail, at 5.3 mi. the AT reaches 4490-ft. Beech Gap, a large grassy area with campsites. A blue-blazed trail goes right for water, and the USFS Beech Gap Trail (also blue-blazed) leads left 2.8 mi., mostly downhill, to USFS 67, 4.0 mi. south of Standing Indian Campground.

After Beech Gap, the AT ascends a bit and then takes a level course along the north side of the ridge. Solid banks of rhododendron line the trail, which is crossed by several small creeks. With some twists and turns, the trail descends to Coleman Gap at 7.1 mi., where the only plant in sight is again rhododendron.

The AT climbs out of Coleman Gap to briefly meet the Tennessee Valley Divide and ridgetop again, offering winter views into the Coleman River valley to the south. The trail returns to the north slope of the basin, curves

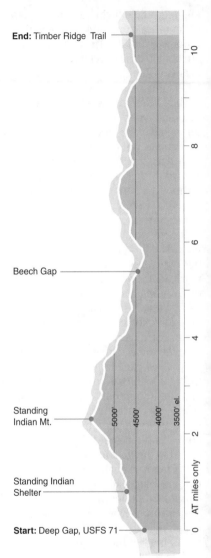

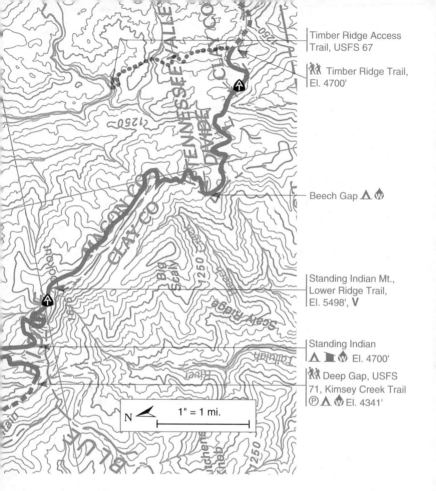

Timber Ridge Access Trail, USFS 67

Timber Ridge Trail, El. 4700'

Beech Gap

Standing Indian Mt., Lower Ridge Trail, El. 5498', V

Standing Indian El. 4700'

Deep Gap, USFS 71, Kimsey Creek Trail El. 4341'

N   1" = 1 mi.

right and then left, and meets the Timber Ridge Trail at 8.1 mi. From here it is 2.3 mi. down to USFS 67.

The foregoing section winds about halfway around the huge mountain basin that sends water down the Nantahala River. Four access trails may be used to design day hikes and overnights, and since this area receives a lot of visitors, the trails are well marked and usually in good condition. You may want to plan hikes that avoid the long and bumpy

Miles N	NORTH	Elev. (ft./m)	Miles S
	Total: 10.4 mi. with access		
2.3	Access: **Timber Ridge Trail** to USFS 67 (2.3 mi.).		2.3
8.1	**End AT miles:** Timber Ridge Trail.	4700/1433	0.0
7.1	**Coleman Gap.**		1.0
5.3	**Beech Gap;** jct. blue-blazed **Beech Gap Trail** to USFS 67 (2.8 mi.).	4490/1369	2.8
2.4	**Standing Indian Mt.;** jct. blue-blazed **Lower Ridge Trail** to Standing Indian Campground (4.2 mi.).	5498/1676	5.7
0.8	**Standing Indian Shelter,** covered picnic table, stream.	4700/1433	7.3
0.0	**Start: Deep Gap,** USFS 71; jct. **Kimsey Creek Trail** to Standing Indian Campground (3.7 mi.).	4341/1323	8.1

SOUTH

drive to Hike # 9's "Start" in Deep Gap on USFS 71. Some suggestions:

• A 10.4-mi. strenuous loop from Standing Indian Campground to Deep Gap on Kimsey Creek Trail, then to Standing Indian Mt. on the AT, and back to the campground on Lower Ridge Trail.

• A 9.9-mi. hike (requiring a 4-mi. car shuttle from Standing Indian Campground to Beech Gap Trailhead on USFS 67), using Beech Gap Trail to reach the AT, turning right to Stand-

ing Indian Mt., then returning to the campground on Lower Ridge Trail.

• A backpacking trip of 14.1 mi., using Kimsey Creek Trail, this 8.1-mi. AT section, and Timber Ridge Trail. Forest Service maps and current condition information are available at the campground and at USFS ranger stations.

Other hikes can be planned combining parts of Hike #9 with parts of Hike #10.

Timber Ridge Trail to Albert Mt.

Maps: ATC Nantahala Nat'l. Forest

Route: Timber Ridge Trail to Carter Gap Shelter to Betty Creek Gap to Albert Mt.

Recommended direction: S to N

Distance: 9.5 mi. total; 6.8 mi. on AT

Access trail name & length: Timber Ridge Trail, 2.3 mi.; Albert Mt. Bypass, 0.4 mi.

Elevation +/-: 4600 to 4500 to 5250 ft.

Effort: Strenuous

Day hike: Yes

Overnight backpacking hike: Optional

Duration: 7 to 8 hr.

Early exit option: Betty Creek Gap, 4.1 mi.; Mooney Gap, 5.0 mi.

Social history feature: Coweeta Hydrologic Laboratory

Other feature: Albert Mt. fire tower

Trailhead access: *Start:* From Franklin, go W on US 64 for 9 mi. Turn L onto Old US 64 at sign for Standing Indian Campground. Drive 2 mi. to Wallace Gap and turn R onto USFS 67 for about 1 mi. to fork. Take the L fork to Backcountry Parking (R fork to campground). From Backcountry Parking, drive 4.4 mi. to Timber Ridge Trailhead on R. *End:* From Timber Ridge Trailhead, continue on USFS 67. Turn L at junction with USFS 83 to large parking area at end of road, about 10 mi. from Backcountry Parking. The AT crosses USFS 83 at Mooney Gap. USFS roads closed in winter.

Camping: Carter Gap Shelter; campsites in Carter, Betty Creek, and Mooney gaps

---

This short AT section swings around the bottom of the Standing Indian Mt. rim and sends the trail north again. The special feature is Albert Mt., with spectacular views and a hands-on climb you will never forget. The rest of the hike could be rated moderate, with excellent trail along pretty ridgetops. Flame azalea, mountain laurel, and rhododendron bloom in profusion when they grow on exposed ridgetops, and a hike here in late May or June will provide a great flower show. Can't hike in the spring? Not to worry. October hiking here will have wonderful fall colors, and winter hiking will offer panoramic views.

Blue-blazed Timber Ridge Trail leaves USFS 67 at its southernmost point and shares a trailhead with (also blue-blazed) Big Laurel Falls Trail (a good side trip of 1.2 mi. with a backtrack to the trailhead). Timber Ridge goes left from the parking lot and climbs Scream Ridge steeply with several switchbacks. After crossing Big Laurel Branch on stepping stones, the trail rises along Timber Ridge to meet the AT in 2.3 mi.

Turn left (north) on the AT, and descend 0.4 mi. to Carter Gap, which

AT trail post

has many level campsites among the patches of rhododendron, though it has been overused. A blue-blazed trail leads right to the new Carter Gap Shelter, a privy, and a good spring.

After Carter Gap, the AT turns left and climbs the north side of Ridgepole Mt. At just under 5000 ft. the trail crosses a ridge and turns right (south) again, descends to a gap between Ridgepole and Little Ridgepole, and then finally turns north for real, leaving the eastern part of the Blue Ridge Mts. From here, the AT goes northwest along the Nantahala Mts. until it turns northeast again in the Smokies, on the western rim of the Blue Ridge. About 0.3 mi. beyond this left swing, at 2.1 mi., look for a trail to a vista 10 yd. to the right. From

it you can look back at Ridgepole Mt. and down into the Chattahoochee National Forest.

The trail makes an easy descent for nearly 2 mi. along a ridgetop of open hardwoods, interrupted by detours through dense rhododendron tunnels where the path dips below the ridgeline. Winter views and an occasional year-round vista point show the steep-sided valley of Betty Creek and Wildcat Branch to the east and Pickens Nose, a high point just across the valley.

At 4.1 mi. the AT descends to Betty Creek Gap, a grassy clearing with large campsites. A blue-blazed trail leads left 0.2 mi. to water as well as to USFS 67. This is the closest the AT has approached a road since Deep Gap and could be a useful access point for a shorter hike or an early exit from this one.

From Betty Creek Gap the AT ascends though more rhododendron, then drops to Mooney Gap to cross USFS 83 and a large parking and camping area. USFS 83 to the left meets USFS 67 in less than a mile; to the right it descends through Coweeta Hydrologic Laboratory to US 441. (USFS 83 may be rough or impassable; check with the Forest Service for current road conditions.) For an excellent side trip to outstanding views and displays of rhododendron and mountain laurel, drive or walk 0.7 mi. right from Mooney Gap on USFS 83 to Pickens Nose Trail on the right. The trail is another easy 0.7 mi., and the best flower time is early June.

Pickens Nose has become popular with climbers, with established routes up a cliff face.

The AT follows an old road out of Mooney Gap. In a few yards the trail turns left from the road and climbs wooden steps to cross a steep cliff face on Big Butt Mt. Many trees fell here in the winter of 1996–97, which required building steps and detours around root masses. While you scramble up and over rocks, look down right into the Coweeta Creek valley. Near the top of this climb is a rock overhang with a convenient sitting boulder just behind the drip line —another place to enjoy the view or the fog.

Descend into Bearpen Gap with USFS 67 visible on the left. Blue-blazed Bearpen Trail crosses the road and descends 2.5 mi. to a lower point on USFS 67 about 3.0 mi. from Backcountry Parking. Another blue-blazed trail follows the road right and serves as a bypass for Albert Mt., which should be considered if there is any chance of a thunderstorm, or if the trail is icy — or if you want to avoid the steepest but most interesting rock scramble the southern AT has to offer.

To continue on the AT, hike parallel to the road until the trail swings away to the right and starts climbing through masses of mountain laurel and rhododendron. The trail becomes nearly vertical in spots, but log steps and well-placed rocks make good foot- and handholds. (Fortunately the trail twists through the rhododendron thickets, so you never have to look at the whole climb all at once.) It will seem like a long 0.3 mi., but then the metal legs of the Albert Mt. fire tower appear on the right at the open, grassy summit.

Albert Mt. was named for Albert Siler, the grandfather of the Rev. Dr. A. Rufus Morgan, an Episcopalian minister born near Franklin. Dr. Morgan founded the Nantahala Hiking Club and during the 1940s almost single-handedly maintained the AT in this section while younger men fought in World War II. He maintained a 55-mi. section well into his seventies, organized and led hikes, and worked for the preservation of these mountains. At age 81 he joined a protest walk of 576 hikers against a road across the Smokies and hiked 17 mi. The road was not built. In his nineties, Dr. Morgan climbed Mt. Le Conte in the Smokies a few more times. If Dr. Morgan could do all this, you can do the 0.3-mi. climb to the top of his grandfather's mountain.

The tower is sometimes open for climbing and sometimes attended. Even without it, the views are spectacular: the steep Coweeta hillsides and the eastern arm of the Blue Ridge beyond, including Fishhawk, Whiteside, and Satulah mts. Rabun Bald stands to the southeast, and the Smokies can be seen to the northwest.

A large sign describes the work of Coweeta Hydrologic Laboratory, the 5400-acre valley just east of Albert Mt. The U.S. Forest Service performs research here on the water cycle and on water quality under different conditions of management and logging practice. Baseline environmental data are also collected in Coweeta, and graduate students go there to study salamanders, insects, plant growth, and other ecological topics.

To leave Albert Mt., continue on the AT across the grassy area past some pussy willows, and take an old road 0.2 mi. down to the blue-blazed bypass trail, which turns left and reaches the parking lot in 0.4 mi. The road is steep, rutted, and rocky but somewhat easier than the climb up the other side; an option in bad weather is to take the bypass around from the south, and then ascend Albert Mt. from the north.

As with Hikes #8 and #9, the excellent trail system of Standing Indian Mt. provides alternatives:

• A 23.8-mi. strenuous two- or three-day backpack loop, starting at Backcountry Parking or Standing Indian Campground and using Kimsey Creek Trail, the AT, and Long Branch Trail.

• A 15.8-mi. backpack loop from Beech Gap trailhead on USFS 67, using Beech Gap Trail, the AT, and Bearpen Trail, with the addition of 1 mi. of road walk.

• Shorter options using Betty Creek or Mooney Gap to reach Mt. Albert, with perhaps a side trip to Pickens Nose.

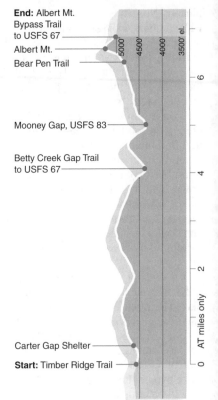

1" = 1 mi.

N

🚶🚶 Albert Mt. Bypass to USFS 67 Ⓟ

— Albert Mt., El. 5250', **V**

Albert Mt. Bypass, Bearpen Trail

Mooney Gap, USFS 83 Ⓟ △ Ⓦ El. 4500'

Betty Creek Gap △ Ⓦ, trail to USFS 67

Timber Ridge Access Trail Ⓟ

🚶🚶 Jct. Timber Ridge Trail

Carter Gap △ ▰ Ⓦ El. 4600'

Miles N	NORTH	Elev. (ft./m)	Miles S
	Total: 9.5 mi. with access trails		
0.4	Access: USFS 67, parking lot.		0.4
6.8	**End AT miles:** Albert Mt. Bypass; to USFS 67.		0.0
6.6	**Albert Mt.,** fire tower, spectacular views.	5250/1600	0.2
6.3	Jct. **Bearpen Trail** to USFS 67 (2.5 mi.).		0.5
5.0	**Mooney Gap,** USFS 83; parking and camping; early exit option; side trip (0.7 mi.) to outstanding views, rhododendron and mountain laurel displays in early June.	4500/1372	1.8
4.1	**Betty Creek Gap,** campsites; jct. blue-blazed trail L to water (0.2 mi.) and USFS 67; early exit option.		2.7
2.1	Spur trail R to good vista.		5.7
0.4	**Carter Gap and Shelter,** good spring, campsites.	4600/1402	6.4
0.0	**Start AT miles:** Jct. **Timber Ridge Trail,** access to USFS 67 and parking (2.3 mi.).		6.8
2.3	Access: Blue-blazed **Timber Ridge Trail.**		2.3

SOUTH

Albert Mt. Bypass to Winding Stair Gap

Maps: ATC Nantahala Nat'l. Forest

Route: Albert Mt. Bypass Trail to Big Spring Gap to Rock Gap to Winding Stair Gap

Recommended direction: S to N

Distance: 9.8 mi. total; 9.4 mi. on AT

Access trail name and length: Albert Mt. Bypass Trail, 0.4 mi.

Elevation +/-: 5250 to 3750 ft.

Effort: Moderate

Day hike: Yes

Overnight backpacking hike: Optional

Duration: 6 to 7 hr.

Early exit option: Rock Gap, 5.7 mi., Wallace Gap, 6.8 mi.

Natural history feature: Flame azalea

Social history feature: Rufus Morgan's Chapel

Trailhead access: *Start:* From USFS parking on USFS 67 (see "Start," Hike #10,) drive about 10 mi. to end of road. Look for blue-blazed gated road at end of parking area. *End:* From Franklin, drive 3.8 mi. W on US 64 to Winding Stair Gap.

Camping: Big Spring Shelter; several campsites

T his hike is mostly downhill on excellent trail and goes along pleasant, peaceful ridges as it directs the AT toward the Smokies in North Carolina. Benton MacKaye had originally envisioned a trail starting at Mt. Mitchell, but as the plans evolved, the Georgia Appalachian Trail Club (GATC) worked hard to build trails through the beautiful Georgia mountains. The Smoky Mt. Hiking Club, of course, insisted that the AT go through the Smokies. After much argument, Horace Kephart, a writer and Smokies park advocate, suggested a compromise that would include both areas in a zigzag. This trail starts the northwest leg—where flame azalea, mountain laurel, and rhododendron bloom profusely in late spring—and it provides good options for shorter day hikes or longer overnight hikes than the section described here.

From the parking lot, follow the blue-blazed road (a bypass of the very steep climb up and down Albert Mt.) around the northern side of Al-bert Mt. At 0.4 mi. the white AT blazes appear and our mileage count begins. To the right is a tough, rocky climb of 0.2 mi. to the Albert Mt. summit and fire tower (see Hike #10). The AT miles for this hike begin to the left on a level stretch of eroded road that goes through rhododendron. The AT turns left off the road, descends through tangles of mountain laurel, and reaches Big Spring Gap in 0.8 mi. In wet weather, parts of the trail become muddy and camping has destroyed much of the ground cover. If you plan to camp, you can find better sites farther down this trail and not add to the impact here.

Big Spring Shelter, here from 1959–2012, was famous for its mice, and in the trail register many hikers have commented on the thriving mouse community. One (2/19/97) advises: "Mice no problem. Wrap one strip of bacon, skewer, and roast. When bacon's crisp, mouse is cooked through. Delicious." Another register comment from a Boy Scout troop (11/16/96) mentions the unusual features of this AT section: the climb up Albert Mt., the rain, the cold, the mice, and a lady backpacker. A later entry on the same day: "Met a Boy Scout troop on the way up. They looked a little confused to see a woman backpacking. Get used to it, boys."

The Nantahala Hiking Club plans to remove Big Spring Shelter (built in 1959) and build a new shelter near Long Branch Trail. These are projects for 2012 or after.

After the gap comes more than 0.5 mi. of level hiking along the top and side of a ridge that has good winter views. Flame azalea bushes (see "Most Gay and Brilliant Flowering Shrub") line the trail and can be seen in all parts of the open oak woods. This azalea blooms in May and June. The blossoms vary from pale yellow to deep red, sometimes on the same bush, and come out when the leaves

Flame azalea and ragwort on Jane Bald

are small. This shrub grows throughout the southern Appalachians at all elevations but is especially abundant on the Standing Indian trails. Many of the shrubs grow more than 18 ft. tall, but if there are blooms within reach, examine the anthers with a hand lens. Many flowers simply expose the pollen to visiting bees, but azaleas and other plants in the heath family keep the pollen in capsules like tiny saltshakers. When the pollinators scrabble around searching for nectar, the pollen is shaken out onto their backs.

The AT starts down the left side of the ridge on excellent trail and easy grade. After some curves, the trail descends to a hemlock and wildflower valley where a small stream fans out across the trail. The new Long Branch Shelter will be left of the AT here, about 400 yds, and will have a privy. Campsites are available near the stream. Another easy descent brings the AT to Glassmine Gap, probably named for a nearby mica mine, at 3.2

mi. Blue-blazed Long Branch Trail descends 2.0 mi. left to U.S. Forest Service parking and Standing Indian Campground. It runs along a creek through groves of large hemlocks and has wonderful spring wildflowers.

From Glassmine Gap the AT climbs on the left side of the ridge to give a little aerobic exercise, but in less than 0.5 mi. it levels again and heads down through rhododendron. It reaches another wide hemlock valley with three easy creek crossings and ascends gently to curve around to the south-facing side of the ridge. Many of the hemlocks have died from attacks of the hemlock woolly adelgid.

Now you will notice a dramatic change in vegetation as the trail crosses this dry, exposed slope. Mountain laurel replaces rhododendron, and the ground is covered with trailing arbutus, galax, and wintergreen. A hard, sandy trail surface replaces the dark, spongy soil of the more sheltered areas. Climb past thickets of mountain laurel to a ridgetop campsite offering winter views and summer glimpses on both sides. To the northeast you can see Whiteside, Satulah, and other mountains around Highlands, North Carolina.

The trail descends a bit, then switches back onto another south-facing slope with several rock outcrops. Look for fence lizards (brown and gray, 6 to 8 in. long) basking here on sunny days. Male fence lizards own territories and advertise their ownership with rapid push-ups. Brilliant blue patches on their throats and sides flash with each push-up, but if another male invades the territory and defeats the owner, the blue patches fade. Fence lizards hide when they hear or see huge predators, but sometimes they give themselves away by scrabbling across the lichens. Sit and wait, and they may come back.

The AT curves around the ridge again, enters deciduous woods, and descends. At 5.7 mi. Rock Gap Shelter

Most Gay and Brilliant Flowering Shrub

The epithet fiery I annex to this most celebrated species of azalea, as being expressive of the appearance of its flowers, which are in general of the color of the finest red lead, orange, and bright gold, as well as yellow and cream color; these various splendid colors are not only in separate plants, but frequently all the varieties and shades are seen in separate branches on the same plant; and the clusters of the blossoms cover the shrubs in such incredible profusion on the hillsides that suddenly opening to view from dark shades, we are alarmed with apprehension of the hill being set on fire. This is certainly the most gay and brilliant flowering shrub yet known. . . . [1791]

From *Travels of William Bartram,* by William Bartram. Yale University Press, 1958.

appears downslope to the left, and the AT crosses a small creek that supplies water. A blue-blazed trail leads to the shelter. People have walked and camped throughout this area; try to stay on the trail. The old shelter has a new veranda, picnic table, privy, and covered cooking area. It is in sight of USFS 67 at Rock Gap and receives a lot of use.

The trail continues down to Rock Gap (5.8 mi., 3750 ft.) and passes in back of a hiker parking lot. A blue-blazed trail leads 0.7 mi. through a forest of medium-sized tulip-trees to the John Wasilik Memorial Poplar (named for an early U.S. Forest Service ranger), a huge old tulip-tree with a split-rail fence around it. A hundred years ago the forest was full of trees like this; now we have one to visit, but it's dead and broken, and the space around it is trampled. The younger tulip-trees grow fast, though, and protected areas will produce giants again.

From Rock Gap the trail is a bit rough and rocky as it passes some wet places, but it soon levels onto a high bench over a wooded valley where you can look down onto the treetops. Christmas fern, shining club moss, and rattlesnake plantain line the trail, which then enters an open, ferny hillside with a large patch of galax.

Descend to 3738-ft. Wallace Gap at 6.4 mi., and cross Old US 64 where USFS 67 comes in from the left. (There is no parking at Wallace Gap.) About 100 yd. to the left on a bank above old US 64 is a small open

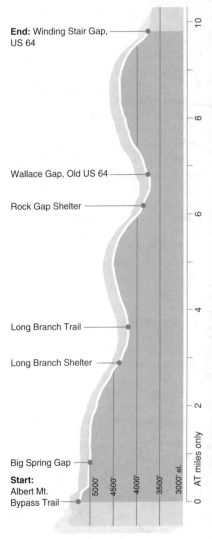

End: Winding Stair Gap, US 64

Wallace Gap, Old US 64

Rock Gap Shelter

Long Branch Trail

Long Branch Shelter

Big Spring Gap

Start: Albert Mt. Bypass Trail

5000' 4500' 4000' 3500' 3000' el.

AT miles only

Winding Stair Gap,
US 64 Ⓟ Ⓦ El. 3750'

Wallace Gap,
Old US 64, El. 3738'

Rock Gap Ⓟ ▬ Ⓦ
trail to John Wasilik
Memorial Poplar 🍁

Glassmine Gap, jct.
Long Branch Trail
to UFSF 67

Long Branch Shelter
▬ ▲ Ⓦ

Big Spring Gap ▲ Ⓦ
El. 5000'

Albert Mt. Bypass

USFS 67, jct. Albert Mt.
Bypass Ⓟ V
El. 5250', V

N
1" = 1 mi.

chapel and a cemetery. Dr. A. Rufus Morgan, an Episcopalian minister who started the Nantahala Hiking Club (see Hike #10), used to preach here.

The AT slants up a grassy bank above the road. On the right, look for pussytoes with gray-green leaves hugging the ground and fuzzy, composite flowers atop stalks. These plants bloom in April and May and don't show off like those gaudy trilliums. They usually grow in mats in sunny areas, and a hand lens will show woolly fur on leaves and stalks plus its composite nature.

The trail climbs wide wooden steps through a hemlock grove. Look for horizontal rows of yellow-bellied sapsucker holes on some hemlock trunks. This small woodpecker drills the holes, feeds on the soft inner bark, and returns later to collect sap and the insects that have been attracted to it. Sometimes as the trees grow they produce scar tissue around the holes, pushing them out into odd shapes.

The AT crosses a ridgetop at 7.4 mi. with winter views to the south and heads down beside a cascading creek crowded with rhododendron. After crossing the creek and an old road, the trail goes up and down through oak woods with American chestnut stumps and logs.

Around the next ridge you can hear traffic noise from US 64 and can soon glimpse the road. The trail goes down to a creek and an old road, then climbs the final ridge above US 64. It descends by long switchbacks and steps through oak woods with flame azaleas to Winding Stair Gap, where you'll find a piped spring and plenty of parking space.

As with Hikes #9 and 10, the access trails provide many alternate hiking options. Some suggestions:

• With an investment of 0.6 mi. (admittedly steep), you can include Albert Mt. summit. Turn right from the bypass trail at the start, climb 0.3 mi., backtrack, and continue the hike.

• For a 10.8-mi. strenuous hike with a short car shuttle, go up Long Branch Trail (not steep), right on the AT, and down Bearpen Trail (steep).

Miles N	NORTH	Elev. (ft./m)	Miles S
Total: 9.8 mi. with access			
9.4	**End:** Winding Stair Gap; US 64, parking, piped spring.	3750/1143	0.0
6.4	**Wallace Gap,** Old US 64. (SR 1448)	3738/1139	3.0
6.8	**Rock Gap,** trail to John Wasilik Memorial Poplar (0.7 mi.); early exit option.	3750/1143	3.6
5.7	**Rock Gap Shelter,** water, picnic table, privy.	3800/1158	3.7
3.2	**Glassmine Gap;** jct. blue-blazed **Long Branch Trail** to Standing Indian Campground, USFS parking (0.2 mi.).		6.2
2.9	**Long Branch Shelter** (2012 or after), privy, water.		6.5
0.4	**Big Spring Gap,** water; jct. trail R to overlook (0.2 mi.).	5000/1524	9.0
0.0	**Start AT miles:** Albert Mt. Bypass to Albert Mt. summit and fire tower (0.2 mi.).	5250/1600	9.4
0.4	Access: **Albert Mt.** parking, USFS 67; profuse azalea, mountain laurel, and rhodondron blooms in May and June.		0.4

SOUTH

Winding Stair Gap to Wayah Bald

Maps: ATC Nantahala Nat'l. Forest

Route: Winding Stair Gap to Siler Bald to Wayah Gap to Wayah Bald

Recommended direction: S to N

Distance: 10.1 mi.

Elevation +/-: 3750 to 5216 to 5342 ft.

Effort: Strenuous

Day hike: Yes

Overnight backpacking hike: Optional

Duration: 8 to 10 hr.

Early exit option: Wayah Gap, 5.9 mi.

Natural history features: Siler Bald and Wayah Bald

Social history features: Wilson Lick historic ranger station; botanists John and William Bartram; Wayah Bald observation tower

Trailhead access: *Start:* Winding Stair Gap on US 64, 8.0 mi. W of Franklin. *End:* From Franklin, drive W for 3.8 mi. on US 64. R after sign for Wayah Bald. Take first L onto Wayah Rd. (NC 1310) for about 8.0 mi. to Wayah Gap. Go R onto gravel USFS 69 for 4.5 mi. to parking area near paved path to tower. USFS 69 closed in winter.

Camping: Siler Bald Shelter, several campsites. *Note:* Camping is not allowed at Wayah Bald.

T his beautiful hike visits two high points of the Nantahala Mts. with panoramic vistas. Though a lot of climbing is required, the trail is well graded and goes by several campsites and springs. Wildflowers flourish in spring and summer; fall and winter provide outstanding views. Described here as a two-car day hike, this trail section, with three access points and some side trips, can be used for a variety of day or overnight trips.

Caution: Siler Bald (an appealing side trip) is an exposed high-elevation meadow and can be dangerous in heavy fog, snow, or electrical storms. There are no blazes on the bald, and fog can be disorienting. In

bad weather, stay on the AT and skip the bald.

From the parking area on the south side of US 64, follow the white blazes on the guardrail to the east, cross the highway, and look for the AT at the end of the guardrail. Turn left into shady woods, and cross a gravel road in 150 ft. Then climb to a wooden bridge across a creek cascade framed by rhododendron. Turn left again to start uphill. A small campsite is under hemlock trees on the right, but nicer ones can be found farther from the highway.

The trail rises gradually beside the creek, then swings left to cross it, passing another small campsite on the left. After climbing and crossing a broad ridge, the trail levels at 1.0 mi. and crosses another creek, with more campsites on the left. Umbrella leaf, a relative of may-apple, grows at the creek edge; look for a leaf the size of a large pizza on a 1- to 2-ft. fleshy stalk. A cluster of white flowers stands above the leaf in June, and the bright blue berries persist into fall. Foamflower, trillium, yellow mandarin, and other spring wildflowers grow here, and as the trail rises along the side of the next ridge, bright summer flowers appear. Fire pink ("pink" for its botanical family, not for its color) has a scarlet flower about as big as a quarter, with five petals with split ends. Evening primrose provides a spot of yellow, and spiderwort is bright blue. These three flowers grow along the trail bank and can be examined almost at eye level with a hand lens. Look for blue hair on the spiderwort stamens.

At 1.1 mi., the AT reaches Swinging Lick Gap. The trail turns north here and climbs to an east-facing slope that offers blackberries in August and a view down the valley toward Franklin in winter. Even if there's no view, you can hear trucks on US 64— maybe not the most welcome sound, but it will help to orient you, especially in fog.

Descend to Panther Gap at 2.0 mi. Camping is possible here, but you will have to carry water. From the gap the trail ascends through quiet woods, passing dead chestnut logs that make good seats for rest stops. After a long, easy ascent to a junction

Wayah Bald observation tower

with the blue-blazed Siler Bald Shelter Loop at 3.7 mi., turn left to climb to Siler Bald or right to visit the shelter. The shelter trail follows an old road down to the right and reaches the shelter in 0.5 mi. There are several springs and seeps along the way and an excellent piped spring and creek at the bottom. The old shelter with a massive cement picnic table has a covered patio and benches and sits in a grassy clearing. There is a moldering privy downhill across a grassy clearing. To keep mud off the floor, the trail maintainers hauled in gravel, which hikers have used for mouse ammunition; sweep before spreading your sleeping bag. Also, hikers have commented in the registry about bears that investigate the shelter at night, and I saw a large bear near the shelter at midday in July.

To continue the shelter loop, follow the blue blazes up a dirt road to another large grassy clearing. The trail goes sharply left on a road from the clearing, and two other roads go right; check for blue blazes. From the clearing, it's a steep 0.5 mi. back to the AT on sometimes muddy road. This is the shortest route from the shelter to Siler Bald, but backtracking to the AT and continuing to Siler Bald that way may be easier, especially in rain.

From the Shelter Loop junction (south end), the AT follows an old road left and in 300 ft. turns right to climb a rocky section that has a few steps to help on the steepest parts. At 4.2 mi. the trail reaches first a huge grassy meadow surrounded by oak trees and then the junction with the north end of the blue-blazed shelter loop. To visit Siler Bald (worth the aerobic challenge), turn left and climb up the meadow on an unmarked but well-worn path. After 0.1 mi. the path reaches a possible campsite with a fire ring and turns right for another 0.1 mi. climb to the top, a sign, a 360-degree view, and another campsite. The lower campsite is sheltered on one side by trees; the upper one is exposed. Neither one is safe in bad weather. The bald is named for William Siler, great-grandfather of the Rev. A. Rufus Morgan, who formed the Nantahala Hiking Club and for decades maintained much of the AT in North Carolina.

Backtrack down to the AT junction, cross the meadow at its narrowest point, and look for familiar white blazes on the other side, going north. From the Siler Bald clearing, the AT descends along a pretty ridge crest crowned with American chestnut sprouts, striped maples, highbush blueberries, flame azaleas, and red oaks. After nearly a mile, the trail turns right and leaves the ridgetop. It descends past springs and tiny creeks that support a rich growth of spring wildflowers.

One summer flower seen here is goatsbeard, a 3- to 5-ft.-tall plant with branched spikes of densely packed white blooms. Peer into the mass of flowers with a hand lens and find a community of beetles crawling in and over the musty-smelling blossoms. Usually a spider or two can be found lurking underneath; they know where the bugs are.

The trail passes muddy spots that may be overgrown with nettles and jewelweed. Then it crosses a creek on a footlog and a jeep road. At 5.9 mi. look for two trails left to Wayah Gap Crest picnic area, which has tables, parking, and a bear-proof trash can. Just past the picnic area, descend to wooden steps and cross paved NC 1310 at Wayah Gap. The gravel road to Wayah Bald (USFS 69) is to the left, and the AT ascends parallel to it through open woods with spring and summer wildflowers. Look for fire pinks and evening primroses in July and blueberries and blackberries in August. After about 0.5 mi., the AT meets the road but stays to the right of it, then reenters

Botanists in the Southern Appalachians

It is hard to imagine today the excitement of the botanical exploration of the so-called New World. People used to know where their food, shelter, and wealth came from, and the vastness and diversity of the continent promised endless possibilities. Once the frenzy for gold and fountains of youth faded, explorers focused on landforms and flora and fauna. The governments of England, France, and Russia sponsored botanical trips and collections. John Bartram (1699-1777) and André Michaux (1746-1842) established gardens to propagate and study new species. Benjamin Franklin, the first three U.S. presidents, and many other early American leaders and scholars visited Bartram's gardens near Philadelphia and kept track of botanical discoveries. Educated people knew plants by their Latin names and botanical family relationships. In 1791 the publication of John's son William Bartram's *Travels* inspired Wordsworth, Coleridge, and other European writers. Audubon's bird prints, which incorporated the natural history and habitat of the subjects, became essential for fashionable drawing rooms.

The names of plants trace some of this history. Fraser fir, Fraser sedge, and Fraser magnolia were named for John Fraser, a Scottish botanist who worked for the Russian czars. Michaux's saxifrage honors André Michaux, a French botanist who made botanical expeditions to England, Spain, Persia, the southern Appalachians, and Madagascar. William Bartram named a beautiful tree, Franklinia, after his friend Benjamin Franklin and a lily, Clintonia, after DeWitt Clinton, first governor of New York. Gray's lily, Catesby's trillium, partridgeberry (Mitchella repens, named for Elisha Mitchell, whose name also graces the East's highest mountain), and twinleaf (Jeffersonia diphylla, named for Thomas Jefferson) are more examples.

Unfortunately, we've lost some of the wonder and much of the diversity. However, parks, public lands, environmental groups, and conservancies are working hard to save the plant and animal diversity that we still have. The wonder can be rekindled by hiking and exploring the wilderness. Carry a flower book (see Bibliography), a hand lens (see "Hiking with a Hand Lens" in Hike #17), and a notebook. It's a fine, lifelong hobby.

---

the woods. There is room for one or two cars to park here.

The AT continues up good dirt trail with both some climbing and some level spots. In wet weather, look for black-and-yellow millipedes that also may be out hiking. If picked up, they exude an almond-smelling cyanide compound—harmless as long as you don't eat the millipede. Mountain people call them cherry bugs, and the millipedes' bright colors warn birds and other predators to leave them alone.

The trail reaches a mowed grassy clearing on the right, with a gated access road on the left. Look for sassafras seedlings along the trail and around the edge of the meadow. Sassafras trees have three leaf shapes: mitten (left- and right-handed), mitten for a three-fingered person, and oval. Younger trees have more of the first two shapes, while older sassafras trees have mostly oval leaves. Leaves, twigs, flowers, fruits, and roots of this tree are aromatic, but each part has a different odor. Sassafras tea is made from the roots, and the dried leaves can be crumbled and used to thicken gumbo. The Cherokee used sassafras root tea for diarrhea and bark tea for "overfatness."

At 7.2 mi the AT meets a blue-blazed trail on the left that leads to the Wilson Lick Ranger Station in about 0.2 mi. This historical site with interpretive signs has reconstructed buildings and exhibits on fire prevention, which was a primary focus of the early Forest Service.

From here, the AT ascends gradually on a rocky logging road with mountain laurel arching overhead. Then, in more open woods, several springs drip on the right and support a large patch of columbine and bee balm. After a rocky scramble on wet trail, reach log steps up to Wayah Bald Rd. (USFS 69) at 7.7 mi. Some 30 ft. up the road is a good piped spring.

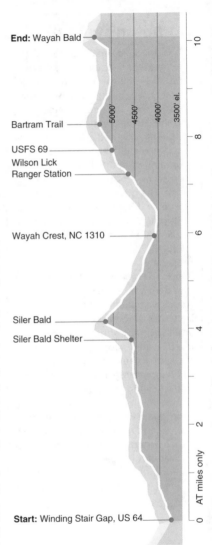

End: Wayah Bald

Bartram Trail

USFS 69

Wilson Lick
Ranger Station

Wayah Crest, NC 1310

Siler Bald

Siler Bald Shelter

Start: Winding Stair Gap, US 64

5000' 4500' 4000' 3500' el.

10

8

6

4

2

0

AT miles only

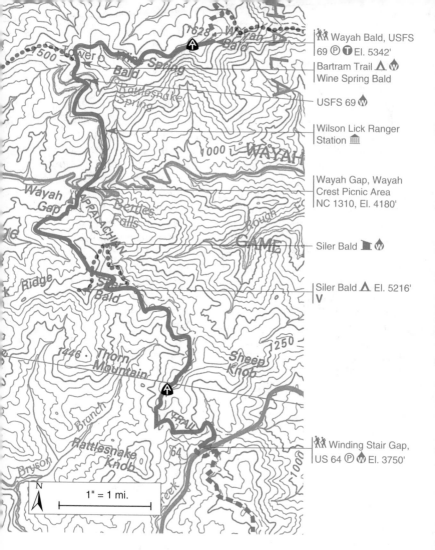

Wayah Bald, USFS
69 Ⓟ Ⓣ El. 5342'

Bartram Trail ⛺ Ⓦ
Wine Spring Bald

USFS 69 Ⓦ

Wilson Lick Ranger
Station 🏛

Wayah Gap, Wayah
Crest Picnic Area
NC 1310, El. 4180'

Siler Bald 🖼 Ⓦ

Siler Bald ⛺ El. 5216'
V

Winding Stair Gap,
US 64 Ⓟ Ⓦ El. 3750'

N
1" = 1 mi.

The trail continues across the road and up more wooden steps. It swings left and loops away from the road for the rest of this hike. Two kinds of bluets grow along the trail. Prostrate bluets, also called Quaker ladies or innocence, have bluish flowers with yellow centers and leaves the size of sesame seeds. The other kind of bluets have pale lilac flowers, stand-up stalks, and opposite leaves nearly an inch long. Both species of bluets have four petals in each flower; creep down to their level and study them with a hand lens.

Becoming grassy and swinging right, the trail passes a pretty campsite with convenient tree limbs for hanging laundry or packs. At 8.2 mi., the Bartram Trail joins from the left in a patch of tassel rue. This plant of the buttercup family has conspicuous white flowers with no petals; the white stalks and knobs that look like petals are actually pollen-producing stamens. From here to just beyond Wayah Bald Tower, the trail is marked by both white blazes and yellow for the Bartram Trail. The Bartram Trail is named for William Bartram (see "Botanists in the Southern Appalachinans"), who in his *Travels* published in 1791 described the amazing plant and animal diversity of the southern Appalachians as well as the gentleness of the Cherokee Indians. The 71-mi., three-state Bartram Trail honors him and provides access to some beautiful wild areas. There are several campsites at the trail junction, and just beyond it on the left is a good spring framed with flat rocks and another campsite. To the right is Wine Spring Bald—visited by Bartram in 1775—now covered with trees.

An old jeep road joins the AT from the left, and after about 100 yd. the road goes right and the AT goes left. It descends through a forest of small beech trees with ferns and billowy grasses. Farther down the slope, seeps

cross the trail at good wildflower patches that include doll's eyes and Solomon's-seal. After crossing a small creek, the AT ascends, crosses another jeep road, passes a Forest Service foot-trail-only sign, and reaches the paved Wayah Bald Tower trail at 10.0 mi. The parking loop is to the right, and the observation tower is uphill to the left, past upscale pit toilets with skylights. About halfway up the paved trail on the left is a large American chestnut that produced a good flower crop in 1997. Check on its health if you like here; dead branches or cracked broken swellings in the bark are signs of chestnut blight.

The observation tower was built in 1935 at the 5342-ft. summit of Wayah (Cherokee for "wolf") Bald by the Civilian Conservation Corps (CCC). On one of my hikes here, in July 1997, I asked an elderly couple for a ride back to my car at Wayah Crest—only to learn that the man had been a member of the CCC crew that hauled the rocks to build the tower, and that he had met his wife at the CCC camp. They come back to visit "his" tower at least twice a year. The tower is dedicated to Nantahala Forest Supervisor John Byrne, who worked here in the 1930s and helped plan the AT route through the Nantahala National Forest.

From the tower, look for Standing Indian Mt. and Albert Mt. to the south, Trimont Ridge and Franklin to the east, Wesser Bald and the Smokies (usually floating in haze if visible

Miles N	NORTH	Elev. (ft./m)	Miles S
10.1	**End: Wayah Bald;** USFS 69, picnic/parking area, observation tower, views, privies; profusion of blooming flame and honeysuckle azalea, mountain laurel, and rhododendron in June and July.	5342/1628	0.0
8.2	Jct. yellow-blazed **Bartram Trail,** good spring on L, campsites; Wine Spring Bald to R.		1.9
7.7	Cross USFS 69; piped spring just past crossing on R.	5000/1524	2.4
7.2	Trail to **Wilson Lick Ranger Station** (0.2 mi.).		2.9
5.9	**Wayah Gap Crest,** picnic area, water, privy, parking; NC 1310; early exit option.	4180/1274	4.2
4.2	**Siler Bald,** trail to summit (0.2 mi.), views.	5216/1590	5.9
3.7	Trail to **Siler Bald Shelter** (0.5 mi.); piped spring, picnic table, tentsites.		6.4
1.0	Creek, campsites.		9.1
0.0	**Start: Winding Stair Gap,** US 64, parking.	3750/1143	10.1

SOUTH

at all) to the north, and the Snowbird Mts. to the west. If you stand at the southwest corner of the tower and look south, you can see Siler Bald on the next mountain south, looking like a partially shaved head. In June and July, flame azalea, honeysuckle (or swamp) azalea, mountain laurel, and rhododendron are in full bloom around the tower. In March, look for pussy willows just north of the tower.

There are many alternate ways to do this hike, especially since cars can be parked at Winding Stair Gap, Wayah Gap, Wayah Bald Rd., and Wayah Bald. Campsites and water are available in many places. Overnight trips could include the Siler Bald Shelter Loop from either Winding Stair Gap or Wayah Gap. For an easy backpacking trip, park at Wayah Gap, hike to the campsite above the road crossing at 7.7 mi., set up camp, and then hike without packs to Wayah Bald and back. Water for this trip is available from the piped spring at the road crossing.

Wayah Bald to Tellico Gap

Maps: ATC Nantahala Nat'l. Forest

Route: Wayah Bald to Cold Spring Shelter to Tellico Gap

Recommended direction: S to N

Distance: 9.3 mi.

Elevation +/-: 5342 to 3850 ft.

Effort: Moderate

Day hike: Yes

Overnight backpacking hike: Optional

Duration: 6 to 7 hr.

Early exit option: None

Natural history feature: Wayah Bald

Social history feature: Wayah Bald observation tower

Trailhead access: *Start:* From Franklin, drive 3.8 mi. W on US 64. Turn R at sign for Wayah Bald for 0.2 mi., then L onto Wayah Rd. (NC 1310). Look for small store/gas station on corner and sign for Lyndon Johnson Work Center. Drive 7.0 mi. to Wayah Gap. Go R onto USFS 69 for about 4.0 mi. to end. For Wayah Crest Campground and another AT access, turn L at Wayah Gap. *End:* From US 19/74 in Beechertown, go 5.0 mi. on Wayah Rd. (NC 1310). Turn L onto Tellico Rd. (NC 1365) for 4.0 mi. to Tellico Gap and a parking area defined by steep banks supported by railroad ties. Tellico Rd. can be reached from US 28 N of Franklin, but this road is very rough.

Camping: Cold Spring Shelter; several campsites

From the 5342-ft. high point of Wayah Bald, this moderate hike descends through rich woods, wonderful wildflower patches, and a large stand of American chestnut. The one long climb, about 0.8 mi. up to Cold Spring Shelter, has good switchbacks. Shuttling a car between Wayah Bald and Tellico Gap can be long, dusty, and bumpy, so you may want to do part of this hike and backtrack or combine part of Hike #12 with part of this hike. But if leaving cars at both ends can be arranged, this hike makes an excellent leisurely day hike, and there are pretty campsites for an overnight.

From the Wayah Bald parking area, go past upscale pit toilets and information signs on a paved path. Crowds may accompany you on this first part of Hike #13, but they won't go much farther than the observation tower, which stands at the summit in a cleared lawn. The stone tower is dedicated to John Byrne, a chief ranger of the Nantahala National Forest who helped plan the AT route. Climb the tower and look for the Smokies to the northwest, Franklin and the Highlands Plateau to the east, and Rabun Bald, Standing Indian Mt., and the hazy mountains of Georgia to the south.

The AT continues on the opposite side of the tower, but the pavement ends. Cross the lawn, look for pussy willows in early spring, and enter a tangle of blackberry bushes as the trail swings left. Bartram Trail (yellow blazes) and the AT (white blazes) share the same path for the next 0.5 mi. William Bartram's *Travels*, published in 1791, described the amazing plant and animal diversity of the southern Appalachians as well as the gentleness of the Cherokee Indians. The 71-mi., three-state Bartram Trail honors him and provides access to some beautiful wild areas.

After some stone steps, the two trails cross an old road and descend a rocky hillside with flame azalea, mountain laurel, and twisted yellow birch. These last trees grow at most elevations, but high in the mountains they get very large, form ringlets from bark curls, and send out crazy roots to anchor themselves among boulders. Yellow birches specialize in germinating on decaying nurse logs, so many of them end up standing on stiltlike roots when the nurse log rots away.

At 0.4 mi. the trail levels at a small campsite and spring, and then the Bartram Trail goes right while the AT goes left. The AT descends through hemlock forest past several springs and seeps and then switches back through rhododendron. On a level ridgetop soon after, there are several more possible campsites.

At 0.7 miles is Wayah Shelter and privy and a blue-blazed trail to a good spring.

The trail ascends gently through a mountain laurel thicket and joins an old road that runs level for several hundred yards. Look on the left side of the road for many American chestnut trees. You can find young healthy trees, older ones with chestnut blight cankers (swollen places on the trunk where the bark dies and splits), and many dead trees, some in clusters from the same root. Some trees here get big enough to produce flowers and fruit; look for long fuzzy catkins in June or for green spiny burrs on the tree or on the ground. In spring or summer you may also find little orange spots of the chestnut blight fungus on the cankers of living trees. The fungus does not affect the root, so as long as the roots stay alive, they continue to send up these hopeful shoots, but the fungus stays alive in the woods, too. In other parts of this hike, look for chestnut snags and logs that died more than 50 years ago.

At about 2.0 mi. the AT swings left and over a ridge to avoid a 1997 mud slide.

The AT reaches 4450-ft. Licklog Gap, a clearing that's an overused campsite, at 2.4 mi. May-apples, with leaves like green umbrellas, and bee balm grow along the trail. Bee balm, or wild bergamot, is a mint, and the leaves and flowers have a refreshing smell.

Ascend from the gap on long, easy switchbacks. A lookout on the right gives a view to the east, and then the trail crosses a ridge to the north side and joins another old road. In the cool, pleasant woods here listen for birds that sing all day in spring and early summer: vireos, ovenbirds, and perhaps a pileated woodpecker.

The next slight descent brings the AT at 3.7 mi. to a six-way intersection of woods roads and paths—a great place for a Pink Panther–style movie of hikers, bears, skunks, or whatever all zooming through and just missing each other. The grassy roadbeds provide fine flat tent sites, but you will have to bring water or fetch it from a stream about a mile farther north on the AT.

The trail goes right, but not sharp right, out of this intersection; check the white blazes. It enters a hemlock and rhododendron tunnel, emerges to go around the end of a ridge, then crosses several seeps and small streams. There may be muddy spots. Large beeches and hemlocks grow here, and along the streams, ramps grow among the spring wildflowers. Ramps are wild onions containing chemicals that repel most sensible herbivores, but some people love the strong garlicky flavor and aroma. Before you put one on your ham sandwich, though, be sure about the identification; ramp leaves resemble leaves of Clinton's lily and false hellebore. Some ramp collectors have been poisoned by false hellebore leaves because after picking a few ramps, everything they picked afterward smelled like ramps, and the hellebore leaves got mixed in.

The deciduous forest gives way to

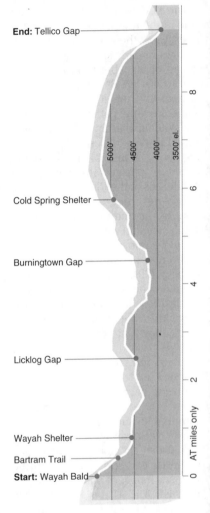

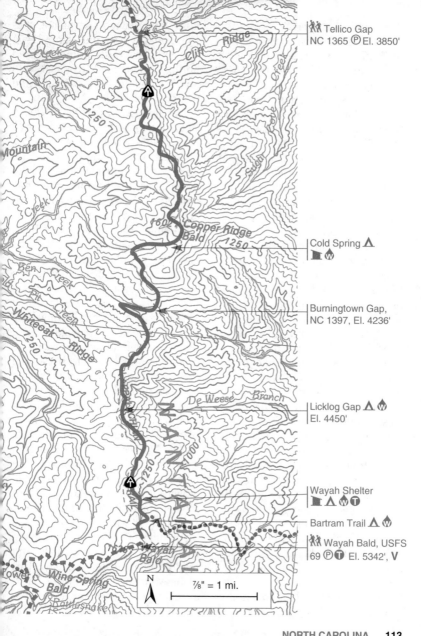

XX Tellico Gap
NC 1365 Ⓟ El. 3850'

Cold Spring ▲
▬ ⓦ

Burningtown Gap,
NC 1397, El. 4236'

Licklog Gap ▲ ⓦ
El. 4450'

Wayah Shelter
▬ ▲ ⓦ Ⓣ

Bartram Trail ▲ ⓦ

XX Wayah Bald, USFS
69 Ⓟ Ⓣ El. 5342', V

N
⋀   ⅞" = 1 mi.

dark hemlocks as the AT descends to 4236-ft. Burningtown Gap at 4.5 mi. NC 1397 enters the gap from the left. This road joins NC 1310, but it may be rough for cars.

Cross the open grassy gap past some old apple trees and look for a Forest Service AT sign that says "AT" or "APP TR" and has pictures of things you can't do here, such as ride your motorcycle. In some places along this trail, these fencepost-style signs take the place of blazes, but always check for white blazes as you proceed.

The AT ascends a roadbed lined with bluets, buttercups, and louse-wort, also called wood betony. Lousewort leaves look like fern fronds, but in April or May the plant produces a hairy flower stalk with yellow to reddish-brown flowers. This is a good flower to investigate with a hand lens, which can reveal many color shades on the lobed petals. Farmers once believed that cows got lice from grazing on this plant; they should have checked with their hand lenses. Lousewort grows best in areas with at least some direct sunlight, such as along old roads.

The trail continues to climb past some springs, a boulder field, and many patches of flame azalea. As the AT levels near the top of the ridge, it's blocked by a building that turns out to be the Cold Spring Shelter at 5.7 mi., the only AT shelter in the Nanta-halas above 5000 ft. Trail maintainers built this small shelter for about five hikers from recycled logs of another shelter. Just beyond is a piped spring

and a faint trail to the right that leads to ridgetop views and campsites. A few hundred yards farther is Cold Spring Gap, marked by a sign, with an excellent grassy campsite and winter views.

The trail swings west of 5200-ft. Copper Ridge Bald and passes a vista of the Little Tennessee River valley. Trailing arbutus, mountain laurel, and wintergreen, three evergreens in the heath family, line the south-facing trail bank here. The AT stays on a ridgetop just west of the watershed divide, bypassing Tellico Bald, Black Bald, and Rocky Bald, all presently tree covered. A comfortable resting rock on the right provides a tree-framed view to the east of Little Tennessee River valley and the Cowee Mts.

The trail now starts a mile-long descent to Tellico Gap. A blue-blazed trail leads right to another rock out-crop vista, and the AT crosses several other rock outcrops. Keep an eye out for mica sparkling in quartz crystals, and at wet rocky seeps, look for black moss and Michaux's saxifrage. This plant, whose Latin name means "rock breaker," grows from moist cracks in rock outcrops. It has a basal rosette of leaves — that is, a circle of leaves all growing from the same point — and a foot-tall stalk with tiny white flowers. A hand lens will show colored sta-mens and yellow dots on some of the white petals. The leaves are hairy and may have bright red margins. This plant was named for André Michaux, a French botanist who explored here in the 1780s. Michaux's saxifrage

Miles N	NORTH	Elev. (ft./m)	Miles S
9.3	**End: Tellico Gap,** NC 1365, parking.	3850/1173	0.0
5.7	**Cold Spring Shelter,** piped spring, views, campsites.		3.6
4.5	**Burningtown Gap,** NC 1397.	4236/1291	4.8
3.7	Six-way intersection, campsites.		5.6
2.4	**Licklog Gap;** stream 0.5 mi. W.	4450/1356	6.9
0.7	**Wayah Shelter,** water, privy, tent sites.		8.6
0.4	Jct. yellow-blazed **Bartram Trail,** good spring on L just past campsite.		8.9
0.0	**Start: Wayah Bald,** observation tower with extensive views, USFS 69, picnic/parking area, privies.	5342/1628	9.3

SOUTH

grows only in the southern Appalachians and only above 4500 ft.

After some rocky steep sections through deciduous woods, the AT goes under a power line and drops into 3850-ft. Tellico Gap through a patch of pussy willows. Tellico Rd. (NC 1365) passes through the gap, where railroad ties reinforce high banks around a parking area.

Tellico Gap to Wesser

Maps: ATC Nantahala Nat'l. Forest

Route: Tellico Gap to Wesser Bald to the Jumpup to Nantahala River

Recommended direction: S to N

Distance: 7.9 mi.

Elevation +/-: 3850 to 4627 to 4100 to 1723 ft.

Effort: Strenuous

Day hike: Yes

Overnight backpacking hike: Optional

Duration: 6 to 7 hr.

Early exit option: None

Natural history features: Mountain laurel and rhododendron blooms

Social history feature: Wesser Bald fire tower

Other feature: Nantahala Outdoor Center (Wesser)

Trailhead access: *Start:* From US 19/74 in Beechertown, take Wayah Rd. (NC 1310) 5.0 mi. Turn L onto Tellico Rd. (NC 1365) for 4.0 mi. to Tellico Gap and parking area defined by steep banks supported by railroad ties. Tellico Rd. can also be reached from very rough US 28 N of Franklin. *End:* Wesser, on US 74/19 where it crosses the Nantahala River. (In summer, Wesser is crowded, but parking is available.)

Camping: Wesser Bald Shelter, A. Rufus Morgan Shelter; campsites; lodging at Nantahala Outdoor Center

---

The great rivers of the southern Appalachians collect water from the eastern Blue Ridge and flow north or northwest, cutting deep valleys through the mountains. This hike descends into the valley of the Nantahala River, the land of the noonday sun. An elevation change of nearly 3000 ft. and several steep, rocky sections make this a strenuous hike in either direction, but the views from Wesser Bald and the Jumpup are excellent, and the displays of mountain laurel and rhododendron blooms are spectacular. Most of the hike runs along sharp ridgetops with no water and few flat places for camping; however, water and camp-

sites are available near the Wesser Bald and A. Rufus Morgan shelters.

The AT ascends from Tellico Gap to the left of an old road. In April, look for pink azalea near the gap. This deciduous relative of flame azalea is less common and usually grows on rocky south-facing slopes. The trail swings left on a well-graded bench, passes through a rhododendron tunnel, and emerges in open, dry woods. Bluets, also called Quaker ladies or innocence, line the trail. Their leaves are smaller than sesame seeds, and a 2-in. stalk holds a four-petal bluish flower with a yellow center. Bluets bloom any time of the year if there are a few warm days. On sunny exposed slopes like this, they can bloom in January, but the flowers are most common in early summer.

As the trail climbs, Wesser Bald Tower becomes visible to the right. At 1.4 mi. a spur trail leads right about 50 yd. from a rock outcrop to the fire tower at 4627 ft.

No longer living up to its name, Wesser Bald has become overgrown with trees, but the old tower stands above them and provides a magnificent 360-degree view. Sturdy metal stairs lead up to a large restored wooden platform, a wonderful place for a nap, lunch, or basking in the sun but a perch to skip in high wind or storms. Look for the Smokies and Fontana Lake to the north, Cheoah Bald to the northwest, the Cowee Mts. to the east, and Wayah Bald to the south. Below the tower is a pleasant grassy spot with some shade. A Dutchman's pipe vine near the base of the tower has champion-sized heart-shaped leaves, and you may be able to find its flowers or seedpods from one flight up the tower. Raspberry and blueberry bushes provide a snack in July or August—but check for stinkbugs before eating a handful of berries. These handsome brown or green beetles seem friendly because of their confidence that you and other big predators know better than to eat them.

The AT descends steeply from Wesser Bald. At 2.0 mi., there is a grassy and dry ridge campsite—also a place to avoid in stormy weather. A blue-blazed trail 0.1 mi. past the campsite leads 125 yd. to a spring, which is the water supply for the upcoming shelter, and the AT turns left to continue down to Wesser Gap at 2.2 mi. and a trail junction. Here a short trail leads left down to the Wesser Bald Shelter, a new "Nantahala Design" building. An extended front overhang covers benches,

Rafting, Nantahala Outdoor Center

shelves, and a picnic table. This shelter was assembled at a more convenient spot by the Nantahala Hiking Club, then airlifted here in sections by Forest Service helicopters. Look for the match-up numbers on the inside walls. A privy was added later. Tenting: Choose the campsite back up the trail (south) toward Wesser Bald; tenters here at the shelter have trampled the front yard.

The blue-blazed Wesser Creek Trail to the right follows an old AT path 3.6 mi. to Wesser Creek Rd. This trail is steep but in good condition and could be used for a loop or an alternative route to Wesser Bald. Wesser Creek Rd. is 0.9 mi. east of Wesser on US 19; the trail starts at a small parking area 2.6 mi. up the road.

From Wesser Gap the trail climbs a dry ridge with chestnut oaks, pines, American chestnut sprouts, and bracken ferns. It stays on the ridgeline as exposed rocky sections (mostly slate and mica) alternate with rhododendron tunnels.

Squaw root and Indian pipe, two flowering plants that have no chlorophyll, can be found in moist areas along here. Squaw root comes up in early spring looking like brown and yellow pinecones stuck in the ground. With a hand lens, you can find fused petals and stamens in the tiny flowers. It gets food from oak roots, and no members of this botanical plant family make chlorophyll. Indian pipe, or ghost flower, looks like a white clay pipe and comes out of the ground flower (bowl of the pipe) first. After it gets pollinated, probably by beetles, the flower turns upward and forms a dry basket that scatters the seeds. Indian pipe absorbs decayed food from the soil.

The ridge now becomes bumpy, and the trail makes several steep ascents and then descends over rocky terrain. At Paint Mt. there's a view down into Silvermine Creek and across to Briertown Mt. to the left. The trail gets rougher, requiring scrambling up and around boulders. The entire ridgetop has a fantastic display of mountain laurel that blooms profusely in May and June. Its tough, leathery leaves can withstand the wind, and mountain laurel is an expert at living on dry pockets of soil, so it has no competition from trees or other bushes in a relatively arid habitat like this. Lower, more sheltered, parts of the same ridge have good displays of rosebay rhododendron, which blooms in late June.

At 3.8 mi. the ridge suddenly ends at an exposed knob, the Jumpup, and the trail makes a sharp right turn. The rocky knob here is surrounded by mountain laurel and provides a wonderful view of Cheoah Bald and the deep valley cut by the Nantahala River over millions of years. It also gives an overview of the steep descent to Wesser and the steep climb to Cheoah Bald in Hike #15. The rock at the bottom of the valley is marble and limestone, both of which are more soluble than the slate or gneiss of the ridgetops.

Water Power

The large rivers of the western slopes of the southern Appalachians flow northwest, cutting 2000- to 3000-ft.-deep valleys and gorges straight through the high ridges of tough metamorphic rock. The rivers established their courses before pre-Jurassic continental collision pushed the sandstone mountains and ridges westward over younger limestones and marbles. The V-shaped river valleys provide much of the beauty and challenge of hiking the AT. They also tell the geologic story by exposing thrust faults, folds, and layers of gneiss, schist, granite, slate, and graywacke (pronounced "gray-wacky," of course, and composed of a mixture of quartz, feldspar, and other darker rocks distributed like chocolate chips throughout the layer).

One way to examine all this geology is to hike the high-elevation ridgelines and knobs, but another way is to run the rapids—bump *into* boulders instead of clambering over them. Views from the ridgetops show the results of millions of years of water erosion, and down on the rivers, you get a chance to feel the power of the water as it rushes down and tumbles great boulders in its path.

The Ocoee, Nantahala, Pigeon, French Broad, and Nolichucky Rivers have free-flowing sections either cross?ing or near the AT where river recreation opportunities have spawned thriving businesses. Family raft trips, canoe and kayak rental, riverside campsites, hiker hostels, restaurants, hiker and river-running shuttles, recreational outfitting, and other services are available. The Ocoee River, which drains the northwestern slopes of Springer Mt. (Hike #1), served as the canoe and kayak venue for the 1994 Summer Olympics in Atlanta. The Nantahala River at Wesser (Hikes #14 and #15) is the home of the Nantahala Outdoor Center (NOC), which also has river rafting outposts on the French Broad and the Nolichucky. The Pigeon River (Hike #25) has a relatively new rafting company in Waterville. In Hot Springs (Hikes #27 and #28), you can hike, camp, raft or canoe, and then soak in riverside hot springs.

Information about river recreation opportunities is available from welcome centers, from the NOC, and at U.S. Forest Service ranger stations. See "Useful Information" for addresses.

After resting at the Jumpup, go down stone steps. For a while the trail down combines hiking with rock climbing among great slabs and boulders as you descend more than 1000 ft. in 1.0 mi. Rock fern caps many of the rocks, and trailing arbutus grows along the trail in open spots. After about a mile the trail levels and has a welcome cushion of pine needles. Mountain laurel and fetterbush, the latter an evergreen shrub with a spike of white flowers, grow here among pine trees. Old man's beard, an appropriately named stringy lichen, hangs from many of the trees.

The trail goes down rough stone steps, enters a thick patch of rhododendron, and resumes a steep descent on the ridge crest. Then it slips to the right of the ridge and descends through richer woods, becoming less rocky but still steep. A wide area surrounded by red oaks and maples could be a campsite, but there is no water nearby. Pink lady's-slippers grow here; they bloom in late April, and the big corduroy leaves remain until fall.

The trail slips farther away from the ridge into a moist sheltered area with spring wildflowers, among them doll's eyes. In spring, the plant produces a round Ping-Pong-ball-sized cluster of white flowers, and during the summer, each flower makes a white seed with a black spot, just right for eyes for a corn-shuck doll. However, the seeds are poisonous, as the other name of this plant—white baneberry—implies. Cucumber root, wood aster, and starry campion also bloom here in summer.

The descent eases again in an open area with black locust saplings and other small trees with unusually big leaves. This area may have been cleared by fire, and many young trees compete for a place in the sun by growing oversized leaves. Treefall from Hurricane Opal in 1995 damaged the next part of the AT, and the trail maintainers relocated it slightly.

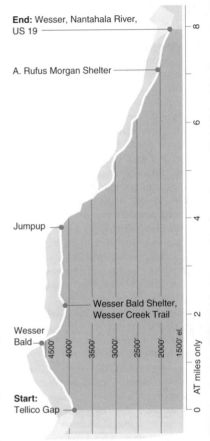

Another rhododendron tunnel at 5.5 mi. leads down to a small creek lined with lots of wildflowers such as umbrella leaf, which has one or two large round leaves up on a tall, fleshy stalk and a cluster of white flowers in May. This plant—a relative of the may-apple—grows only in the southern Appalachians and

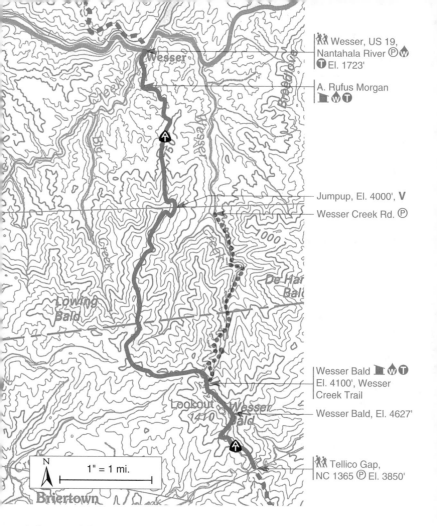

Wesser, US 19,
Nantahala River Ⓟ🅦
🅣 El. 1723'

A. Rufus Morgan
▰🅦🅣

Jumpup, El. 4000', **V**

Wesser Creek Rd. Ⓟ

Wesser Bald ▰🅦🅣
El. 4100', Wesser
Creek Trail

Wesser Bald, El. 4627'

Tellico Gap,
NC 1365 Ⓟ El. 3850'

only in steep hillside creeks. Its near-est botanical relative lives in similar habitats in Japan.

At about 6.5 mi. the AT skirts a steep, dry, sandy knob and then con-tinues down the side of the ridge. At 7.1 mi., the trail enters a clearing with the A. Rufus Morgan Shelter uphill 200 ft. to the right in a shade-dappled cove; a stream across the AT to the left of the shelter provides water. Dr. Morgan, an Episcopal min-ister, founded the Nantahala Hiking Club and worked on AT building

Miles N	NORTH	Elev. (ft./m)	Miles S
7.9	**End: Wesser, Nantahala Outdoor Center,** US 19; parking, food, water, lodging, and river rafting.	1723/527	0.0
7.1	**A. Rufus Morgan Shelter,** stream for water, privy.		0.8
3.8	**Jumpup,** rocky promontory with views of valley.	4000/1219	4.1
2.2	**Wesser Bald Shelter,** picnic table, spring 0.1 mi. back on blue-blazed trail; jct. **Wesser Creek Trail** to Wesser Creek Rd. (3.6 mi.).	4100/1250	5.7
1.4	**Wesser Bald,** rebuilt fire tower.	4627/1410	6.5
0.0	**Start: Tellico Gap,** parking on NC 1365.	3850/1173	7.9

SOUTH

and maintaining for most of his long life.

The last mile of descent is graded with a few steep spots. On summer weekends the sounds of buses, motorcycles, and people will reach you as you approach the recreational complex of Wesser on the banks of the Nantahala River. Watch for traffic as you cross US 19. Across the road and left are a pedestrian bridge over the river and shops and restaurants; the AT continues on the other side of the big parking lot at Nantahala Outdoor Center. Wesser is hiker-friendly and provides shuttle service, lodging, scenic autumn train rides to Bryson City, as well as river expeditions. Call for schedules and reservations (See "Water Power").

Stecoah Gap to Wesser

Maps: ATC Nantahala Nat'l. Forest

Route: Stecoah Gap to Cheoah Bald to Sassafras Gap to Nantahala River (Wesser)

Recommended direction: N to S

Distance: 13.6 mi.

Elevation +/-: 3165 to 5062 to 1723 ft.

Effort: Strenuous

Day hike: No

Overnight backpacking hike: Yes

Duration: 10 to 11 hr.

Early exit option: None

Natural history features: Cheoah Bald; flame azalea

Other feature: Nantahala Outdoor Center, Wesser (See Hike #14)

Trailhead access: *Start:* From US 129 in Robbinsville, drive 8.6 mi. E on NC 143 (Sweetwater Creek Rd.) to Stecoah Gap (NC 143 meets NC 28 at 3.0 mi. to the E). *End:* US 74/19 in Wesser, where it crosses the Nantahala River. In summer Wesser is crowded, but parking is available.

Camping: Sassafras Gap Shelter; several campsites; lodging at Nantahala Outdoor Center

C heoah Bald is the highest point of the Cheoah Mts. and the only 5000-ft. peak between the Nantahala and Little Tennessee rivers. Mountain laurel covers the ridgetops on this hike, and flame azalea grows abundantly throughout the woods. Hike #15 to the bald (actually an area at the summit cleared by the U.S. Forest Service) is strenuous in either direction, but as described here (north to south) it has an elevation gain of about 1900 ft. Northbound long-distance hikers have no choice and must climb nearly 3500 ft. from the Nantahala River valley to Cheoah Bald. Water is available at the shelters and at some gaps, but for camping at the bald or on the ridgetop, you will have to carry water.

At Stecoah Gap there is a large parking and picnic area, and a Forest Service road to the left of the AT leads 0.1 mi. down to a piped spring. The AT starts at steps to the right of the gravel road. It climbs quickly on several switchbacks, passing large rock slabs on the left and a rock overhang that could be useful in heavy rain. The trail ascends along a hillside to another ridge that sports red oaks, black locusts, and winter views of the road below. As soon as you reach one ridgetop you descend for a few steps and then ascend to the next ridge, like a surfer heading out through the waves. Finally, after almost a mile, the trail levels and descends to a saddle and a possible campsite. On a curve there's a good winter view of Cheoah Bald looming ahead.

After a series of small knobs—steep, rocky bumps on a ridgeline that don't show on trail profile maps—the trail descends on an easy grade to Simp Gap at 2.1 mi. The knobs repeat on the other side of the gap until the trail reaches a narrow, rocky ridgetop with big red oaks and mountain laurel on exposed areas. The next few knobs feature sourwood trees and masses of galax on the trail banks. This evergreen plant, with rounded heart-shaped leaves, grows only in the southern Appalachians and probably can be seen on every AT hike described in this volume. In some places the leaves turn a rich burgundy color in fall; in others, they remain dark green. People used to harvest and sell galax leaves for Christmas decorations, and the plant became rare in some areas. Fortunately, it recovers quickly, and wholesale galax harvesting seems to be out of style now. In spring, look for miniature galax leaves with shiny, iridescent surfaces. They come out of the ground folded in half like a valentine card. In May or June, galax flowers appear on spikes up to two feet tall. Look at the flowers with a hand lens to see five creamy petals around each tiny blossom.

Finally you reach a knob that you don't have to climb; the AT skirts right on a south-facing slope. Beside the trail, look for a crop of even-age oak seedlings. They probably all started growing in a spring after an acorn harvest so heavy that the squirrels, hogs, bears, turkeys, and other acorn eaters couldn't eat them all. Seedlings like this are often seen lining the trail or along abandoned roads because the clearing gives them a chance to get started. Oak trees produce big crops in good years and scant crops in poor years. When American chestnuts reigned in these woods, the mast (a general word for high-food-value tree nuts) crops were more reliable, and the forest supported more wildlife, especially those that need mast to fatten up for winter.

The trail descends through thick laurel and a few pine trees. Lining the trail is trailing arbutus, which blooms in March. The flowers smell wonderful, but you have to get down to their level to smell them, although you may get a whiff that tells you to lift up the leathery last-year leaves to look for the flowers.

At 3.1 mi., the AT reaches Locust Cove Gap with a level campsite and a blue-blazed trail that leads right 150 yd. to an unreliable spring. There are a few old black locust trees here with deeply furrowed bark and finely divided compound leaves. Locust trees germinate best in disturbed areas, so the presence of locusts indicates that the forest has been cut, and the fact that they are dying out indicates that the forest is recovering nicely.

Ascend to the right from the gap along a north-facing slope, and cross

Grazing, Lightning, or What?

Grass balds are mysterious. Why don't trees grow there? Did Cherokee and Catawba Indians set fires and graze elk up there? Did the glaciers scrape off all the soil? The glaciers didn't even come this far south, and at any rate, the last glacier left 12,000 years ago. And then there's the botanical enigma: Why are the balds shrinking? Only two balds in the Smokies stay the same size year after year, and that's because park rangers burn or cut the trees around the edge. The biggest balds, on Roan Mt., get smaller every year, and the man-made balds, such as Max Patch on the Tennessee / North Carolina border, and Silers Bald, near Franklin, North Carolina, have to be mowed each summer to prevent shrubs and trees from creeping in from the edges. The U.S. Forest Service does what it can to maintain some grass balds with cows, and sometimes goats, pastured in strategic spots. Most ecologists would agree that grazing patterns of recorded history, especially the practice of driving livestock to high elevations in the summers, maintained the balds. But what started them?

The Cherokee believed that a giant hornet, the Ulagu, swooped above villages and snatched unwary children. Brave warriors went up into the mountains after the Ulagu. The Great Spirit sent lightning and fire, allowing the warriors to trap the beast in its den and kill it. The trick worked, but the tops of mountains lost their trees in the process. Botanists from John Bartram on have blamed acid soil, toxic roots, seasonal permafrost, elks and woolly mammoths.

Ecology graduate students continue to write dissertations on grass balds, and still nobody knows for sure.

Meanwhile, all you can do is enjoy the view and keep off Beauty Spot, Big Bald, Little Hump, and the other fine balds during thunderstorms.

---

a creek with large boulders and many spring wildflowers, including foamflower, trillium, and several kinds of violets. Then cross the ridge to another south-facing slope, and follow rocky, narrow trail through a bank of flame azalea. Look for fungus galls—light green or white lumpy growths—on the azalea stems. These fungi take water and nutrients from the azaleas until they turn dark and produce spores that travel with the wind to other azaleas. When the galls are fresh, they have a slightly sour taste, somewhat like watermelon rind. Cherokees and other travelers used them to appease thirst.

From here to Cheoah Bald, the trail keeps to the rocky ridge crest, passing mountain laurel and thick rhododendron patches. Twists and turns are well marked with blazes. After a steep, rocky climb, blackberry bushes appear—a sign that you are near the top of Cheoah Bald at 5.5 mi. Cheoah Bald is an artificial bald, established and maintained by the Forest Service to provide views and a grazing area for wildlife. Look right for an opening to the mowed field; then look left a little farther along for a spur trail to a rocky viewpoint. The bald is a wide and steep grassy slope that faces south, giving an excellent view to the Nantahala and Snowbird mts., Wayah Bald, and possibly Standing Indian Mt. and Albert Mt. Smoke signals from any point on the AT south to Springer Mt. could be viewed from here. A gated Forest Service road gives access to the bottom of the mowed area; don't be surprised to see a mountain biker or two creeping up or hurtling down the bald.

The left side view is of the Cheoah Mts. and the Smokies beyond, and you can look down dramatic cliffs into forested coves and the Nantahala River Gorge, this hike's destination. Just past the left spur trail, the AT meets the edge of the field at a level spot and a good campsite; the nearest water is either in your pack or 1.2 mi. farther at Sassafras Gap Shelter. Blueberry and blackberry bushes will provide dessert in August.

To continue on the AT, descend a steep, rocky ridge crest past yellow birches with bark curls. These trees grow at most elevations, but they seem to stand out more at 5000 ft. In winter, look for inch-long catkins, or male flowers, growing in clusters high in the tree. In April, these catkins expand to several inches in length, scatter their pollen, and then fall off. If you're not allergic to pollens, find

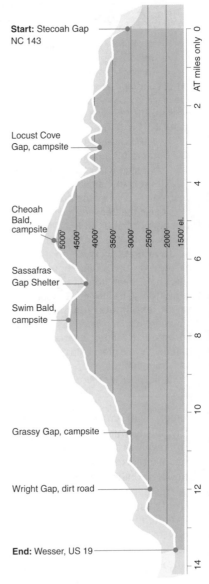

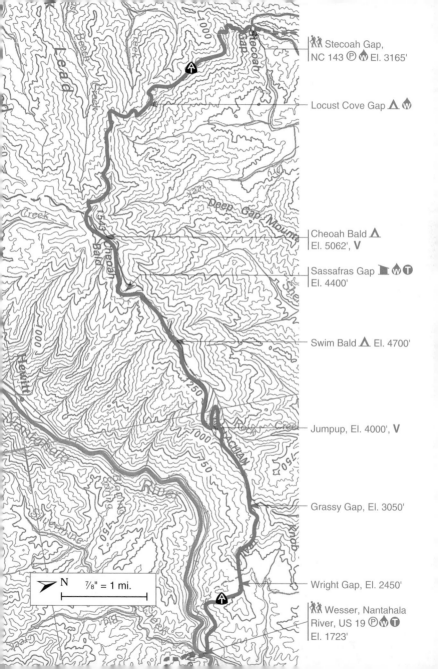

🚶 Stecoah Gap,
NC 143 Ⓟ 💧 El. 3165'

Locust Cove Gap ▲ 💧

Cheoah Bald ▲
El. 5062', **V**

Sassafras Gap ◣ 💧 🅣
El. 4400'

Swim Bald ▲ El. 4700'

Jumpup, El. 4000', **V**

Grassy Gap, El. 3050'

Wright Gap, El. 2450'

🚶 Wesser, Nantahala
River, US 19 Ⓟ 💧 🅣
El. 1723'

N   ⅞" = 1 mi.

fresh catkins on the trail and look for the bright yellow pollen—if there's any left—with a hand lens.

The AT turns left and descends to Sassafras Gap (6.7 mi.) with a shelter, piped spring, and privy on a side trail. This shelter was rebuilt in 2002 and sleeps 12.

Climb out of the gap and descend on top of or beside the ridge crest for nearly a mile Big red oaks and abundant flame azaleas grow here. At 7.6 mi. the AT reaches the summit of 4700-ft. Swim Bald, which is no longer a bald and provides only winter views. About 50 yd. east is a pleasant campsite and a wet-weather spring; in summer, you may need to collect water at Sassafras Gap to camp here. Cattle and hogs probably grazed here in the last century, and Swim Bald may have looked like Cheoah Bald. Give your legs a rest here. From Swim Bald to the Nantahala River, the AT loses 3000 ft. in a little more than 5 mi.; your knees may notice.

Watch the blazes carefully in the open woods of this area, especially if leaves have fallen. The AT goes east from Swim Bald and curves around the Jumpup, two viewing spots on a rocky ridgetop where you can jump up on rocks to get a better view of the Nantahala River valley and some of the communities along it. The trail makes a sharp left at 8.3 mi., then a sharp right at 8.8 mi., through a rocky area with many fallen oaks. In March, trail maintainers from the Smoky Mt. Hiking Club bring chain saws to cut tree trunks; in winter, hikers may have to climb over hurricane or ice storm blowdowns.

Openings along the trail give closer views of the Nantahala Gorge as it seems to rise up to meet the AT. The rocks that form the walls of the gorge contain marble and mica and are about 500 million years old, much younger than the harder rock of the ridgetops. The marble is slightly soluble, and the Nantahala River has had plenty of time to cut this deep, relatively straight, gorge. Marble is mined about a mile upstream from Wesser, where the AT crosses the Nantahala River.

At Grassy Gap (10.5 mi.) the AT turns left and starts to ascend out of the gap, but it skirts right around the next knob and plunges down again. On the left, a memorial plaque dated December 7, 1968, honors Forest Ranger Wade Sutton, who died near here fighting a fire, "That you might more fully enjoy your hike along this trail." A level spot provides a good campsite with big rock slabs split into layers and a small rock shelter.

Descend along a ridge crest and rest your braking muscles with an easy ascent on a dry piney ridge that looks is if it may have burned recently. A spur trail leads to an overlook of the Nantahala Gorge, where the steep sides show why the Cherokee named this *Nantahala*—"the land of the noonday sun." To the left are open fields and Christmas tree farms.

The AT descends through thick mountain laurel, another open, dry

Miles N	NORTH	Elev. (ft./m)	Miles S
13.6	**Start: Stecoah Gap,** parking and picnic area; piped spring 0.1 mi L of AT on USFS service road.	3165/965	0.0
10.5	**Locust Cove Gap,** campsite, unreliable spring 150 yd. to R.		3.1
8.1	**Cheoah Bald,** campsite, views.	5062/1543	5.5
6.9	**Sassafras Gap Shelter,** privy, piped spring 120 yd. R.	4400/1341	6.7
6.0	**Swim Bald,** campsite, unreliable spring 50 yd. E of summit.	4700/1433	7.6
3.1	**Grassy Gap,** campsite.	3050/930	10.5
1.6	**Wright Gap,** dirt road.	2450/747	12.0
0.0	**End: Wesser, Nantahala River,** US 19, parking and services at Nantahala Outdoor Center.	1723/527	13.6

SOUTH

ridge, and then at 12.0 mi. into Wright Gap with a gravel road. Cross the road, ascend through Flint Ridge (with blackened tree trunks and other signs of a more recent forest fire), and pass under power lines. The trail becomes very rocky and offers a few views of the river to the right.

When it can't go down any farther, the trail crosses railroad tracks at 13.6 mi. into a large parking area. Buildings on the left are housing for employees of Nantahala Outdoor Center, the river outfitters. Turn right across the parking lot to reach the bathrooms, ice cream shop, and a bridge where you can watch Olympic kayakers running the gates. (For more information on the rafting-kayaking center, which is also hiker-friendly, see Hike #14.)

An excellent one-car alternative to this hike would be to hike from Stecoah Gap to Cheoah Bald and then backtrack to the car. This 11-mi. hike could be an overnight or a day hike and would be strenuous either way.

Stecoah Gap to Yellow Creek Gap

Maps: ATC Nantahala Nat'l. Forest

Route: Stecoah Gap to Brown Fork Shelter to Yellow Creek Gap

Recommended direction: S to N

Distance: 7.6 mi.

Elevation +/-: 3165 to 3912 to 2980 ft.

Effort: Moderate

Day hike: Yes

Overnight backpacking hike: Optional

Duration: 6 to 7 hr.

Early exit option: None

Natural history features: Mountain laurel displays; boulder field

Trailhead access: *Start:* From Robbinsville, go E on NC 143 E for 8.6 mi. to Stecoah Gap. At the intersection of NC 29 and NC 143, drive W on NC 143 for 3.0 mi. *End:* From Fontana Village go S on NC 28 for 9.0 mi., then W (R) onto Yellow Creek Mt. Rd. (NC 1242, also called Tuskeegee Creek Rd.). Drive 4.0 mi. to Yellow Creek Gap. Park on S side of gap on Wauchecha Bald Rd. From the gap, Yellow Creek Mt. Rd. goes 10.0 mi. W to US 129.

Camping: Brown Fork Gap Shelter; several campsites

T his short hike between two gaps provides a few ridgetop views and pleasant, quiet woods. Though Hike #16 is rated "moderate," there are several short, steep ascents on knobs of the Cheoah Mts.

From Stecoah Gap, climb a steep road bank and continue up the side of a ridge to the crest. Descend into Sweetwater Gap at 1.0 mi., where a large, inviting campsite is surrounded by tulip-trees. Then the AT climbs steeply up the side of a ridge on trail that may be slippery. At a switchback to the right, look for a spur trail left to a cliff top with views of NC 143 below and the Snowbird Mts. to the west.

The rock outcrop here has many types and colors of lichens as well as a few potholes, probably formed when pebbles settled into a slight depression and swirled around when water ran over the rock. If there has been a recent summer rain, check the water in the potholes for mosquito larvae. Mix up the water, scoop out a handful and look for wrigglers in your palm (perhaps after several tries). Drain out most of the water and examine your catch with a hand lens. Mosquito larvae have big heads, stiff bristles along the body, a flexible segmented abdomen, and a rigid extension from the tail. Unlike gilled aquatic insect larvae, mosquitoes breathe air, and the tail extension serves as a snorkel. They float up through the water, head down, until the snorkel breaks through the surface tension, hanging there until something big scares them down into the mud.

Wish the mosquito larvae well (you'll be long gone before they pupate) and climb another 0.2 mi. to a narrow rocky ridge crest with winter views on both sides.

After a few ups and downs along the same ridge, the AT descends and turns left. A signed side trail at 2.4 mi. goes right some 200 ft. to Brown Fork Gap Shelter, which has a spring about 75 yd. to the right. The U.S. Forest Service and the Smoky Mt. Hiking Club built this shelter in 1994 from trees that fell in storms in the area. They cut the trees, let them season for a year, and then assembled the shelter with rot-resistant locust logs at the bottom and mostly tulip-tree logs on the sides. Large pillars in front hold up an overhanging roof to cook and eat under. There are benches, a fire ring, and a shake (oak shingles) roof. The privy (with smaller pillars) is down the hill on a switchback trail; unfortunately, people have cut across the switchbacks, causing erosion on the steep hillside.

From the shelter trail, the AT descends and then ascends the first of a series of knobs—steep bumps of erosion-resistant rock on a ridge-line that don't show on trail profile maps. For the next 3.0 mi., Hike #16 has a mild case of knobs, and the trail maintainers relocated parts of the trail in 1998 and 1999 to reduce erosion on fragile rocky sections.

At 2.5 mi. a blue blaze on a large black locust tree marks the descent to a gap. A path on the right leads to a small spring in about 50 yd. Black locust trees grow best in sunny, open areas. The presence of one here shows that this forest was once cleared. As the forest becomes mature again, most of the black locusts die as other trees shade them.

After another small knob, descend into Brown Fork Gap and climb up and down more knobs. One knob is flat on top and makes a nice campsite, but there is no water nearby. The next knob has a steep, hard climb, and the narrow rocky top is covered with mountain laurel and blueberry bushes. Laurel blooms in May, and exposed sunny ridges like this have the best displays. Blueberries ripen in August. Flame azalea, blooming in May and June, lines the trail between knobs.

After another knob and the 3912-ft. high point of this hike at 3.3 mi., the trail descends steeply to Hogback Gap at 4.4 mi. and turns right. An old trail goes left to Wauchecha Bald (4385 ft.) and rejoins the AT at Cody Gap. The trail is currently overgrown, but if it gets cleared and reblazed, it will loop to the left of the AT and have a spur trail to the top of the bald, which is also overgrown.

From Hogback Gap, the AT leaves the ridgetop and descends a side-hill trail through thick stands of rhododendron. It emerges from the rhododendron tunnel at the bottom of a boulder field where you can look up into a tangle of rhododendron as thick as what you just came through and imagine the work of early trail-blazers. Silverbell trees, Dutchman's pipe vines and many wildflowers grow among the rocks. Hearts-a-bustin with love—a small green-stemmed shrub—grows inconspicuously for most of the year, but in September it produces a preposterous magenta seedpod with bright orange seeds popping out. More reserved botanists call it strawberry bush or bursting heart.

The AT curves right and enters Cody Gap at 5.2 mi. (A trail on the left leads to a spring 200 yd. down and continues—though overgrown—on to Wauchecha Bald and Hogback Gap, as above.) From Cody Gap bear right and climb again to the ridge crest, which has a grassy knob with a flat place for resting or camping, but no water. At 5.6 mi. the AT again swings left of the ridge crest along a sheltered north-facing slope. Two orchid species can be found here: putty root orchid and downy rattlesnake plantain. Both live in dense shade, have leaves of a pale dollar-bill shade of green, and seem to have too little leaf area to support any flowers at all. They are semiparasitic; their pale leaves produce some food by photosynthesis, but they get sugars and amino acids from the roots of other plants, usually trees. And they don't even do the dirty work themselves. Their roots associate with mycorrhizae, or fungus roots, which

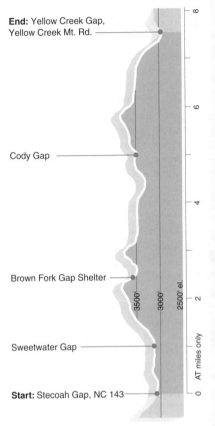

steal from the rich tree roots and transport the goods to the orchid roots. The orchid leaves are somewhat like some tax shelters: not profitable, but good investments because of underground arrangements.

The AT goes once more to an open, dry ridge crest with mountain laurel, galax, blueberry bushes, and greenbrier, plus an occasional view of Cheoah Bald to the southeast. In

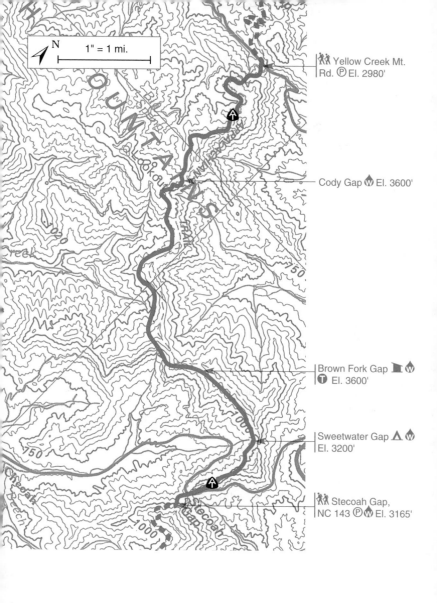

N   1" = 1 mi.

🏃🏃 Yellow Creek Mt.
Rd. Ⓟ El. 2980'

Cody Gap Ⓦ El. 3600'

Brown Fork Gap ▰ Ⓦ
Ⓣ El. 3600'

Sweetwater Gap ▲ Ⓦ
El. 3200'

🏃🏃 Stecoah Gap,
NC 143 Ⓟ Ⓦ El. 3165'

Miles N	NORTH	Elev. (ft./m)	Miles S
7.6	**End: Yellow Creek Gap,** Yellow Creek Mt. Rd., parking on gravel road.	2980/908	0.0
5.2	**Cody Gap,** spring 200 yd. down side trail on L.	3600/1097	2.4
4.4	**Hogback Gap,** AT turns R.		3.2
3.3	Hike high point.	3912/1192	4.3
2.4	**Brown Fork Gap Shelter;** privy, spring 75 yd. to R.	3600/1097	5.2
1.0	**Sweetwater Gap,** large campsite.	3200/975	6.6
0.0	**Start: Stecoah Gap,** NC 143; parking and picnic area.	3165/965	7.6

SOUTH

1997, an American chestnut in this section produced fruit but had cankers of the chestnut blight on its trunk. It may have died, but other sprouts along here may get old enough to reproduce. Look for golf-ball-sized prickly burrs on the ground.

At 6.2 mi. the trail goes down the left side of the ridge on a narrow sidehill trail and descends for about a mile. At 7.2 mi. it crosses a small creek with a pretty upstream cascade. Wood and Christmas ferns and many wildflowers live along the creek. Soon you will be able to see a gravel road below, and then the AT reaches steps leading down to Wauchecha Bald Rd. These steps were designed and built as an Eagle Scout service project with the supervision and help of the trail maintainers. To the left is a gravel Forest Service gate, and to the right is paved Yellow Creek Mt. Rd. Parking is available along the gravel road, but don't block the gate.

Yellow Creek Gap to Fontana Dam

Maps: ATC Nantahala Nat'l. Forest

Route: Yellow Creek to Cable Gap, to US 28, to Fontana Dam

Recommended direction: S to N

Distance: 7.8 mi.

Elevation +/-: 2980 to 3786 to 1800 ft.

Effort: Moderate

Day hike: Yes

Overnight backpacking hike: Optional

Duration: 6 to 7 hr.

Early exit option: None

Natural history feature: Fontana Lake

Social history feature: Fontana Dam

Trailhead access: *Start:* From Fontana Village go S on NC 28 for 9.0 mi. Turn W (R) onto Yellow Creek Mt. Rd. (NC 1242, also called Tuskeegee Creek Rd.) 4.0 mi. to Yellow Creek Gap. Park on S side of gap on Wauchecha Bald Rd. (From the gap, Yellow Creek Mt. Rd. goes 10.0 mi. W to US 129.) *End:* From the junction of US 129 and NC 28, go E past Fontana Village for 2.0 mi. Turn L at sign for Fontana Dam. Hiker parking available near boat dock on S side of the dam and where AT enters.

Camping: Cable Cove Shelter; Fontana Dam Shelter (registered long-distance hikers only); campsites

The Little Tennessee River carved a deep valley between the Yellow Creek Mts. and the Smokies, now filled by Fontana Lake, which was created by the damming of the river as part of the TVA system. This short but strenuous hike climbs and crosses part of the Yellow Creek Mts., a long east-west ridge parallel to the Snowbird and Cheoah mts. and to the spine of the Smokies looming to the north, passing peaceful valleys, rugged boulder piles, and windy ridgetops, with wonderful views and wildflower displays.

Hiker parking is available at Yellow Creek Gap, the Fontana Dam Boatdock, and the Fontana Dam visitor center, where this hike ends (parking at the Fontana Boatdock reduces the distance to 6.4 mi.). Most of the terrain is too steep for camping, but excellent campsites can be found at Cable Cove and at creeks on the northern slope of the Yellow Creek Mts. Long-distance hikers (50 mi. or more) can stay at the Fontana Dam Shelter (also called the Fontana Hilton).

From Wauchecha Bald Rd., cross paved Yellow Creek Mt. Rd. and look for a post with a white blaze. The AT slants up the road bank on rough wooden steps, which may be hidden by tall grass. Continue up sandy, dry trail, cross a low ridge with mountain laurel and pines. Descend on a more sheltered north-facing slope sporting hemlocks and rhododendron, and

David Emblidge

Black bear, foraging

then cross a shallow creek on stepping stones.

At 0.9 mi. pass Cable Gap Shelter to the left, which is made of big logs and a shingle roof and has a low sleeping platform. It offers a reliable water source and a privy nearby. The area receives a lot of use, probably because it is so close to a road, but attempts have been made to reduce the impact by having separate camping areas. The shelter and campsites have theme trees: Beyond the privy is the hemlock section, behind the shelter is the tulip-tree camp, the shelter itself has black gum trees, and a pretty campsite up the creek has mixed deciduous growth.

Above the shelter, turn right and climb to a ridgetop, then climb again on steep trail that can be slippery with ice or wet leaves, depending on the season. At 1.1 mi., the AT starts the climb up 3786-ft. High Top and turns sharply left onto a well-graded path with easy ups and downs. Hurricane Opal (October 1995) and other storms knocked down many trees on this exposed ridge.

The trail climbs again to a jumble of huge boulders. Blazes on rocks show the way to scramble through without tackling the highest rocks. Look right at about 2.0 mi. for the first views of Fontana Lake and the solid wall of the Smoky Mts. to the north. Fall colors are great from this hike any time in October because the view includes elevations from 1800 to 6000 ft. This ridge is part of High Top, the highest point on the Yellow Mts., but the AT skirts south of the summit.

Descend to Black Gum Gap at 2.3 mi. and then ascend along the ridgeline to the second-highest point of this hike at 3720 ft. (3.1 mi.), with another rock jumble. Turn left and follow the same ridge down through a weedy area that may be overgrown in summer with blackberries. A little farther down, flame azaleas and blueberry bushes line the trail.

Curve right to another ridge crest with many American chestnut logs and stumps. Large oak trees are growing to take the place of the massive chestnuts, but many fall in hurricanes and in winter storms. Try to imagine this ridge as it looked 100 years ago, before logging and before the chestnut blight. In one area of the Smokies, about 40 percent of the ridgetop trees were found to be chestnuts in a 1905 study, at about the same time chestnut blight fungus was discovered at the Bronx Zoo. New York City imported Chinese and

Hiking with a Hand Lens

Some of the best views on the AT require no blue sky: the hairy underside of a lousewort leaf, the downy silencer of a discarded owl feather, the bloodsucking gear of a mosquito.

I always carry a 10X hand lens in my pack. It weighs less than my compass and has a string so that I can hang it around my neck. Most nature centers and college bookstores sell hand lenses.

Make sure you get one that magnifies at least ten times. Plastic 3X or 5X lenses don't help much, though they are easier for small children to use. A glass lens that slides into a protective case will last the longest. You can also buy 16X lenses that require more light and a bit of practice or compact field microscopes with about 30X magnification and their own light source.

To use a 10X hand lens, place the lens close to your eye, almost touching your eyebrow, and bring, say, the owl feather closer and closer until it's in focus—usually within a few inches. If you want to look at flowers or mosses, get down to their level; don't pick them just to get a good look at them.

Look at *everything*. For example, whether a flower is new to you or you're reacquainting yourself with a familiar one, look at its stamens and pistil. Look at each plant part to find out why botanists need so many words for "hairy."

Hand lenses are cheaper and lighter than binoculars, and you will get views you never knew were there.

Japanese chestnuts for landscaping around 1900, bringing with them the chestnut blight fungus. American chestnuts had no defenses against the blight, and the disease spread by fungal spore production for the next 30 years. In the southern Appalachians, high-elevation and ridgetop American chestnuts were the last to succumb; good chestnut crops were reported as late as 1938.

The AT descends at 3.7 mi. to Walker Gap (3450 ft.) and a trail intersection. From here the Yellow Creek Mt. Trail goes straight 2.7 mi. to Fontana Village, but at the time of this writing it was overgrown and difficult to follow. The AT goes right and descends, leaving the high ridges of Yellow Mt. At 3.9 mi. the trail curves a bit more to the right, crosses a tiny creek, and then at 4.1 mi. crosses a larger creek on a footlog near an excellent campsite.

The trail descends along the creek, which runs almost flat and has an unusual creek marsh, with tall grasses, rushes, sedges, ferns, and mosses. Most mountain creeks tumble over stones and have no time for this kind of growth, but this creek slows down enough to deposit soil that supports plants and probably frogs and turtles. It also provides a quiet place to reproduce for those hiker's banes—mosquitoes and gnats.

Creek and trail descend together, the creek speeding up to reach its junction with a larger stream. The trail crosses on good stepping stones and continues down parallel to the creek before ascending to a small ridgetop at about 4.0 mi., with a tiny campsite surrounded by mountain laurel, sourwood trees, and black-cherry trees. Black cherry is the largest native cherry, and mature trees have tall, straight trunks with nearly black bark divided into scales with upturned edges. The white flowers clustered along short stalks are usually too high to be seen, but squirrels may chew the twigs and drop them onto the trail in April or May. The fruits mature in September, but they are usually too good to last long enough to be seen; birds and squirrels get them first. Loggers searched the forest for black-cherry trees because of the strong, mahogany-colored wood, and for many years, the sight of a large cherry tree was rare. Now, after several decades of forest protection, these trees are returning to their former role as forest dominant and wildlife food provider. On this ridge as on the higher ridges of the Yellow Mts., you can also see many American chestnut skeletons throughout the woods among the thriving maples, cherries, and red oaks.

Views to the right show Fontana Lake, the dam, and the powerhouse

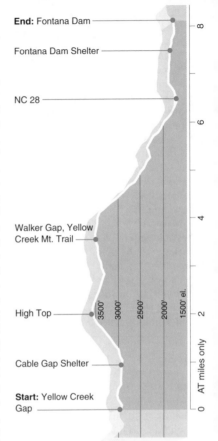

below the dam. From this lower ridge and the subsequent switchbacks, you can hear the hum of the generators. Fontana Dam backs up 29-mi. Fontana Lake, which forms the southern border of the Smokies. The dam, part of the Tennessee Valley Authority (TVA) system, was built between 1942 and 1945 to speed the production of aluminum

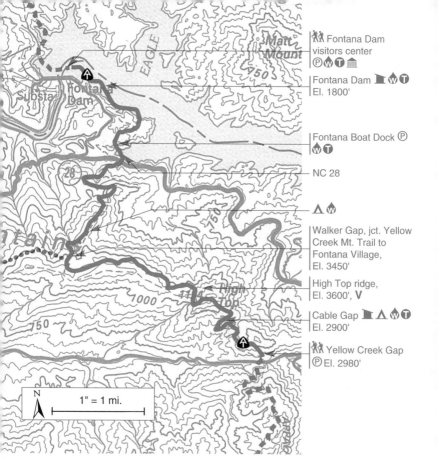

Fontana Dam
visitors center
Ⓟ Ⓦ Ⓣ 🏛

Fontana Dam ◼ Ⓦ Ⓣ
El. 1800'

Fontana Boat Dock Ⓟ
Ⓦ Ⓣ

NC 28

⛰ Ⓦ

Walker Gap, jct. Yellow
Creek Mt. Trail to
Fontana Village,
El. 3450'

High Top ridge,
El. 3600', **V**

Cable Gap ◼ ⛰ Ⓦ Ⓣ
El. 2900'

Yellow Creek Gap
Ⓟ El. 2980'

N
1" = 1 mi.

at Alcoa, Tennessee, and to supply Oak Ridge with electricity for the development of enriched uranium and other nuclear bomb components. Work started in Fontana Dam less than a month after the bombing of Pearl Harbor and continued around the clock under lights for 3 years. The dam is 480 ft. high, nearly twice the height of Norris Dam, which was the first TVA dam. The TVA was established by New Deal legislators as a long-range project to bring electricity to rural areas of the Tennessee River Valley, and TVA dams were authorized to both control flooding and provide a source of hydroelectric power.

The trail descends steeply with switchbacks and narrow passages through rock clefts at 4.7 mi. Look for upthrust slabs of sandstone with vertical cracks you can see through. When this rock formed 600 million to a billion years ago, these cracks were horizontal lines between sedimentary layers. The mountain-building continental collisions of 300 million or so years ago thrust these rocks up and over younger rocks somewhat like a bulldozer pushing paving stones. Also look for rock tripe, a flaky lichen, and rock fern, an evergreen that looks like a small version of Christmas fern, growing on the tops and sides of rocks. Rock tripe needs no soil, and rock fern needs just a little; these are pioneer plants of rock surfaces and will make soil for mosses and other plants to follow.

The trail continues to descend along rocks and on stone or log steps. It squeezes between two large basswood trunks and then goes down more steeply on a rocky section that may be slippery. At a small gap with a resting log, it turns left and goes down a sheltered creek valley. Bloodroot and hepatica bloom here in March, as do many other spring flowers in April.

At a rocky creek crossing, the water runs under the rocks and can be heard but not seen. In April and May, look for two heartleaf plants here: wild ginger on the ground and pipe vine up in the trees, both members of the birthwort family. Wild ginger usually grows in large colonies from underground rhizomes. Each individual has two heart-shaped leaves and a three-lobed brown flower where the leaf stalks join. Pipe vine, also called Dutchman's pipe, has some leaves as big as a medium pizza, smooth woody vines, and flowers that look like small, curved clay pipes. Most flowering plants offer payments such as nectar and pollen for pollination services, but many birthworts operate a scam. They produce odors of rotten meat to attract beetles or flies, then hold them captive until the pollen is ready to go. Wild ginger goes a step further. It attracts fungus gnats that would normally lay their eggs on a dead animal. The gnats get covered with pollen while they lay their eggs in the fleshy tissue of the flower and then visit nearby flowers. When the larvae hatch, not only is there no rotten meat, but poisons in the plant kill them.

The trail moves from the moist sheltered creek valley to a drier south-facing slope with mountain laurel, trailing arbutus, white pine, and galax. False foxglove, a 3-ft.-tall plant with bright yellow flowers, blooms here in August and persists throughout the fall.

A double blaze at about 6.0 mi. indicates a left turn off the ridge, and the trail drops into another creek valley with even more spring wildflowers. Cross a grassy roadbed, and continue down to stone steps on the bank of NC 28 at 6.4 mi. Civilization reappears. Across the road, the trail goes down more steps, passes public toilets, and crosses a road from the Fontana Lake boat dock on the right

Miles N	NORTH	Elev. (ft./m)	Miles S
7.8	**End: Fontana Dam** (north bank); visitor center with free showers, phones, exhibits, parking.	1800/548	0.0
7.5	**Fontana Dam Shelter**, picnic area, water, restrooms, path to lake.		0.7
6.4	NC 28; public toilets, road to boat dock and public swimming pools.		1.8
4.7	Sandstone slabs.		3.5
3.7	**Walker Gap**, jct. **Yellow Creek Mt. Trail** to Fontana Village (2.7 mi.).	3450/1052	4.5
2.3	**Black Gum Gap.**		5.0
2.0	**High Top**; exposed ridge, views.	3600/1107	6.2
0.9	**Cable Gap Shelter**, campsites, reliable water, privy.	2900/884	7.3
0.0	**Start: Yellow Creek Gap**, parking.	2980/908	7.8

SOUTH

and the public swimming pool on the left. At 7.1 mi. it then climbs a small ridge and descends to the paved Fontana Dam access road. Turn right and ascend on this road.

Fontana Dam Shelter (dubbed the "Fontana Hilton") is on a side trail at 7.5 mi. through the picnic area to the right. The shelter has two sleeping areas, a breezeway in between, a view of the lake, a trail down to the lake for swimming, and bathrooms nearby. The shelter is for AT long-distance hikers only; you can't drive to the dam and sleep in the shelter. Reg-istration forms for Smoky Mts. AT shelters are available here. (Fontana Village, built in 1942 to house the dam construction workers, provides food, lodging, laundry, and other services for hikers; it is 2.0 mi. west of the Fontana Dam Road on NC 28.) Past the shelter side trail, the road leads to a large parking area on the south side of the dam. Across the road is the Fontana Dam Visitor Center, with showers, phones, and interpretive exhibits. From here you can walk across the dam. A security camera may take your picture.

Fontana Dam to Shuckstack and Doe Knob

Maps: Trails Illustrated: Great Smoky Mts. Nat'l. Park, TN–NC

Route: Fontana Dam to Shuckstack Mt., to Birch Spring Shelter, to Doe Knob, and on to Cades Cove (optional)

Recommended direction: S to N

Distance: Shuckstack RT 8.0 mi.; Doe Knob 7.5 mi.; Sassafras Gap RT 8.6 mi.; Cades Cove 14.5 mi.

Access trail name and length: Gregory Ridge, then Gregory Bald Trail, 6.9 mi.

Elevation +/-: 1700 to 4520 ft.

Effort: Strenuous

Day hike: Yes

Overnight backpacking hike: Optional; permits required

Duration: 6 to 7 hr. to Doe Knob; 5 to 6 hr. for RT to Shuckstack

Early exit option: None

Natural history features: Bears; rock outcrop

Social history features: Fontana Dam; Shuckstack fire tower

Trailhead access: *Start:* From Fontana Village on NC 28, go E about 1.0 mi. Turn N onto Fontana Dam Rd. for 2.3 mi., crossing Fontana Dam. Park at hiker parking at end of pavement. *End:* For full hike to Cades Cove, from the Townsend entrance to the Smokies, turn R onto Laurel Creek Rd. for 7.0 mi. to Cades Cove. Follow Cades Cove Loop Rd. 5.5 mi. to Forge Creek Rd., just past Cable Mill. (Forge Creek Rd. goes straight when Cades Cove Loop Rd. turns L.) Drive 2.2 mi. to end of road; look for Gregory Ridge Trail sign.

Camping: Birch Spring Campsite; hiker shelter at Fontana Dam is for long-distance hikers only. Check at park visitor centers for information on backcountry regulations for campsites on access trails. Permits required for campsites and shelters; long-distance hikers can fill out permit forms at a self-service box near Fontana Dam Shelter.

W elcome to the Great Smoky Mts. National Park, established in 1934 and visited annually by more people than any other national park. The AT to the north and Fontana Lake to the south frame the valleys of Hazel and Eagle Creeks, which supported Cherokee hunters, Scots-Irish settlers, two cop-per mines, a few gold and silver prospectors, several logging companies, and many moonshiners. Much of this area was incorporated into the park in 1945 after the construction of Fontana Dam. The copper mine lands didn't become part of the park until 1983. For more information about the founding of the park, see

"National Parks History Lesson" in Hike #21.

From Fontana Dam on the Little Tennessee River up to the crest of the Smokies is quite a climb, but it's made easier by good trail and long switchbacks, and the view from Shuckstack is worth the effort. Chances of seeing a bear are good in this quiet part of the park, called "the back of beyond" by writer Horace Kephart (see "Horace Kephart, Honorary Highlander" in Hike #19). On one September hike here I saw seven bears—a mother with four cubs and two lone bears that looked like adolescents. The bears are shy; they are most likely to look you over and then scamper off, but be very cautious if you see a bear with cubs. If you see them from a safe distance, stop and wait; the mother will probably hustle the cubs over a ridge. Turkeys, ruffed grouse, and pileated woodpeckers might also show themselves. Ruffed grouse sometimes burst out from behind a log with an explosive whir as you walk along a quiet trail. (This antipredation strategy works so well that you may shake for a while afterward.) If you see a ruffed grouse female clucking and moaning to get your attention in summer or early fall, she has chicks somewhere nearby. They freeze until she gives them the all-clear cluck.

There are two popular day hikes on this section of the AT: to Shuckstack Mt. and back (8.0 mi.), and to Sassafras Gap, the Lost Cove loop, and back (13.0 mi.). Long-distance hikers will want to continue on to Doe Knob, where the AT reaches the crest of the Smokies and the North Carolina/Tennessee border, and eventually to Cades Cove (14.5 mi. from start). The most accessible part of the hike is the first 5.2 mi., up to Birch Spring Shelter (another possible turnaround point).

The original AT route entered the Smokies near the state line, but crossing the Little Tennessee River was a problem. After Fontana Dam was completed, the AT was rerouted east to cross the dam. This AT section is the only Smokies AT hike that lies entirely in North Carolina. Trail junctions in the Smokies are well marked with park service signs that include mileages to landmarks, roads, or other junctions.

Our mileage count starts at the trailhead parking area north of Fontana Dam. There is also a large parking area and visitor center on the south side of the dam. If you hike from here and cross the dam, add 0.6 mi. Fontana Dam was completed in 1944 and provided electricity for the production of war materials from Oak Ridge and Alcoa, Tennessee. At 480 ft. it is the highest dam in the eastern U.S. (For more information about Fontana Dam, see Hike #17.)

The trail starts on the left of the parking area and ascends through thin, dry woods of oak, pine, dogwood, and sourwood. A fire in 1995 killed many trees and cleared out understory plants. This south-facing slope can be hot; take plenty of water

David Emblidge

Lichen

(available at the dam's visitor center and the picnic area near Fontana Dam Shelter) and plan for rest stops. The long switchbacks take you into the woods and back to a lake view, repeating this pattern until you reach a ridgetop at about 1.6 mi. Some parts of this climb are rocky. In summer, your own personal escort of gnats may explore your eyes and ears. The best protection is a long-billed hat or a stiff breeze.

On the ridgetop, the trail becomes level and shaded by chestnut oaks and maples. Turn left and cross an area of fallen trees, eager saplings, and pretty trail-side flowers: violets and foamflower in spring, and yellow coneflower and wood aster in summer. From here, instead of going back and forth on switchbacks, you will go up exposed small ridges and down across moist valleys with ferns and wildflowers. The fire did not cross these ridges, and the cove woods are rich, with thick undergrowth.

At about 3.0 mi. the trail skirts the south side of Little Shuckstack and becomes a rocky bench with a beautiful rock face on the right. Exposed here are the sedimentary layers of this Precambrian sandstone, now decorated with multicolored lichens. The layers formed under an ancient sea to the east, and the resultant rock was pushed westward millions of years later by continental collision, folding and cracking as it was thrust up over younger sedimentary rock. Fence lizards and garter snakes live here, and possibly other snakes. The snakes will mind their own business and slide out of sight silently, but the fence lizards may give themselves away by skittering noisily across the rock face. If you stop and watch, you may see one peering back at you from a high, safe ledge. Fence lizards are territorial, and dominant males advertise their ownership by performing rapid push-ups and flashing iridescent blue throat patches.

A common flower here is Michaux's saxifrage, with a rosette of furry, toothed leaves, sometimes red on the underside, and a straight stalk holding many tiny white flowers in late spring. It grows in cracks where soil from moss and lichen has collected and can trap water flowing down the rock. *Saxifrage* is Latin for "rock-breaker," a good name for these plants that help recolonize bare rock. André Michaux, a French botanist, came to the southern Appalachians in 1785. He spent several years collecting specimens but lost them in a shipwreck in 1797.

After you study the rocks, lichens, and lizards, turn around for a good view to the south of Santeetlah Lake and Joyce Kilmer/Slickrock Wilderness, which is not on the AT but is well worth a side visit on another day.

The trail ducks back into the woods to a moist rocky area with many spring and summer wildflowers. A weedy, rocky ascent leads to a switchback onto a narrow ridge. At 4.0 mi. a 0.1-mi. spur trail to Shuckstack Mt. goes straight, and the AT veers down left. The spur trail climbs steeply to a level spot with a chestnut sitting log and then starts a series of switchbacks on very rocky trail. At the top is an open grassy area with an old house foundation and a fine stone chimney on the left. Ahead to the right is the Shuckstack fire tower.

The tower, built in 1932, is in poor repair, with rusty, unstable handrails and old steps that look as if they were made of chestnut planks. Warn children not to approach the tower without adult supervision. Trees have grown up around the clearing, limiting the view — you may be able to climb a few steps of the tower to get above the trees; check for safety first. Either above or through the trees, you will get a glimpse of the Smokies Crest extending northeast, with Thunderhead Mt., Silers Bald, and Clingmans Dome as the highest visible points. The valleys of Hazel and Eagle creeks, between here and Fontana Dam, once sheltered over 2000 settlers. After your view and snack, backtrack on the spur trail to the AT.

For the Shuckstack day hike, turn left and backtrack to the hiker parking near Fontana Dam. To continue on the AT, turn right to follow an old road down through rhododendron from the spur junction. At 4.3 mi. reach 3653-ft. Sassafras Gap and the junction with Twentymile (left) and Lost Cove (right) trails.

From this point, you can make a round-trip by turning right down Lost Cove Trail. Then turn right again onto Lakeshore Trail, and hike back to your car. This loop is 13 mi. total, but once you have climbed to Shuckstack, the rest is easy.

From Sassafras Gap the AT travels an easy mile left of a ridgetop and then along it, a good place to look for bears or signs of them. In September, if you hear something high in an oak tree making far too much noise to be a squirrel, it might be a bear gathering acorns. Just look and walk by quietly, but don't be surprised if the bear scrambles to the ground, makes huffing noises, and dashes away. Bears also leave deep claw slashes on trees as high as they can reach, apparently to say: "If you can't scratch this high, you'd better stay out of here."

European wild hogs also leave signs here. These exotic pests root with their tusks and snouts to eat plant bulbs, especially spring beauty, trout lily, and Turk's cap lily. The ridgetop from here to Silers Bald, where settlers used to bring domestic hogs to forage, is now being rototilled by the wild hogs. Coyotes, recently arrived in the southeast, may prey on hoglets.

Ascend a little and then at 5.2 mi. drop into Birch Spring Gap. On the right is the Birch Spring Campsite, with several pleasant tent pads. Water can be collected from a spring on the left. Horses are allowed here; about half of the AT in the Smokies is open to horse traffic.

The AT climbs steeply from Birch Spring Gap and ascends steadily toward Doe Knob, sometimes on the ridgetop and sometimes just left of the backbone of jumbled rocks that support good crops of rock tripe lichen. This section is narrow, steep, and little used. Parts of it may become overgrown with blackberry bushes in summer, and it may take the trail maintainers a while to clear it. However, if large trees fall across the AT in winter storms, trail workers must either remove them during a 2-week "chainsaw window" in March or use hand tools to remove them later; the park service does not allow power tools on the AT except for emergencies. Doe Knob is at 7.5 mi. from the start of the hike.

To follow the access trails from here to Cades Cove, turn left onto Gregory Bald Trail, hike 2.0 mi. (mostly level), and turn right onto Gregory Ridge Trail (mostly downhill). At 6.9 mi. from Doe Knob, reach the hiker parking area at the end of gravel Forge Creek Rd. (Get someone to pick you up in Cades Cove; a car shuttle would take most of your hiking day.) This would give you about 14 mi. of hiking, half up and half

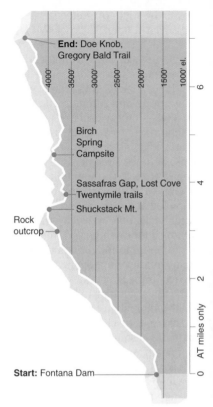

down. If you choose this alternative, you will need a Smokies hiking map (available at Cades Cove and other visitor centers) because the access trails are beyond the scope of this book. Tent camping is permitted only at specified backcountry sites on trails other than the AT; permits are required. Parsons Branch Rd., a

Doe Knob, Gregory Bald Trail

Birch Spring Gap, Birch Spring △

Sassafras Gap, Twentymile Trail, El. 3653'

Lost Cove Trail

Shuckstack Mt., El. 4020', **V**

Rock outcrop, **V**

Lakeshore Trail

Fontana Dam Ⓟ

N
⅞" = 1 mi.

Miles N	NORTH	Elev. (ft./m)	Miles S
	Total: 14.5 mi. with access trail		
7.6	Access: **Gregory Bald Trail** to Gregory Ridge Trail (2.0 mi.), then **Gregory Ridge Trail** to **Forge Creek Rd.** (4.9 mi.) at Cades Cove; parking.		0.1
7.5	**End AT miles: Doe Knob**; jct. **Gregory Bald Trail.**	4520/1378	0.0
5.2	**Birch Spring Gap and Campsite,** spring, creek.	3834/1170	2.3
4.3	**Sassafras Gap**; jct. **Lost Cove** and **Twentymile trails,** R for Lost Cove loop hike.	3653/1113	3.2
4.0	Spur trail to **Shuckstack Mt.** (0.1 mi.), fire tower; turnaround point for Shuckstack day hike.	4020/1225	3.5
3.0	Rock outcrop.		4.5
0.0	**Start:** Trailhead at **Fontana Dam** visitor center; parking, phones, water, toilets, free showers, exhibits.	1700/518	7.5

SOUTH

seasonal gravel road, leads one way from Cades Cove to US 129 a few miles west of Fontana Dam. It could shorten a car shuttle for this hike; check with the park service for maps and current conditions.

HIKE #19
Doe Knob to Spence Field

Maps: Trails Illustrated: Great Smoky Mts. Nat'l. Park, TN–NC

Route: From Forge Creek Rd. up Gregory Ridge to Doe Knob, to Mollies Ridge Shelter, to Russell Field Shelter, to Spence Field, and back to Cades Cove

Recommended direction: S to N

Distance: 19.6 mi. total; 7.5 mi. on AT

Access trail name and length: *Start:* Gregory Ridge and Gregory Bald trails, 6.2 mi.; *End:* Bote Mt. and Anthony Creek trails, 5.2 mi.

Elevation +/-: 4520 to 3842 to 4850 ft.

Effort: Strenuous

Day hike: No

Overnight backpacking hike: Yes

Duration: 14 to 15 hr.

Early exit option: Russell Field Trail, 6.1 mi. from Doe Knob

Natural history features: Gregory Bald azaleas

Social history features: Former high-elevation grazing lands; Ekaneetlee Pass used by Cherokee

Trailhead access: *Start:* From the Townsend entrance to the Smokies, turn R onto Laurel Creek Rd. for 7.0 mi. to Cades Cove. Follow Cades Cove Loop Rd. 5.5 mi. to Forge Creek Rd., just past Cable Mill. (Forge Creek Rd. goes straight when Cades Cove Loop Rd. turns L.) Drive 2.2 mi. to end of road; look for Gregory Ridge Trail sign. *End:* From Laurel Creek Rd., turn L before the Cades Cove Loop Rd. and drive 0.1 mi. to ranger station and parking beside camp store. Trailhead at the back of picnic area.

Camping: Mollies Ridge Shelter; Russell Field Shelter; signed campsites on Gregory Ridge and Russell Field trails (reservations required for shelters; permits required for any overnight stay)

In 1924 Mrs. Willis P. Davis of Knoxville, Tennessee, just back from a long, beautiful trip to western national parks, said, "Why can't we have a national park?" Her question focused the efforts of citizens in Tennessee and North Carolina who knew the wonder of the mountains and also saw the devastation wrought by lumber and coal companies. For 10 years, park advocates raised money, tackled legal issues, and ran political mazes. John D. Rockefeller Jr. promised a $5 million matching grant, and in 1934, in the midst of the Depression, the Great Smoky Mts. National Park (GSMNP) was established. It was dedicated in 1940 by President Franklin D. Roosevelt on the eve of another national crisis, World War II. The GSMNP covers 508,000 acres along the state line and receives more than 11 million visitors a year. Most of those people drive through, however, and hikers can still find quiet, remote forest.

The AT in the GSMNP follows the Smokies crest for 68.6 mi., crossing only one road (US 441 at Newfound Gap). It includes the highest point of the entire AT (Clingmans Dome, 6643 ft.) and the longest stretch of trail above 5000 ft. Segments of the AT between access trails are described here; trail maps for the park are available for a nominal fee from visitor centers in the park. In some cases, the access trails are as long as the AT segments themselves. Tent camping is prohibited on the AT in the Smokies (except at Birch Spring Gap), and shelter space is by permit only; reservations may be made 1 month in advance. Some of the access trails have backcountry campsites for tents; permits are required there as well. Dogs are not allowed on trails in the park.

At 4520-ft. Doe Knob, the crest of the Great Smokies, the AT reaches the Tennessee/North Carolina border and sticks with it for more than 200 mi., zigzagging northeast along high ridge crests. This 7.5-mi. section is beautiful and remote; no roads come closer than 5 mi. Much of the crest along this hike was cleared for grazing and foraging at least a century before the park was established. Gregory Bald, on the access trail to this hike, famous for its abundance and variety of flame azalea blooms in late June, is worth a side visit. The National Park Service maintains this bald by clearing encroaching trees,

whereas the other balds along the route of the AT in the park are becoming forested.

There are four shelters on 10 mi. of AT, including the three shelters on this section, and shelter space is in high demand from horseback riders, thru-hikers, scout troops, and overnighters. Make reservations early, and on spring or fall weekends, be prepared to choose another hike, such as a day hike from Clingmans Dome (Hike #20) or Newfound Gap (Hike #21 or #22).

From the parking area on Forge Creek Rd., it is a 4.9-mi. climb to Gregory Bald Trail on the Gregory Ridge Trail. At the signed junction, turn right for a 0.5-mi. side trip to 4948-ft. Gregory Bald, and then backtrack to the sign. Or turn left at the junction of Gregory Ridge and Gregory Bald trails for the easy, level, 2.0-mi. connection to the AT. Before Fontana Dam was built, the AT took this route into the Smokies, but in 1948 it was relocated to cross the dam (see Hike #17) and climb Shuckstack. The Benton MacKaye Trail meets the AT here and provides an alternate route to Springer Mt. along the western rim of the southern Appalachians.

Finally, after 6.9 mi. of access trail (more with the side trip to Gregory Bald), you reach the AT in open woods just below Doe Knob. The AT miles of this hike start here. Grasses and blackberries are signs of former clearings. Farmers drove cattle, hogs, sheep, and goats up here to graze

Horace Kephart, Honorary Highlander

Horace Kephart, a librarian and scholar, moved to Sugar Creek, near Bryson City, North Carolina, in 1904, partly to explore the vast and undescribed eastern forests and partly to escape his own alcoholism and conflicts with his wife and six children. He earned a little money from magazine articles but lived simply, camping and learning about the land and its inhabitants. An ardent campaigner for a Smokies national park, he died penniless in 1931 a few months before the park movement acquired enough land deeds to make the park possible. Two of his books, *Our Southern Highlanders* and *Camping and Woodcraft,* are still earning royalties today.

Here is a tale from the Smokies, collected by Kephart:

It was here I first heard of "tooth-jumping." Let one of my old neighbors tell it in his own way:

"You take a cut nail (not one o' those round wire nails) and place its squar p'int agin the ridge of the tooth, jest under the edge of the gum. Then jump the tooth out with a hammer. A man who knows how can jump a tooth without it hurtin' half as bad as pullin'. But old Uncle Neddy Cyarter went to jump one of his own teeth out, one time, and missed the nail and mashed his nose with the hammer. He had the weak trembles. . . . Some men get to be as experienced at it as tooth dentists are at pullin'. They cut around the gum, and then put the nail at jest sich an angle, slantin' downward for an upper tooth, or upwards for a lower one, and hit one lick."

"Will the tooth come at the first lick?"

"Ginerally. If it didn't, you might as well stick your head in a swarm o' bees and ferget who you are."

—Horace Kephart,
Our Southern Highlanders, 1913

and forage; high productivity on the sunny meadows gave the livestock more food than the mountain hollows could provide.

The AT swings into Tennessee, descends to Mud Gap at 4260 ft., climbs gently to Powell Knob (4439 ft.), and then begins the descent to Ekaneetlee Gap. This gap, used by the Cherokee to cross to the Overhill Towns of the Tennessee Valley, has an elevation of 3842 ft., the lowest point on the Smokies crest until after Mt. Cammerer. Traces of the old trail across the gap and into Cades Cove still can be found. The influx of European settlers gradually pushed many Cherokees off their Tennessee lands until the Ekaneetlee Gap road was no longer needed. Chief Yonaguska (Drowning Bear), who successfully resisted attempts to remove the Cherokee, used this trail, as did Cades Cove settlers and traders visiting the Carolinas. In 1817, Chief Yo-naguska adopted a white boy, Will Thomas, who grew up to be a businessman and lawyer and held land titles for the Eastern Band of the Cherokee until they were granted the rights of citizenship and could own the lands they had lived on for hundreds of years. James Mooney, in his 1900 book about Cherokee myths, reported that Yonagusta had little use for Christian missionaries or their Bible and had remarked, "Well, it seems to be a good book—strange that the white people are not better, after having had it so long."

The AT curves south, and at 1.8 mi., you'll have earned back all the elevation lost at Ekaneetlee and will reach Devils Tater Patch. This open, windy 4775-ft. ridgetop with twisted trees must have been a spooky place for farmers looking for their livestock in the fog. Now, of course, domestic animals are not allowed, but one type of livestock comes up here on its own. European wild hogs, escaped from sport hunters, invaded the Smokies from the south in the 1920s. The hogs found protected lands to their liking: no big predators, open forests, and plenty of wildflower bulbs to eat. Along many parts of this trail, look for areas that seem plowed. The wild hogs root with their snouts and tusks, and they wallow in muddy spots and creeks (they may keep water sources infected with *Giardia* and other pathogens). When encountered, they are usually timid and scamper away with their tails straight up, but they can be dangerous when cornered; keep a safe distance. The park tries to control the wild hog population.

On a high, windy corner of the open space sits Mollies Ridge Shelter at 2.5 mi. According to Cherokee legend, Mollie loved White Eagle and searched for him when he did not return from a hunting trip. She froze to death on top of this ridge—but may be searching still.

Mollies Ridge Shelter, with an inside fireplace and two sleeping platforms, has room for fourteen people. A piped spring on the Tennessee side provides water. The Smoky Mt. Hiking Club has remodeled all of the old CCC-built shelters, adding verandas and high windows.

Chances of seeing bears are good, partly because these high, open areas provide berries and nuts and partly because careless hikers have introduced bears to junk food. Most black bears run when they see or hear people. Try this if you see a black bear: Stop, back up several paces, and stand quietly. You may be able to watch the bear for a while. When you're ready to go on, ask permission in a loud voice, and the bear will probably look up, startled, and leave the trail. *Do not approach a mother bear with cubs.*

After Mollies Ridge, the AT remains level for a bit and then drops to Big Abrams Gap (4080 ft.), with a small knob to climb before starting up the other side. Abram was a Cherokee chief of a village on Little Tennessee

River, now under the waters of Chilhowee Lake. The trail climbs through beech forest to a level stretch and at 4.9 mi. arrives at Russell Field Shelter, which can hold fourteen people, on the edge of another open area. A spring can be found 150 yd. down Russell Field Trail, which joins on the left and leads down to Cades Cove Picnic Area in 5.3 mi. In summer, you may meet an Appalachian Trail Conservancy (ATC) caretaker. These dedicated volunteers offer advice and emergency help, keep the shelters clean (a job that should be done by the hikers), instruct hikers on no-trace trail use, and report problems to the park service or to the ATC.

The AT swings right from the shelter and climbs to McCampbell Knob and Mt. Squires on about 1 mi. of easy grade through open beech and yellow birch woods. Mountain oat grass grows along this section, especially under the beech trees, and forms billows and mounds. Spring beauty, trout lily, and violets bloom in early spring.

From the top of Mt. Squires (named for a North Carolina park promoter of the 1920s), the grassy area expands across the broad ridgetop of the largest bald in the Smokies, Spence Field. Russell, Spence, and McCampbell were early settlers of Cades Cove and had hunting or herding cabins up here on the ridge. Look for mountain ash trees in the open areas. This small tree has compound leaves, white flowers in May, and clusters of shiny red fruits in fall. It grows only on high-elevation balds and may die out here as the forest becomes thicker. Sarvisberry, or shadbush, also grows on the bald and around the edges. This tree blooms in March before any leaves appear and encourages thru-hikers surprised by late-spring snowstorms. Highbush blueberries flourish here and ripen in August and September, but you will have to share them with bears.

Now the AT descends through the grassy area to the intersection with Eagle Creek Trail at 7.5 mi. To the right about 0.2 mi. is Spence Field Shelter, looking like a clone of the other Smokies crest shelters but with the added convenience of a fine privy. This shelter is the most heavily used on this section, with Russell Field Shelter a close second. A short way down the Eagle Creek Trail is a good piped spring. Within sight of the Eagle Creek junction is the Bote Mt. Trail junction, the end of this AT section.

Bote Mt. Trail (the access trail to the end of Hike #19) is an old road that goes down to paved Laurel Creek Rd. in 7.2 mi. It is said that the Cherokee work crew that built the road were asked to vote for a route. There being no *V* sound in Cherokee, they "boted" for this route. Bote Mt. Trail meets Anthony Creek Trail in 1.7 mi., which then leads to Cades Cove Picnic Area in 3.7 mi. Parking is available at the entrance to the Cades Cove Campground.

Gregory Ridge, Russell Field, and Anthony Creek trails have backcountry campsites (permits required) that could be used in planning a 1- or 2-night trip on this AT section. One possibility would be to park at Forge Creek Rd., hike 2.0 mi. to Campsite 12 and set up camp, and then visit Gregory Bald and Mollies Ridge and backtrack to camp. Similar overnights could be arranged from campsites on the other access trails, but in any case, it would be wise to take turns hiking and have one person remain at the campsite to entertain any hungry skunks and bears. Reservations for campsite and shelter space may be made 1 month in advance (423-436-1231). Consecutive-night stays in shelters are not allowed, but campers may stay in backcountry sites for up to 3 nights.

A possible one-car day hike (but an ambitious one) from Cades Cove would begin at the campground and picnic area at the junction of Cades Cove Loop Rd. and Laurel Creek Rd., ascending into the mountains on Anthony Creek Trail to Russell Field Trail, to the AT (go north, left), then to Spence Field, and down again on Bote Mt. Trail and Anthony Creek Trail. Round-trip: 12.3 mi., with about a 2900-ft. gain in elevation.

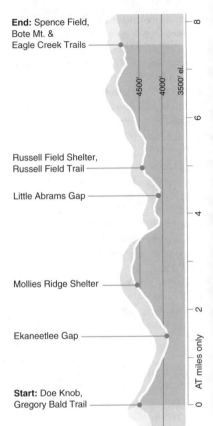

End: Spence Field, Bote Mt. & Eagle Creek Trails

Russell Field Shelter, Russell Field Trail

Little Abrams Gap

Mollies Ridge Shelter

Ekaneetlee Gap

Start: Doe Knob, Gregory Bald Trail

4500'   4000'   3500' el.

AT miles only

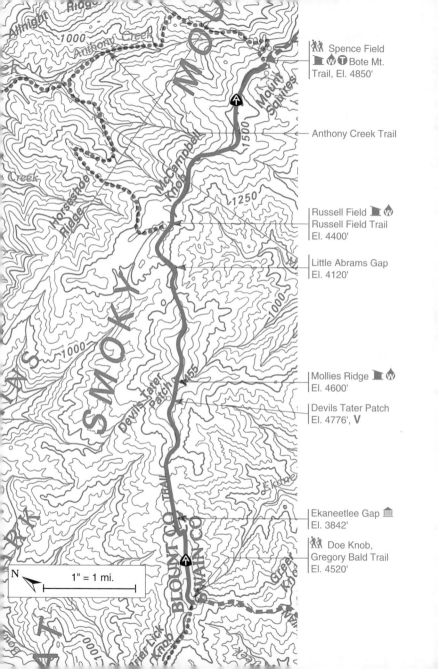

Spence Field
Bote Mt.
Trail, El. 4850'

Anthony Creek Trail

Russell Field
Russell Field Trail
El. 4400'

Little Abrams Gap
El. 4120'

Mollies Ridge
El. 4600'

Devils Tater Patch
El. 4776', **V**

Ekaneetlee Gap
El. 3842'

Doe Knob,
Gregory Bald Trail
El. 4520'

N

1" = 1 mi.

Miles N	NORTH	Elev. (ft./m)	Miles S
	Total: 19.6 mi. with access trails		
5.2	**Access: Bote Mt. Trail** to Anthony Creek Trail (1.7 mi.), then **Anthony Creek Trail** to **Cades Cove Picnic Area** (3.5 mi.), parking.		5.2
7.5	**End AT miles: Spence Field Shelter,** privy; jct. **Eagle Creek Trail,** piped spring; **Bote Mt. Trail** to **Anthony Creek Trail.**	4850/1478	0.0
4.9	**Russell Field Shelter** and **Trail,** spring 150 yd. down trail; jct. **Russell Field Trail;** early exit option.	4400/1341	2.6
4.2	**Little Abrams Gap.**	4120/1256	3.3
2.5	**Mollies Ridge Shelter,** piped spring.	4600/1402	5.0
1.8	**Devil's Tater Patch;** open ridgetop.	4775/1455	5.7
1.4	**Ekaneetlee Gap,** water 100 yd. down Tennessee side of slope.	3842/1171	6.1
0.0	**Start AT miles: Doe Knob**	4520/1378	7.5
6.9	**Access: Gregory Ridge Trail** from Forge Creek Rd. (4.9 mi.), then **Gregory Bald Trail** (2.0 mi.) to AT.		6.9

SOUTH

Clingmans Dome to Spence Field

Maps: Trails Illustrated: Great Smoky Mts. Nat'l. Park, TN–NC

Route: From Clingmans Dome to Double Spring Gap Shelter, to Silers Bald Shelter, to Thunderhead Mt., to Spence Field Shelter and down to Cades Cove

Recommended direction: N to S

Distance: 22.1 mi. total; 16.4 mi. on AT

Access trail name and length: *Start:* Clingmans Dome Trail, 0.5 mi. *End:* Bote Mt. and Anthony Creek Trails to Cades Coves Campground, 5.2 mi.

Elevation +/-: 6643 to 4900 ft.

Effort: Strenuous

Day hike: No; shorter day hikes optional

Overnight backpacking hike: Yes

Duration: 12 to 13 hr.

Natural history features: Southern end of boreal spruce-fir forest; balds; highest point on AT

Social history feature: Observation tower

Trailhead access: *Start:* From Newfound Gap, go 0.2 mi. E into NC on US 441. Turn R onto Clingmans Dome Rd. for 7.6 mi. to parking area. *End:* From Townsend Wye, go R on Laurel Creek Rd. toward Cades Cove for about 7.0 mi. Turn L into campground, and park in the lot beside registration booth.

Camping: Double Spring Gap Shelter; Silers Bald Shelter; Derrick Knob Shelter; Spence Field Shelter (reservations and permits required)

Millions of people visit the Smokies every year, and most of them drive to Clingmans Dome (named for Thomas Lanier Clingman, Civil War general, U.S. senator, explorer, prospector, and the man who first claimed that the Smokies had higher peaks than anything in New Hampshire). However, just a few minutes of hiking will get you out of the crowds (but not necessarily out of the clouds) and onto a remote ridge crest with not one road crossing for 31 mi. For this book, we have divided the stretch between Clingmans Dome and Fontana Dam

into three overnight hikes (#18, #19, and #20) because of available access trails. But you don't have to carry a big pack or spend 3 days to enjoy the Smokies AT. Here are some day-hike alternatives using this description of Hike #20:

• Follow this narrative from Clingmans Dome to Silers Bald, and then backtrack for a moderate day hike of 9.8 mi.

• Arrange a car shuttle between Elkmont Campground and Clingmans Dome. Follow the AT from Clingmans Dome to Goshen Prong

A Day in the Life of an AT Maintainer

The Appalachian Trail is maintained by volunteers from thirty-one regional hiking or maintaining clubs affiliated with the Appalachian Trail Conference (ATC). The ATC also provides maps, guides, and other publications, regional representatives, ridgerunners and shelter caretakers, and volunteer work crews who build shelters, bridges, and new trail.

The Smoky Mts. Hiking Club (SMHC), one of the seven clubs south of the Tennessee/Virginia state line, maintains the AT from Davenport Gap in the Smokies to the Nantahala River in the Cherokee National Forest. Volunteers perform routine maintenance such as brush cutting on "their" section of trail (and some have had the same section for 20 years or more),

but bigger jobs such as fallen tree cutting or relocation are done by groups of club members.

On Saturday, May 4, 1996, SMHC member Dick Ketelle of Oak Ridge, Tennessee, joined Dennis Fulcher, Jim Goddard, and Morgan Briggs to work on the AT in the Smokies north of Sam's Gap. When working as a trail maintainer, Dick carries a chain saw, fuel, oil, block and tackle, a pulaski (a mattocklike tool for cleaning water bars and building trail), and other tools on a steel frame with backpack straps. He also carries his hard hat, ear protectors, chain-saw chaps, water, rain gear, and lunch. Here is part of his account of the day:

"I leave home at 5 a.m., heading to Tremont. Arrive there about 6:30, embark via mountain bike (with

Trail, and then follow Goshen Prong Trail down to Little River Trail for a one-way hike of 13.6 mi. ending at Elkmont Campground. The upper 4.0 mi. of Goshen Prong Trail are very rocky, but the rest is easy walking. In May, lower Goshen Prong Trail is one of the best wildflower walks in the park. This alternative could be combined with car camping at Elkmont Campground.

• Start at Cades Cove, the end point of this narrative. Hike 5.2 mi. up to the AT on Spence Field, following Anthony Creek and Bote Mt. trails. The grass bald spreads about 1.0 mi.

in each direction from the trail junction. Backtrack to your car for a day hike of 10 to 12 mi., depending on how far you hike on the bald.

For any of these alternatives, be sure to get a trail map from the visitor center for more information about trails, mileages, shelters, and designated campsites.

Hike #20 is a long, difficult, beautiful hike, and by the end, you will have your own definition of a southern Appalachian knob. The trail follows an easy descent for about 3 mi.; then a short rocky climb to Silers

permission from park service) on Tremont Road. . . . Ride 1.8 miles up the Middle Prong Road and lock my bicycle to a tree. . . . At 10 a.m. I stroll into the clearing in front of Derrick Knob Shelter, having covered the first 10.5 miles of my day's journey and having climbed 3500 feet in about 3 hours and 20 minutes. . . . Dennis, Morgan, Jim, and I clear blowdowns to Starkey Gap or beyond [about 2 mi.]. We work along at a good pace, I with the saw and the others throwing brush and logs as I cut. . . . After lunch we continue up Brier Knob to clear trees remaining on that section. Dennis's thermometer registers 85 degrees in the sun, and I'm starting to feel the work. We drop the chain saw and fuel container at the western summit of Brier Knob and walk to Mineral Gap and back. The views are spectacular.

"Shouldering the pack frame fully loaded with saw and trail gear, I head back down the steep trail from Brier Knob to Starkey Gap for a taste of things to come. Dennis hands me the fuel bottle with about a gallon of gas and oil mix and most of a quart of oil. . . . I head off the mountain down into the headwaters of Sam's Creek. . . . My descent is largely a matter of stamina and balance—having the stamina to carry the pack and having the balance to rock hop across the full flowing stream in several places.

"My load makes the bike ride back down the gravel road much faster than the pedal up. I use the brakes most of the way for steering control and to ease the painful bouncing of my tailparts. . . . At 5:40 I am back at my car at the end of the paved road, having traveled about 21.75 miles since 6:30 a.m."

Bald gives a warning of the climbs to come. After Buckeye Gap, the knobs start, some of which might be called stealth knobs because they aren't big enough to show on a trail profile. Also, since they are knobs and not mountains, they don't get switchbacks, so this trail requires plenty of time (the knobs aren't too bad if you rest often). Camping is not allowed along the AT in the park, but the four shelters provide enough options for a good hiking schedule. Reservations are required for the shelters and for designated campsites on side trails.

From the Clingmans Dome parking lot, there are two ways to get to the AT. You can hike 0.5 mi. up the paved path to the observation tower, and after visiting the tower for a panoramic view, turn left at the AT sign, then turn left again in 20 yd. at the next AT sign. Or you can drop down behind the parking lot water fountain on Forney Ridge Trail, and after 0.2 mi., turn right at a switchback for a private 0.5-mi. connector up to the AT. The connector is rocky, but it is less traveled than the paved path. Both options are well signed.

An AT sign at the junction of the connector and the AT stands across from a 45-degree sandstone thrust fault overlooking a wonderful view of Tennessee at 0.9 mi. These sandstone slabs came from east of here and were laid down under a Precambrian ocean called Iapetus. According to current theory, collision with Africa about 65 million years ago thrust these flat sedimentary rocks up and over younger rocks. These hard sandstones and the white quartz sometimes filling their cracks have resisted millions of years of erosion.

The trail descends the flank of 6582-ft. Mt. Buckley, named for Samuel Buckley, who helped Clingman measure elevations in the 1850s. For about 0.5 mi. the trail stays on exposed ridge crest with grasses, blackberries, huckleberries, serviceberry trees, and mountain ash trees. Serviceberry (or shadbush) trees bloom early in spring, before any leaves appear. Settlers of the 1800s could see them up on the mountains and knew it was time for circuit-riding ministers to come and start services again and conduct the marriages, funerals, and christenings that were put on hold over the long winter. Views from this open area include both sides of the park, Clingmans Dome to the back, dark with spruce and fir trees, and Silers Bald and Thunderhead Mt. ahead (or south on the AT). Clingmans Dome appears almost flat on top from this view, and it's easy to see why New Englanders found it hard to accept that this

dome is higher than craggy Mt. Washington. Look for heath balds on ridgetops or sharp ridge edges.

The trail slips into Tennessee at about 1.6 mi. and enters quiet forest with a good dirt-pack tread. At 2.3 mi., Goshen Prong Trail goes right, reaching Elkmont Campground in 11.3 mi. At 3.4 mi., after a short rise, the trail reaches a grassy opening and Double Spring Gap Shelter, notable for an especially fine chimney rock and a large buckeye tree arching over one corner. In September, the bonging of buckeye nuts on the metal roof adds to the drama of thunderstorms. You can get water from the North Carolina spring, some 50 ft. left of the shelter, or from the Tennessee spring, about 100 ft. to the right, but the Tennessee spring is likely to be muddy.

The trail ascends from Double Spring Gap through a beech forest with one or two spruce trees and almost no firs. This is the southern boundary on the AT of the spruce-fir forest. As the last glaciers moved south 15,000 years ago, boreal plant and animal communities retreated into the southern mountains. When the glaciers receded, this spruce-fir community recolonized the great forests of the eastern United States and Canada but survived only on high, cool ridges of the South. In the beech forest, look for beech drops — parasitic plants that get all their food from beech roots — which bloom in late summer. Standing 6 to 10 in. high, they look like brown twigs stuck into the ground and are especially abundant here.

The trail levels after a short climb. Billowy grass covers the ridgetop, and in autumn prickly beechnuts drop. Pry one open to find the triangular seeds. Beeches are related to chestnuts, and the nuts have a similar sweet taste when roasted. Farmers used to drive their cows and pigs up here to graze and forage. The hollows provide water and shelter, but food for livestock is limited there, and crops don't grow well. To survive, the mountaineers needed ridgetop grasses and nuts to support livestock. The challenge of moving animals up and down the rugged slopes contributed to the strength and independence of the Scots-Irish settlers.

The trail slips to the right around a small rocky knob with a lot of quartz veins in the sandstone. Then the trail rejoins the ridge crest at the Narrows (4.0 mi.), a rocky ridgetop where you can stretch your arms and drop beechnuts deep into Tennessee and North Carolina at the same time. You can see Gatlinburg, Tennessee, and Pigeon Forge to the right, Clingmans Dome and Mt. Le Conte in back, Silers Bald ahead, and Fontana Lake and waves and waves of parallel ridges to the left (south) in North Carolina. But watch your step, too.

Common here and on many high open ridges is a vine called carrion flower. Related to greenbrier, it has heart-shaped leaves and tennis-ball-sized clusters of white flowers in spring. They smell like dead bodies

Doris Gove

Dick Ketelle, trail maintainer

and attract those fans of dead bodies, flies, as pollinators. In fall, the blue berries form conspicuous spherical clusters.

At the end of the Narrows, a trail to the right through a steep rocky section begins the ascent to Silers Bald. (Welch Ridge Trail goes left at 4.7 mi. to connect with Hazel Creek, Jonas Creek, and Bear Creek trails, which wind through the huge roadless area between Fontana Lake and the AT.) After a few switchbacks you emerge on Silers Bald (at 4.9 mi., 5607 ft.), named for a landowner who grazed livestock here. Blazes and arrows on a rock indicate a left turn, which leads through a thick patch of short beeches, probably dwarfed by the strong winds that sweep across the bald. After the beeches comes an open area with soft grass, blueberries in season (August), ferns, meadow flowers, serviceberries, and blackberries. A small trail leads left for a better view of Fontana Lake, the Yellow Creek Mts., and the Nantahalas. Sunken squares in the grass show where cabins used for herding or hunting once stood.

Return to the AT and descend, passing larger beeches, and enter a grassy clearing with the stone Silers Bald Shelter at 5.1 mi. (This shelter, too, has a buckeye tree hanging over it.) A spring can be found about 300 ft. down a side trail.

Beyond the shelter, the AT winds through open beech woods with gentle ups and downs. After a short scramble on the left side of the ridge, look for black cherry trees—tall trees with black, flaky bark and leaves that look somewhat silvery. The wood is valuable for furniture because of its color and strength, and loggers depleted the population of black cherry in many parts of the park. As the trail climbs over a small knob, other trees appear: silverbells, striped maples, yellow birches, and tulip-trees.

At 7.8 mi. the trail descends to Buckeye Gap (4817 ft.), marked by an old sign on a cluster of yellow birch trunks. Next comes a steady climb on good trail to the junction with Miry Ridge Trail at 8.0 mi.

A steep ascent and left turn start the roller-coaster part of this hike—the famous knobs. In winter you can see the knobs ahead; in summer you

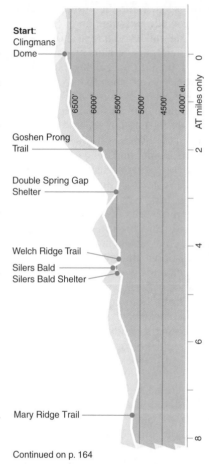

Continued on p. 164

are spared that sight. At first, just a few roots obstruct the dirt trail, but as the knobs get steeper, the trail gets rockier and becomes quite difficult. In fall roots and rocks may be more treacherous under wet leaves; in any season allow plenty of time for the next 4.0 mi.

At 10.4 mi., Greenbrier Ridge Trail

K￼ Clingmans Dome ℗
w **T** El. 6643', **V**

Clingmans Dome
Bypass Trail

Mt. Buckley, El. 6582',
V

Goshen Prong Trail,
El. 5800'

Double Spring Gap
■ **w** El. 5507'

Welch Ridge Trail

Silers Bald, El. 5607', **V**

Silers Bald ■ **w**

N ◄ ⅞" = 1 mi.

Miry Ridge Trail,
El. 5420'

joins from the right at Sams Gap. This side trail leads to Middle Prong Trail and (8.3 mi. down) to a gravel road to Great Smoky Mt. Institute at Tremont, an environmental education camp with programs for students, elder hostelers, teachers, and the general public.

Just 0.2 mi. farther, at 10.6 mi., is Derrick Knob Shelter on the edge of the former Big Chestnut Bald. This bald may have been created by grazing, and the shelter—which, like the others on this hike, sleeps twelve on built-in bunks—sits on the site of a cabin used by a herder. The beech forest has taken over since the park was established in 1934, but the trees are still small. A spring is located about 150 ft. from the shelter on the Tennessee side of the slope.

The trail angles left after the shelter on a pleasant ascent through sugar maples. Then comes a steep descent with many roots across the trail, ended by a level stroll with chestnut snags and logs. A short descent leads to Sugar Tree Gap at 4455 ft. (11.7 mi.). A big hollow chestnut log lies in the gap, and a sign announces that Thunderhead Mt. is 3.5 mi. ahead.

The next ascent is steep, long, and rocky, with a welcome level spot on top, and then comes another rocky plunge to Starkey Gap, with a set of log resting benches. The next hard climb goes left of 5215-ft. Brier Knob, with soft grass cushions for another rest. From here, look down into Bone Valley. One spring in the 1870s, livestock were herded up to the balds,

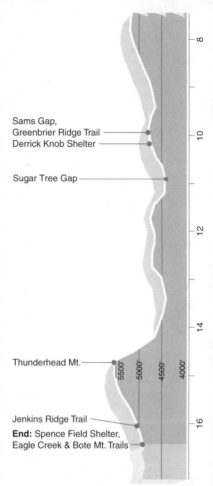

Sams Gap,
Greenbrier Ridge Trail
Derrick Knob Shelter

Sugar Tree Gap

Thunderhead Mt.

5500' 5000' 4500' 4000'

Jenkins Ridge Trail
End: Spence Field Shelter,
Eagle Creek & Bote Mt. Trails

but a late blizzard sent them searching for shelter. Many cattle got trapped on their way down and died in the deep valley just below here.

As you start down Brier Knob at 13.3 mi., look for a twisted yellow

Sams Gap, Greenbrier
Ridge Trail
Derrick Knob
El. 4840'

Thunderhead Mt.,
El. 5527', **V**

Rocky Top, El. 5441', **V**

Jenkins Ridge Trail, **V**

Spence Field
Bote Mt. Trail,
El. 4900'

N ◄ ⅞" = 1 mi.

birch on the left that resembles a charging rhino. The trail soon levels on a rocky ridge dotted with fire cherry. and pagoda dogwood, and offering excellent views of 5527-ft. Thunderhead Mt. Then the trail turns right down a narrow, rocky, ankle-twisting section that requires special caution if the rocks are wet. Sharp edges of upthrust Thunderhead sandstone in the trail are interesting geologically, but slippery. Many spring flowers grow along this sheltered wet area.

Entering a rhododendron thicket, the trail reaches Beechnut Gap at 14.9 mi. with a spring 75 yd. down to the right. Here the trail starts a longer but easier ascent than those pesky knobs, now behind you. Switchbacks through rhododendron ease the way up Thunderhead Mt., but the trail is still quite rocky.

The first peak of Thunderhead is Laurel Top, an open space at 15.2 mi. in a heath bald with a benchmark (5527 ft.) and a small rock pile on the left to stand on for a view. An easy descent down a grassy meadow and a short steep climb through beech trees leads to the second peak of Thunderhead Mt., where names are chiseled into the rock outcrop. To the left are Fontana Lake and the Nantahala Mts., and Cades Cove lies down to the right. Geologists call Cades Cove a "limestone window"; the bedrock there is much younger than the mountain sandstone that was pushed over it from the east. Before the park was formed, Cades Cove was a prosperous farming community because of fertile soils and flat fields. The park service now maintains it as open farmland with the help of the numerous deer. Native black bears, self-introduced coyotes, and many wild turkeys can be seen in the fields.

A short ascent leads to the third Thunderhead peak, Rocky Top (15.7 mi.), with an even better view of Fontana Lake and with rock outcrops like the foreheads of Easter Island faces. For the next 2.0 mi. the trail is overused and sinks into thick grass. Sometimes water rushes down it, but locust log steps improve the tread. After a short descent and ascent through beech forest, the trail comes out to an expanse of grassland spotted with sarvisberry trees, tall blueberry bushes, azaleas, and small clumps of other trees moving in from the edge. When used for grazing, this bald was much bigger, the biggest one in the Smokies. In a few years it will probably be tree-covered like Big Chestnut Bald. The park maintains two high-elevation grass balds, Andrews and Gregory, but others will be allowed to grow over.

At 16.5 mi. Jenkins Ridge Trail goes left. (Note that from here to the end of the hike, the white blazes are painted on rocks, not trees.) This rough trail leads to the vast drainages of Eagle and Hazel creeks. Many isolated settlers lived down there during the 1800s and early 1900s. Horace Kephart—writer, folklorist, and park advocate—joined them in 1904, described their lives, wrote about woodcraft and natural history, and publicized the logging practices that were destroying the southern Appalachians.

The AT descends across grassland and enters a sparsely wooded area at the junction (16.9 mi.) with Bote Mt. Trail, which this hike uses as an access trail to reach its conclusion. Bote Mt. Trail is a rocky but well-graded old road leading to Anthony Creek Trail, which leads to Cades Cove Picnic Area, the end point.

Spence Field Shelter is 0.2 mi. farther south on the AT beyond the Bote Mt. Trail junction, on a side trail to the left. A good piped spring is down to the right of the shelter, and a privy sits to the left. The privy was built in 1991 with a special feature: planks extending from the base so that it can be moved over a new hole when necessary—though it still takes a large crew of maintainers to move it. A recent privy relocation on National Trails Day, June 7, 1997, was performed by volunteers of Smoky Mts. Trail Riders and Smoky Mts. Hiking Club. A large family of mice living in the privy thought it was the end of the world as they knew it.

Miles N	**NORTH**	Elev. (ft./m)	Miles S
	Total: 22.1 mi. with access trails		
0.5	**Access: Clingmans Dome parking lot,** water, toilets. Follow trail to AT. (or use bypass trail)	6643/2025	0.5
16.4	**Start AT miles:** Jct. access trail and AT.		0.0
16.0	**Clingmans Dome Bypass Trail,** trail to parking lot (0.7 mi.)		0.4
14.5	Jct. **Goshen Prong Trail** to **Elkmont Campground** (11.3 mi.).	5800/1768	1.9
13.5	**Double Spring Gap Shelter,** two springs.	5507/1679	2.9
12.2	Jct. **Welch Ridge Trail.**	5450/1661	4.2
12.0	**Silers Bald,** spur trail to good views.	5607/1709	4.4
11.8	**Silers Bald Shelter,** spring 300 ft. R on spur trail.	5400/1646	4.6
8.9	Jct. **Miry Ridge Trail.**	5420/1652	7.5
6.5	**Sams Gap;** Jct. **Greenbrier Ridge Trail.**	4840/1475	9.9
6.3	**Derrick Knob Shelter,** spring 150 ft. R.	4880/1487	10.1
5.2	**Sugar Tree Gap.**	4455/1357	11.2
3.6	**Brier Knob.**		12.8
2.2	**Beechnut Gap,** spring 75 yd. R.		14.2
1.7	**Thunderhead Mt.**	5527/1685	14.7
1.2	**Rocky Top.**	5441/1658	15.2
0.3	Jct. **Jenkins Ridge Trail.**		16.1
0.0	**End AT miles: Spence Field Shelter;** water, privy.	4900/1494	16.4
5.2	**Access: Bote Mt. Trail** to Anthony Creek Trail (1.7 mi.), then **Anthony Creek Trail** to **Cades Cove Picnic Area** (3.5mi.)		5.2

SOUTH

HIKE #21
Newfound Gap to Clingmans Dome

Maps: Trails Illustrated: Great Smoky Mts.
Nat'l. Park, TN/NC

Route: From Newfound Gap to Indian
Gap, to Mt. Collins, to Clingmans Dome

Recommended direction: N to S

Distance: 7.9 mi.

Elevation +/-: 5045 to 6643 ft.

Effort: Moderate

Day hike: Yes

Overnight backpacking hike: No

Duration: 5 to 6 hr.

Early exit option: Indian Gap, at 1.7 mi.

Natural history feature: Boreal spruce-fir
forest; highest point on the AT

Social history features: Founding of
GSMNP; forest health and human activities

Other feature: Observation tower

Trailhead access: *Start:* Newfound Gap

parking area: From Sugarlands Visitor
Center in TN, drive 15.0 mi. S on US
441. From Oconaluftee Visitor Center
in NC, drive 18.0 mi. N on US 441. The
trail starts across US 441 from the
Rockefeller Memorial; look for trail
sign at R end of stone retaining wall.
End: Clingmans Dome parking area:
From the observation tower, walk 0.6
mi. down a wide paved path to parking area.

Note: Clingmans Dome Rd. closes for
the season sometime in late November,
and Newfound Gap Rd. may be closed
when it snows. For a recorded announce-
ment of park road conditions, call 423-
436-1200.

Camping: Mt. Collins Shelter

Twelve thousand years ago, the
Wisconsin glacier melted, leaving lifeless rock piles and lakes
in the northern part of this continent.
But the plants and animals that lived
in New England, the upper Midwest,
and Canada found refuge in the
South. As the piles of rocks warmed,
pioneer species, such as lichens,
algae, and mosses, crept northward
and made new soil. Larger plants
and the animals could then follow.
Further warming killed the cold-
adapted species in the valleys of the
southern Appalachians, but some,

including spruce and fir trees, northern flying squirrels, ravens, and a
strange little spruce-fir spider, stayed
on the mountaintops. On this hike to
Clingmans Dome, the highest point
of the entire AT, you will pass through
part of this refuge.

You'll see hundreds of people at
the beginning (and perhaps even
more at the end) but very few on
the trail itself. Steep spots near
Newfound Gap and a long rocky
climb at the end make Hike #21 a
challenge, but most of the trail is
well graded and has steps or cross

David Emblidge

AT and side trails, Great Smoky Mts. National Park

logs for rough spots. The trail parallels Clingmans Dome Rd., whose traffic can be heard in some places, but most of the hike has a private feeling to it because it's on the other side of the ridge from the road. This section of the AT is one of the best places to experience the boreal spruce-fir forest and to see the changes occurring in it.

From the Rockefeller Memorial (where the national park was dedicated by Franklin D. Roosevelt on September 2, 1940), cross the road and swing left down a narrow trail along the base of an impressive limestone-block retaining wall. The construction rock was brought here; there is no high-elevation limestone in the Appalachians, and some of the rock surface has partly dissolved in just 50 years, perhaps accelerated by acid rain. The Thunderhead sandstone underlying the AT here is much more resistant and will long outlast this wall.

At first, deciduous northern hardwoods line the trail, but at 0.2 mi. the

AT ascends through large red spruces and a few Fraser firs. Spruce needles are square in cross-section and sharp on the ends; fir needles are flat and rounded on the ends (spruce: sharp; fir: friendly). As you hike from the only gap with a road in the Smokies to the highest elevation of the AT, you can see the proportion of firs increasing in the forest. When this was a healthy forest, just 25 years ago, firs dominated at the higher elevations and created a cathedral-like atmosphere with subdued light and open shaded spaces. However, a combination of air pollution and an imported insect pest, the balsam woolly adelgid, has killed most of the mature firs and damaged other dominant plants here, so nowadays you will see dead standing trees, lots of blowdowns, and tangles of blackberries and other invasive plants.

Hike #21's first climb is over in less than a mile, and then the trail descends to a beech gap. This small dip in a mountain crest funnels the wind and has deeper soil; these factors favor the deep-rooted, sturdy beech trees. Ground plants here include grasses and many wildflowers, such as trout lily, spring beauty, and trillium. This beech gap has a 150-yd.-wide hog exclosure, a fenced-in area to keep wild hogs out. Hikers can walk up a metal grate and enter and leave the exclosure, but the hogs' feet slip through the bars. The wild hogs are descendants of European wild boars that were introduced for hunting in the 1920s. They

National Parks History Lesson

President Abraham Lincoln gave Yosemite Valley to California for use as a state park.

1872 — Yellowstone established, the first national park in the world.

1906 — California gave Yosemite Valley back to the federal government to be included in Yosemite National Park.

1916 — President Woodrow Wilson signed a bill creating the National Park Service to run the growing number of national parks.

1919 — Acadia National Park in Maine established, first national park in the East.

1923 — Mrs. Willis Davis of Knoxville, Tennessee, asked: "Why can't we have a national park in the Great Smokies?"

1926 — President Calvin Coolidge signed a bill authorizing a national park in the Smokies, but there was a catch: Before the park could be actually established, park commissions in Tennessee and North Carolina had to purchase at least 400,000 acres of mountain land from private citizens and commercial owners and transfer the deeds to the federal government.

The bill also authorized Mammoth Cave and Shenandoah National Parks.

1928 — John D. Rockefeller Jr. offered a $5 million matching grant for land acquisition as a memorial to his mother, Laura Spelman Rockefeller.

1933 — President Franklin D. Roosevelt allotted $1.5 million and Rockefeller added another $500,000 when the park commissions ran out of money to buy the last tracts.

1934 — The Little River Lumber Company agreed to sell its 76,507-acre holdings at an affordable price ($3.57 per acre) only if they could continue to cut timber for five years after park establishment. This was dubbed "conservation with an axe" by Edward Meeman, editor of the *Knoxville News,* but the deal was signed. After much controversy, Meeman changed his mind and supported the park and its organizers. Logging and road building between Elkmont and Tremont (north of Hike #19) went on until 1939.

1934 — Great Smoky Mts. National Park formally designated.

1940 — President Roosevelt dedicated the park at Newfound Gap on September 2.

root in the soil, cause erosion, compete with native black bears for food, pollute streams (possibly shedding *Giardia* parasites into the water), have no natural predators, and eat bulbs of rare flowers. Though the hogs are environmental bad news, they are not dangerous; they run and hide when hikers approach. The park service removes many hogs each year and uses exclosures like this one to measure the extent of environmental damage. Between here and Doe Knob on the AT, muddy wallows near the trail and areas that look as if they have been rototilled indicate the presence of these exotic animals. By contrast, the trail inside the exclosure is carpeted with spring beauties and trout lilies in April.

The trail descends steeply on the right to Indian Gap at 1.7 mi. From here, Road Prong Trail drops into Tennessee, marking the path of the Oconaluftee Turnpike, which was used for cross-mountain trade and for Civil War troop movements. As a toll road, the turnpike charged a few cents for each cow, pig, horse, wagon, and chicken. Tennessee farmers faced a rough trip bringing their livestock to the better markets of the Carolinas.

Cross the grassy patch, and try to ignore the whizzing traffic of Clingmans Dome Rd. on the left. The AT now enters dark spruce forest and ascends on log steps with switchbacks. As the trail levels, it widens and is lined with huckleberry bushes and a small patch of rhododendron. On a short descent, many stark dead fir trunks stand sentinel to the right. Look for young fir trees; some show brown needles that may be a sign of stress or disease.

The trail becomes level and easy, with footlogs to cross muddy spots. Hurricane Opal, in October 1995, blew down many trees along this ridge. Unfortunately, most of them were large, healthy spruce trees, while the dead firs, with no needles to catch the wind, remain standing. You will get an intimate view of the

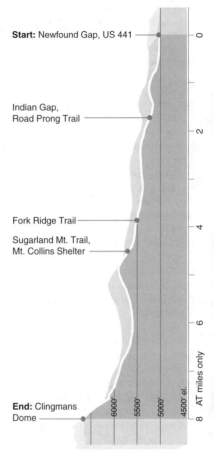

undersides of roots and see how they have to spread out in this thin soil; the bedrock prevents them from going down.

At 4.1 mi., the AT meets the Fork Ridge Trail on the left, which crosses Clingmans Dome Rd. and plunges into Deep Creek Valley of North Carolina. About 0.4 mi. later, the trail

🚶🚶 Newfound Gap,
US 441 Ⓟ🅦🅣
El. 5045'

Indian Gap, Road Prong
Trail Ⓟ

Fork Ridge Trail;
Mountains-to-the-Sea
Trail joins AT

Sugarland Mt. Trail,
Mt. Collins 🏠🅦🅣

🚶🚶 Clingmans Dome
Ⓟ🅦🅣 El. 6643', **V**

N

1" = 1 mi.

meets Sugarland Mt. Trail on the right, which leads to Mt. Collins Shelter in 0.5 mi. — it sleeps twelve on built-in bunks and has a nearby spring — and then follows a ridge crest for 12.0 mi. down to Little River Rd. The AT then swings left and starts a long, rocky climb with a few level relief spots. To the right are occasional views of Tennessee ridges stretching north. From a narrow, open ridge at about 7 mi., you can see the radio tower on the broad curve of Clingmans Dome, and just one more climb with a few switchbacks will get you to the observation tower. Before you see it, however, you will hear voices seemingly coming from the sky and the sound of children running down the concrete ramp.

After the last switchback to the right, look left and give a little wave because someone on the tower is bound to take your picture. Continue on below the tower, and turn left at the next trail sign to reach the base of the tower. The Mountains-to-the-Sea Trail goes from here to the North Carolina Outer Banks (900+ mi.).

At 6643 ft., Clingmans Dome is the second-highest point in the East, after Mt. Mitchell at 6684 ft., but this odd corkscrew-shaped tower takes you higher than Mt. Mitchell. The 360-degree view is spectacular when available, but thick fog, rain, or snow is common, even if you've been hiking in sun all day. Signs and diagrams around the tower identify Tennessee and North Carolina peaks. Silers Bald and Thunderhead Mt. (see Hike #20) are prominent in the southwest. Even when it's foggy, from the tower you'll be able to see large fir trees with their upright cones. In this area, the park service can treat the trees for woolly adelgid infestation with a soapy solution that doesn't harm other plants or animals. The treatment can only be done along a road or paved path because tank trucks of water are needed.

The AT continues south here toward Silers Bald. But to end this hike, follow the paved path from the base of the tower down to the Clingmans Dome parking area, where you'll find toilets, water, a park information center, and all those people who drove by while you hiked.

A pleasant alternative to the paved path is the Clingmans Dome Bypass Trail. Continue on the AT past the tower for 0.2 mi. A park sign indicates a sharp left turn for the connector, while the AT turns right. Descend a rocky 0.5 mi. to Forney Ridge Trail, and ascend left for 0.1 mi. to reach the parking area.

A good one-car alternative hike would be to park at Indian Gap (1.5 mi. from Newfound Gap on the Clingmans Dome Rd.). Find the AT to the left of a grassy area below the parking lot (Road Prong Trail goes straight down the hill), and hike 5.2 mi. to Clingmans Dome and back, for a round-trip of 10.4 mi.

A small parking area at the Fork Ridge trailhead (3.5 mi. from Newfound Gap on Clingmans Dome Rd.)

Miles N	NORTH	Elev. (ft./m)	Miles S
7.9	**Start:** Newfound Gap; US 441, parking, toilets, water.	5045/1538	0.0
6.2	**Indian Gap;** jct. **Road Prong Trail;** early exit option to Newfound Gap Rd. (3.3 mi.), parking.	5200/1584	1.7
3.8	Jct. **Fork Ridge Trail;** Mountains-to-the-Sea Trail joins AT.		3.8
3.4	Jct. **Sugarland Mt. Trail** to **Mt. Collins Shelter** (0.5 mi), spring and privy.		4.5
0.0	**End:** Clingmans Dome, observation tower; 0.6-mi. path to parking, toilets, water, visitor center.	6643/2025	7.9

SOUTH

offers a shorter one-car round-trip. Cross Clingmans Dome Rd. from the parking lot, and hike 0.1 mi. to the AT. Turn left and hike 3.6 mi. to Clingmans Dome (7.2 mi. with a backtrack to the car).

One side trail worth a visit is the 0.7-mi. Spruce-Fir Nature Trail on the other side of Clingmans Dome Rd.

from the AT, about 2 mi. beyond Indian Gap.

Another excellent side trip is the 2.0-mi. hike from the Clingmans Dome parking area on the Forney Ridge Trail to Andrews Bald, a high-elevation grass bald with flame azalea, Catawba rhododendron, and delicious blueberries.

Newfound Gap to Charlies Bunion
to Cosby Campground

Maps: Trails Illustrated: Great Smoky Mts. Nat'l. Park, TN/NC

Route: From Newfound Gap to Icewater Spring, to Charlies Bunion, to Pecks Corner, to Snake Den Ridge, to Cosby Campground

Recommended direction: S to N

Distance: 24.7 mi. total; 19.4 mi. on AT

Access trail name and length: Snake Den Ridge Trail, 5.3 mi.

Elevation +/-: 5045 to 6250 to 5750 ft.

Effort: Strenuous

Day hike: Optional shorter section

Overnight backpacking hike: Yes

Duration: 16 to 18 hr.

Early exit option: None

Natural history features: Anakeesta slate, 2.5-mi. stretch above 6000 ft.

Social history features: Cherokee boundary land; damage from 1925 logging fire

Trailhead access: *Start:* Newfound Gap parking lot on US 441, 16.0 mi. from Gatlinburg, TN, and 18.0 mi. from Cherokee, NC. At Newfound Gap, the AT starts between the Rockefeller Memorial and the paved path to the toilets. *End:* Cosby Campground: Enter the park at Cosby entrance on TN 32, drive 2.0 mi., and park at hiker parking behind registration building. Walk up into campground and look for trail sign near Campsite B-55.

Camping: Icewater Spring Shelter; Pecks Corner Shelter; Tricorner Knob Shelter (reservations required); Cosby Campground

O n September 2, 1940, here at the Rockefeller Memorial, President Franklin D. Roosevelt dedicated the Great Smoky Mts. National Park, which had been authorized by Calvin Coolidge in 1926 and established by Congress in 1934. It was fortunate that Roosevelt came when he did; soon after, he was busy running a war. The Smokies was the first American national park that required fund-raising and acquisition of land from private own-ers. Schoolchildren gave pocket money to help match a $5 million challenge grant from John D. Rocke-feller Jr. Park advocates persuaded, negotiated, and condemned land to acquire the tracts. The effort took more than 10 years, but eventually more than 6600 tracts of land—from tiny vacation lots to huge lumber company holdings—were bought.

The first 4.0 mi. of this AT section, from Newfound Gap to Charlies Bun-ion, is a good choice for an 8.0-mi.

one-car round-trip day hike. Beyond Charlies Bunion, the AT passes along a remote ridge crest with very few access trails. Reservations are required for shelter space and may be made a month in advance. Off-season and weekday hikes are least crowded, and on clear fall and winter days, views from the ridge crest are spectacular.

The trail starts to the right of the Rockefeller Memorial with a vigorous climb through spruce-fir forest. Many park visitors are intrigued by the AT sign at the memorial, which promises Maine in just 1958 miles, but most of these hikers turn back in less than a mile. In 1995 Hurricane Opal toppled many trees here. Trail volunteers couldn't clear the trail because of the danger involved, so the park hired skilled logging crews and closed this section for several months. Some upright stumps are cut 10 to 15 ft. from the ground. If you wonder why trail workers cut them so high, it turns out they didn't. The roots of a partially uprooted horizontal tree can pull the stump upright after the heavy trunk is sawed off, adding to the danger of the job.

The AT slips to the north side of the ridge and continues its ascent. In some places here, the path slopes downhill, and trail ice can be hazardous. After 1.5 mi. the trail levels and becomes grassy with yellow birches and spruce trees. At 1.7 mi., Sweat Heifer Creek Trail goes right and in 3.7 mi. descends to Kephart Prong Shelter—which sleeps four-

teen and offers water from a creek—and to Newfound Gap Rd. in 5.7 mi. This is a good spring-wildflower trail that got its odd name from the annual spring cattle drives up to the grassy balds. If you climb Sweat Heifer Creek Trail just after a lazy winter, you will sympathize with the cows. A twisted yellow birch and a trail sign mark the junction.

Smooth, easy trail descends a bit and at 2.7 mi. reaches the junction with Boulevard Trail. This trail leads left 5.3 mi. to Mt. Le Conte, the third-highest peak of the Smokies at 6593 ft. (There's a heap of stones at the highest point that you can add to if you want to help Le Conte become higher than 6643-ft. Clingmans Dome.) Rustic Le Conte Lodge provides meals and cabin accommodations. A 13-mi. hike (with car shuttle) could be arranged with the AT, Boulevard Trail, and Alum Cave Trail down to the Alum Cave parking lot on US 441. In 1997 three peregrine falcons fledged near Alum Cave Trail, the first successful nesting of this endangered bird in the park in 50 years.

The AT goes right from the Boulevard Trail junction and looks like a side trail; watch the blazes. The rebuilt Icewater Spring Shelter and composting latrine are to the right after a short descent. Facing south and surrounded by thick, soft grass—a good place for a break—the shelter sleeps fourteen and receives heavy use because it's so close to Newfound Gap.

After the shelter, the piped Icewater Spring flows onto the rocky trail from the left at 3.1 mi. Ice on the broken pieces of flat slate in the eroded gully can be treacherous in winter. But the trail levels onto a narrow ridge in about 0.5 mi., and an open area with a sunny rock gives a wonderful southern view of the deep Oconaluftee valley and the North Carolina mountains beyond. On some clear days, meringue clouds fill the valley. Just a short distance farther is a left view of Mt. Le Conte, the Jumpoff (a rocky spur), and Greenbrier Valley. Charlies Bunion, a large knob of exposed rock, is visible ahead to the right.

At 4.0 mi., the trail forks. The right fork is the AT; the left fork leads out on a narrow, rocky ledge to the Bunion, then rejoins the AT in 0.2 mi. (The Bunion was named by Horace Kephart in honor of the sore foot of Charlie Conner, a local mountaineer who helped Kephart and photographer George Masa inspect fire and storm damage in 1929, before the convenience of trails.)

In foggy, wet, icy, or stormy weather, the Bunion trail can be dangerous; use extreme caution or save it for another trip. The rock here is Anakeesta Formation slate; because it has a high iron content, exposed rock turns red from oxidation. The slatey rock, far less stable than the sandstone of Clingmans Dome, breaks into slabs and is slippery. Hikers have fallen here, some to their death. Be very careful, and rein in the kids.

The Bunion was once covered by heath bald, but a logging fire in 1925 destroyed the plants, and a subsequent cloudburst removed the unprotected soil. Lichens and mosses colonize some cracks, and rhododendron, mountain laurel, and sand myrtle are doing their best to get established. Sand myrtle bushes stand 1 to 2 ft. tall, have sunflower-seed-sized evergreen leaves, and produce tiny white and pink flowers in May. From the Bunion, the view includes Mt. Le Conte, Brushy Mt. (a large heath bald), Greenbrier Valley, Mt. Sequoyah, Mt. Guyot, and the Sawteeth (jagged chunks of Anakeesta slate that form the next AT section). For the day-hike option, sunbathe awhile, and then backtrack to Newfound Gap. If the sunbathing is not so good (windchill of minus 50 degrees or a downpour), come back to Charlies Bunion some other time.

Shortly after Charlies Bunion, the trail passes through spruce woods and then enters a south-facing grassy hillside with blackberries, bush honeysuckle, and exposed spruce and fir trees with branches on the leeward side of the trunk. You can scramble up this steep, rocky meadow to sit on beautiful, usually private, rocks thrust out over Porters Flat. Before the park was established, a thriving community lived down there, large enough for a 200-student school, a hotel, stores, and a few moonshiners.

The AT next goes right of the ridgetop through a thick patch of spruces and then into a small beech gap. Some of the Porters Flat settlers crossed the mountains here with livestock and wagons full of household goods. It's no wonder they stopped at the next reasonably flat place.

A sign on the right at 4.2 mi. marks the junction with Dry Sluice Gap Trail and connections to Smokemont Campground (8.5 mi. down) and Kephart Prong Shelter (3.5 mi. down via Dry Sluice Gap Trail and Grassy Branch Trail). From the sign, the AT ascends on a rock ledge left of the ridgetop, which supports green, white, pink, and orange lichens on the surface and clumps of moss in cracks. The ledge becomes narrower and at 4.4 mi. rises to the section of jagged Anakeesta slate called the Sawteeth. The AT runs over some of the sawteeth and around others.

Porters Gap (5500 ft.; 5.8 mi.) and False Gap (5400 ft.; 6.5 mi.) provide some relief from the narrow, rocky trail; then the AT curves left and climbs the side of Laurel Top at 7.5 mi. In May and June mounds of sand myrtle blooms cover the sides of the trail. In some years, this tough little shrub blooms again in October.

Providing views on both sides, the AT slips back and forth along the state border. At 9.1 mi. it passes Bradleys View, a long rock bench (with a USGS benchmark) on the right where you can dangle your feet over North Carolina and look down into the Bradley Creek watershed. Back to the right, Mt. Kephart, Mt. Collins, and Clingmans Dome can be seen, and ahead to the left, Hughes Ridge rises to meet the crest of the Smokies.

Hughes Ridge starts in Qualla Boundary, the land that surrounds Cherokee, North Carolina. A few Cherokee families that lived on Hughes Ridge

David Emblidge

Charlies Bunion

successfully resisted the Indian Removal of 1838. Fugitives from the Trail of Tears joined them to become the present Eastern Band of Cherokee. Will Thomas, a white man raised in a Cherokee family, held deeds to Qualla Boundary lands after the 1838 Cherokee Removal, when Cherokees were not allowed to own land. When the Cherokees were granted citizenship in 1924, the deeds were returned to them.

The AT drops right of the ridge and follows an old logging road. Look for drill-core marks on the mossy rock face on the left. Red spruce and Fraser fir grow here in a few pockets of old-growth forest that the loggers and their fires didn't reach.

After a left turn, the trail ascends, crosses the crest of Hughes Ridge at 10.2 mi., and goes down a rocky section to a trail junction and sign at 10.4 mi. Pecks Corner Shelter, which sleeps twelve and has a good spring and a privy, is 0.4 mi. down Hughes Ridge Trail, opposite a grassy patch where horses may be tethered. (Horses are allowed on the AT from here north to Davenport Gap.)

Beyond Hughes Ridge the AT becomes easier for about a mile, with gentle ups and downs along the ridge crest and some level spots. Look for yellow Clintonia, or bluebead lilies, on the trail bank. Three or four oval basal leaves surround a leafless stalk with delicate yellow-green flowers (especially beautiful in a hand lens view) in May or June; in August, bright blue inedible berries hang from the stalk.

Continued on p. 182

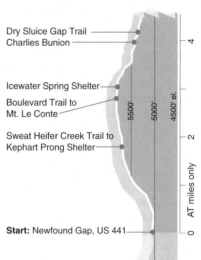

After a rocky climb, perch at Eagle Rocks (5849 ft.; 11.3 mi.) over Eagle Creek valley. Look for Mt. Le Conte to the left, but don't lean out too far. To the north, across the valley of Ramsay Prong, is Greenbrier Pinnacle, where captive-bred peregrine falcons were released. Thanks to these reintroduction efforts, peregrine falcons are nesting in the park.

The AT then swings left through a recent blowdown area with plenty of bare rock for pioneering lichens. Descend to Copper Gap, and then at 13.1 mi. ascend to 6000-ft. Mt. Sequoyah, named for a Cherokee silversmith who developed written Cherokee by analyzing the sounds and assigning symbols to them. Completed in 1821, this is the only

N   1" = 1 mi.

Dry Sluice Gap Trail
El. 5375'

Charlies Bunion
El. 5400', **V**

Icewater Spring
El. 5750'

Boulevard Trail to
Mt. Le Conte

Sweat Heifer Creek Trail
to Kephart Prong

Newfound Gap,
US 441
El. 5045'

Alum Cave Trail to
Mt. Le Conte

known case of a written language being created by one person. Many schools and communities, the largest tree species in the world, and a western national park are also named for Sequoyah (or Sequoia).

There is a good view south across the tops of blackberry bushes. Look for conglomerate rock along the trail with small blue quartz crystals and for quartz chips in the trail. The Anakeesta slate of Charlies Bunion and the Sawteeth is replaced here by sandstone, which makes rounder mountain shapes and less jagged trail rocks. Large visible crystals indicate that this rock was subjected to enough heat and pressure to melt the quartz until it flowed like soft plastic.

After Mt. Sequoyah comes a steep, rocky climb to Mt. Chapman (14.6 mi.), the fourth-highest peak of the Smokies at 6250 ft. named for Colonel David Chapman, park promoter in the 1920s and first chairman of the Tennessee Park Commission. The top of Mt. Chapman lies slightly west of the AT; a spur trail to the top is overgrown.

Descend along rocky trail to Tricorner Knob at 15.6 mi. and then the junction (15.8 mi.) with the Balsam Mt. Trail, one of the more remote trails in the park. Three ridge crests and three county lines meet here. The Tricorner Knob Shelter, which sleeps twelve on built-in bunks, lies in a hollow 300 ft. to the right and has an unreliable spring and a new privy.

Tricorner Knob was named by Arnold Guyot, a Swiss geographer who carried fragile barometers up

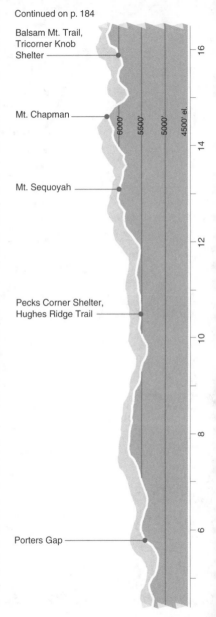

Continued on p. 184

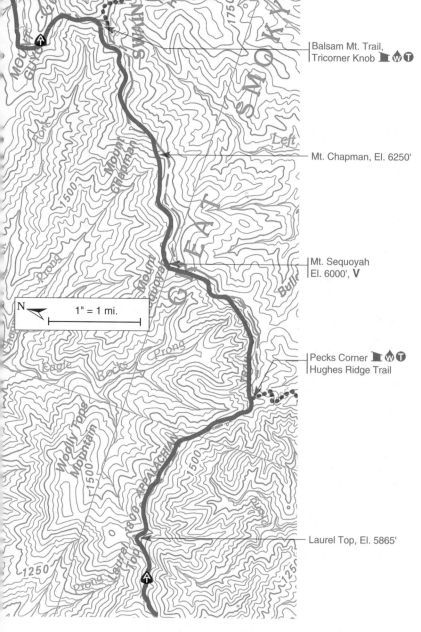

Balsam Mt. Trail,
Tricorner Knob

Mt. Chapman, El. 6250'

Mt. Sequoyah
El. 6000', **V**

Pecks Corner
Hughes Ridge Trail

Laurel Top, El. 5865'

these mountains before there were trails. Guyot's measurements of elevation were quite accurate and gave the first indication that these southern mountains might rival the New England peaks. Guyot (a professor at Princeton University) and his countryman Louis Agassiz (of Harvard University) were early proponents of the theory of continental glaciation.

The AT ascends left from the junction, passes a horse rail, and stays above 6000 ft. for 2.5 mi. As it regains the ridge crest at about 16.5 mi., there are views left of English Mt. and the village of Cosby, with Douglas Lake in the distance looking oddly higher than the mountains in front of it. The rounded dome of Mt. Guyot, visible to the east about 0.4 mi. from the AT, is studded with dead Fraser fir trees, killed by the balsam woolly adelgid, an introduced insect that entered the park in the 1950s.

The AT levels again between mossy banks; in fall, some of the moss turns bright red. At Deer Creek Gap (18.5 mi.), a high grassy open spot, there is an old concrete helipad. To the left, the sharp ridge of Maddron Bald, covered with thick heath, extends into Tennessee. From here there is a rocky descent past Inadu (Cherokee for "snake") Knob at 19.1 mi. Look on the right for chunks of gray airplane fuselage from an Air Force jet that crashed in 1984.

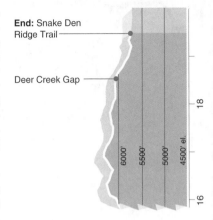

At 19.4 mi., Snake Den Ridge Trail comes in from the left, next to slabs of sandstone rippled from the ancient ocean that once covered them. The AT turns right from the junction to continue on to Low Gap (Hike #23). Snake Den Ridge Trail goes left 5.3 mi. down to Cosby Campground. This pleasant, all-downhill walk passes through old-growth forest and then along Inadu Creek. Somewhere on the lower part of Snake Den Ridge Trail is Tater Hill, a rocky area where young men drafted into the army during the Civil War hid gold for safekeeping. Some of them never came back for their gold.

The trail enters Cosby Campground at Campsite B-55. Turn left on the paved road, and follow it down and right to the hiker parking area, which is 2.0 mi. from TN 32.

Cosby Campground
🅿 ⛺ 🚿 🚻

🚶🚶 Snake Den Ridge
Trail, El. 5750'

N

1" = 1 mi.

Deer Creek Gap
El. 6020', **V**

Miles N	NORTH	Elev. (ft./m)	Miles S
	Total: 24.7 mi with access trail		
5.3	Access: Snake Den Ridge Trail to Cosby Campground.		5.3
19.4	**End AT miles:** Jct. Snake Den Ridge Trail.	5750/1753	0.0
18.5	Deer Creek Gap; helipad.	6020/1835	0.9
15.8	Jct. Balsam Mt. Trail to Tricorner Knob Shelter, 300 ft. R; unreliable spring and privy.	6000/1829	3.6
14.6	Mt. Chapman; fourth-highest Smokies peak.	6250/1905	4.8
13.1	Mt. Sequoyah, view.	6000/1829	6.3
11.3	Eagle Rocks, view.	5849/1782	8.1
10.4	Pecks Corner Shelter, spring and privy; jct. Hughes Ridge Trail.		9.0
9.1	Bradleys View; USGS benchmark, views.		10.3
7.5	Laurel Top.	5685/1732	11.9
5.8	Porters Gap.	5500/1676	13.6
4.2	Jct. Dry Sluice Gap Trail to Kephart Prong Shelter (3.5 mi.).	5375/1638	15.2
3.9	Trail to Charlies Bunion, exceptional views.	5400/1646	15.5
3.0	Icewater Spring Shelter, privy.	5750/1753	16.4
2.7	Jct. Boulevard Trail, to Mt. Le Conte, Mt. Le Conte Lodge (5.3 mi.).		16.7
1.7	Jct. Sweat Heifer Creek Trail to Kephart Prong Shelter (3.7 mi.), water from creek.		17.7
0.0	**Start:** Newfound Gap, US 441; Rockefeller Memorial.	5045/1538	19.4

SOUTH

HIKE #23

Cosby Campground to Low Gap

Maps: Trails Illustrated: Great Smoky Mts. Nat'l. Park, TN/NC

Route: From Cosby Campground to Snake Den Ridge, to Cosby Knob Shelter, to Low Gap, to Cosby Campground

Recommended direction: S to N

Distance: 12.4 mi. total; 4.6 mi. on AT

Access trail name & length: Snake Den Ridge Trail, 5.3 mi.; Low Gap Trail, 2.5 mi.

Elevation +/-: 4242 to 5750 ft. on AT; 2400 to 5750 ft. with access from Cosby Campground

Effort: Strenuous

Day hike: Optional

Overnight backpacking hike: Yes

Duration: 8 to 10 hr.

Early exit option: None

Natural history feature: Dramatic elevation change

Social history features: Logging fire of 1925

Trailhead access: *Start:* From Cosby Campground (TN 32), enter the park and drive 2.0 mi. to hiker parking. Hike up road into campground, turn R at pay phone, and look for the Snake Den Ridge Trail sign at Campsite B-55. *End:* Hiker parking, Cosby Campground

Camping: Cosby Knob Shelter; Cosby Campground

The AT doesn't really lend itself to loop hikes, but Hike #23, with the inclusion of Snake Den Ridge Trail (up) and Low Gap Trail (down), provides a strenuous one-car outing on a little-used part of the AT. In general, this end of the Smokies doesn't receive much traffic, so when the Newfound Gap and Cades Cove roads are bumper-to-bumper (which may be any April-through-October weekend with good weather), head for Cosby. At hiker parking there's a map station to help with itinerary planning and usually a park volunteer who knows the trails and can answer questions or make suggestions. Both Snake Den Ridge

and Low Gap Trails are steep and somewhat rocky; Snake Den Ridge Trail gains (or loses) over 3000 ft. in 5.3 mi. This three-trail loop can be done as a long day hike or as an overnight at Cosby Knob Shelter (crowded in spring and on weekends; reservation required); the best way might be to camp at Cosby Campground (rarely crowded), and start early the next morning. The dramatic elevation change helps procrastinators—early summer at Cosby Campground can be pushed back nearly a month by climbing to the Smokies crest, which will still have cool weather and spring flowers.

We describe this as a south-to-north hike, but of course at the start and end you're heading south.

From Cosby Campground, follow Snake Den Ridge Trail for about 1 mi. on an old road that starts just downhill from Campsite B-55. Then climb steadily for more than 3 mi. to the junction with Maddron Bald Trail, which goes right and descends to US 321 in 7.2 mi. Turn left (still on Snake Den Ridge Trail), and hike 0.7 mi. to the AT just below Inadu (Cherokee for "snake") Knob. At 5750 ft., this trail junction is the highest elevation of the loop. Look for Catawba rhododendron (purple blooms in June), a moutain ash tree (clusters of red berries in fall), and great slabs of upthrust Thunderhead sandstone.

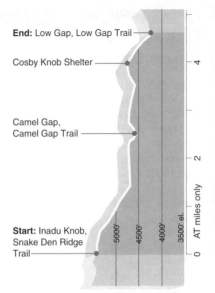

From here turn left (north on the AT), and descend on good trail for about 0.5 mi. through thick rhododendron. The woods open as the AT regains the ridgetop, with yellow birches, grass-lined trail, mounds of reindeer moss, and more upthrust sandstone slabs. Use a hand lens to examine the fractal pattern of a piece of reindeer moss (which is actually a lichen, not a moss), with its ever-smaller repetitions of tiny branches. Mathematicians use geometrical patterns like this to describe and measure nonlinear systems.

A few young Fraser firs grow along the trail among the laurel and spruces. The lower limit of firs in the park is about 5000 ft., so as this section descends, they will disappear.

The AT enters an open crest—dotted with fire cherry, mountain ash, and blueberry bushes—named Hell Ridge for the result of a fire in the 1920s that swept up the valley from a logging camp and burned miles of this ridge. Private logging companies left slash (branches, roots, and any wood they didn't want) in the woods, and piles of slash fueled disastrous fires in many parts of the southern Appalachians. Fire cherry, mountain ash, and brushy plants of the laurel family germinate first on burned areas and persist as tangles (hells) until the soil can support the original forest.

A view of Camel Hump Knob, Mt. Sterling, and Luftee Knob opens on the right. The state line and the AT follow a lower part of the Smokies crest here, dropping to about 5000 ft.

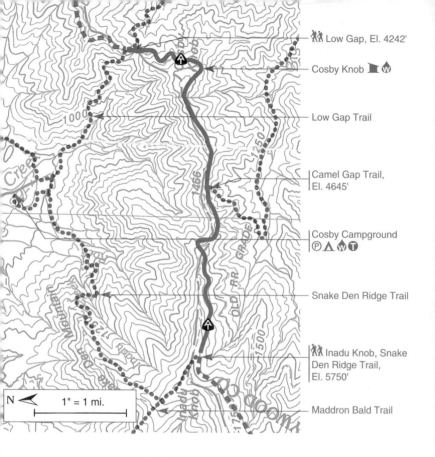

Low Gap, El. 4242'

Cosby Knob

Low Gap Trail

Camel Gap Trail,
El. 4645'

Cosby Campground

Snake Den Ridge Trail

Inadu Knob, Snake
Den Ridge Trail,
El. 5750'

Maddron Bald Trail

N   1" = 1 mi.

Luftee Knob and other peaks of the Balsam Mts. are higher, over 6000 ft., and were measured by Swiss geographer Arnold Guyot in 1860. A peak just west of Luftee is named Thermo Knob because one of Guyot's thermometers broke there (no trivial matter when the thermometers and barometers were large glass instruments that had to be carefully carried through rhododendron and mountain laurel hells). Guyot measured the elevations of these mountains on a state-line journey; he either made a wrong turn at Tricorner Knob, or he thought these peaks should have been the state line. The AT section described here follows the real state line. Another peak between Thermo Knob and Tricorner Knob is named Yonaguska (Drowning Bear), for the Cherokee chief of Oconaluftee who resisted Cherokee removal and exhorted his people to cherish their religious traditions.

The AT slips to the right of the ridgetop into a rhododendron tunnel. Princess pine, a club moss, can be seen all year here, and painted trillium blooms here in May. This high-elevation white flower with a deep pink triangle "painted" across the inner base of the petals ranges with boreal spruce-fir forest from the Smokies to Maine and Canada.

After about a mile from Snake Den Ridge Trail (at 6.3 mi. into the loop hike), the AT levels along a ridge with excellent stone work, built by a Civilian Conservation Corps crew in the 1930s. Then the trail shifts to the left side of the ridge (into Tennessee) and descends toward Camel Gap. Look for Indian pipe in shaded places under mountain laurel or rhododendron. This ghostly white plant gets its food from decaying matter in the soil and makes no chlorophyll. It looks like a thin clay pipe with the mouthpiece stuck in the ground, but after pollination the "bowl" of the pipe straightens and disperses the seeds. It blooms in June or July, but the gray or black capsules can be seen during fall. As the trail descends, more wildflowers bloom in moist areas. In summer, dodder twines its yellow or orange stems around jewelweed, snakeroot, or other trailside flowers. Dodder gets food, water, and support from other plants and has no leaves or roots. The Cherokee name for dodder is love-in-a-tangle. Look at the tiny white flowers with a hand lens.

At 2.4 mi., reach Camel Gap; Camel Gap Trail goes right and leads to several remote trails around Mt. Sterling and the Cataloochee area. The AT continues straight through a blackberry patch. These blackberries have thorns; higher-elevation blackberries have no thorns or just tiny ones.

Ascend alongside ferns, mountain oat grass, and black snakeroot that has masses of white blooms in late summer. Hydrangea bushes grow on the left. As the trail levels, look for three members of the lily family: Turk's-cap lily, Solomon's-seal, and false Solomon's-seal.

Beyond Cosby Knob (5160 ft.; 3.4mi.), a short rocky, steep trail leads right to Cosby Knob Shelter (3.9 mi.), which sleeps twelve and looks like the other Smokies crest shelters: three sides built of stone, a covered veranda, and two levels of sleeping platforms. The shelter sits in a pleasant grassy clearing and has bear cables for food bags.

Back on the AT, the trail has fine rock steps as it descends to Low Gap at 4.6 mi. (9.9 mi. from Cosby Campground). In summer, yellow coneflower, scarlet bee balm, yellow jewelweed, and other tall flowers grow at eye level along this weedy part of the trail, a good place to stop and look with a hand lens. Bee balm, also called wild bergamot, has large flowers above the leaves, and is the only bright-red flower here in summer. It is in the mint family and smells

Miles N	CIRCUIT HIKE	Elev. (ft./m)	Miles S
Total: 12.4 mi. with access trails			
2.5	Access: **Low Gap Trail** to **Cosby Campground**.	2400/731	2.5
4.6	**End AT miles:** jct. with **Low Gap Trail**.	4242/1293	0.0
3.9	Side trail to **Cosby Knob Shelter,** spring.	4750/1448	0.7
3.4	**Cosby Knob**.	5160/1572	1.2
2.4	**Camel Gap;** jct. with **Camel Gap Trail**.	4645/1416	4.7
0.0	**Start AT miles:** Just below **Inadu knob**; head L (N) on AT.	5750/1750	4.6
5.3	Access: **Snake Den RIdge Trail** from **Cosby Campground**.	2400/731	5.3

CIRCUIT HIKE

like spicy lemon. Pinch a flower gently (no need to pick it) and smell your fingers. In late summer, jewelweed crowds the trail, and its swollen green seedpods may explode to disperse their seeds as you brush past them. Find an unexploded seedpod, capture the seeds in a cupped hand as they fly out, and eat them. They taste like black walnut.

Low Gap is a large open area with logs for resting and a major trail intersection. This is the lowest point of the Smokies AT going north since Big Abrams Gap, 50 mi. south of here. Turn left to complete the loop: Low Gap Trail will reach Cosby Campground in 2.5 (steep) miles along Cosby Creek. To the right, Low Gap Trail descends to Walnut Bottoms and two backcountry campsites in 2.5 mi. The AT goes ahead, north, to Mt. Cammerer as described in Hike #24.

HIKE #24
Cosby Campground to Davenport Gap

Maps: Trails Illustrated: Great Smoky Mts. Nat'l. Park, TN/NC

Route: From Cosby Campground to Low Gap, to Mt. Cammerer, to Davenport Gap

Recommended direction: S to N

Distance: 9.8 mi. total; 7.3 mi. on AT; 11.0 mi. with side trip to Mt. Cammerer

Access trail name & length: Low Gap Trail from Cosby Campground, 2.5 mi.

Elevation +/-: 2400 to 4928 to 1975 ft.

Effort: Strenuous

Day hike: Yes

Overnight backpacking hike: Optional

Duration: 8 to 9 hr.

Natural history feature: Sandstone slabs

Social history feature: Rebuilt stone fire tower

Trailhead access: *Start:* From Cosby Campground (TN 32), enter the park and drive 2.0 mi. to hiker parking. Across the parking lot from camper registration building a trail parallels the road to the campground and connects with a nature trail, Lower Mt. Cammerer Trial, and Low Gap Trail. (Camper registration has maps, other information, and often a backcountry camping volunteer who helps with permits and information.) *End:* From I-40 to Waterville, NC (Exit 451), turn R, cross bridge, then go L for 1.0 mi. past Waterville plant and Mountain Moma's store. At four-way intersection, go R for 0.8 mi. to Davenport Gap for short-term parking or go straight 0.2 mi. to Big Creek Ranger Station and overnight parking. Big Creek Campground is 0.8 mi. past ranger station.

Camping: Cosby Campground; Davenport Gap Shelter (reservations required); Big Creek Campground

Hike #24 has a certain symmetry: about 5.0 mi. up with some steep rocky parts and about 5.0 mi. down with some steep rocky parts. The AT section starts at Low Gap but first requires a strenuous 2.5-mi. access climb from Cosby Campground. Mt. Cammerer, the high point in the middle, rewards hikers with wonderful views, especially in October, from a rebuilt fire tower perched on massive rocks. A trip to Mt. Cammerer and back (10.4 mi. total) makes an excellent one-car day hike; the entire hike as described here requires two cars. Short-term parking is available at a gravel pullout just beyond Davenport Gap; safer long-term parking is available at Big Creek Ranger Station. Low Gap Trail and this AT section receive heavy horse and hiker use and have rough spots.

From hiker parking, walk up a paved road to the upper campground loop. Low Gap Trail starts as an old gated road past stone walls and other signs of settlement. The trail crosses Cosby Creek (whose dense rhododendron thickets hid many moonshine stills before the park was established) and follows it steeply through hemlock woods and then closed oak forest. At 2.5 mi., with nearly 1000 ft. elevation gain per mile, it meets the AT at Low Gap (4242 ft.), a wide, trampled intersection with grass and resting logs around the edge. In summer, yellow coneflowers, nettles, and jewelweed grow shoulder high.

The AT turns left (north) from the gap, and our AT mileage count begins here. On the gradual climb, more flowers add color in summer: blue lobelia, red bee balm, orange Turk's-cap lily. At about 1.0 mi., the trail levels at Sunup Knob and swings around a sandstone outcrop. On the knob, galax, mountain laurel, blueberries, and red oaks—plants adapted to dry southern exposure—predominate. Rufous-sided towhees, robin-sized birds with dark (black for male and brown for female) backs and orange sides, own territories on knobs like this and open areas like Mt. Cammerer. The males sing *drink-your-tea* or *chareee* to declare ownership. Towhees search for insects under leaves by scratching backward with both feet at the same time (try it; it's quite a trick), and the surprising amount of noise they make in the woods sounds as if something big is coming.

Fractured sandstone lines the right side of the trail as it continues along a level ridge. To the left, watch ahead through the trees for views of the sheer rocks of Mt. Cammerer. Yellow birches grow here—look for yellow bark that curls horizontally in ringlets. At least one along here hosts a white blaze. Birches, like most trees, have a fiscal year that starts in summer (on or about July 1) with the production of flower buds for next spring. The buds (catkins, in the case of birches) stand up to ice, snow, and winter storms. In April or May, the male catkins elongate, flop around in the wind like little cattails, release masses of yellow pollen, and then fall off the twigs. On the trail, they look like yellow-green caterpillars, and a hand lens will show the tiers of stamens and maybe a bit of leftover pollen. The female buds expand a little, capture pollen that lands on them, and then swell into cone-shaped bundles of winged seeds. As the seeds get ready to disperse, the buds for the next year grow.

The trail ascends through rhododendron to another dry area and goes along gentle ups and downs through waves of grass. It then turns left uphill and splits with several eroded pathways around a tree. After the next rise, the AT descends on a grassy eroded gully. A double white blaze indicates an upcoming intersection: At the junction, Low Gap is 2.1 mi. back (south); Davenport Gap is 5.2 mi. ahead (north); and Mt. Cammerer is 0.6 mi. left on a sandy spur trail. In stormy weather, follow

Painted trillium

the AT to the right here; it bypasses the exposed mountaintop.

To visit Mt. Cammerer, turn left, climb to large rocks, and then pass through a heath of mountain laurel, Catawba rhododendron, and high-bush blueberries, with wintergreen and reindeer moss lichen lining the trail. After a steep, rough descent, reach a horse rail in the shadow of huge slabs of sandstone. From here scramble up wet rocky trail through tall heath of mountain laurel, blueberries, and rhododendron to the exposed boulders of the summit. Climb over and between sandstone slabs marked with straight quartz veins and sharp quartz pebbles. Heat and pressure from continental collision cracked the ancient sandstone, and quartz flowed into the cracks and crystallized there. Quartz resists erosion better than sandstone does and sometimes protrudes where the

sandstone has worn away. Quartz in the southern Appalachians tells stories of rock metamorphosis and mountain building events. The 1997 Mars Pathfinder mission has found evidence of quartz in Martian rocks, indicating a geological history more similar to Earth's than was formerly believed.

Above the heath, big rocks make you feel like an ant scurrying along. Look for a benchmark and a good picnic spot on the left. Rock steps help with the climb to the round fire tower straight ahead, looking like shingled outgrowth of the native rock. The stone tower, which tops out at 5025 ft. above sea level, was built in the 1930s by a Civilian Conservation Corps (CCC) crew but fell into disrepair until it was rebuilt with funds from Friends of the Smokies in 1995. You can walk around the balcony or take in the view from the glassed-in central room. To the northwest is the Valley and Ridge province—a series of parallel ridges that extend from Pennsylvania to Alabama just west of the Appalachians. To the southwest are Mt. Guyot and other Smokies peaks. Mt. Sterling's fire tower should be visible to the south, and Snowbird Mt. to the east has a white aviation tower on top. The town of Cosby and road cuts for the Foothills Parkway can be seen to the north. A closer view shows fire cherry, mountain ash, red maple, and red spruce surrounding the summit. In July, yellow-flowered bush honeysuckle blooms around the base of the tower. In spring and summer the resident rufous-sided towhees sing, and dark-eyed juncos hop around to check what you have for lunch. Juncos know all about Canadian climate zones in the Smokies and practice vertical migration. They breed in boreal spruce-fir forest and spend the winters at lower elevations. During blizzards they pop down to Gatlinburg or Knoxville for sunflower seeds, and people who don't get out much call them snowbirds.

Mt. Cammerer was renamed from White Rock to honor Arno B. Cammerer, the third director of the U.S. National Park Service. Cammerer helped draw the boundaries of this national park and advised his friend John D. Rockefeller Jr. in conservation philanthropy, part of which made the Great Smoky Mts. National Park possible.

After lunch, sightseeing, and sunbathing, backtrack 0.6 mi. to the AT on the spur trail. To return to Low Gap, turn right (south). To continue on the AT, turn sharp left (north) and descend on steep, wide steps. About 0.5 mi. from the Cammerer spur trail, the trail twists between house-sized rock slabs and improves a bit. The sandstone here is conglomerate (pebbles of quartz and other materials are visible), and about here is the Greenbrier Fault, a junction of two sandstone masses deep under the surface. The upper Thunderhead sandstone that makes up Mt. Cammerer and most of the Smokies crest is about 2 million years older than the lower Elkmont sandstone.

The AT turns left at about 3.0 mi. and descends between a rock face on the left and a fine supporting rock wall on the right, built by CCC crews. It switches back through a boulder field—a hillside covered with blocky boulders pushed out from the bedrock by freeze-thaw erosion during the Pleistocene, about 20,000 years ago. When the glaciers receded, 12,000 years ago, these boulders must have looked like a Martian landscape, but now they sport caps of rock fern, shrubs, wildflowers, and long-rooted trees.

After the boulder field, the trail improves and runs through good wildflower patches. Look for clusters of Fraser magnolia trunks with horizontal lines of yellow-bellied sapsucker holes. These little woodpeckers drill the holes and then return to lap up the sap and any small insects attracted to it, like working a trap line.

At 3.5 mi., the AT meets Lower Mt. Cammerer Trail on the left. This trail leads 7.4 mi. back to Cosby Campground and has a backcountry campsite about halfway, so it could be used for an 11.9-mi. overnight or day-hike loop.

After the intersection, the AT continues down, and the air starts to feel much warmer. Trail quality improves again; most of the horse traffic turns off to Lower Mt. Cammerer. The trail alternates between thick rhododendron and open deciduous forest with a few stands of pine trees in drier areas. A mile past the intersection (5.4 mi.), Chestnut Branch Trail goes right to Big Creek Ranger Station (2.0 mi.) and may be a shortcut to your ride if you parked overnight there.

The AT becomes level, easy, and peaceful, with purple irises along the footpath and rhododendron arching overhead. Sourwood, sassafras, and tulip-trees surround a moist, flowery cove with squirrel corn, trillium, and great chickweed. Then the AT curves right and starts down the final descent of the Smokies with winter views left into a deep valley and its treetops. At 6.4 mi. the Davenport Gap Shelter appears on the left in the valley; if in use, campfire smoke may be the first clue. Hikers have beaten an eroded path straight down to the shelter, but continue on the AT for a safer, more sensible official side trail at a sign. Sitting in an old homesite surrounded by tall, straight tulip-trees and black locusts—both experts at reforesting once-cleared fields—this shelter is only 1.0 mi. from the road and receives heavy use. It's the standard Smokies design: rock walls with a veranda and room for twelve. A good spring provides water.

Hikers doing the whole Smokies AT haven't seen poison ivy since Hike #18 from Fontana Dam; now the trail has lost enough elevation (3000 ft. since Mt. Cammerer) to support this fair-weather plant. Also look for American chestnut sprouts, white pines (pines with five needles in each cluster), hemlocks, and dog-

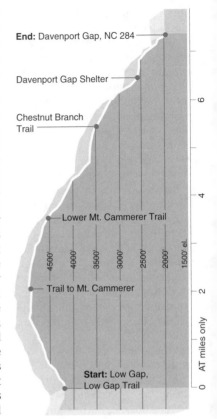

woods. The AT becomes dry and sandy on the last descent to Davenport Gap on paved TN 32.

As mentioned above, Hike #24 could be done as a day hike to Mt. Cammerer, with backtracking to Cosby Campground. Or it could be combined with Lower Mt. Cammerer Trail for a loop to Cosby. Both Cosby

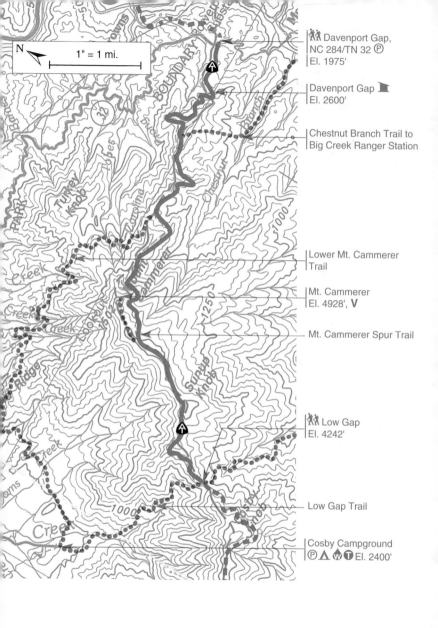

N
1" = 1 mi.

Davenport Gap,
NC 284/TN 32 Ⓟ
El. 1975'

Davenport Gap
El. 2600'

Chestnut Branch Trail to
Big Creek Ranger Station

Lower Mt. Cammerer
Trail

Mt. Cammerer
El. 4928', **V**

Mt. Cammerer Spur Trail

Low Gap
El. 4242'

Low Gap Trail

Cosby Campground
Ⓟ ▲ ⓦ Ⓣ El. 2400'

Miles N		NORTH	Elev. (ft./m)	Miles S
Total: 9.8 mi. with access trail				
7.3	**End: Davenport Gap,** NC 284, limited parking; overnight parking at ranger station.		1975/602	0.0
6.4	**Davenport Gap Shelter,** spring.		2600/792	0.9
5.4	Jct. **Chestnut Branch Trail,** R to Big Creek Ranger Station (2.0 mi.)			1.9
3.5	Jct. **Lower Mt. Cammerer Trail** L , back to **Cosby Campground** (7.4 mi.).			3.8
2.1	Trail to **Mt. Cammerer** (0.6 mi.); lookout tower, excellent views.		4928/1502	5.2
0.0	**Start AT miles: Low Gap;** turn L (N) onto AT.		4242/1293	7.3
2.5	Access: **Cosby Campground,** parking, phone, toilets, information. Follow **Low Gap Trail** E, strenuous climb to AT.		2400/732	2.5

SOUTH

and Big Creek Campgrounds are excellent park service areas with little crowding; they provide informative signs, a variety of hiking opportunities, and large wooded campsites. Hiker parking is available all year; check with the park about open dates for camping.

HIKE #25
Davenport Gap to Max Patch

Maps: ATC Map 3, Sams Gap to Davenport Gap

Route: From Davenport Gap to Pigeon River, to Deep Gap, to Max Patch

Recommended direction: S to N

Distance: 16.0 mi.

Elevation +/-: 1975 to 4629 ft.

Effort: Strenuous

Day hike: No

Overnight backpacking hike: Yes

Duration: 10 to 11 hr.

Early exit option: Green Corner Rd., at 1.9 mi.

Natural history features: Parasitic plants; Max Patch grassy bald

Other feature: Snowbird Mt. FAA tower

Trailhead access: *Start:* From I-40 Exit 451, Waterville, NC, turn R, cross bridge, turn L, and drive 1.0 mi. past Waterville power plant. Go R at four-way intersection for 0.8 mi. to Davenport Gap for short-term parking or straight 0.2 mi. for Big Creek Ranger Station and overnight parking. Because of vandalism, overnight parking is not advisable at Davenport Gap. Big Creek Campground is 0.8 mi. beyond the ranger station. *End:* From I-40 Exit 432, Newport, TN, head N for 15.2 mi. through Newport and across French Broad River. Turn R (W) onto NC 107 for 6.0 mi., recrossing river and going through Del Rio. Go L onto gravel road (continuation of NC 107) at sign for Lemon Gap and Rattlesnake Gap, then L at the fork, indicated by a USFS camping sign. At 6.0 miles pass Round Mt. Campground; at 8.0 mi. pass Lemon Gap; at 11.8 mi. arrive at Max Patch parking area on L. Or, in NC the same road becomes NC 1182, which can be reached from I-40 Exit 7 (Harmon Den exit). Take Cold Springs Rd. (USFS 148) N for 6.2 mi. to junction with USFS 1182. Left for 1.8 mi to the Max Patch parking area on R. (For current conditions of forest service roads, call French Broad Ranger District Office at 704–622–3202.)

Camping: Big Creek Campground in GSMNP; USFS Round Mt. Campground; Groundhog Creek Shelter; several campsites

Because of distance and several long ups and downs, the rating on this hike is "strenuous," but in general the grade is good with no difficult or rough spots. The trail passes through peaceful second-growth forest with sheltered coves and exposed ridges. The shortage of views along the trail is more than made up by the panoramic vistas at Max Patch, a grassy bald that looms over the nearby mountains. The best camping option is at Deep Gap at 9.6 mi., with both a shelter and nice campsites, but some closer campsites are noted below.

The hike begins at 1975-ft. Davenport Gap, where gravel NC 284 meets paved TN 32. The gap is on both the state border and the Great Smoky Mountain National Park boundary. Arranging this hike may be as challenging as doing it. A key-swap or car shuttle would involve many miles of driving. The best way might be to get a friend to drop hikers off at Davenport Gap and pick them up at Max Patch. This would also allow for shortening the hike by 2.0 mi. by starting at Green Corner Rd. near the I-40 exit. (Some hikers might be able to do this as a strenuous 14-mi. day hike.) The gravel road to Lemon Gap and Max Patch is steep, rough, and not well signed. It probably won't damage vehicles, but it will take at least 30 min. and may startle passengers who get a view of the steep hillside.

At Davenport Gap, the AT from the Smokies is on the left, with an open area, National Park Service signs, and posts to discourage parking. From there, walk 20 yd. back into North Carolina, cross the gravel road, climb steps to a wooden fence, and enter the woods. A few yellow-fringed orchids grow near the end of the fence. These orchids, which are actually orange, send up a 2-ft.-tall stalk in June and bloom through July and August.

Pine needles cushion the narrow trail, which ascends about 0.1 mi. to the ridgetop through white pines, red and white oaks, and mountain laurel. Plenty of white blazes mark the AT in both directions, and double blazes warn of turns, old road crossings, or side trails.

After a steep descent through rhododendron, the trail crosses under a power line at 0.7 mi. Look down the power-line clearing for a view of Pigeon River Valley and Snowbird Mt., the next big climb. If you hear rumbling, it might be an approaching storm, or it might just be trucks on the interstate.

After crossing the clearing, check the blazes to avoid other paths. The trail continues down and crosses State Line Branch. Big tulip-trees grow in this sheltered cove, and ferns, violets, trilliums, and other spring flowers line the trail. After some rock steps, look right for a tiny campsite across the creek — probably not useful in high water. Farther down, at 1.1 mi., is a better campsite in a field and former homesite. A blue-blazed trail leads left to a good spring in an old springhouse.

The AT ascends right for about 50 yd. and then descends more steeply as State Line Branch tumbles over ever-larger boulders. The trail rocks and steps may be slippery. Switchbacks beside the creek cascades lead to a paved road near the Pigeon River Bridge, and State Line Branch disappears into a culvert.

Turn left and look for AT blazes on bridge guardrails across the road. After crossing the Pigeon River, turn right and follow the blazes about 75 yd. up the I-40 east entrance ramp. Turn left off the ramp and go under I-40, cross the entrance ramp on the other side, and hike straight up gravel Green Corner Rd. (probably unmarked). After 500 ft., look for a double blaze on a rock face on the left, and climb a fine stone staircase with sturdy handrails. At the top, an AT sign gives destinations and mileages for 30 mi. in both directions. Your hike could start here, but only if you can be dropped off on Green Corner Rd., 1.9 trail miles from Davenport Gap.

After the sign, the AT swings right through open woods. At 0.5 mi. after leaving Waterville School Rd., the trail descends to the road again on switchbacks with good stone steps. The road ditch has a good rock stepover. Turn right on the road, descend 200 ft., and turn left on a woods road. The trail turns right in front of a big blazed oak and switches back into a dark pine forest.

After two more switchbacks, the trail passes rhododendron, striped maple, hemlock, and a few poison ivy vines that look like orangutan arms climbing tree trunks. The I-40 noise fades as you reach a ridgetop. Flame azalea and mountain laurel form an understory, and galax, Virginia creeper, and trillium line the trail. Over the ridge, the soil holds more moisture and supports many flowers.

Henry Lafleur

Shelter in winter

Squawroot, a parasitic flowering plant common along this part of the AT, makes no chlorophyll and sucks sugar and other nutrients from the roots of oak trees. It comes up in clusters in early spring, looking like scruffy small ears of corn with the wide-spaced "kernels" being the flowers. Later in summer it turns black and fibrous, and then looks like scruffy pine cones. Watch also for rattlesnake plantain, an orchid that has an evergreen rosette of round leaves with a lacy network of white veins. In early summer, each plant produces a stalk with delicate white flowers.

At 4.3 mi., an old road joins the AT from the left. The trail follows a ridgetop with mountain laurel, chestnut oak, and black gum trees and in 0.3 mi. approaches Painter Branch (possibly named from sightings of panthers) and a small campsite on a creek island. More campsites appear 100 yd. farther along the creek, and a blue-blazed trail leads right to a spring a few yards from the creek. Orange paint on trees and small metal signs indicate the boundary of the North Carolina Wildlife Management Area.

The trail turns left away from Painter Branch and ascends nearly 1.0 mi. up a steep hillside, where you can look down onto the tops of oak-hickory woods. Look for living and dead American chestnuts. The living ones are just saplings, 8 to 12 ft. tall. As soon as they get big enough for the bark to crack, the chestnut blight

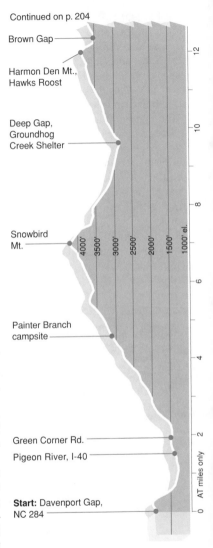

Continued on p. 204

Brown Gap

Harmon Den Mt.,
Hawks Roost

Deep Gap,
Groundhog
Creek Shelter

Snowbird
Mt.

Painter Branch
campsite

Green Corner Rd.

Pigeon River, I-40

Start: Davenport Gap,
NC 284

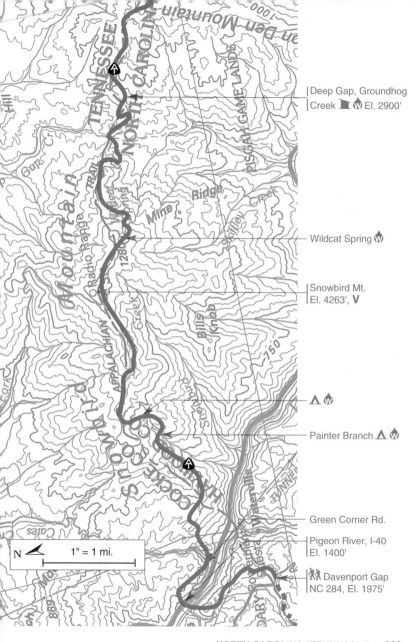

Deep Gap, Groundhog Creek El. 2900'

Wildcat Spring

Snowbird Mt. El. 4263', **V**

Painter Branch

Green Corner Rd.

Pigeon River, I-40 El. 1400'

Davenport Gap NC 284, El. 1975'

N 1" = 1 mi.

NORTH CAROLINA / TENNESSEE   203

that killed the giant chestnuts will kill them, too. The blight fungus, which survives on other trees and is transported through the forest by wind or birds, does not hurt the chestnut tree roots, so they keep sending up hopeful sprouts.

The trail crosses a draw and ascends, with another old road coming in from the left. At 6.4 mi. it reaches the ridge of Spanish Oak Gap and then ascends another 1.0 mi. up a main ridge of Snowbird Mt. Near the top, a weedy trail leads left down to a gravel road to the Snowbird Mt. FAA tower, but you can continue on the AT and take the next left trail to the tower at 7.0 mi. and 4263 ft. On a cold but sunny day this would make a warm rest spot. The trees around the clearing have been cut to provide long-distance views. The gravel tower access road goes down 11 mi. to Hartford, Tennessee.

From the tower, the trail descends Snowbird Mt., passing first mountain laurel and then rhododendron. A small campsite on the left about 0.1 mi. from the summit has an elegant quartz fire ring. After an easy ascent to another Snowbird Mt. ridge, the trail heads down for real. Look for Wildcat Spring at 7.8 mi. on the left, protected by good rock masonry. Mosses and liverworts live on the wet rocks, and the spring water runs down across the trail, supporting a rich growth of spring and summer flowers, including anemone, foamflower, and geranium in April and bee balm and starry campion in midsummer.

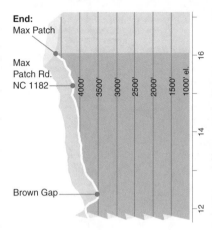

An even steeper descent leads into 2900-ft. Deep Gap at 9.6 mi. Large white pines surround a nice flat campsite. An overgrown road comes up on the left just past the campsite from Deep Gap Creek, Tennessee. To the right, a pretty trail leads through hemlocks for 0.2 mi. to Groundhog Creek Shelter, which has room for five or six people, good logs to sit on, and a stream nearby.

The AT rises out of the gap through thick rhododendron onto an open ridge crest. On the other side of the ridge is a patch of buffalo-nut bushes. These shrubs, which are partly parasitic — they make some food with chlorophyll and get some from the roots of trees — have small yellowish flowers in May and a poisonous, oily green fruit in summer. Early settlers used the oil to harden beef fat to make candles.

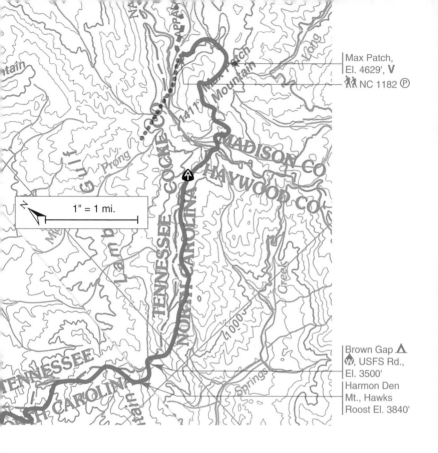

Max Patch,
El. 4629', **V**
🏕 NC 1182 Ⓟ

Brown Gap ▲
Ⓦ, USFS Rd.,
El. 3500'
Harmon Den
Mt., Hawks
Roost El. 3840'

1" = 1 mi.

At 11.4 mi., the trail joins an old lumber road on the left and ascends left from the road on log steps after 100 ft. At the top of the next ridge, the Rube Rock Trail, choked with nettles and poison ivy, goes right to the tree-covered summit of Harmon Den Mt. The AT descends some log steps and a huge tree trunk with a step cut through it. At 12.0 mi., a spur trail leads left 350 ft. to Hawk's Roost, a rocky overlook of State Forest land that is recovering from clearcutting by former private owners.

For the next 0.5 mi. the AT descends through pleasant woods with cucumber magnolia, striped maple, and ash trees. At Brown Gap (12.5 mi. and 3500 ft. elevation) the AT crosses a gravel road, then heads steeply up the other side of the gap. Reasonably good gravel roads converge here from Deep Gap, Max Patch Rd., and

Cold Springs Rd. from I-40 at Harmon Den. A large campsite and spring are on the left under white pines.

After rising steeply, the trail levels off briefly, then rises again. An open field at the ridgetop contains blue lobelia, nettles, jewelweed, and tangled masses of dodder. This is another parasitic flowering plant, but it steals right out in the open, not underground. The yellow strands twine up other plants and grow into their stems to get nutrients. Look for the white dodder flowers in summer, each about the size of an apple seed. Inside most flowers are tiny beetles, aphids, or spiders, but you may need a hand lens to see them.

Near a large gnarled buckeye tree on the left, the trail meets the ridgetop and then slides down the right side of it. In a saddle at 14.0 mi. there's a good resting spot on the right, with logs arranged like sofas in a square. Ascend twice more through open woods. At a left curve of the AT at 15.0 mi., the signed Cherry Creek Trail goes off right and drops down to USFS 148 in 2.5 mi. At 0.2 mi. after the trail junction, the AT goes down some steps to Max Patch Road (NC 1182). To the right is the gravel road down to I-40 at Harmon Den. To the left is the road to the Max Patch parking area in 0.5 mi. Cross the road, pass through a stile, descend to a possibly muddy creek, and climb a thinly wooded, fern-filled hillside. After less than 0.5 mi., the trail reaches a smaller gravel road. Cross it, walk right for 10 yd.,

and look for the AT sign and blazes on the left. The gravel road and a Forest Service trail lead sharply left to the Max Patch parking area. In stormy weather turn left here to bypass the exposed top of the bald; continue to the USFS parking lot and rejoin the AT on a 0.2-mi. path from the left of the Forest Service sign.

The AT takes a longer and prettier route, swinging around the back of Max Patch under a power line and then through a cluster of maple, oak, sassafras, and locust saplings that are eagerly waiting for the grassy bald to be abandoned so they can take over. After crossing a bright-green patch of lady fern, the trail climbs 0.3 mi. up the steep grassy hillside. Blazes are on flexible wands or posts, since there are no trees. Big rocks, strawberries, and a few blackberry bushes line the trail along with the grass.

At the top (4629 ft.) the view is wonderful. From up here, those fern patches look like mysterious crop circles in the darker grass. The Smokies appear to the southwest, Mt. Mitchell to the east, and other mountains in every direction. Max Patch was privately owned and used for grazing until recently. The bald and the rerouted AT were dedicated on July 9, 1983, after years of efforts by hiking clubs and the USFS to preserve Max Patch. The AT crosses the summit and continues down the north side of the bald. About 0.2 mi. past the summit, a worn trail on the left leads down to the parking area.

Miles N	NORTH	Elev. (ft./m)	Miles S
16.0	**End: Max Patch,** parking, USFS information display, extensive views.	4629/1411	0.0
15.2	Max Patch Rd., NC 1182.	4250/1295	0.8
12.5	**Brown Gap,** campsite.	3500/1067	3.5
12.0	**Harmon Den Mt.;** spur trail (350 ft.) to **Hawks Roost,** view on L.	3840/1170	4.0
9.6	**Deep Gap,** trail to **Groundhog Creek Shelter** (0.2 mi.); stream, campsites.	2900/884	6.4
7.8	**Wildcat Spring.**		8.2
7.0	**Snowbird Mt.,** FAA Tower; campsite 0.1 mi. from summit.	4263/1299	9.0
4.6	**Painter Branch,** campsites; blue-blazed trail R to spring.		11.4
1.9	Stone steps from **Green Corner Rd.;** early exit option.		14.1
1.5	Pigeon River & I-40; cross over river and under 1-40.	1400/427	14.5
1.1	Campsite; blue-blazed spur trail L to good spring.		14.9
0.0	**Start: Davenport Gap,** NC 284, limited parking; safer parking at Big Creek Ranger Station in 0.8 mi.	1975/602	16.0

SOUTH

HIKE #26
Lemon Gap to Max Patch

Maps: ATC 3, Sams Gap to Davenport Gap

Route: From Lemon Gap to Roaring Fork to Max Patch

Recommended direction: N to S

Distance: 5.8 mi. total; 5.4 mi. on AT

Elevation +/-: 3550 to 4629 ft.

Effort: Moderate

Day hike: Yes

Overnight backpacking hike: Optional

Duration: 3 to 4 hr.

Early exit option: None

Natural history features: Max Patch grassy bald

Trailhead access: *Start:* From I-40 Exit 432, Newport, TN, go 15.2 mi. E on US 25/70 through Newport and across French Broad River. Turn R onto TN 107 for 6.0 mi., recross river, and go through Del Rio. Turn L onto Round Mt. Rd. (a continuation of TN 107) at sign for Lemon Gap and Rattlesnake Gap. L at fork, indicated by a USFS camping sign. At 6.0 mi., pass Round Mt. Campground on L, and at 8.0 mi., reach Lemon Gap on L. *End:* From Lemon Gap, go 3.8 mi. on USFS 1182 and look for USFS Max Patch parking area on L.

Camping: Roaring Fork Shelter; campsites; car camping at Round Mt. Campground, 2.0 mi. NW of Lemon Gap on TN 107.

Hike #26 ascends from Lemon Gap (3550 ft.) to Max Patch (4629 ft.) through a sheltered, winding valley. The trail runs roughly parallel to the road—but separated from it, so there is little car noise—and crosses many side creeks and Roaring Fork on footlogs. A few muddy spots and the climb provide some challenge, but it isn't steep, and trail quality is good. This hike could be combined with camping at Round Mt. Campground, a good U.S. Forest Service camp with large sites, water, and toilets.

The gravel road to Lemon Gap is steep and rough in spots, but not bad enough to damage a vehicle. Other hikes in the area are Walnut Mountain, which connects the campground with the AT, and the AT from Lemon Gap to Hot Springs (Hike #27). Short-term parking is possible at Lemon Gap, but the safest parking is in the USFS parking area at Max Patch.

For a short while past Lemon Gap, USFS 1182 is visible on the right, but soon a deep valley separates the road from the trail. Several old roads cross the trail and connect with the gravel road; watch the blazes carefully. At 0.2 mi. the trail enters a rhododendron stand and crosses the first creek and an old road. A small trail to the right leads to a creekside campsite.

Leave No Trace Sanitation

Do the math—several hundred thru-hikers, a few thousand section hikers, thousands of day hikers and overnighters, and all those scout troops—it adds up to *many* hiker days. And still, we need to strive for Leave No Trace hiking to protect our wilderness areas, not to mention making possible a pleasant experience for those we share these areas with.

Most of the shelters in this volume and on many other parts of the AT now have moldering privies. Developed in the late 1990s, these privies are a simpler version of the composting toilet and promote aerobic decomposition of feces (faster and less smelly than the old pit privies). Many of the moldering privies are two-holers, and the maintainers alternate the toilet seat once or twice a season to help those wonderful bacteria keep up with their job. Hikers can help by following the instructions posted in the shelters and in the privies themselves. Moldering privies are usually out of sight from the shelter, but just a short walk. (Check it out before settling in for the night.)

However, while camping or hiking far from a shelter, hikers have to make their own arrangements. This gives us a great opportunity to practice and teach good wilderness stewardship.

Peeing in the woods is encouraged, as long as you stay away from trails and water sources. But defecation in the woods involves health and aesthetic concerns. Human solid waste must be buried in catholes, under at least 6 inches of soil so soil microorganisms can work in peace. Toilet paper should be packed out, not left in little colored clumps that remind future hikers that you were there. All other waste and trash should also be packed out. Carry extra plastic bags for tampons, sanitary napkins, and diapers—it takes too long for them to break down even when buried. Catholes for feces should be at least 100 feet from trails, water sources, and shelters or campsites; farther if possible. They should also be camouflaged after use by returning leaves, rocks, and logs. Pet feces also should be buried; bears do it in the woods, but since the result is called scat, it's interesting rather than disgusting. (What was that bear eating, anyway?) An essential piece of equipment is a digging tool. You can pack an old garden trowel or buy a Day-Glo one from a hiking outfitter and hook it to your pack as a badge of wilderness ethics. If you are not convinced that this is an important issue, check out the classic reference on the subject: *How to Shit in the Woods* by Kathleen Meyer.

Both Fraser and cucumber magnolia grow here, along with sourwoods, oaks, white pines, maples, and hemlocks. Wood betony, or lousewort, lines the trail in spots. This flowering plant has leaves like fern fronds and produces orange blossoms in May. The name "lousewort" comes from an old European belief—brought over by early settlers—that cows got lice from grazing on this plant. Brush your hand across the louseworts and check for lice with a hand lens.

The trail curves up through woods of big tulip-trees and thick patches of rhododendron. In moist parts of the trail where more deciduous trees grow, a large variety of flowers bloom in April and May. One of these is doll's eyes, or white baneberry. In April, it produces a rounded cluster of tiny white flowers. By late summer, each fertilized flower grows into a pea-sized white berry on a bright red stalk. Each berry has a dark spot on the end—just the thing for the eyes of a corn-shuck or rag doll. But the berries are poisonous, as the name "baneberry" would imply.

At 1.1 mi. a large rock on the right supports stonecrop, Virginia creeper, ferns, mosses, and rock tripe. This lichen, olive green on top and velvet black on the bottom, grows very slowly, radiating out from an attachment point on the rock, and is said to be edible if you are desperate.

Many buckeye trees grow here, especially along the creeks. They are usually the first trees to leaf out in spring and may get frostbitten, forc-

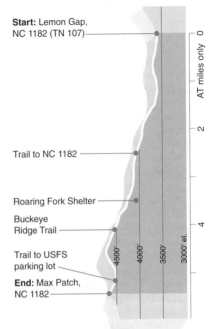

ing them to start over. In dry summer weather, they also drop their leaves early. In late August, you might find a buckeye nut that the squirrels have missed. Its color is a rich chestnut brown, and it has swirly woodgrain lines around it. A round spot where the nut was attached to the inside of the husk looks like the pupil of a large animal eye. Buckeyes are said to bring good luck—as long as you don't eat them; they are poisonous.

After some switchbacks and a few more creek crossings, the trail ascends to hemlock woods with large

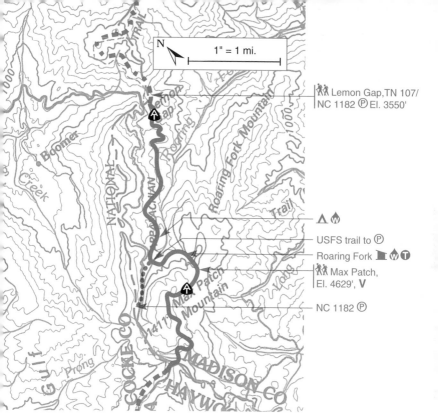

N
1" = 1 mi.

🚶🚶 Lemon Gap, TN 107/
NC 1182 Ⓟ El. 3550'

△ 🌼

USFS trail to Ⓟ
Roaring Fork 🏠🌼🚻
🚶🚶 Max Patch,
El. 4629', V

NC 1182 Ⓟ

Fraser magnolia trees at 2.5 mi. Canada mayflower and painted trillium bloom in May in open areas. At a footlog with a handrail, look upstream for umbrella leaf. This relative of the may-apple lives in shady creeks and can grow to 3 ft. tall with pizza-sized leaves. It has a cluster of small white flowers in May and blue fruits in summer.

At 3.5 mi., near Roaring Fork Shelter, the trail becomes a little steeper, but switchbacks and log or rock steps help. After passing a clearing and a rhododendron tunnel, the trail goes through a stile, crosses a grassy roadbed, and goes through another stile. To the right is a row of big red oaks, and the next blaze is on an apple tree. Ahead and left you can see the open expanse of Max Patch, a grassy bald that is currently maintained by Forest Service clearing. Blackberries and blueberries line the trail, and in summer, harebells, Turk's-cap lily, yarrow, Queen Anne's lace,

Miles N	**NORTH**	Elev. (ft./m)	Miles S
	Total: 5.8 mi with access trail		
5.4	**Start: Lemon Gap,** NC 1182 (TN 107), parking.	3550/1082	0.0
1.8	**Roaring Fork Shelter,** privy, streams.		3.5
1.1	Jct. **Buckeye Ridge Trail**		4.1
0.2	Trail to USFS parking lot, USFS information; spur trail to creekside campsite.		5.2
0.0	**End AT miles: Max Patch,** views.	4629/1411	5.4
0.4	Access: NC 1182, parking.	4629/1411	0.4

SOUTH

and virgin's bower bloom. Buckeye Ridge Trail, a ski/horse/hiking trail, goes left at 4.1 mi. and runs parallel to the AT for nearly 0.5 mi. After the signed junction, the AT enters a dark rhododendron tunnel through the meadow. Ground pine and fluffy moss line the trail.

Cross a seep, enter a grove of big maples, and ascend a fern-filled hillside to a large, open campsite on the left. Then follow blazes on posts or flexible wands up to the rounded slopes of Max Patch. A trail to the right leads to the USFS parking area, and the AT leads left to the summit, with a great view of the Smokies, Mt.

Mitchell to the east, and mountains upon mountains all around.

Until recently, Max Patch was privately owned and used for grazing. It also had a sports club and a landing strip. The Forest Service acquired the land in the 1970s and has maintained the bald by mowing since then. Without the mowing, trees would invade it in a few years.

From the summit of Max Patch, you can see the parking lot and the trail leading to it (0.4 mi.). The trail swings to the right as it descends, and the Forest Service asks you not to use the most direct path down because of erosion damage.

HIKE #27
Lemon Gap to Hot Springs

Maps: ATC Map 3, Sams Gap to Davenport Gap

Route: From Lemon Gap to Walnut Mt., to Garenflo Gap, to Deer Park Mt., to Hot Springs

Recommended direction: S to N

Distance: 14.0 mi.

Elevation +/-: 3550 to 4686 to 1330 ft.

Effort: Strenuous

Day hike: No

Overnight backpacking hike: Yes

Duration: 9 to 10 hrs.

Early exit option: USFS road at Garenflo Gap, at 7.4 mi.

Natural history feature: Rocky ridge crest

Social history feature: Hot Springs historical area

Other feature: Hot Springs Spa (call 704–622–7676 for year-round reservations and information)

Trailhead access: *Start:* From I-40 Exit 432, Newport, TN, drive E for 15.2 mi. on US 25/70, through Newport and across French Broad River. Turn R onto Round Mt. Rd. (continuation of TN 107) at sign for Lemon Gap and Rattlesnake Gap. Go L at fork, indicated by a USFS camping sign. At 6.0 mi. pass Round Mt. Campground Rd. on L, and at 8.0 mi. reach Lemon Gap on L. *End:* Hot Springs, NC

Camping: Walnut Mt. Shelter; Deer Park Mt. Shelter; many campsites (best campsite for 1 overnight at Deer Park Mt., 10.8 mi. from Lemon Gap); car camping at Round Mt. and Hot Springs

---

Running east along the Tennessee / North Carolina border through the Bald Mts. — an irregular range between the Nolichucky and Pigeon rivers — this trail does most of its climbing in the first 4 mi. and then begins a long descent to the town of Hot Springs on the banks of the French Broad River. The open woods of this hike are mostly on ridgetops, and some spots are weedy, unless trail volunteers have been at work recently. Nettles, thistles, poison ivy, and just plain wet stuff can be a problem. During fall and winter, though, there are excellent views of mountains to the south and north.

Since Lemon Gap is not a good place for overnight parking, an alternative would be to camp at Round Mt. Campground and take the 2.0-mi. Walnut Mt. Trail up to the AT at the summit of Walnut Mt. This would add 0.7 mi. to the total hike length. Another option is an 8.6-mi. round-trip day hike from the campground to Bluff Mt. and back. The Walnut Mt. Trail starts from TN 107 about 20 yd. north of the entrance to Round Mt.

War and Peace in Hot Springs

Today Hot Springs is one of the friendliest towns on the Appalachian Trail. Here long-distance hikers can rest up, tourists can take the waters and eat gourmet food, and artists can work far from big-city hassles. But in years past, peaceful Hot Springs (or Warm Springs, the more honest earlier name) played an important part in America's wars.

At the start of the American Revolution, the Cherokee sided with the British because King George, in the Treaty of 1763, had promised to protect Cherokee lands from settler encroachment, even though he wasn't in much of a position to do so. In 1776, General Rutherford led an army across the French Broad River, struggled over the mountains, and destroyed Cherokee towns and crops. Those men, women, and children not shot were sold into slavery. In 1780, after the Battle of King's Mountain, John Sevier, in pursuit of a Cherokee war party, crossed the French Broad, sent a few soldiers ahead, and arranged the rest in a semicircle in the thick woods. The advance men lured the whole Cherokee force into the trap, and Sevier's soldiers killed most of them.

During the Civil War, Hot Springs families joined the Confederacy, while their relatives and friends in Tennessee fought for the Union. Betrayals and ambushes resulted in conflicts unresolved by war's end. A large memorial to General Robert E. Lee stands near the Jesuit hostel.

During World War I, some 2800 German POWs were interned at the Warm Springs Hotel. They performed concerts for the townspeople and built a merry-go-round, a beautiful stone church, and other fine structures, all of which were later destroyed. Upon hearing a rumor that they might be transferred to Alabama or Mississippi, they put poison in the hotel's water system to render themselves too ill to move. Some of them died.

World War II saw an influx of people to work in Oak Ridge and Knoxville for the war effort. Their presence created a demand for moonshine, which benefitted Hot Springs and many other local communities. And since sugar was needed for the fermenting but rationing was severe, beekeepers, too, enjoyed an increased business.

Campground. This hike begins where the AT ascends, about 0.5 mi. from Lemon Gap (3550 ft.), north past a green "Hikers Welcome" sign and a weedy patch of nettles and yellow jewelweed. You will see metal North Carolina Wildlife Game Lands markers, some of them half inside the trees they were nailed to years ago. The open woods include black locusts, red maples, striped maples, and sourwoods. Ascending along the right side of a creek, the trail enters rhododendron and hemlock woods with a groundcover of galax, trailing arbutus, and painted trillium.

At 0.7 mi., the trail crosses two creek branches. A small campsite here is surrounded by yellow birch, black gum, and witch hazel. This last small tree has the odd habit of blooming between November and February. Its petals look like tiny yellow ribbons, and on warm winter afternoons a few sleepy bees come out of hibernation and pollinate them. During the summer, look for last year's seedpods (hard, green or dark brown, and the size of a garbanzo bean) and next year's flower buds (lighter brown and each one the size of a sesame seed).

At 1.1 mi., near the crest of Walnut Mountain (4280 ft.), is Walnut Mt. Shelter and the junction with Walnut Mt. Trail. The shelter sits right on the trail in a weedy clearing. It was built in 1938, and the ATC had planned to remove it when Roaring Fork Shelter, on the other side of Lemon Gap, was built. However, it is still there and maintained because of the relocation of Roaring Fork Shelter to 3.5 miles south of Lemon Gap.

The Walnut Mt. Trail starts behind the shelter and heads left down to Round Mt. Campground in 2.0 mi. A trail to the right leads about 50 yd. to a good spring.

The AT descends Walnut Mt. to Kale Gap (3700 ft.) at 2.1 mi., past oak, hickory, sassafras, and ash trees. In late summer, thistles, nettles, and jewelweed may grow taller than most hikers, and some blazes may be hard

Michael Warren

Box turtle near Pump Gap

to see. Go straight across the gap, ascend an old road on the other side, and head up to the right above the road. On the long, steady climb up Bluff Mt. there are a few rough, rocky spots and some excellent wildflower patches. Look for the fernlike leaves and creamy white flowers of squirrel corn and Dutchman's-breeches in spring.

You'll reach Catpen Gap at 2.8 mi. The trail stays to the left of this large open grassy area, but if you wish, go right to check the apple trees or the view. A rutted road comes up from the Tennessee side and disappears into the woods across the gap. The trees block much of the view, but if you enter the clearing and look back to the right, you can see the angular shape of Max Patch, a U.S. Forest Service–maintained bald named for its former owner.

At 3.7 mi. you'll reach Bluff Mt. (4686 ft.) This peak has no views in summer, but you can rest with the satisfaction that you have reached the highest elevation of this hike, and there are some lichen-covered rocks to lounge on. Big oak, yellow birch, and buckeye trees grow along the flat summit, and filmy angelica and Turk's-cap lilies (check the freckles on the petals) bloom in summer. From here, there is a 3.7-mi. descent to Garenflo Gap (2550 ft.), two slight rises, then a steep descent to Hot Springs (1326 ft.).

The descent from Bluff Mt. is steep at first, but the trail is good. At a switchback (4.2 mi.), a blue-blazed side trail leads left 80 yd. to a spring. The trail crosses several old roads though mostly oak, hickory, and ash woods. Look for a small muddy cave on the left at about 4.6 mi. after some new log steps. Lampshade spiders—named for the shape of their web—hang on the underside of the cave rock. A seep after the cave supports foamflower, mandarin, Clintonia lily—named for DeWitt Clinton first governor of New York and a patron of botanical exploration—and blue cohosh.

Good new trail steps and rocks on the downhill edge protect the next part of the trail. After a switchback, there is a small creek with boulders and umbrella leaf, brook lettuce, and other spring flowers. The AT crosses another old road into a moist area of hepatica and Jack-in-the-pulpit, buckeye trees, and a tangled grape arbor. A large basswood tree on the right sports eight main trunks and many root sprouts.

At 6.6 mi., the trail crosses a junction of two USFS gravel roads and descends into a rhododendron tun-

Continued on p. 218

Garenflo Gap

Bluff Mt.

Catpen Gap

Kale Gap

Walnut Mt., Walnut Mt. Trail

Start: Lemon Gap, NC 1182/TN 107

4000' 3500' 3000' 2500' 2000' 1500' 1000' el.

AT miles only

nel. Then it climbs a little to a broad ridgetop. A blue-blazed trail leads right to a view of the French Broad valley. The AT crosses the ridge, then descends to the left through a stand of small white pines and large patches of ground pine. After more pine and hemlock woods, the trail drops to an old road and then goes right to 2500-ft. Garenflo Gap (at 7.4 mi., it's halfway between Lemon Gap and Hot Springs on Garenflo Gap Rd.).

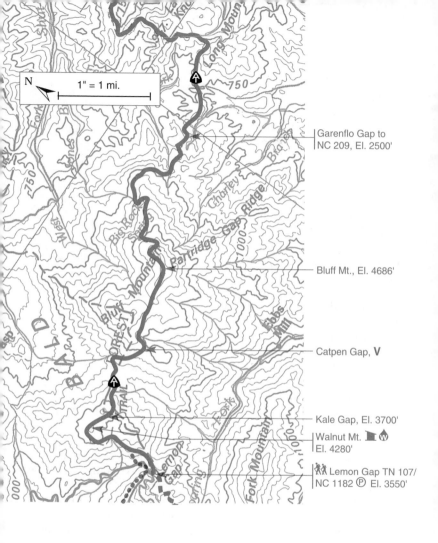

N   1" = 1 mi.

Garenflo Gap to
NC 209, El. 2500'

Bluff Mt., El. 4686'

Catpen Gap, **V**

Kale Gap, El. 3700'

Walnut Mt.
El. 4280'

Lemon Gap TN 107/
NC 1182 ℗ El. 3550'

From Garenflo Gap, the AT ascends the grassy road bank and steps to the left. An old AT sign appears after power lines: "Hot Springs, 6.52 mi." The trail continues up through rhododendron, mountain laurel, and white pine. A roadbed goes right; the AT stays left and descends, crossing two footlogs. After a deep draw, the trail ascends to a dry ridgetop campsite on the right at about 8.0 mi. The big trees here are chestnut oaks, with huckleberries and American chestnut saplings as undergrowth. Follow the curve of the ridge left and then a gentle up and down through dry woods with southeastern views to the right of a deep creek valley.

After a sandy, open ridgetop with huge chestnut oaks, the trail takes a rhododendron tunnel down to Gragg Gap, where there's a sign for water to the left and shelter to the right. The Deer Park Shelter (at 10.8 mi.) is not visible from the trail and sits on a rise above more rhododendron. People have camped on a flat packed-dirt area behind the shelter; camping is also possible near the trail sign and causes less damage there.

On the left, 30 yd. beyond the sign, are the graves of George and Eva Gragg, former landowners in the national forest. Then the trail continues through dry white pine and chestnut oak woods, with a few pink lady's-slippers.

The next ridgetop, Canebrake Ridge at 12.0 mi., is a jumble of beautiful rocks with all sorts of

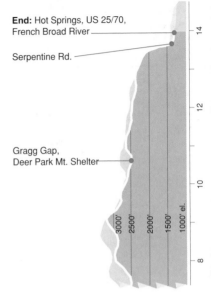

End: Hot Springs, US 25/70, French Broad River

Serpentine Rd.

Gragg Gap, Deer Park Mt. Shelter

3000' 2500' 2000' 1500' 1000' el.

14 12 10 8

lichens. The trail builders (probably the Civilian Conservation Corps crew that camped at Hot Springs during the 1930s) used many of these rocks to reinforce the treadway. Lift up a flap of rock tripe lichen (the big leathery ones with black velvet undersides) to look for wingless bristletails or other small insects and tiny spiders.

The trail then starts a steep descent through a moist area with ferns, small sassafras trees, and spring flowers near seeps. As you go down a series of switchbacks, you will start to hear the dogs and machines of Hot Springs and get glimpses of the town and the French Broad River through the trees.

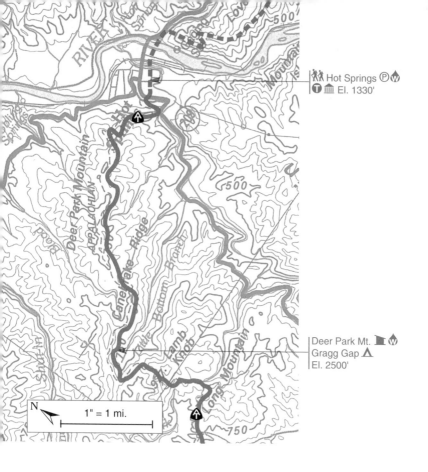

Hot Springs Ⓟ Ⓦ
Ⓣ 🏛 El. 1330'

Deer Park Mt. ◤ Ⓦ
Gragg Gap ▲
El. 2500'

N
1" = 1 mi.

When European explorers of the 1700s saw this broad river flowing toward the French lands, they called it the French Broad. It joins the Holston above Knoxville to form the Tennessee River, which flows south past Chattanooga, then swings north past Shiloh, and at Paducah, Kentucky, joins the Ohio. Until the Tennessee Valley Authority (TVA) built

dams in the 1940s, the French Broad and its fellow rivers rose in great floods, especially after the logging companies stripped the mountains. The drainage areas for these rivers are so large that a storm two or three counties away can cause surprise flooding. In 1916, one hurricane from the Gulf of Mexico and another from the Atlantic hit the mountains in the same week. The resulting floods damaged Knoxville and almost swept away Chattanooga. The TVA dams (and reforestation; the TVA can't take all the credit) have controlled floods while providing electrical power. The dams also covered thousands of acres of Tennessee's most productive farmland, but during World War II, power for Oak Ridge and other war supply industries was considered the priority.

Finally at 13.7 mi. — but not before the ends of your toes are bruised — you reach an open area of mowed grass, a nice shady parking place, a Forest Service information board, and an AT bronze plaque erected by the Carolina Mt. Club. Walk in front of the USFS information sign, cross the road, climb down stone steps beside a rock face, and turn left onto NC 209. Follow this road 0.2 mi. to the junction with US 25/70. The AT goes through the town of Hot Springs on the south side of 25/70, as shown by the AT signs and blazes embedded in the sidewalk. To drive, turn left onto Serpentine Rd., right onto US 25/70, and left at the traffic light where NC 209 joins from the right. There are restaurants, a post office, and other services here; the Hot Springs Spa and Campground are about 100 yd. farther up US 25/70. They are open year-round (reservations are recommended), and the mineral waters at the spa will cure your sore muscles and mashed toes.

Miles N	**NORTH**	Elev. (ft./m)	Miles S
14.0	**End: Hot Springs,** jct. NC 209, US 25/70; restaurants, spa, campground.	1330/405	0.0
12.0	**Canebrake Ridge,** rocky ridge crest.		2.0
10.8	**Gragg Gap, Deer Park Mt. Shelter,** L to water.	2500/762	3.2
7.4	**Garenflo Gap,** halfway point of hike; early exit option.	2500/762	6.6
4.2	Blue-blazed spur trail to spring (80 yd.).		9.8
3.7	**Bluff Mt.,** winter views.	4686/1428	10.4
2.8	**Catpen Gap,** view.		11.2
2.1	**Kale Gap.**	3700/1128	11.9
1.1	**Walnut Mt.;** jct. **Walnut Mt. Trail** to **Round Mt.** **Campground** (2.0 mi. on L); spring (50 yd. on R).	4280/1305	12.9
0.0	**Start:** Lemon Gap, NC 1182/TN 107; parking.	3550/1082	14.0

SOUTH

Hot Springs to Tanyard Gap

Maps: ATC Map 3, Sams Gap to Davenport Gap

Route: From Hot Springs to Lovers Leap, to Pump Gap, to Tanyard Gap

Recommended direction: S to N

Distance: 5.3 mi.

Elevation +/-: 1326 to 2100 to 2278 ft.

Effort: Moderate

Day hike: Yes

Overnight backpacking hike: No

Duration: 3½ hr.

Early exit option: Lovers Leap Trail, at 0.9 mi.

Natural history features: Lovers Leap; French Broad Valley; thermal springs

Social history features: Hot Springs Spa; river rafting

Trailhead access: *Start:* From Hot Springs, NC (US 25/70), drive E on US 25/70, cross French Broad River, and turn L onto paved road. Bear L and loop down under bridge to Silvermine Creek Rd. Park here or go left about 0.5 mi. farther to USFS parking lot for hikers on L. If walking from Hot Springs, follow the blazes across French Broad River bridge, and climb over guardrail on R to find the rocky, steep trail down to Silvermine Rd. The AT continues straight where Silvermine Creek Rd. swings L away from the river. *End:* Tanyard Gap. Drive 3.0 mi. E out of Hot Springs on US 25/70. Pass under hiker bridge (green AT sign), turn L onto paved road, immediately turn L again, and go back 100 yd. to end of bridge. Park on R, out of the way of bridge traffic.

Camping: Two campsites on trail; USFS Group Camp (available to groups with a reservation)

The AT, heading north from Hot Springs, climbs steeply from the French Broad River to the ridge that it cut through the mountains on its way from Asheville to Knoxville. The climb lasts 2.0 mi., with the first mile rough and possibly hazardous in wet or icy weather. But the view is worth the effort, and after the first mile the trail passes through dry pine-oak forest and becomes well graded with easy ups and downs.

Many side trails run through this area, and the AT can be combined with some of them for loop hikes. Hike #28 could be done with a car shuttle, leaving one car at Tanyard Gap and the other at Silvermine Creek Rd. for a one-way 5.3 mi. walk, or you can backtrack to Silvermine Creek Rd. (10.6 mi. round-trip).

Silvermine Creek Rd. passes several river-raft outfitters. If you're interested in combining some river

Northern water snake

rafting with your hiking, these companies provide transportation, instruction, and equipment. After the rafting companies, Silvermine Creek Rd. turns sharply left. The AT crosses a small bridge and then runs on a sandy road between an outpost of the Nantahala Outdoor Center (see "Water Power" in Hike #14) and the river. If you park at the U.S. Forest Service parking lot, walk back down Silvermine Creek Rd. to the curve. The blazes are clear in this area. Mileages in this narrative start from where the AT goes straight as Silvermine Creek Rd. curves left.

The AT runs between a cliff face on the left and a series of river rapids on the right. An old concrete bridge support is covered with poison ivy, a plant that indicates low elevation and environmental disturbance. At 0.4 mi., turn left up the dry, rocky, narrow trail, and start the first of many sharp switchbacks. A blue-blazed trail to the right leads to a small overlook. The steep hillside is messy with loose rocks and erosion channels from people cutting across the switchbacks. Some seedling pines are trying their best to anchor the trail; please don't step on them. Red oaks and sourwood also grow here, but new trees will have trouble getting started. Side trails to the left lead to rocks overlooking the river.

At 0.9 mi. the AT meets Lovers Leap Trail coming up from Silvermine Rd. Left of the junction is Lovers Leap, a large flat ledge jutting out over the cliff face 500 ft. up from the river. It is a pleasant place to rest and view the town of Hot Springs, the spa, Deer Park Mt. (where the AT goes south), and the French Broad River flowing off to the northwest. Use caution near the edge, especially if your love life is not going well:

Have You Thanked a Snake Today?

Only two venomous snakes live in the Appalachians: timber rattlesnakes and copperheads. The risk of snakebite is extremely small, much smaller than the risk of falling trees or lightning strikes. Here are some suggestions to make the risk even smaller:

1. Before your next hike, study pictures of these two reptiles in a good guidebook. Both are thick-bodied snakes with patterns on the back, have vertical slit pupils, and move slowly. Compare them with the non-venomous snakes of the same area. Most guidebooks also have maps to show where each species lives.

2. When stepping off a trail, watch where you put hands, feet, other body parts, or gear. Look around a log or rock before sitting on it.

3. If you see a snake, keep a respectful distance. It will do the same or will leave in a hurry. If it's sunning right in the middle of the trail, wait for it to leave or detour around it.

4. Look for the following characteristics, any *one* of which means nonvenomous snake: solid color with no pattern (could be black, green, gray, or brown); stripes along the body (could be yellow, white, light brown or gray against a dark background color); skinny body; narrow head; round pupils. Some nonvenomous snakes mimic venomous ones by rattling their tails or puffing out their cheeks to make their heads look triangular. Some nonvenomous snakes, such as corn snakes and water snakes, do have bands or patterns on their backs, and when a snake is moving, it

---

A legend tells of a Cherokee maiden who leaped to her death here after her lover was killed by a rival. The ledge that you sit on is the same kind of blocky quartzite that forms the rapids below, and the French Broad probably established this route before the mountains were pushed up by continental collision. The process of mountain building was slow enough that the moving water could erode even the resistant sandstones and quartzes and cut this huge bite out of the ridge.

You may be able to watch rafts, canoes, and kayaks sliding over the ledges below. The French Broad has small rapids and is excellent for family or group water trips provided by the river outfitter companies. At one time, though, there were plans for power navigation on this river. In 1876, Congress allocated money to "improve" the French Broad near Asheville. The Army Corps of Engineers deepened the channel, constructing jetties and other structures to maintain it. A developer built the *Mountain Lily*, a small sidewheel steamboat to transport pleasure rid-

can be hard to pick out the details.

The snakes seen most often on the AT are garter snakes and black rat snakes. Garter snakes and their relatives, ribbon snakes, have stripes along their bodies (see above) and may dash across the trail as you approach. Or they may freeze, probably thinking that you don't see them (yes, snakes think). Stop and look for a while; you may get to see the black, red, and white tongue. Black rat snakes can be seen draped on tree branches or climbing straight up a tree trunk, but if they get surprised by hikers on a trail, they sometimes kink their bodies and look like a stick.

The most common snake near creeks, rivers, swamps, and ponds is the northern water snake, a nonvenomous fish eater. Water moccasins can't live near any part of the AT; they need a warmer climate. In both numbers and variety, there are more snakes in the southern Appalachians than farther north, and there are more snakes at lower elevations. Northern New England has no venomous snakes, and the most common nonvenomous snakes there are green snakes and garter snakes.

All snakes eat meat (mouse meat, bug meat, slug meat, etc.) and are good citizens of the environment. They hold down full-time jobs in pest control and rarely go on strike, even though they are treated incredibly unfairly. Do not hassle them, harm them, or say mean things about them. And if you and your food and equipment make it through a night at a shelter without too many mouse problems, thank a snake.

ers as well as agricultural products from isolated areas. The *Mountain Lily* was launched with great fanfare, but only 3 days later a downpour in distant Transylvania County drove the steamboat into a sandbar and destroyed the jetties.

After Lovers Leap the AT trail turns up into rhododendron and oak woods. It becomes well graded and easy going though still ascending. A blue-blazed trail at 1.3 mi. leads 40 yd. right to another overlook of the river and Bluff Mt. At the top of the ridge, the trail levels at a pretty campsite with separate cooking and sleeping areas and a river view. Pine, maple, dogwood, and sassafras trees surround the campsite, and lady's-slippers and heartleaf ginger flowers can be found nearby. There is no water source; you'll have to carry water to camp here.

At 2.2 mi. the trail continues left down a sheltered, moist section with many large Fraser magnolias. The trail enters Pump Gap at 2.8 mi. and crosses the yellow-blazed Pump Gap Loop Trail, also coming up from Silvermine Rd. Here the AT drops down to the right and meets an old logging road and some faint trails. Watch for the white blazes, and then enter a rhododendron tunnel. The AT crosses Pump Gap Loop Trail again as it loops back down to Silvermine Rd.

A wide place in open woods might be a possible campsite, but continue on toward a concrete dam at 4.3 mi., climb steps on the left side, and come out at a pond. There are benches around the pond and excellent tent sites on the opposite side. Turtles, frogs, fish, salamanders, harmless water snakes, and dragonflies live here, and in fall, jewelweed, cardinal flower, Joe-Pye weed, and ironweed bloom. Beyond the pond is another unusual sight for the AT: a large kudzu patch. This invasive vine, with August-blooming purple flowers that look like wisteria and smell like grape Kool-Aid, was brought over from Asia and used to stabilize road banks. Unfortunately, it has infested cleared land all over the South. As you can see here, kudzu climbs trees at the edge of a forest, shades the tree leaves with its own big thick leaves, and kills the host trees because they don't have enough light for photosynthesis. With the edge trees dead, kudzu can move deeper into the forest and work on the next line of trees. A piped spring runs into a muddy spot to the right of the kudzu tangles.

A short climb takes you to a grassy meadow with many wildflowers. Proceed to the gravel road at 4.5 mi., turn left, and follow the road as it swings right through another meadow.

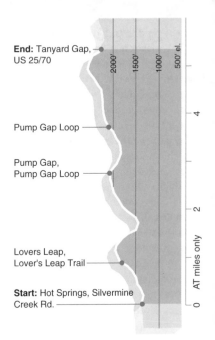

End: Tanyard Gap, US 25/70

Pump Gap Loop

Pump Gap, Pump Gap Loop

Lovers Leap, Lover's Leap Trail

Start: Hot Springs, Silvermine Creek Rd.

2000' 1500' 1000' 500' el.

AT miles only

Ascend to the open grassy top of 2600-ft. Mill Ridge, which was bought from tobacco farmers by the U.S. Forest Service in 1970. The USFS manages this area for wildlife, clearing it and planting trees and bushes that attract turkey and ruffed grouse. Turn left after the Mill Ridge sign, and descend the gravel road. In about 50 yd. two sets of double blazes signal where the AT leaves the road with a steep, short scramble up the right bank. Then the trail runs level above the road and drops down to join it

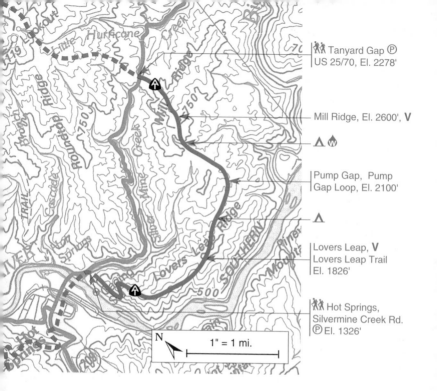

Tanyard Gap Ⓟ
US 25/70, El. 2278'

Mill Ridge, El. 2600', **V**

△ ♨

Pump Gap, Pump
Gap Loop, El. 2100'

△

Lovers Leap, **V**
Lovers Leap Trail
El. 1826'

Hot Springs,
Silvermine Creek Rd.
Ⓟ El. 1326'

N
1" = 1 mi.

again in Tanyard Gap at the concrete bridge over US 25/70 at 5.4 mi. This looks like a hiker's bridge, but cars use it also, and sometimes rather fast, so watch for traffic.

The 5.5-mi. Pump Gap Loop Trail offers an alternative route if you plan to backtrack to your car at Hot Springs. From Tanyard Gap, hike back (south on the AT) past the pond and turn right onto the yellow-blazed loop trail. It drops off the ridgetop and joins Pump Branch, going upstream to Pump Gap, and crosses the AT

again. Then it follows Silvermine Creek valley down to the Forest Service Group Camp. From there you can walk down the road to your car or take one last short, steep climb up to Lovers Leap (0.6 mi.) and return on the AT switchbacks.

Another option is to make a reservation at the Hot Springs Spa (704-622-7676) before you leave. A soak in mineral water does wonders for sore muscles or whatever else ails you. The springs, discovered in 1778, once attracted health seekers from Asheville. A turnpike and a rail line

Miles **N**	**NORTH**	Elev. (ft./m)	Miles **S**
5.3	**End:** Tanyard Gap, US 25/70; parking on old US 25.	2278/694	0.0
4.3	Pond and campsite, spring.		1.0
3.7	Jct. **Pump Gap Loop**		1.6
2.8	**Pump Gap,** jct. yellow-blazed **Pump Gap Loop** (5.5 mi.).	2100/640	2.5
0.9	**Lovers Leap,** jct. **Lovers Leap Trail** to **Silvermine Trail** (0.6 mi.); early exit option.	1826/557	4.4
0.0	**Start:** Hot Springs, Silvermine Creek Rd.; river rafting, USFS parking.	1326/404	5.3

SOUTH

brought weekend crowds to a large hotel with a European-style bathhouse. The resort fell into disuse early this century, and German prisoners of war were housed in the hotel in 1917. They built a model Bavarian village (see "War and Peace in Hot Springs" in Hike #27), which was destroyed when the war ended. A Civilian Conservation Corps (CCC) camp next occupied the area and CCC crews worked on the AT and other trails. In 1991 the mineral baths were reopened with individual sites on the riverbank rather than a large central bathhouse. The waters contain sulphate of magnesia, lime, potassium, silica, and other minerals and are said to correct anemia and help nerves, muscles, bones, and teeth. The spa office has enlarged photographs of the various hotels that have occupied the site and some of the activities here. A fountain provides free mineral water to drink, and there is a fee to use the baths. Reservations are recommended, especially on weekends.

HIKE #29
Tanyard Gap to Allen Gap

Maps: ATC Map 3, Sams Gap to Davenport Gap

Route: From Tanyard Gap to Rich Mt., to Spring Mt., to Allen Gap

Recommended direction: S to N

Distance: 8.9 mi.

Elevation +/-: 2278 to 4100 to 2234 ft.

Effort: Moderate

Day hike: Yes

Overnight backpacking hike: Optional

Duration: 6 hr.

Early exit option: Hurricane Gap, at 3.5 mi.

Natural history features: Abundant spring wildflowers

Other features: Rich Mt. fire tower

Trailhead access: *Start:* From Hot Springs, drive E on US 25/70 for 3.0 mi. Passing under hiker bridge (green AT sign), turn L onto paved road, immediately turn L again, and go back 100 yd. to end of hiker bridge. Park on R, out of the way of bridge traffic. *End:* From Hot Springs, go E on US 25/70 for 6.0 mi., then N on NC 208 for 9.0 mi. to Allen Gap. From Greeneville, go S, then E on TN 70 for 15.0 mi. TN 70 crosses AT 0.1 mi. W of gap crest.

Camping: Spring Mt. Shelter; several campsites

This hike is a low-elevation walk that winds through second-growth woods, white pine stands, and sheltered creek valleys. The high point, at the Rich Mt. fire tower, offers views of the surrounding higher mountains, and many wildflowers grow in the valleys. The hike as described here requires two cars and a 15-mi. car shuttle on winding roads. A good one-car alternative would be to hike from Tanyard Gap to Rich Mt. and backtrack (4.0 mi. round-trip). A two-car hike with a short car shuttle could be arranged by combining the Rich Mt. section of this hike with Hike #28 for a hiking total of 9.3 mi.

Midsummer hiking here can be hot, but spring and fall are pleasant, and main-road access would make this trail a good winter choice. Spring wildflowers are especially abundant between Rich Mt. and Deep Gap; bring a wildflower guidebook and a hand lens.

Hike #29 starts in North Carolina but rejoins the Tennessee/North Carolina border after Rich Mt. and then follows the ridgetop boundary between the Cherokee National Forest (Tennessee) and the Pisgah National Forest (North Carolina).

At 2278-ft. Tanyard Gap, park on old US 25, which becomes gravel. To start head along the roadbed and look for log steps up to the right. Fire rings indicate that groups have camped here, but quieter places can be found on the trail. Ascend through mountain laurel and then rhododendron, and climb the left slope of a ridge. Wintergreen and trailing arbutus grow on the trail banks. Wintergreen leaves are waxy and rounded at the end and available for chewing all year. The bright-red berries also taste good.

Turn left and descend into a white pine plantation. Watch the blazes as the AT crosses old roads and faint trails. Another set of log steps at about 0.5 mi. leads up right to a roadbed; then switchbacks lead up the side of a ridge. Over the ridge, two footbridges cross branches of a creek. Near the second bridge, look for a large patch of cinnamon fern, with 3-ft.-tall fronds growing in a circle. In spring, the central reproductive frond that produces spores has a cinnamon color, hence the name. This fern grows beside many mid-elevation creeks or wet places along the AT.

The trail then crosses several small ridges, but it generally climbs and passes open areas with views back across US 25/70. At 1.5 mi. look for a good spring (and lots more cinnamon fern) to the right. Then the AT tops another ridge and descends to log steps down an old road bank. It follows the road for 50 ft., turns right, and then rises to the junction with yellow-blazed Roundtop Ridge Trail (USFS 295) on the left at 2.0 mi. This

was the old AT route from Hot Springs and is still maintained by the U.S. Forest Service. It leads 3.1 mi. back to NC 1304 about 0.5 mi. north of the US 25/70 bridge over the French Broad River. Roundtop Ridge Trail could be used for a 5.1-mi. two-car hike with one car at Tanyard Gap and the other at Silvermine Rd. (NC 1304). Another possibility is a loop of 11.0 mi. starting at Silvermine Creek Rd., taking the AT 2.0 mi. past Tanyard Gap, and then returning on Roundtop Ridge Trail to NC 1304 (Silvermine Creek Rd.).

Just past the trail junction, a spur trail leads left for 0.2 mi. to the 3643-ft. summit of Rich Mt. This steep trail can be weedy in summer, with nettles, jewelweed, and blackberries to push through. Tangled mats of dodder grow on these tall plants. This yellow-stemmed plant has no roots or leaves; it gets all of its food from other plants. Look for its suckers and pretty white flowers, and use a hand lens to check inside the flowers for aphids, tiny beetles, or crab spiders.

On the spur trail and for the rest of this hike, watch for shagbark hickories. The name says it all: long strips of bark split and curl out from the bottom so that the main trunk looks shaggy. Shagbark hickories produce catkins (pollen-making flowers) and large sweet nuts with fleshy green hulls, eaten by squirrels, chipmunks, turkeys, bears, and even deer. The wood, like that of all hickories, is tough and is used for hoe and ax handles. The nut hulls and leaves are aromatic when crushed or pinched.

At the summit of Rich Mt., an open mowed area surrounds an old fire tower, and tall meadow wildflowers, such as sunflowers, Joe-Pye weed, and starry campion, lean in from the edges. You can climb partway up the tower to get a great view of the Smokies (southwest), the Blacks including Mt. Mitchell (southeast), and Camp Creek Bald (just 12 mi. ahead to the northeast). To the west is the deep French Broad River valley and the Bald Mts. on the other side. Here, too, is a picnic table, a Pisgah National Forest sign, two vine-covered abandoned buildings, and huge yellow letters to tell airplane pilots and aliens where they are.

Backtrack to the AT from Rich Mt. and turn left (north) down a steep stretch to a spring on the left with a tiny pool and a pipe to help fill water bottles. A campsite on the right has sassafras trees and cold running water. About 100 yd. farther there is another campsite on the right with its own blackberry patch.

The trail descends the north side of Rich Mt. through open woods, a nettle field, and more shagbark hickories. Christmas and maidenhair ferns flourish, along with Solomon's-seal, mandarin, and many other spring wildflowers on this north-facing slope. One summer flower common here is false hellebore, a poisonous plant with large parallel-veined leaves and a branched spike, up to 5 ft. tall, of tiny greenish flowers. Each flower

has three petals and three sepals and forms a perfect star about the size of a snowflake. In fall, hard green seedpods form.

After steeper descent, the trail enters a rhododendron tunnel and then reaches the Rich Mt. Fire Rd. Don't cross the first road; follow the blazes right along it, past a green Forest Service welcome sign for about 100 yd. to a gravel crossroad in Hurricane Gap at 3.5 mi. Cross USFS 422/467, and then climb the road bank into mountain laurel and pine woods. About 100 yd. past the gap is a memorial stone for Rex Pulford, who died here of a heart attack during a thru-hike in April 1983.

Ascend between patches of poison ivy to an open ridgetop with a few large maples, oaks, and tulip-trees. Sunflowers, jewelweed, Joe-Pye weed, and milkweed take advantage of the summer sun here, and grapevines and witch hazel make tangles of undergrowth.

Look for "Bear Sanctuary" signs on the right. Tennessee has five bear sanctuaries in the Cherokee National Forest; bear hunting is allowed in other places but only for a short time in December, after pregnant females are thought to have retreated into their winter dens. Each July, Tennessee Wildlife Resources agents run bait lines of open sardine cans in trees. Scratch marks on the tree bark and licked-out cans indicate bear visits (squirrels don't scratch, and birds don't lick out the corners), and comparing the number of visits from year to year gives an estimate of the bear populations. The sardine survey of 1997 estimated the bear population to be at an all-time high (at least since the surveys started); the southern Appalachian regional estimate is 3000 to 4000 bears. In 1996 some 116 bears were shot during the legal bear-hunting season.

At 5.2 mi. and 3300 ft., Spring Mt. Shelter appears beside the trail on the left, surrounded by tall weeds in summer. A narrow trail just beyond the shelter leads left to the moldering privy. The wooden shelter, which has room for five or six people, offers a picnic table, a fire ring, and, 75 yd. down a path to the right, opposite the shelter, a spring. In July and August blueberry and blackberry bushes beyond the shelter provide dessert — after your lunch of sardines. . . . Many American chestnut stump sprouts grow here.

Descend after the shelter through another wet area that has wonderful spring flowers, with bloodroot and hepatica starting the show in March. The trail climbs over a low ridge and continues down. At 6.7 mi. look for a spring a few yards to the left, tucked into a rhododendron ravine. Just 0.2 mi. farther is Deep Gap, with two campsites and a hearty chorus of cicadas in August. Little Paint Creek Trail goes left 2.5 mi. to USFS 31.

Ascend Buzzard Roost Ridge, and cross high on the side of a deep valley, where you can look down into the treetops. Then the trail starts the descent to Allen Gap through pleas-

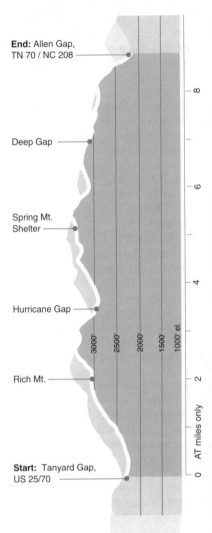

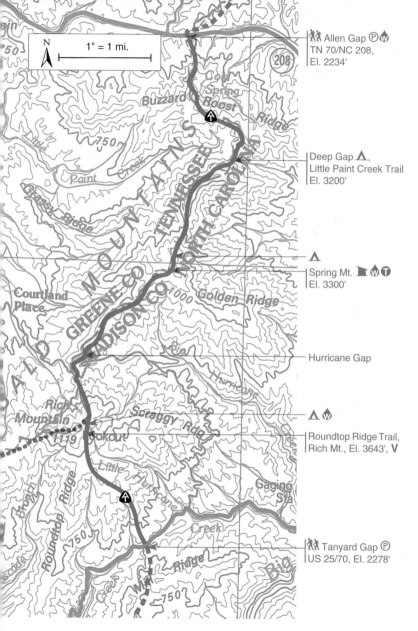

N
1" = 1 mi.

Buzzard Spring
Boost
Ridge

🚶🚶 Allen Gap Ⓟ🔥
TN 70/NC 208,
El. 2234'

Deep Gap 🔺,
Little Paint Creek Trail
El. 3200'

Little
Paint Creek

Grassy Ridge

M O U N T A I N S

T E N N E S S E E

N O R T H C A R O L I N A

G R E E N E C O.

M A D I S O N C O.

🔺

Spring Mt. 🔭🔥🚻
El. 3300'

Courtland
Place

Golden Ridge

1000

Hurricane Gap

Rich
Mountain

1119

Lookout

Scraggy Ridge

🔺🔥

Roundtop Ridge Trail,
Rich Mt., El. 3643', **V**

Little Hurricane

Gaging
Sta

Branch

Roundtop Ridge

750

Creek

🚶🚶 Tanyard Gap Ⓟ
US 25/70, El. 2278'

Gabes Mtn. Ridge

750

Big

Miles N	NORTH	Elev. (ft./m)	Miles S
8.9	**End:** Allen Gap, TN 70/NC 208; parking.	2234/681	0.0
6.9	Deep Gap, campsites, **Little Paint Creek Trail**.	3200/975	2.0
5.2	**Spring Mt. Shelter,** spring (75 yd. R) and privy.	3300/1006	3.7
3.5	Hurricane Gap; cross USFS 422/467; early exit option.		5.4
2.0	Jct. yellow-blazed **Roundtop Ridge Trail;** spur trail (0.2 mi.) to **Rich Mt. fire tower** (3643 ft.); campsites and spring just past spur trail.		6.9
0.0	**Start:** Tanyard Gap; US 25/70, parking.	2278/694	8.9

SOUTH

ant woods of Fraser magnolia, black gum, and tulip-tree. Again look for cinnamon fern beside creeks.

After a drier, level area, the trail turns down through thick rhododendron. Dog hobble, a low-elevation understory evergreen not seen on higher parts of the AT, grows under the rhododendron. It forms a tangle of arching branches that is said to hobble bear-hunting dogs because their skinny feet slip down into the tangle. Meanwhile, the bears, with their big footpads, walk right across the top.

Reach 2234-ft. Allen Gap, the end of this hike, at 8.9 mi. Cross a gravel road and go about 30 yd. through a patch of hemlock trees to reach TN 70. The AT continues straight across TN 70 for a few yards right of a large Forest Service sign. The state line is a short distance east of where the AT crosses TN 70/NC 208. Park in the tiny one- to two-car pullout at the U.S. Forest Service sign just west of the AT crossing. In summer, tall weeds make the AT difficult to locate from a moving car; park at the state line and walk back (west) 0.1 mi. along TN 70.

Allen Gap to Devil Fork Gap

Maps: ATC Map 3, Sams Gap to Davenport Gap

Route: From Allen Gap to Camp Creek Bald, to Jerry Cabin, to Flint Mt. Shelter, to Devil Fork Gap

Recommended direction: S to N

Distance: 20.2 mi.

Elevation +/-: 2234 to 4844 to 3107 ft.

Effort: Strenuous

Day hike: No

Overnight backpacking hike: Yes

Duration: 15 hr.

Early exit option: Round Knob Rd., at 3.0 mi.

Natural history features: Rock outcrops

Social history features: Shelton graves

Trailhead access: *Start:* From Hot Springs, go E on US 25/70 for 6.0 mi. Then drive N for 9.0 mi. on NC 208 to Allen Gap. From Greeneville, go S and then E on TN 70 for 15.0 mi. TN 70 crosses AT 0.1 mi. W of gap crest. *End:* From Hot Springs, drive 6.0 mi. on US 25/70. Turn L on NC 208, go 3.0 mi., and then turn L on NC 212 for 15.0 mi. to Devil Fork Gap on the NC/TN border. A large gravel parking area is on R. From Erwin, go S on US 23 to Rocky Fork. Turn R on TN 352 for 4.2 mi. to Devil Fork Gap; park on L. AT crosses road S of parking area.

Camping: Little Laurel Shelter; Jerry Cabin Shelter; Flint Mt. Shelter; several campsites

T he northern half of Hike #30 borders the Bald Mt. Ridge Scenic Area in the Cherokee National Forest, and the AT runs along a rugged, isolated crest. Outstanding high views, masses of rhododendron and mountain laurel, plus good campsites and shelters make this an excellent choice for a 2- or 3- day backpack. With increasing demand for outdoor recreation and the extension of I-26 to upper east Tennessee, access to trails in this area may become easier, but for now it's remote. On one beautiful fall hike here I met only two other hikers, one from Germany and one from Ireland.

Caution: The AT is well blazed and well maintained throughout this section and is easy to follow, but side trails vary in difficulty and conditions. Do not attempt them without current maps and information from the U.S. Forest Service. Contact the Nolichucky Ranger District (Tennessee trails) or the Appalachian Ranger District. Most Forest Service trails are marked with yellow rectangles, but their presence on a map does not mean they are maintained.

To get started, from the crest of

Hiker with trusty companion

Allen Gap walk about 0.1 mi. north on TN 70, and look for AT blazes and a stone Forest Service sign on the road bank. Ascend, swing left, and then turn left again on a small ridge parallel to the road below. Other trails wind through this area, part of which is private land. Watch the white blazes carefully. After cresting two more ridges, the trail descends and crosses Log Cabin Rd. at 1.6 mi. with two log houses on the right. The AT ascends, with one level rest spot, for the next 3.0 mi. on well-graded sidehill trail. White pines, hemlocks, and red oaks predominate in quiet woods. Occasional winter views to the left show Paint Creek Valley and Green Mt.

At 4.9 mi. the trail reaches Little Laurel Shelter, a low stone shelter on the right that faces away from the trail, accommodates five or six, and has a picnic table and a fire ring. A blue-blazed trail leads left about 100 yd. to a piped spring.

After the shelter, there is another mile of climbing, and the trail now becomes rocky in spots. The forest changes with higher elevation: white pines disappear, and red maples and American beeches become common. Beeches have elegantly toothed leaves and smooth gray bark (sometimes marred with initials; please don't carve yours—leave that to the bears, whose claw marks you may see on beech trunks). The leaves turn a golden-bronze color in fall, and some young trees show the same color in their first spring leaves. In September, beeches drop large quantities of triangular nuts in spiny husks. They taste as sweet as chestnuts when roasted but require more work. In winter, beeches are recognizable by the smooth bark and the buds that are pointed like spines. The nuts of the beech family (including beeches, chestnuts, and oaks) provide mast, or high-energy food, for many animals. Bears depend on mast for hibernation fat, and turkey, grouse, squirrels, and other animals feed on mast all winter. The chestnut blight had profound effects on animal populations of eastern woods, but oaks and beeches are providing more mast as protected forests are allowed to mature.

The trail gets rockier, goes through switchbacks, descends a bit, and at 6.2 mi. reaches a junction with a rocky side trail that leads left 0.2 mi. to Camp Creek Bald. At 4844 ft., Camp Creek Bald is the highest point on the AT since Mt. Cammerer in the Smokies. A large communications tower (not climbable) has replaced the old fire tower, and a rough road from the Tennessee side brings caretakers up to the bunker next to the tower. About 0.2 mi. down the road from the tower is Jones Meadow, a several-acre grassy area with excellent views of the Smokies and the Black Mts. of North Carolina. A developer built Viking Mt. Resort around Jones Meadow, but it failed, and the Forest Service acquired the land. Camping is possible on Jones Meadow, but you'll have to carry water.

Backtrack to the AT, and turn left (north); the trail swings left around the summit of Camp Creek Bald and descends to cross an old road at 6.9 mi. The AT then enters a thick stand of rhododendron, and at 7.0 mi. a side trail leads 100 yd. left to a jeep track — another way up to Jones Meadow.

The AT continues to circle below the summit and then ascends on switchbacks past a spring at 7.9 mi. At 8.0 mi., a short side trail leads to White Rock Cliffs with an excellent view to the southeast of Mt. Mitchell and the Black Mts.

The AT ascends, and at 8.2 mi. it passes two spur trails to Blackstaff Cliffs on the left. Each climbs about 100 yd. through tangled rhododen-dron to rock promontories surrounded by mountain laurel, blueberry bushes, and Catawba rhododendron. The view is across a deep gulf to Camp Creek Bald and Jones Meadow. The rock of these cliffs is white quartz with a healthy population of lichens. Beyond Camp Creek Bald is a view north of the Green Mts., the Nolichucky Valley, and the long, straight ridges of east Tennessee.

The trail continues through rhododendron, on a raised trailbed. Along this ridgetop, with no shade trees and acidic soil that holds water, the rhododendrons produce masses of blooms in July. A blue-blazed side trail leads L to Jones Meadow.

At 8.4 mi. the trail reaches Bearwallow Gap (3940 ft.) and a junction with Jerry Miller Trail, which leads down to USFS Hickey Fork Rd. in about 4.0 mi. I don't know if bears wallow here, but I have met several bear-hunting dogs on this trail. The dogs wear radio collars that send a signal when the dog stands on its hind legs, which it is most likely to do when it has treed a bear. While the dogs are doing all the work, the hunters relax at a campground until they get a signal.

The trail forks after Bearwallow Gap. The left, blue-blazed fork is the old AT, which swings north of the ridgetop. The current AT (right fork) climbs on boulder steps through twisted rhododendron and mountain laurel and in less than 0.5 mi. emerges onto the exposed quartzite rocks of the Firescald, so called because of the logging fires that cleared it nearly a century ago. For almost a mile the trail follows this ridge crest with a few rocky scrambles. Shrubby Catawba rhododendron blooms lavender in spring, and blueberries get ripe in August. Views of Tennessee and North Carolina are spectacular, one of the main benefits of moving the trail to this ridgetop.

However, hikers will be the tallest objects, and the narrow ridge offers no retreat. In stormy, icy, or foggy weather, use the left fork bypass trail, which rejoins the Firescald in 1.5 mi.

As you return to the woods after the Firescald, look for little brown jug, a type of wild ginger, around the bases of some of the boulders. It has leathery, evergreen, heart-shaped leaves that smell like ginger when crushed. The "jugs," also called little pigs, are fleshy brown flowers that attract fungus gnats or small beetles for pollination, some of which get trapped on the sticky inner surface and never get out.

The trail returns to the ridgetop, and at 10.6 mi. a jeep road merges from the left. This road leads 2.0 mi. down to Round Knob Picnic Area on Round Knob Road (USFS 88). This pleasant Forest Service facility has a covered pavilion, toilets, and hiker parking. USFS 88 is rough but usually passable by cars. It could be used as access to day hikes, but check with the Forest Service for maps and current conditions.

The AT and the jeep road continue together along the ridgetop, ascend

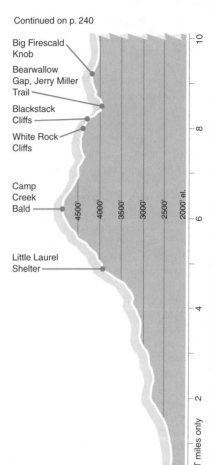

Continued on p. 240

Big Firescald Knob

Bearwallow Gap, Jerry Miller Trail

Blackstack Cliffs

White Rock Cliffs

Camp Creek Bald

Little Laurel Shelter

Start: Allen Gap, TN 70

AT miles only

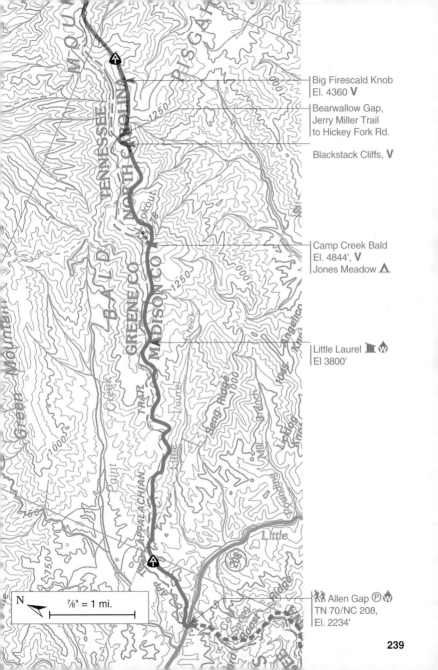

Big Firescald Knob
El. 4360 **V**

Bearwallow Gap,
Jerry Miller Trail
to Hickey Fork Rd.

Blackstack Cliffs, **V**

Camp Creek Bald
El. 4844', **V**
Jones Meadow ▲

Little Laurel 🏕️ 💧
El 3800'

Allen Gap Ⓟ 💧
TN 70/NC 208,
El. 2234'

N   ⅞" = 1 mi.

239

past tall white pines, and meet the Fork Ridge Trail coming in from the right at 11.4 mi. This steep, rough trail leads 2.0 mi. down to gravel USFS 111.

From the Fork Ridge trail junction, the AT descends past oaks, yellow birches, and big gnarled sugar maples. After a patch of mountain laurel, the trail opens into a broad grassy area at 11.6 mi. The Jerry Cabin Shelter is on the right, with water, privy, and possibly social events. Sam Waddle, a trail volunteer from Chuckey, Tennessee, maintained this shelter from 1972–2004. A trail to the right behind the cabin leads 20 yd. to the privy, and a trail on the other side of the AT goes 100 yd. to the spring. Please don't camp at Jerry Cabin — the grass looks nice and shouldn't be flattened under a tent. Just 100 yd. farther on the AT is Chestnut Log Gap with good campsites.

Beyond Chestnut Log Gap, the jeep road goes left and the AT turns right and climbs the ridge via stone steps and switchbacks. Open areas on Coldspring Mt. provide views of the Nolichucky River Valley and Greeneville, named for Revolutionary War General Nathanael Greene. The AT rises for about a mile, then descends to the right into a rocky ravine that requires some scrambling. At 13.5 mi. the trail climbs steeply and meets a 30-yd. side trail up the rocky face of well-named Big Rock (4838 ft.). Greeneville spreads out at the foot of the mountain; Camp Creek Bald is visible to the southwest, fog willing,

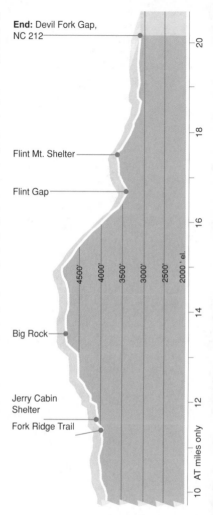

End: Devil Fork Gap, NC 212

Flint Mt. Shelter

Flint Gap

Big Rock

Jerry Cabin Shelter

Fork Ridge Trail

AT miles only

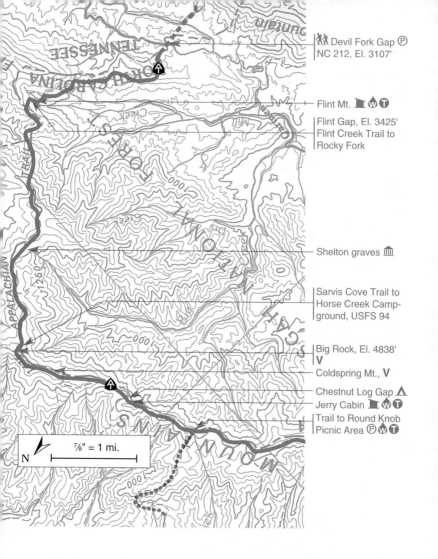

XX Devil Fork Gap Ⓟ
NC 212, El. 3107'

Flint Mt. ◼ⓌⓉ

Flint Gap, El. 3425'
Flint Creek Trail to
Rocky Fork

Shelton graves 🏛

Sarvis Cove Trail to
Horse Creek Camp-
ground, USFS 94

Big Rock, El. 4838'
V

Coldspring Mt., **V**

Chestnut Log Gap △

Jerry Cabin ◼ⓌⓉ

Trail to Round Knob
Picnic Area ⒫ⓌⓉ

⅞" = 1 mi.

N

and Unaka and Roan Mts. may be visible to the east. In August, look for blueberries.

Scramble down Big Rock, and continue on the AT to meet a dirt road 100 yd. ahead. Trail and road cross a large meadow, partly grown up with brambles, with more excellent views of the Nolichucky River valley on the left. Blazes are on isolated buckeye trees. In fall, look for the apple-sized buckeye hulls containing two or three mahogany-colored buckeyes. Rub one in your hands or on oily parts of your face to make it glow with an even richer color. In deep woods the squirrels grab buckeyes almost before they leave the tree, but out in the open the nuts fall on the ground.

Look for a small pond to the right of the grassy area. Probably dug for cattle when grazing was permitted, it now raises frogs and mosquitoes.

The AT approaches Big Butt Mt. and reaches a blue-blazed trail to the left with a sign for Sarvis Cove Trail. The Horse Creek Campground Trail intersects the AT just past the Sarvis Cove Trail in a mowed meadow. The AT turns right and passes another blue-blazed trail to the right that leads to a spring in about a 5-min. walk. Then it enters a stand of white pines on a possibly muddy jeep road.

At 15.0 mi. the AT passes the Shelton graves on the right in a wide cleared area. William and David Shelton were Union soldiers in the Civil War, as were men from many East Tennessee mountain families. To return home on leave, they had to pass through Confederate towns in the North Carolina valleys. The Sheltons and a boy were ambushed and killed near here. There were many similar events along this border, which divided sympathies as well as states. Folklorist Sheila Kay Davis sings a ballad from nearby Sodom, North Carolina, in which a Union soldier comes home because his wife's baby is due. After the successful birth, he tries to slip away at dawn but is caught and killed.

The AT ascends easily for another 0.5 mi., swings left, and descends steeply on a rocky road with switchbacks. Watch blazes carefully in this section; several other roads cross the AT, but double white blazes mark the intersections. If you notice logs across the trail or branches at face level, stop and look for a blaze. If none is visible, backtrack until you see one.

At 16.3 mi. the AT turns left from the road and descends steep trail to 3425-ft. Flint Gap at 16.7 mi. Flint Creek Trail goes left from the gap and passes several waterfalls on its way down to Rocky Fork in 4.0 mi.

The AT then ascends from Flint Gap about 0.5 mi. to a rocky ridge crest and continues down a sandy, south-facing slope to Flint Mt. Shelter at 17.5 mi. This attractive log shelter, which faces east, was built by the Carolina Mt. Club in 1988. A table, benches, fire ring, and a moldering privy complete the amenities, and water is available from a creek and piped spring about 100 yd. beyond the shelter on the AT.

From the shelter the AT meanders down across a series of ridges with easy ups and downs. Many chipmunks live in a boulder field about a mile beyond the shelter. Look for their holes near the trail, and listen for their sharp metallic squeaks as you interrupt their peace. If you sit quietly for a while, you may see one dash across the trail with a hickory nut.

At 19.0 mi. the AT turns left onto an easy railroad grade and follows it for nearly a mile through forest of maple, hickory, and Fraser magnolia. At 19.6 mi. the AT leaves the grade and climbs steeply on log steps to get over the last large ridge of this hike. Again, watch the blazes. The trail then traverses a series of smaller ridges through a patch of white pines, a rhododendron thicket, and finally thin woods before a set of log steps leads down to Devil Fork Gap at 20.2 mi. The AT continues directly across the road, and the large gravel parking area is up to the left.

Miles N	**NORTH**	Elev. (ft./m)	Miles S
20.2	**End: Devil Fork Gap,** NC 212; parking.	3107/947	0.0
17.5	**Flint Mt. Shelter,** privy, piped spring 100 yd. down AT.	3570/1088	2.7
16.7	**Flint Gap;** jct. **Flint Creek Trail** to Rocky Fork (4.0 mi.); waterfalls.	3425/1044	3.5
15.0	**Shelton graves.**		5.2
13.5	Side trail 100 ft. on R to **Big Rock.**	4838/1475	6.7
11.7	**Chestnut Log Gap;** campsite, water.		8.5
11.6	**Jerry Cabin Shelter,** privy 20 yd. R, spring 100 yd. NW.	4150/1265	8.6
11.4	Jct. **Fork Ridge Trail** to USFS 111 (2.0 mi.).		8.8
10.6	Jct. jeep road to USFS **Round Knob Picnic Area** on Round Knob Rd./USFS 88 (3.0 mi.) toilets, picnic area, parking; early exit option.		9.6
9.2	**Big Firescald Knob**		10.8
8.4	**Bearwallow Gap;** jct. **Jerry Miller Trail** to USFS Hickory Fork Rd. (4.0 mi.).	3940/1201	11.8
8.2	Spur trails to **Blackstack Cliffs** (100 yd. L), view.		12.0
8.0	Spur trail to **White Rock Cliffs,** excellent view.		12.2
6.2	Steep, rocky trail to **Camp Creek Bald** (0.2 mi.), communications tower (not climbable); spur trail to **Jones Meadow** (0.4 mi.), view and camping.	4844/1476	14.0
4.9	**Little Laurel Shelter;** blue-blazed spur trail 100 yd. L to piped spring.	3620/1103	15.3
1.6	Cross Old Hayesville Rd.		18.6
0.0	**Start: Allen Gap,** TN 70/NC 208; parking, grocery store.	2234/681	20.2

SOUTH

HIKE #31
Devil Fork Gap to Sams Gap

Maps: ATC Map 3, Sams Gap to Davenport Gap

Route: From Devil Fork Gap to Rice Gap, to High Rock, to Sams Gap

Recommended direction: S to N

Distance: 8.2 mi.

Elevation +/-: 3107 to 4460 to 3800 ft.

Effort: Strenuous

Day hike: Yes

Overnight backpacking hike: Optional

Duration: 6 to 7 hr.

Early exit option: Rice Gap, at 4.9 mi.

Natural history features: High Rock; old-growth trees

Social history feature: Southern Appalachian farms

Trailhead access: *Start:* From Hot Springs, NC, go 6.0 mi. E on US 25/70. Turn L on NC 208 and go 3.0 mi. Turn R on NC 212 (at Shelton Laurel Massacre historical sign) and go 15.0 mi. to Devil Fork Gap on the NC/TN border, marked by state border signs. A large gravel parking area is on the R. From Erwin, TN, take US 23 S to Exit 12. Turn L to go under US 23 and immediately turn R onto US 19W/TN 352. In 1.0 mi. go straight on TN 352 (US 19W turns L) for 5.0 mi. to Rocky Fork. Turn R to continue on TN 352 for 4.2 mi. to Devil Fork Gap; park on L. The AT crosses the road W (NC side) of the parking area. Look for a blazed wood-plank stile into a pasture over a barbed-wire fence that shows AT crossing. Look for AT Parking where US 23 goes under I-26 at Sams Gap. *End:* From Erwin, take US 23 S for 20.0 mi., or 12.0 mi. from junction with NC 352. From Asheville, take I-26 about 31.0 mi. N to Wolf Laurel, Exit 3. Turn L and go 5 miles on US 23 to AT parking.

Camping: Hogback Ridge Shelter; several campsites

Everything is backward on this AT section: You hike south to go north, Tennessee lies east of North Carolina, and one of the best views is from a gap. The state border that this hike follows also defines the border of the Cherokee National Forest (Tennessee) and the Pisgah National Forest (North Carolina). Hike #31 covers a pleasant and little-used section of the AT through ridgetop woods that were grazing lands just a few decades ago. In many cases, cleared farmlands saved adjacent pockets of mature woods from logging, and here the trail alternates between rapidly growing new forest and old-growth areas of large trees. Additionally, the area's knobs provide plenty of aerobic exercise. In April, fringed phacelia flowers cover the ground on parts of this section like a spring snowfall. Take a hand lens along to see the lavender anthers and the exquisite lacy fringes of their five petals.

Note: The AT at Sams Gap, the northern end of this hike, goes under I-26. During the construction of this interstate, the AT was relocated several times, and negotiations between the Federal Highway Administration and the ATC led to the safe and pleasant current AT route. Regional planner Benton MacKaye envisioned the AT in 1921; he also helped draw plans for the interstate highway system—so this hike provides the opportunity to observe a surprising junction of two of MacKaye's visions.

From the North Carolina side of the Devil Fork Gap parking area, cross a barbed-wire fence on a stile with white blazes. Watch for cows and check for apples on an old tree left of the stile. The AT curves right, ascends through a pasture along blazed posts, and in 0.1 mi. enters white-pine woods. It then crosses two more stiles about 100 yd. apart, reaches a ridgetop at 0.2 mi., descends on switchbacks, and crosses paved Rector Laurel Rd. at 0.5 mi., with houses on the left. This crossing is 1.3 mi. from TN 352 (to the left) and may be obscured in summer with head-high weeds. Go straight across the road, and then cross a creek on a footbridge.

The trail becomes level as it traverses an overgrown field and old road, passes under a power line, and

enters a thick patch of rhododendron, hopping over the creek again on stepping stones. After passing a sturdy old barn on the right, the trail climbs a steep hillside on log steps and turns right to a tiny cemetery at 0.8 mi. It reaches the next ridge crest, descends to and crosses a creek, then ascends past a sagging old barn and the remains of a log cabin.

The trail continues snaking up ridges and crossing creeks, sometimes on stepping stones and twice on footlogs. Steps and excellent trail work make this steep climb easier. At about 1.4 mi. bear left and pass a large open campsite demarked by barbed wire on the far side. The AT enters thin woods. Watch for a large rock on the left that looks like a rhino-sized guinea pig facing up the trail. Another flat rock in front of the "guinea pig" provides a good viewing bench for this upthrust-and-subsequent-erosion artwork, while across the trail is a good-flowing spring.

Ascend through beech woods with beech drops, twiggy brown parasitic flowers that get food from beech roots. At 1.8 mi. the AT reaches 4000-ft. Sugarloaf Gap, a level, open area adorned with some very old apple trees, blackberries, and sumacs that turn fiery red in the fall. Old fields extend down each side from the gap, and there's a good view northeast of No Business Knob and the Unaka Mts.

At 2.1 mi. the AT ascends along a

Southern AT Peak Experiences

- **The best flame azalea blooms:** Deep Gap to Standing Indian Mt. (Hike #9)
- **The best mountain laurel blooms:** Tellico Gap to Wesser (Hike #14)
- **The best rhododendron blooms:** Carvers Gap to Roan High Bluff (Hike #37) or Iron Mt. (a private showing) (Hike #42)
- **The best aerobic challenge:** Unicoi Gap to Dicks Creek Gap (Hike #6) or Hughes Gap to Roan High Knob (Hike #36)
- **The best waterfall:** Laurel Creek Falls (Hike #40)
- **The best view:** Hump Mt. (Hike #38)
- **The biggest shelter:** Overmountain (Hike #38)
- **The smallest shelter:** near McQueens Gap (Hike #45)
- **The highest elevation:** 6643 ft. at Clingmans Dome (Hike #20 and Hike #21)
- **The lowest elevation:** 1326 ft. at Hot Springs (Hike #28)
- **The most likely for bear sightings:** Fontana Dam to Shuckstack (Hike #18)
- **The best blueberries:** Deep Gap (Hike #34) or Spence Field (Hikes #19 and #20)
- **The best spring wildflowers:** Lemon Gap to Max Patch (Hike #26)
- **The best fall colors:** Charlies Bunion (Hike #22)
- **The best cross-country skiing:** Roan High Knob (Hike #37)

barbed-wire fence on a smooth dirt path that may be slippery when wet. It climbs steeply, with trees on the right and tall weeds and blackberries on the left. After crossing an old road twice at a level spot, it climbs again to the summit of Frozen Knob at 3.3 mi. From Flag Pond and other nearby communities, Frozen Knob appears as a pointed peak, and it probably gets covered with frost or snow when it is still warm in the valley. A view to the northeast of the Bald Mts. from Frozen Knob is partially obscured by young trees.

Turn right and walk down the middle of a ridge on rocky trail. In about 0.5 mi. reach level Big Flat, with a camping area on the left but no nearby water source.

The trail continues down, switching back on steeper parts. The old AT went straight down to the next gap, but a relocation has more switchbacks and less erosion. It's still a long way down. Along the way in March, look for spring beauty and hepatica. When a Cherokee maiden wanted a man to fall in love with her, she surreptitiously scattered powdered hepatica leaves on his clothes. We disclaim all responsibility for use of this information.

At 4.9 mi., the trail swings right on a level spot and then descends a roadbank into 3800-ft. Rice Gap. To the left, the gravel road descends to Flag Pond in about 6.0 mi. The AT goes straight across the road and passes over big earthen bumps (sometimes called tank stoppers) that prevent erosion and off-road-vehicle use.

The trail climbs gently for 0.3 mi. out of the gap, becomes level, and at 6.0 mi. reaches a blue-blazed side trail that leads 0.1 mi. right to Hogback Ridge Shelter and a spring (about 450 yd. west of the shelter) and a privy with a view.

From the shelter the AT climbs a series of knobs and at 6.5 mi. reaches a 150-yd. side trail to 4460-ft. High Rock, a rock outcrop with excellent winter views to the east. Red maples and other trees obscure the view in summer. Then the trail starts the descent to Sams Gap along an old fence line. A relocation has moved the trail slightly south of its original route because of the interstate construction. At a patch of small black locust trees, the trail turns right and crosses the old fence into a weedy meadow. There are a few blazes on posts, and the trail is well worn. It swings left and crosses the top of the open area that has a view to the right down a cleared valley. Tulip-trees, hickories, and black locusts are growing fast in this field; soon some of them will be large enough to hold blazes.

The trail turns right along a wall of trees, descends about 0.1 mi., then switches back to the left to enter a

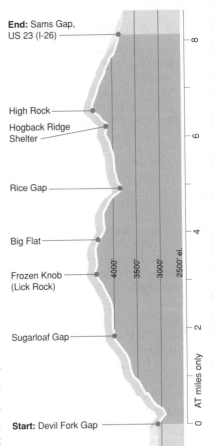

1" = 1 mi.

N

🏃🏃 Sams Gap ⓟ US 23
(I-26), El. 3800'

High Rock, El. 4460', **V**

Hogback Ridge ▮ Ⓦ Ⓣ
El. 4300'

Rice Gap, El. 3800',
road to Flag Pond

Big Flat ▲

Sugarloaf Gap
El. 4000'

Rector Laurel Rd.

🏃🏃 Devil Fork Gap ⓟ
TN 352/NC 208,
El. 3107'

strip of woods. Look for giant (2 to 3 ft. tall) Jack-in-the-pulpits here. The AT continues down, switches back right again, and then turns toward the highway. The trail passes a fenced atmosphere testing station, goes right for 100 ft. down a steep dirt road to US 23. Turn right and in about 200 ft, go under I-26 for AT parking on right.

HIKE #31 Itinerary

Miles N	**NORTH**	Elev. (ft./m)	Miles S
8.2	**End:** Sams Gap; US 23, parking.	3800/1158	0.0
6.5	Side trail to **High Rock** (150 yd.); excellent winter views.	4460/1359	1.7
6.0	Blue-blazed side trail to **Hogback Ridge Shelter** (0.1 mi.), spring and privy.	4300/1310	2.2
4.9	**Rice Gap;** jct. rough gravel road to Flag Pond (6.0 mi.); early exit option.	3800/1158	3.3
3.8	**Big Flat,** campsite.		4.4
3.3	Summit, **Frozen Knob.**		4.9
1.8	**Sugarloaf Gap,** old apple trees, view.	4000/1219	6.4
1.4	Large, open campsite.		6.8
0.0	**Start:** Devil Fork Gap, TN 352/NC 208, parking.	3107/947	8.2

SOUTH

Sams Gap to Spivey Gap

Maps: ATC Map 2, Moreland Gap to Sams Gap

Route: From Sams Gap to Street Gap, to Big Bald, to Spivey Gap

Recommended direction: S to N

Distance: 13.6 mi.

Elevation +/-: 3800 to 5516 to 3200 ft.

Effort: Strenuous

Day hike: No

Overnight backpacking hike: Yes

Duration: 9 to 10 hr.

Natural history features: Big Bald; High Rocks

Social history feature: Birth of an interstate

Trailhead access: From Erwin, take US 23 S for 20.0 mi., or 12.0 mi. from junction with NC 352. From Asheville, take I-26 about 31 mi. N to Exit 3 (Wolf Laurel). Turn L and go 5 mi. on US 23 to AT parking. Look for AT sign and blazes on a stile on other side of US 23. *End:* From Erwin, go S on US 23 to Exit 12. Turn L under US 23, and immediately turn R on US 19 W/TN 352. In 1.0 mi., turn L (S) on US 19W (Spivey Gap Rd.) for 7.6 mi. Pass state border signs at gap crest and go 0.3 mi. farther to large gravel pullout on R. AT crosses 20 yd. N of pullout. Blazes are hard to see from the road; look for log steps up the bank for AT going N and a narrow path directly opposite for AT going S. A 30-yd. side trail from N edge of parking area also connects to southbound AT.

Camping: Big Bald Shelter; several campsites

R emote high-elevation forest, over a mile of grassy bald with panoramic views, and masses of spring wildflowers make Hike #32 inviting. High-meadow Big Bald, halfway between Sams Gap and Spivey Gap, is awash with summer flowers and, of course, blueberries and blackberries in August. This section of the AT runs northeast, and the first few miles are moderate hiking with little elevation change. The knobs toward Spivey Gap add a little more challenge. Mileage starts at Sams Gap on the state line and includes a 0.1-mi. road walk to the trailhead. Parking is plentiful at both Sams and Spivey gaps. A good one-car option would be to hike from either gap to Big Bald (13.6 mi. round-trip either way). The hike from Sams Gap to Big Bald would be the easier one, with less elevation change.

Caution: Big Bald can be dangerous in bad weather. Check the weather report before starting on this hike, and use the Big Bald bypass trail for safety if conditions turn bad.

From the AT parking area near the crest of Sams Gap, cross US 23 and look for stile and AT sign. Climb about 100 yd. up a gravel road, then turn left onto a grassy roadbed that twists and turns up a south-facing slope with oak, sassafras, hickory, and cucumber magnolia. Swing left and cross a ridge crest at 0.6 mi. The trail heads up the right side of a deep valley with two good springs and several smaller seeps on the left. Maidenhair ferns, which spread out like horizontal fans from skinny black stalks, thrive here.

Just before the trail reaches the ridgetop and an old fence, it swings right at 1.6 mi. onto what seems to be a land bridge across the top of the valley. Talc (magnesium tetrasilicate) was mined here, and a lot of earth was pushed around to get at it. This mineral, a type of soapstone, forms when two kinds of metamorphic rocks are crushed against each other for a long period, and it gets the lowest score on a mineral hardness scale. (Quartz, common along the southern AT, gets a seven, and diamonds, not so common, get a perfect ten.) Trees and vines have now covered the excavations.

The AT takes switchbacks up the other side of the valley and ascends past sugar maples. At 2.0 mi., the trail crests a hill with a small campsite on the right, then emerges to a cleared field with a view ahead of Big Bald and the Wolf Laurel development. Descend through an overgrown field crowded with sumac, Queen Anne's lace, goldenrod, and brilliant purple ironweed in late summer. Turn right and descend through the field with woods on left and continue down.

At 2.6 mi. swing left into 4100-ft. Street Gap with a gravel road across it. (To the left in about 6.0 mi. is Flag Pond; to the right for 0.6 mi. the road is steep, but it becomes passable Puncheon Fork Rd., which heads south to US 23 in about 5.0 mi.)

The AT follows a gated dirt road out of the gap and climbs to a powerline clearing. A fence demarking private property borders the AT on the right.

At 3.7 mi. the AT curves left, away from the road, and descends along the side of a ridge. At 3.8 mi. there's a campsite in open beech woods, and a blue-blazed trail leads 20 yd. left to a spring.

The trail ascends easily through a north-facing slope of mixed hardwoods and then more open beech woods with ferns. Trout lilies and spring beauties are part of the first wave (in March) of flowers here. Trout lilies have mottled leaves and yellow flowers with dark-red stamens. When the flower is ready to open, it hangs down from a stalk like a banana, and if enough sun hits it, it opens petal by petal like a banana peeling itself. At night or if the day turns cold, it closes back up to repeat the process until it gets pollinated. Spring beauty has a white flower with pink candy stripes on each petal to guide pollinators to the nectar. The second wave of spring flowers here (in April) includes trillium, blue cohosh, and Jack-in-the-pulpit.

At 4.0 mi., the AT almost reaches 4300-ft. Low Gap, 50 yd. to the right on the ridge crest. An old road from the left joins the AT for an easy descent, with private land and the ridge crest to the right. Deciduous trees and moist soil encourage, trillium, fringed phacelia, Solomon's-seal, and a carpet of other spring flowers.

At about 4.5 mi. the trail meets the ridgetop, which provides another view ahead of Big Bald. There's a campsite in open beech woods, and a blue-blazed trail leads right to a spring.

After the campsite, pass electric lines to the right, and follow easy level trail for about a mile through even more spring flowers. Their strategy is simple: Bloom in the spring sunlight before the hardwoods grow their leaves and shade the forest floor.

Look for black cherry trees: tall straight trunks with almost black scales with upturned edges. Flower clusters appear in April, and many birds eat the cherries in late summer. This is the largest native cherry, and when the unrestrained loggers of the early decades of this century didn't have time to harvest everything, they searched out the black cherries because the red-streaked wood makes strong and beautiful furniture. Along the AT corridor and in other protected areas, black cherries are growing big again.

At 6.0 mi. the trail climbs, passing a blue-blazed trail on the left that leads about 300 ft. down to a spring. At 6.1 mi. the AT goes to the left of a signboard (empty at the time of this writing) and the blue-blazed Big Bald bypass trail goes right. Big Bald is high, exposed, and dangerous in snow, ice, dense fog, and thunderstorms. Take the bypass in bad weather.

After the trail junction, the AT enters beech woods and climbs a rocky section. Some of the rock here may be 1.1 billion years old, formed during Precambrian times, before our familiar continents split apart.

A short climb through rhododendron brings you to the edge of Big Bald at 6.5 mi. Follow blazes on short posts for a steep climb through meadow grasses, tall summer flowers, and short trees. The most common tree is hawthorn, which displays long thorns and haws, the hawthorn berries, which look like little apples. The haws may hang on the trees all winter—or until a flock of hungry cedar waxwings visits.

At 6.8 mi. the AT reaches the high knob of Big Bald at 5516 ft., the highest point on the AT since the Smokies, marked by a post and a U.S. Geological Survey benchmark. A road climbs Big Bald from the left, and vehicles might be parked at the summit. If you want a private lunch spot (or if the wind thinks your sandwich is a kite), go past the mowed area and hide in the blueberry bushes.

The view to the east is the dark spruce cap of Unaka Mt., with the lighter Beauty Spot Bald in front and Mt. Mitchell—at 6684 ft. the highest point east of the Mississippi—more distant to the right of Unaka Mt. The Smokies, Erwin, No Business Knob, Temple Ridge, Pisgah National Forest, and the ski slopes of the Wolf Laurel development are also visible. The closer view is of a classic southern Appalachian bald with shrubs and windswept trees. The trees around the edge creep in a little each year, and this bald may be forested soon, leaving only the mystery of how the balds formed in the first place.

Descend on switchbacks, and at 7.0 mi. cross gravel Wolf Laurel Rd., where the blue-blazed Big Bald bypass trail rejoins the AT from the right. A trail on the right leads 0.3 mi. to a spring and campsite.

The trail continues straight through a meadow of tall grasses, filmy angelica, goldenrod, and ironweed. Serviceberry, a small tree in the rose family, blooms on the bald and the hillsides before most trees produce leaves. When people in the valleys saw its white bloom, they knew it was about time for the preacher to ride up the mountain to perform the weddings, funerals, or baptisms that had to wait until winter was over.

The trail descends, passes boulders on the left, and goes down log steps to cross a roadbed. It then enters woods of gnarled beech and yellow birch.

Stillman Hanson

View from an Appalachian bald

At 7.9 mi., after a steep, rocky section, a sign indicates AT mileages and a trail to the left to Bald Mt. Shelter, built by volunteers in 1985. This shelter is larger than most in this area; it has room for ten people and a generous overhanging roof for cooking and eating in wet weather. The three-sided privy is 50 yd. behind the shelter.

Descend past large yellow birches with an understory of viburnum, or hobblebush —so called because its branches bend over and tend to root where they touch the ground. The resulting snares can hobble, or trip, off-trail hikers. Beech and viburnum grow in high-elevation forests; yellow birches grow at all elevations, but they seem most exuberant up here around 5000 ft.

At 8.3 mi. a short trail goes left to a campsite among beeches. Water is available from a creek across the AT or from a spring 0.2 mi. farther down the side trail. The AT continues down the ridge and joins an old roadbed. This ridgetop is windy and a rough place for trees; broken crowns and branches, burls, and twisted shapes show long-term wind pressure.

After gentle ups and downs, the AT climbs to 5185-ft. Little Bald at 9.3 mi. Now tree-covered, it has impressive rock slabs pointing northwest and large red oaks. Descend steeply at first and then easily along the crest of a ridge to Whistling Gap (perhaps named for the wind blowing through it, which has been strong every time I've hiked here) at 11.2 mi. There's a level campsite here, and water is available on a 0.1-mi. side trail to the left.

At 11.6 mi. reach a blue-blazed trail that leads right 0.1 mi. to High Rocks, an exposed rock basin about the size of a motel room. When dry, it is about as comfortable as rock can be and a good place to sunbathe, eat lunch, and look back on the big climbs of this hike, visible to the west and now behind you.

From High Rocks it's all downhill to Spivey Gap, but some of it is through jumbles of rocks and along the base of a cliff. Look for pink quartz and thick quartz veins, and

Continued on p.258

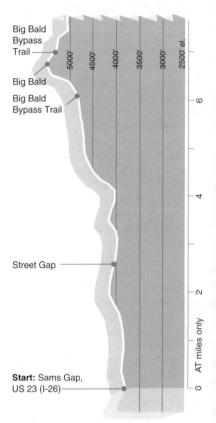

notice how the trail workers integrated level, convenient steps with the outcrops and slabs. At about 12.2 mi. the descent becomes easier and passes through deciduous moist woods of tulip-tree, red maple, and striped maple. Rocky wet areas have Christmas ferns and many trilliums.

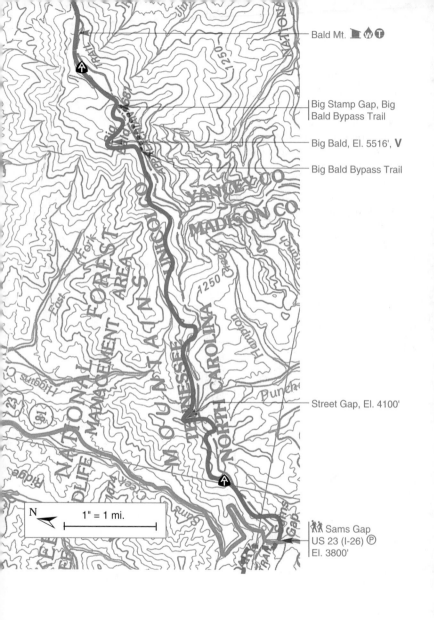

Bald Mt.

Big Stamp Gap, Big Bald Bypass Trail

Big Bald, El. 5516', **V**

Big Bald Bypass Trail

Street Gap, El. 4100'

Sams Gap
US 23 (I-26) Ⓟ
El. 3800'

N
1" = 1 mi.

Descend on more artistic rock and log steps and cross tiny creeks. A ridgetop opening provides a view, left, of the Nolichucky River valley, and then the trail enters hemlock and white pine woods. Look for deer or rabbits in a game clearing (maintained by the Forest Service to increase game populations) to the left at 13.4 mi., and then cross a creek on stepping stones and ascend to US 19W at 13.6 mi. To reach the parking area, turn right just after the creek. To continue north on the AT, cross US 19W to steps on the opposite bank.

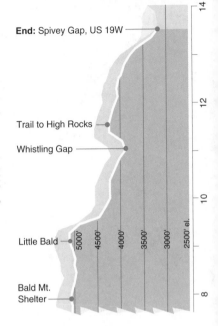

End: Spivey Gap, US 19W

Trail to High Rocks

Whistling Gap

Little Bald

Bald Mt. Shelter

5000' 4500' 4000' 3500' 3000' 2500' el.

14

12

10

8

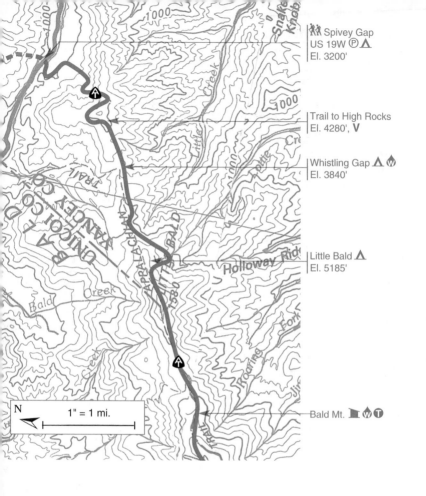

Spivey Gap
US 19W Ⓟ ⛺
El. 3200'

Trail to High Rocks
El. 4280', **V**

Whistling Gap ⛺ ⓦ
El. 3840'

Little Bald ⛺
El. 5185'

Bald Mt. 🏠 ⓦ Ⓣ

N
1" = 1 mi.

Miles N	NORTH	Elev. (ft./m)	Miles S
13.6	**End: Spivey Gap;** US 19W, parking, USFS campsite.	3200/975	0.0
11.6	Blue-blazed spur trail to **High Rocks** (0.1 mi.), view; trail continues R to rejoin AT..	4280/1305	2.0
11.2	**Whistling Gap,** campsite; water 0.1 mi. on side trail L.	3840/1170	2.4
9.3	**Little Bald,** rock slabs.	5185/1611	4.3
8.3	Spur trail to campsite; creek; spring 0.2 mi.		5.3
7.9	Spur trail L to **Bald Mt. Shelter,** spring, privy, great view.	5100/1555	5.7
7.0	**Big Stamp Gap,** jct. **Big Bald Bypass Trail;** spur trail to spring, campsite (0.3 mi.).		6.6
6.8	**Big Bald,** USGS benchmark, good views.	5516/1681	6.8
6.1	Jct. blue-blazed **Big Bald Bypass Trail.**		7.5
4.5	Campsite; blue-blazed trail R to spring.		9.1
4.0	**Low Gap** 50 yd. R on ridge crest.	4300/1310	9.6
3.8	Campsite; blue-blazed trail L 20 yd. to spring.		9.8
2.6	**Street Gap,** jct. gravel road.	4100/1250	11.0
0.0	**Start: Sams Gap;** US 23 (I-26), parking.	3800/1158	13.6

SOUTH

HIKE #33
Spivey Gap to Nolichucky River

Maps: ATC Map 2, Moreland Gap to Sams Gap

Route: From Spivey Gap to No Business Knob, to Chestoa Bridge, Nolichucky River

Recommended direction: S to N

Distance: 10.4 mi.

Elevation +/-: 3200 to 3710 to 1700 ft.

Effort: Strenuous

Day hike: Yes

Overnight backpacking hike: Optional

Duration: 8 to 10 hr.

Early exit option: None

Natural history feature: Nolichucky River valley

Trailhead access: *Start:* Spivey Gap: From Erwin, I-26 to Exit 43. Turn L to go under I-26, and immediately turn R onto US 19 W/TN 352. In 1.0 mi. turn L onto US 19W (Spivey Gap Rd.), and go S for 7.6 mi. After passing state border signs at gap crest, go 0.3 mi. farther to large gravel pullout on R. AT crosses 20 yd. N of pullout. Blazes are hard to see from the road; look for log steps up the bank for the AT going N and a narrow path directly opposite for the AT going S. There is also a 30-yd. side trail from the N edge of the parking area that connects to the southbound AT. *End:* Chestoa Bridge: From I-26, take Exit 40 (Jackson-Love Hwy.), turn L at stop sign, cross over I-26, and turn immediately R onto an unsigned road with a Holiday Inn visible from the intersection. Drive past the Holiday Inn for about 0.3 mi. to Jones Branch Rd. with USFS signs for Chestoa Recreation Area. In 0.4 mi. turn L, cross the Nolichucky River on Chestoa Bridge, and turn R onto River Rd. Park in the gravel lot on the corner. To find the northbound AT, follow blazes across the Chestoa Bridge, turn L on Unaka Springs Rd., and walk 50 yd. Look across the road for steps up into the woods.

Camping: No Business Knob Shelter; some campsites

The view into the Nolichucky River valley will reward you for the steep climbs and rock scrambles of Hike #33, which undulates between Flattop Mt. and No Business Knob but never reaches the top of either. Traveling along the sides of these mountains shows the contrast between moist ravines with cove hardwood forest and exposed ridges with pine and mountain laurel. Wildflowers are abundant, and the 2.0-mi. descent into the Nolichucky Gorge has a wonderful mountain laurel display in June. Rough, rocky sections and a few steep climbs make this hike strenuous, and water sources may be dry in summer; carry plenty of water.

To begin, climb the stone steps on the north bank of US 19W to a grassy road. Turn left onto the road for 90 yd., and then turn right and climb on dirt trail through rhododendron, hemlock, and white pine. After a switchback, ascend along the left side of Oglesby Branch, named for Frank Oglesby, founder of the Tennessee Eastman Hiking Club (TEHC), who fell in. TEHC maintains 135 mi. of the AT between Spivey Gap and Damascus, Virginia. At 0.4 mi. cross the same creek on a footbridge.

The AT becomes rocky, ascends along another creek, and crosses it at 0.6 mi. on a footbridge. In summer this may be the best water source for the next 2 to 3 mi. since other creeks and springs may be dry. The trail then turns left away from the creek and continues to climb. It crosses a grassy road, ascends log steps, and finally becomes level after curving left along a ridgetop at about 1 mi.

Hemlock and chestnut oak live on this ridgetop, the eastern edge of Flattop Mt. and the highest part of this AT section. Botanists divide the several species of oaks into two groups: white oaks and red oaks. Chestnut oak, a white oak, has leaves shaped like those of American chestnut but with rounded lobes on the leaf margin instead of pointed ones. Like other white oaks, chestnut oaks produce large starchy nuts that can be roasted and ground into flour.

Red oak acorns are smaller and have too much tannic acid to be useful as human food, but they do have more protein. Chestnut oak acorns germinate almost as soon as they hit the ground, while red oak acorns wait until the next spring. Squirrels, of course, know all this, even without graduate degrees in forestry; they eat chestnut oak acorns on the spot and bury red oak acorns for later. Blue jays and wild turkeys depend on white oak acorns for winter fat, and passenger pigeons used to flock to ridges like this to feed on acorns and the American chestnuts that once lived here. Black bears climb white oak trees in the fall to gather nuts before the tree is ready to let them go.

The AT proceeds through minor ups and downs and enters a mountain laurel thicket. At 1.5 mi. it drops to cross a rough gravel road from Spivey Gap. The AT follows the left fork of the road for about 100 yd., turns left just before a gate, and then descends on switchbacks. Striped maple, a common understory tree, thrives here and can be recognized by its smooth, striped greenish bark. Older striped maples have gray, furrowed bark, but the stripes can still be seen on the branches. Crested iris patches cover the trail banks.

Look for pileated woodpecker holes on dead tree trunks in this forest. This crow-sized bird has a loud cackling call that echoes in forested hollows. The bird anchors itself with strong toes (two forward and two back) and hammers at dead wood in search of insect larvae, which it catches with its sticky tongue. Pileated woodpecker holes are oblong, roughly the size and shape of an AT blaze.

At the valley bottom, cross a small creek (dry in summer) and ascend to a ridge crest and the state line at 2.2 mi. At 2.3 mi. cross a gravel road and small campsite at Devils Creek Gap. Ascend past a green AT welcome sign. The trail becomes level along the side of the ridge, approaches the nose of the ridge, goes over and descends on the other side, then approaches the next ridge—a theme with variations that continues along the side of No Business Knob. Imagine the ridges like fingers spread out from the crest of the mountain, and you have to clamber over each one. In each valley runs a tiny creek, a tributary of Devil's Creek, which flows into the Nolichucky River. On the top of each knuckle, mountain laurel, pines, galax, trailing arbutus, and other dry-adapted plants grow, and in the moist ravines the trail is lined with ferns, mosses, and spring wildflowers such as bloodroot, hepatica, and violets. Occasional views to the east show Flattop Mt., the deep Nolichucky River valley, and Unaka Mt. to the northeast.

After one ridgetop switchback, the AT descends on stone steps to a rocky creek at about 3.5 mi. and crosses on another footbridge. One knuckle farther, the AT starts the ascent to the side of No Business Knob (apparently named by someone who struggled through tangled mountain laurel and rhododendron and declared that he had no business being up there). The trail becomes very rocky and climbs through shady hemlock woods.

At 4.7 mi. a blue-blazed hemlock on the left indicates a 20-yd.-long trail to a piped spring that runs well for much of the year but may be dry in summer. Climb to the right from the creek, and take two switchbacks up to a broad ridgetop and open area. No Business Knob Shelter is to the left at 4.9 mi. and typifies another TEHC architectural style: sturdy cinder-block box with metal roof—not rustic but serviceable. The shelter has an overhanging front roof to permit cooking and eating out of the rain.

To continue on the AT, hike 25 yd. past the front of the shelter and turn sharply left. (An unblazed trail straight ahead goes to a gravel road to Unaka Springs, but the AT is well blazed. If you don't see any white blazes, backtrack to the shelter and try again.) Ascend steeply, and then descend on rocky trail with some washed-out sections. The trail resumes its knuckle-climbing pattern but on a higher contour. Creeks and seeps support violets, foamflower, toothwort, and other early-spring flowers. At about 6.0 mi. the trail crosses a rocky hillside that, though level, requires careful rock hopping. Pause and look down on the right into a rich ravine. Beyond a tangle of grapevines you can see the tops of Fraser magnolias. In spring you'll have an eye-level view of their creamy, waxy, dinner-plate-sized flowers. In fall, look for their magenta fruits. The magnolia's flowers, fruits, and seeds all have a sweet, spicy smell when crushed or punctured with a finger-nail.

At 7.3 mi. an old road joins the AT from the right and continues with it for 50 yd. to Temple Hill Gap (2850 ft.), where the AT turns right onto a rougher old road and climbs steeply through open woods to a ridge crest. Then the trail curves left into rich woods of chestnut oak, sourwood, and pipe vine. After a short rhodo-dendron tunnel, the AT reaches Temple Ridge at 8.0 mi. An old fire road continues left to the wooded 3220-ft. summit, which used to have a fire tower and cleared area. The AT turns right and passes a good resting log on level trail.

The trail keeps going on the ridg crest, descends to a saddle, and then climbs. The ridge falls off steeply on both sides; trees and shrubs soften the view for three seasons, but in winter you may feel as if you are on a high bridge with no guardrails.

From here the trail climbs three small knobs and then begins its plunge down to the Nolichucky River. Alongside the trail among mountain laurel, look for the pink lady's slip-per orchids, which bloom in May or June. Each plant has two large dark-green oval leaves that look like wide-wale corduroy. The leaves curl up around the flower stalk in spring but lie flat on the ground in summer and persist well into winter. They grow in

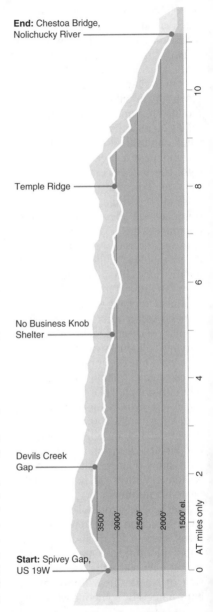

End: Chestoa Bridge, Nolichucky River

Temple Ridge

No Business Knob Shelter

Devils Creek Gap

Start: Spivey Gap, US 19W

3500' 3000' 2500' 2000' 1500' el.

AT miles only

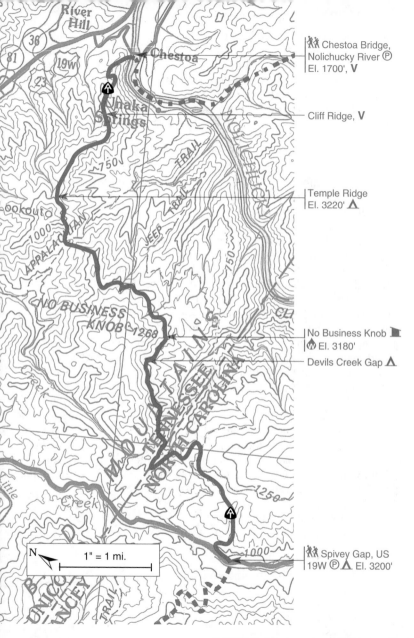

🥾 Chestoa Bridge,
Nolichucky River Ⓟ
El. 1700', **V**

— Cliff Ridge, **V**

Temple Ridge
El. 3220' ▲

No Business Knob 🔳
Ⓦ El. 3180'

— Devils Creek Gap ▲

🥾 Spivey Gap, US
19W Ⓟ ▲ El. 3200'

N

1" = 1 mi.

colonies, so if you find one, look for others. Leaves smaller than 8 in. long are probably adolescents and won't have blooms. Lady's-slippers require special conditions and have become rare because people try to transplant them. They have a symbiotic relationship with mycorrhizae, or fungus roots. In a new habitat that doesn't meet all the complex needs of both the orchid and the fungus, both will die. So if you want to enjoy lady's-slippers at home, take a picture, not a plant.

The AT used to follow the narrow ridge crest down, but erosion and crumbling rocks became a problem. Now trail relocations switch back from the sharp rocky edge of the ridge to moist creek ravines. The new trail cuts through rhododendron tangles and is well graded and reinforced with rock walls. You can appreciate here the work that trail maintainers do to keep the AT safe and enjoyable.

The best view on this hike is from Cliff Ridge. Carolina hemlocks grow here, but they, as well as the more common eastern hemlock, are being killed by the hemlock woolly adelgid. Piratebush, a rare endemic shrub, can be seen on Cliff Ridge. This shrub is parasitic on the roots of hemlock and will become even rarer as the hemlocks die. Piratebush (*Buckleya*) is a member of the mostly tropical sandalwood family, and its closest relatives live in Japan and China.

Each ridge view is slightly closer to the river and Unaka Springs community below. You may see what from up here looks like a model train inching along the tiny tracks, and ravens or hawks may be riding thermals in the steep Devils Creek valley. The next view seems to look right down the chimneys, and soon the view takes in the Nolichucky River in both directions and Erwin to the north. You might also see what the folks in Unaka Springs are growing in their gardens, and the sound of roosters may float up the ridge.

At 10.2 mi. one last switchback leads to level trail and, 0.2 mi. farther on, to steps down to paved Unaka Springs Rd. The AT crosses the road, turns left, then crosses over the Nolichucky River on the Chestoa Bridge sidewalk. Just across the bridge is a war memorial and parking space for several cars.

Miles N	NORTH	Elev. (ft./m)	Miles S
11.2	**End: Chestoa Bridge,** Unaka Springs Rd., parking.	1700/518	0.0
8.0	**Temple Ridge;** old fire road L to wooded summit, campsite.	3220/981	2.4
4.9	**No Business Knob Shelter.**	3180/969	5.5
4.7	Blue-blazed spur trail to piped spring (20 yd.).		5.7
2.2	**Devils Creek Gap,** campsite.	3400/1036	8.2
1.8	**Cliff Ridge.**		9.4
0.6	Creek; good water source.		9.8
0.0	**Start: Spivey Gap,** US 19W; parking, USFS campsite, stream.	3200/975	11.2

SOUTH

HIKE #34
Nolichucky River to Iron Mt. Gap

Maps: ATC Map 2, Moreland Gap to Sams Gap

Route: From Nolichucky Gorge Campground to Indian Grave Gap, to Beauty Spot, to Unaka Mt., to Iron Mt. Gap

Recommended direction: S to N

Distance: 17.8 mi.

Elevation +/-: 1700 to 5180 to 3723 ft.

Effort: Very strenuous

Day hike: No

Overnight backpacking hike: Yes

Duration: 9 to 10 hr.

Early exit option: Indian Grave Gap, at 7.0 mi.; Beauty Spot, at 9.3 mi.

Natural history features: Bald at Beauty Spot; spruce forest of Unaka Mt.

Trailhead access: *Start:* From I-26, take Exit 43 (Jackson-Love Hwy.), turn L at stop sign, cross over I-26, and take immediate R onto unsigned road with a Holiday Inn visible from the intersection. Go past the Holiday Inn for about 0.3 mi. Turn L and follow USFS signs for Chestoa Recreation Area. In 0.4 mi., turn L, cross Chestoa Bridge over the Nolichucky River, and turn R onto Jones Branch Rd. Go 1.4 mi. to a R turn and a fork; the R fork goes to a commercial rafting company, the L fork crosses a small bridge to the campground and hiker hostel. Park with permission and look for the AT to L of road just before fork. *End:* From Unicoi, TN, go E for 10.0 mi. on TN 107. From Buladean, NC, go N on NC 226 for 4.0 mi. Iron Mt. Gap is marked by TN/NC border signs; a large parking area is on S side of road. Look for AT crossing on gravel road E of parking area. *Intermediate access:* From Erwin, head W on TN 107 to traffic light at 10th Street (TN 395). Turn R for 6.1 mi. to Indian Grave Gap on TN/NC border. The AT crosses the W side of parking area.

Camping: Nolichucky Gorge Campground; USFS Rock Creek Campground (3.3 mi. from AT on TN 395); Curley Maple Shelter; Cherry Gap Shelter; campsites

Between the Nolichucky River and Iron Mt. Gap lies a remote protected region, mapped as parcels of land with different names and federal designations — recreation area, primitive area, wilderness — but the bears and trees don't care. The forest is recovering vigorously from logging in the 1930s and fires in the 1950s, and the bear population is as high as modern wildlife biologists have ever measured it. Halfway between the river and the gap is Beauty Spot, a natural grass bald that features outstanding views and an all-you-can-eat berry feast in August. If you have the time and energy to climb from the Nolichucky River to the top of Unaka Mt., the reward might be nearly 18 mi. of private trail.

Described here as a strenuous backpack, this hike can also be broken into smaller segments. Paved TN 395 from Erwin crosses the AT at Indian Grave Gap, and rough gravel USFS 230 runs somewhat parallel to it for 12.5 mi. One possibility is to leave a car at Nolichucky Gorge Campground, drive to Indian Grave Gap, and hike 7.0 mi. (north to south) back to the car. A good family one-car day trip would be to hike from Indian Grave Gap to Beauty Spot (2.3 mi.) and then backtrack. Either option could be combined with car camping at the U.S. Forest Service Rock Creek Campground. Located 3.3 mi. west of Indian Grave Gap on TN 395, this large campground has a swimming pool and wooded creekside campsites.

From the Nolichucky Gorge Campground, walk 25 yd. toward Jones Branch Rd., turn right on a grassy road, and enter woods. Look for AT white blazes in about 10 yd. The AT going north is straight ahead, while the AT going south turns left and runs for 1.3 mi. parallel to Jones Branch Rd., crossing it again at the Chestoa Bridge. That 1.3-mi. AT section between the end of Hike #33 and the start of Hike #34 crosses a railroad track and passes through thin woods. It isn't described here in detail because it parallels the road, but it's well blazed and easy to follow.

Swing to the left, cross an elegant wooden bridge, and reach the junc-

David Emblidge

Giant oyster mushroom

tion with Nolichucky River Trail at 0.1 mi. to the right. This little-used Forest Service trail runs along the river for 2.0 mi. Camping is possible near the trail junction and in other flat places here; once the AT starts climbing the side of the gorge, there will be no flat sites for about 3.0 mi.

The AT wanders through a stand of hemlocks and white pines, crossing Jones Branch four more times on bridges. Part of the trail is rocky creek bed with tall nettles in late summer. Look for Jack-in-the-pulpit and foamflower in spring and deep red cardinal flower near the water's edge in July. Water-loving sycamore trees, easy to recognize with large patches of peeling bark, grow along the creek.

The AT moves away from the creek at about 1.0 mi. and rises gently through moist, rich woods. Fraser's sedge, a rare plant with dark-green leathery leaves about as wide as a belt, grows on the trail bank. Hike past large hemlocks and a few patches of rhododendron and doghobble. On late spring mornings and

The Wood Thrush (*Turdus mustelinus*)

How often . . . when far from my dear home, and deprived from the presence of those nearest to my heart, wearied, hungry, drenched, and so lonely and desolate as almost to question myself why I was thus situated, when I have seen the fruits of my labours on the eve of being destroyed, as the water, collected in a stream, rushed through my little camp, and forced me to stand erect, shivering in a cold fit like that of severe ague, when I have been obliged to wait with the patience of a martyr for the return of day, trying in vain to destroy the tormenting moschetoes, silently counting over the years of my youth, doubting perhaps if ever again I should return to my home, and embrace my family!—how often, as the first glimpses of morning gleamed doubtfully amongst the dusky masses of the forest-trees, has there come upon my ear, thrilling along the sensitive cords which connect that organ with the heart, the delightful music of this harbinger of day!—and how fervently, on such occasions, have I blessed the Being who formed the Wood Thrush, and placed it in these solitary forests, as if to console me amidst my privations, to cheer my depressed mind, and to make me feel, as I did, that never ought man to despair, whatever may be his situation, as he can never be certain that aid and deliverance are not at hand.

— John James Audubon
Ornithological Biography (1831)

evenings, listen for the flutelike song of the wood thrush with a trill at the end of each song. This bird nests only in mature woods. Another bird call, the loud *teach-teach-teach* of the ovenbird, can be heard all day.

At 1.8 mi. the trail turns sharply left and begins to climb out of the river plain on switchbacks. Watch blazes carefully because old roads and trails continue straight at many of the switchbacks. If you think you might have missed a turn (a sudden branch in your face is a good clue), backtrack until you see a white blaze.

The trail becomes steep and rocky as it zigzags up the ridge. Take a rest from time to time, and look back across the valley at Temple Hill and No Business Knob. To the northwest is Buffalo Mt. The Nolichucky River flows northwest through the ridges and valleys here, suggesting that its course was established before the formation of the Appalachians. The mountains grew slowly as continental collision sent waves through the ancient rocks, and the rivers maintained their courses by eroding their beds faster than the ridges rose.

As you climb from 2500 to 3000 ft., oak and mountain laurel replace hemlock and rhododendron. In October, watch out for white oak acorns hiding like marbles under dry leaves, lying in wait to roll you back down the trail.

Approach Jones Branch again, and at 2.9 mi. reach Curley Maple Gap Shelter on the right. It has wood siding and a metal roof and a large covered area in front with a picnic table. Remodeled and enlarged in 2011, it has room for 10. Water is available from a spring on the right 100 ft. south on the AT, but if that spring is dry, backtrack about 0.1 mi. to Jones Branch.

Climb another 0.1 mi. to Curley Maple Gap (at 3080 ft., nearly twice the starting elevation), a grassy open area with an old road crossing. A rectangular concrete foundation on the left is all that remains from a Civilian Conservation Corps (CCC) shelter from the 1930s. The climb becomes a little steeper through rocky woods as the trail crosses a tiny creek at about 4.0 mi. and then approaches a ridgetop. Rockcap fern, or polypody, grows on the rocks. With a hand lens, look for brown dots on the undersides of the fern fronds. These reproductive structures produce spores inside cells that explode in wet weather, propelling the spores—perhaps onto the moss mat of a new rock. Lucky spores will grow on moist spots into green specks called gametophytes. Eggs and sperm develop on the gametophytes, and on another wet day, the sperm swim to the eggs to form the next generation. On rainy hikes, think about all this microscopic activity taking place beneath your feet.

At about 5.5 mi. reach a gap with a grassy campsite and old trails on both sides. Follow the blazes straight, and then turn sharply right at 6.3 mi. onto good trail carpeted with pine needles. The AT continues on minor ups and downs with some rocky sections, crosses a rough gravel road, descends past an AT sign, and at 7.0 mi. drops to a gravel road at Indian Grave Gap. (This road continues across Indian Grave Gap as USFS 230, allowing a passable ride to Beauty Spot and other points on this hike. It reaches TN 107 after 12 rough miles.)

Cross paved TN 395 with the "Welcome to North Carolina" sign to the right, beyond which TN 395 is called NC 197. The AT reenters the woods at a paved parking area, passes a sign for Beauty Spot and Cherry Gap Shelter, and climbs through a rhododendron tunnel. It levels off at 7.5 mi. in open woods of chestnut oak, Fraser magnolia, American chestnut saplings, and sourwood.

At 7.7 mi., the AT crosses a powerline clearing dotted with blackberries and Catawba rhododendron; there's a view left of Erwin nestled between two ridges. As the trail reenters woods, an old road joins it from the right for an easy descent to a (usually) dry creek bed. AT, old road, and creek bed ascend together to a level grassy spot, and at 8.1 mi. the AT crosses USFS 230. To the right down the gravel road is Indian Grave Gap in 0.9 mi.

After 0.1 mi. the AT turns left and

follows a gently ascending ridge for about 0.5 mi. There are glimpses of the North Carolina mountains to the right (south). Witch hazel blooms along this ridge in winter, as do many wildflowers at other times: false Solomon's-seal and squawroot in spring; bee balm, blue lobelia (once believed to cure syphilis), spiderwort, and starry campion in summer; and asters and goldenrod in fall. Patches of lady fern and New York fern stretch from both sides of the trail. New York fern is easy to recognize because the frond tapers at both top and bottom.

Just beyond a group of small shagbark hickory trees at 8.9 mi., the AT emerges onto an open meadow, the edge of Beauty Spot bald. (To the left, a track leads down to USFS 230 in about 100 yd.) Turn right past a double-blazed weathered post, and follow the well-worn path through tall grass. Blazes on the bald are green metal fence posts with white tops, barely taller than the plants. In fog or snow they may be invisible; be careful, especially if you step off the path. Highbush blueberries are a few yards off the trail on both sides, and blackberries offer their fruit right beside the trail. Camping is possible on both sides of the trail, but you will have to carry water. If you do camp on the bald, make it look as if you hadn't before you leave.

Some meadow flowers, such as Indian plantain, goldenrod, and yarrow, compete for sunlight by growing tall. Yarrow was brought here from

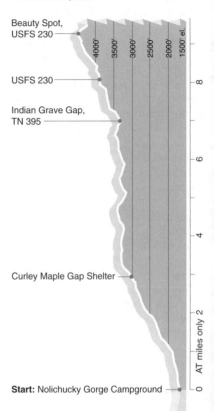

Continued on p. 274

Beauty Spot, USFS 230

USFS 230

Indian Grave Gap, TN 395

Curley Maple Gap Shelter

Start: Nolichucky Gorge Campground

AT miles only

Europe and found some habitat to its liking in almost every state. Its Latin name is *Achillea millefolium* because Achilles was said to have used it to treat his soldiers' wounds during the siege of Troy. Also called staunchwort and soldier's woundwort, yarrow was used by Civil War soldiers and countless others to stop bleeding. Rub a bit of yarrow leaf to get a spicy smell.

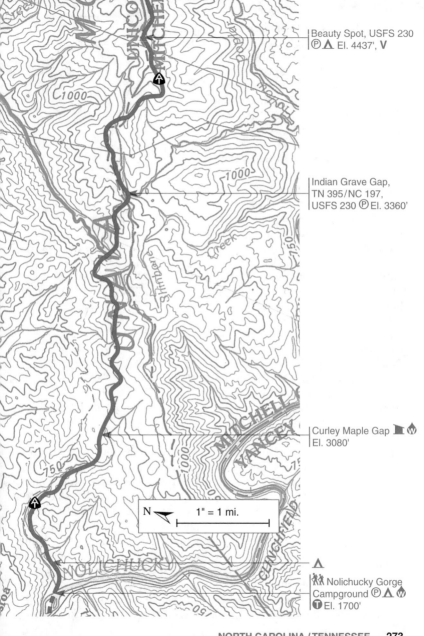

Beauty Spot, USFS 230
Ⓟ ▲ El. 4437', **V**

Indian Grave Gap,
TN 395/NC 197,
USFS 230 Ⓟ El. 3360'

Curley Maple Gap 🛏 ⓦ
El. 3080'

N ➤   1" = 1 mi.

▲

🚶🚶 Nolichucky Gorge
Campground Ⓟ ▲ ⓦ
Ⓣ El. 1700'

Some flowers climb other plants to bask in the sun. Clematis, or virgin's bower, covers some bushes on the bald, and dodder, a parasitic plant, spreads out on its host blackberries like a tattered orange blanket. The dodder doesn't even need the sun since it doesn't make its own food, but it seems to enjoy getting a tan. Using a hand lens, look into the dodder's tiny white flowers; mites, aphids, beetles, and all sorts of other mini-beasts might be crawling around inside.

A third flower strategy, practiced by cinquefoils and gentians, is to grow next to a path or opening and reach out for the sun. Gentian root extract is an ingredient of the soft drink Moxie and is said by some herbalists to be a general restorative.

Climb to the 4437-ft. summit of the bald, with great views, at 9.3 mi. Unaka Mt. looms straight ahead with Roan and Mitchell Mt. to the right of it. Erwin and Buffalo Mt. are to the left. A cleared spot with a fire ring provides an on-trail campsite, but it is best to use a stove and not build a fire at all. A path leads 100 yd. left to a parking area on USFS 230.

Watch for those skinny fence-post blazes, and descend on an old road for 0.2 mi. to the edge of thin woods. USFS 230 is visible to the left, and a blue-blazed trail leads 50 yd. left through a gate and across USFS 230 to a spring. To the right of the trail is a small campsite in the shade of a huge gnarled white pine. Continue between a wooden fence and the road, descending a little.

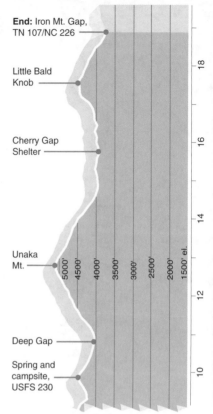

End: Iron Mt. Gap, TN 107/NC 226

Little Bald Knob

Cherry Gap Shelter

Unaka Mt.

Deep Gap

Spring and campsite, USFS 230

5000' 4500' 4000' 3500' 3000' 2500' 2000' 1500' el.

18 16 14 12 10

At 9.8 mi. there's a larger campsite on the left between the AT and USFS 230. The AT continues level on an old road, crosses a wooden stile into a mowed field, and descends along the right side. It then climbs steeply over a small knob and reaches 4100-ft. Deep Gap, at 10.8 mi., with campsites and a spring just across USFS 230.

After the gap the AT climbs steeply on switchbacks and excellent rock steps up the side of Unaka Mt. Large

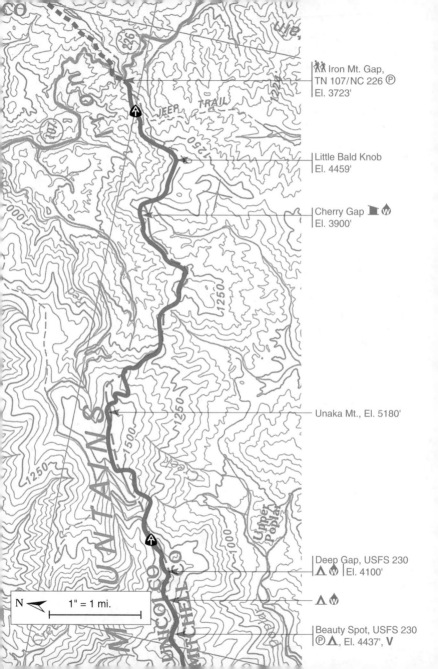

Iron Mt. Gap,
TN 107/NC 226 Ⓟ
El. 3723'

Little Bald Knob
El. 4459'

Cherry Gap
El. 3900'

Unaka Mt., El. 5180'

Deep Gap, USFS 230
△ Ⓦ El. 4100'

△ Ⓦ

Beauty Spot, USFS 230
Ⓟ△, El. 4437', V

N   1" = 1 mi.

sugar maples grow here, some with enormous burls and hollow centers that you could crawl into. At 11.3 mi. the trail reaches a ridge crest, and suddenly there's USFS 230 to the left again.

The AT swings right and ascends steadily but not so steeply on switch-backs. At 11.6 mi., it turns left to an open area with scattered highbush blueberry bushes and deciduous holly trees. Ascend across the open-ing and turn right into dark spruce woods. The AT twists among the big trees along a needle-covered path; in some cases the blazes are the only guide—keep one in sight at all times.

At Unaka Mt.'s 5180-ft. summit (12.6 mi.) you'll find a small campsite and a survey marker. Then the trail starts down a rocky section through open beech and yellow birch woods, crosses another patch of spruces with a few mountain ash trees, and con-tinues down Unaka Mt. on switch-backs. Some rocks have prominent quartz veins and pink quartz crystals.

A section of switchbacks and steep trail leads down to Low Gap at 14.7 mi. From here to Iron Mt. Gap the AT skirts a series of steep knobs, on a sidehill trail with abundant wild flow-ers. The steep climb out of Low Gap is

about 0.5 mi., and just down the other side on the right is the cinder-block Cherry Gap Shelter at 15.9 mi. A blue-blazed trail leads 250 yd. left from the shelter to a spring.

Descend 0.3 mi. to Cherry Gap (3900 ft.) and another chance to take an old road 0.8 mi. left to USFS 230. The next 1-mi. climb offers a wel-come level spot about halfway, and twists and turns at the top take you past 4459-ft. Little Bald Knob at 16.6 mi. Grazing once kept this bald open, and some grass is left beside the trail, but trees now obscure the views. Great slabs of erosion-resistant metamorphic rock slant toward the northwest, indicating how these rocks, formed on an ocean floor half a billion years ago, were pushed up over younger rocks.

Descend steadily along a rusty barbed-wire fence, and look for glimpses of Roan Mt. through the trees to the right. After two switch-backs, a crop of huge boulders on the right, and a small weedy gap, descend and cross a grassy roadbed. Turn right into woods. At 18.8 mi. you'll reach the gravel road again at Iron Mt. Gap at the state border. Paved TN 107 / NC 226 is just a few yards to the right.

Miles N	NORTH	Elev. (ft./m)	Miles S
18.8	**End: Iron Mt. Gap;** TN 107/NC 226, parking.	3723/1135	0.0
17.4	**Little Bald Knob;** rock slabs.	4459/1359	1.2
15.9	**Cherry Gap Shelter;** blue-blazed trail to spring 250 yd. L.	3900/1189	3.1
12.6	**Unaka Mt.,** campsite.	5180/1579	6.4
10.8	**Deep Gap;** campsite, water.	4100/1250	8.0
9.8	Blue-blazed trail to spring and campsite, USFS 230.		9.0
9.3	**Beauty Spot;** USFS 230, campsite, parking; early exit option.	4437/1352	9.5
8.1	Cross USFS 230.		10.7
7.0	**Indian Grave Gap;** TN 395/NC 197, USFS 230, parking; Rock Creek Recreation Area is 3.3 mi. W.	3360/1024	11.8
5.5	Grassy campsite.		13.4
2.9	**Curley Maple Gap Shelter;** spring 30 yd. back on AT; 0.1 mi. to **Curley Maple Gap.**	3080/939	15.9
0.1	Jct. **Nolichucky River Trail,** parallels river for 2.0 mi.		18.7
0.0	**Start: Nolichucky Gorge Campground;** camping, water, hiker hostel; Jones Branch Rd. to Chestoa Bridge (1.3 mi.).	1700/518	18.8

SOUTH

Iron Mt. Gap to Hughes Gap

Maps: ATC Map 2, Moreland Gap to Sams Gap

Route: From Iron Mt. Gap to Greasy Creek Gap to Hughes Gap

Recommended direction: S to N

Distance: 8.1 mi.

Elevation +/-: 3723 to 4918 to 4040 ft.

Effort: Moderate

Day hike: Yes

Overnight backpacking hike: Optional

Duration: 5 to 6 hr.

Early exit option: None

Natural history feature: Little Rock Knob

Social history feature: Birthplace of Davy Crockett near Iron Mt. Gap

Trailhead access: *Start:* From Unicoi, go 10.0 mi. E on TN 107; from Buladean, go 4.0 mi. N on NC 226. Park W of the crest. The AT going N starts across from the parking area on an old gravel road. *End:* From Roan Mt., go S for 5.3 mi. on TN 143. At Burbank, across from a small store, turn R onto Cove Rd., cross bridge, and bear R onto Hughes Gap Rd. Go 3.1 mi. to state line sign (just before pavement ends), and park on R. AT from the S comes down into this parking lot and crosses the road. To reach Hughes Gap from Iron Mt. Gap, drive 4.0 mi. on NC 226 to Buladean. Turn L onto Hughes Gap Rd. for 4.5 mi. to Hughes Gap at state line. Park on L.

Camping: Clyde Smith Shelter; campsites

D avy Crockett, king of the wild frontier, wasn't born *in* the mountains but certainly within sight of some—Unaka, Roan, and the smaller ones you'll climb on this pleasant hike. The AT heads northeast from Iron Mt. Gap, then swings south with the state border toward Roan Mt. Hike #35 is a mid-elevation section that connects two of the highest east Tennessee mountains. It is remote and little used, providing excellent views of the higher peaks and superb spring wildflower displays. For a two-car moderate day hike, leave one car at Hughes Gap, drive around through Buladean, North Carolina (not to be confused with Buladeen, Tennessee, which is closer to the northern end of Hike #43), and start hiking from Iron Mt. Gap. A good one-car 12-mi. day hike or overnight could be done from Iron Mt. Gap to Clyde Smith Shelter (which receives little use except by thru-hikers, mostly in April and May) and back. The shorter possibility from Hughes Gap is another day-hike option, but Hughes Gap is not a good place to leave a car overnight. Hike #35 is an excellent winter hike—the low elevation provides shelter from

Rime ice

extreme weather and views of snow and ice on higher spots. In late summer, the gaps and open spots of this hike can become weedy, with spectacular stands of stinging nettles — bring or wear long pants.

From the wide sandy parking area at Iron Mt. Gap, cross paved TN 107 to a gated gravel road. Ascend left of the ridge crest, and reach it in about 0.5 mi. An open area has good views if you stop and look back. To the west looms the dark bulk of Unaka Mt. (dark because of thick spruce woods on the summit). The pretty valley to the west contains Limestone, the birthplace of Davy Crockett (August 1786). The valley also holds Greeneville, named for the Revolutionary War general Nathanael Greene and home of two Tennessee presidents, Andrew Jackson (of 1838 Cherokee Removal Trail of Tears infamy) and Andrew Johnson (before the Civil War, a Unionist senator from a secessionist state; later, Lincoln's vice president and successor; and later still, almost impeached for his sympathies with the South during Reconstruction). Other notables who spent time in Greeneville: the Marquis de Lafayette and English author Frances Hodgson Burnett (*Little Lord Fauntleroy*, *The Secret Garden*).

Cross the crest, leave the gravel road (watch for double blazes), and descend to a gap at 1.2 mi. Scraggly Christmas trees and a few old apple trees remain from tree farming, and rusty barbed-wire fences line the trail. In fall, look for deer munching on heritage apples.

Ascend from the gap a few yards

to a blue-blazed trail that leads 0.1 mi. right to a stream, which may be dry in August. Continue ascending through open woods past greenbrier tangles. After a 4426-ft. summit (2.3 mi.), topped by a huge overhanging rock slab, descend to Lowly Martyr Gap at 3.0 mi. Though Tennessee seceded from the Union in 1861, many of the mountain counties, once part of the independent state of Franklin, remained loyal to the Union. Confederate conscriptors from North Carolina crossed through some of these gaps and captured men and boys and impressed them into the army. Deserters from both sides found haven in these mountains, and some of them formed bands of renegades, or bandits, who ambushed travelers in the gaps.

After a few rocky ups and downs, offering occasional ridgetop views, reach a blue-blazed trail at 3.8 mi., just past an overgrown field. It goes left for about 0.2 mi., passing a spring and grassy campsite before rejoining the AT at 4034-ft. Greasy Creek Gap (4.0 mi.). This pleasant name probably came from the practice of skinning, dressing, and gutting bears at the creek nearest where they were shot so that the pieces would be easier to carry. A bear in fall has a lot of grease (fat stored for winter) that can wash down to the homesites below. Woods roads (presently impassable by car) cross this gap. To the right, a rutted road goes down to Buladean.

From Greasy Creek Gap, the AT runs nearly level for more than 1 mi.

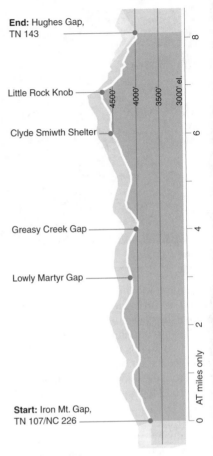

along the north side of the ridge crest. Cool, moist soil supports masses of spring flowers: foamflower, hepatica, toothwort, violets, trilliums, and many more. At 4.9 mi., pass between a house foundation and a row of huge gnarled sugar maples. There's a flat, grassy campsite beside the trail

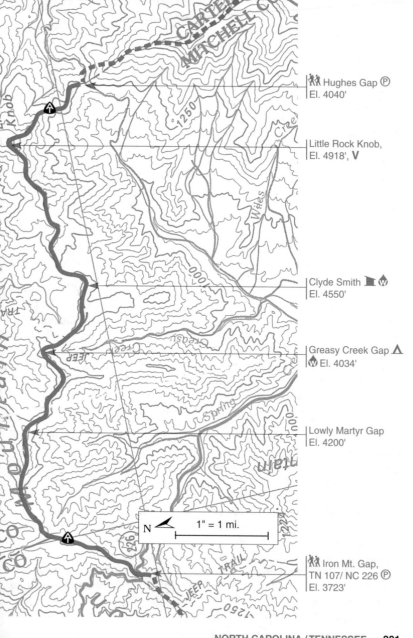

人 Hughes Gap Ⓟ
El. 4040'

Little Rock Knob,
El. 4918', **V**

Clyde Smith ▄ ⓦ
El. 4550'

Greasy Creek Gap ▲
ⓦ El. 4034'

Lowly Martyr Gap
El. 4200'

N ◤ 1" = 1 mi.

人 Iron Mt. Gap,
TN 107/ NC 226 Ⓟ
El. 3723'

and a sluggish spring 100 yd. down to the left, along with plenty of blackberries to eat in August.

The AT ascends to the top of the broad ridge and continues climbing gradually through oak and maple woods. A common trailside plant here is shining club moss, looking like green furry fingers growing 2 to 3 in. up from an equally furry runner. Club mosses were the first land plants to develop cells that could transfer water to other cells, and the combination of water transport and a shiny waterproof cuticle on the tiny leaves allowed these plants to invade land. About 250 million years ago, before the formation of these mountains, some species of club mosses grew more than 100 ft. tall. There were no herbivores to eat them, and their trunks and branches piled up in layers that became much of Appalachia's coal deposits. Ferns, conifers, and flowering plants evolved more efficient water transport cells and other adaptations for dry-land living; the only club mosses today are ground creepers like this one. They produce masses of oily spores for reproduction, and people have used the spores for gunpowder and flash cameras.

At 6.0 mi. a blue-blazed trail goes left 200 yd. to Clyde Smith Shelter in an open, sunny clearing surrounded by beech trees. The shelter accommodates about eight hikers, and was named for the first national park ranger in Cades Cove in the Smokies. From behind the shelter there is a view through trees of Little Rock Knob, and a trail behind the shelter leads down to a spring in about 100 yd. (If it's dry, you can continue down the same hollow for a lower spring or creek.) Hurricane Opal blew down many trees here, and a jumble of potential firewood sits in front of the shelter.

From the shelter side trail, ascend a few hundred yards to another knob, and then descend to a gap at 6.4 mi. and a grassy campsite. A steep trail leads left about 0.1 mi. to a small spring.

The trail then ascends on a steep and rocky ridge crest to 4918-ft. Little Rock Knob, the highest point on Hike #35, at 7.0 mi. Relocation and repair of eroded sections of the trail on both sides of this knob were completed in 1997 by the Tennessee Eastman Hiking Club, an AmeriCorps crew of college students doing national service in exchange for partial tuition, and the Konnarock ATC trail crew.

The rocky promontory offers a view left (north) of Ripshin Lake — Limestone Cove may be visible to the far left — Christmas tree farms (possibly with Fraser firs planted from seeds collected on Roan Mt., Hike #37), pastures, and hayfields. In May and June millions of mountain laurel blooms frame the views; in winter, this is a good place to see horizontal clusters of rime ice, which forms on the windward sides of twigs and branches when wind blows supercooled fog across them. On cold mornings, the rime ice crystals may be more than 1 in. long, and as the

Miles N	NORTH	Elev. (ft./m)	Miles S
9.1	**End:** Hughes Gap, parking.	4040/1231	0.0
7.0	**Little Rock Knob,** promontory, views.	4918/1499	2.2
6.4	Grassy campsite; steep trail L 0.1 mi. to small spring.		2.6
6.0	Blue-blazed trail L 200 yd. to **Clyde Smith Shelter;** spring 100 yd. behind shelter.	4550/1387	3.1
4.9	Campsite, spring 100 yd. L.		4.1
4.0	**Greasy Creek Gap.**	4034/1230	5.0
3.0	**Lowly Martyr Gap.**	4200/1280	6.0
2.3	Summit; huge rock slab.	4426/1349	6.8
0.0	**Start:** Iron Mt. Gap; TN 107/NC 226, parking.	3723/1135	9.1

SOUTH

sun warms them, they fall with tinkling noises and crunch underfoot. If you hike early enough, collect a few off trees and eat them.

Descend the eastern side of Little Rock Knob on switchbacks through stands of mountain laurel and rhododendron. Flame azalea, fetterbush, galax, wintergreen, and trailing arbutus line the trail, and larkspur, trillium, and ramps grow in wet areas. At 8.2 mi. the trail reaches an old field with small trees. A short ascent along an old fence leads to a summit and a rutted dirt road. A winter view straight ahead shows Roan Mt., close and very big. After one more small knob, the road and trail swing right and at 9.1 mi. descend though open oak woods to Hughes Gap.

Hughes Gap to Roan Mt. Cloudland Hotel Site

Maps: ATC Map 2, Moreland Gap to Sams Gap

Route: From Hughes Gap to Ash Gap to Cloudland Hotel Site

Recommended direction: S to N

Distance: 2.6 mi.

Elevation +/-: 4040 to 6150 ft.

Effort: Strenuous

Day hike: Yes

Overnight backpacking hike: Optional

Duration: 2 to 3 hr.

Early exit option: None

Natural history feature: Transition from deciduous to spruce-fir forest

Social history feature: Cloudland Hotel site

Trailhead access: *Start:* From Roan Mt. go 5.3 mi. S on TN 143. At Burbank, across from store, turn R onto Cove Rd., cross bridge. Bear R onto Hughes Gap Rd. 3.1 mi. to state line sign (just before pavement ends). Parking lot on R at gap crest. The AT crosses the road a few yards N of the gap crest. *End:* From US 19E in Roan Mt., TN, turn R on TN 143 for 12.8 mi., passing through Roan Mt. State Park. Go R at Carvers Gap (before state line sign) onto USFS 1348 (at sign for Rhododendron Gardens) for 1.0 mi. to Cloudland parking area on R. AT runs behind Cloudland Hotel site at the R end of parking area. Note: USFS 1348 is closed in winter; TN 143 may be closed because of snow.

Camping: Ash Gap campsite

With an elevation change of nearly 1000 ft. per mi., Hike #36 is an aerobic challenge going up and difficult and challenging coming down. It is separate from the adjacent hikes because it's so different from them. The south-to-north ascent is the safest course, and the rewards for the climb include the Rhododendron Gardens, Roan High Bluff, and cool boreal spruce-fir forest (see Hike #37 for the easy way there). The hike goes straight up the northwestern wall of the Roan Massif, a 15-mi.-long series of 5500- to 6000-ft. peaks and balds. This short hike is best done with two cars or with someone dropping hikers off at Hughes Gap. It can be combined with parts of Hike #37 or a side trip to the Rhododendron Gardens or Roan High Bluff.

Caution: Conditions at 6000 ft. may be colder, wetter, or icier than at the start of this hike. Carry warm clothes and rain gear. When it's sunny in the valley, the mountaintop may be shrouded in fog, sleet, or snow in almost any season. Check with the U.S. Forest Service or Roan Mt. State Park for current weather and road conditions. (See "Useful Information" for phone numbers.)

From the parking area, cross Hughes Gap Rd., and look for white blazes to the left of the gap crest. Start up a steep, eroded dirt road and look for an AT mileage sign. This climb out of the gap faces north and receives plenty of rainfall, so weed growth is especially luxurious. Expect head-high nettles, grasses, and orange jewelweed in summer as well as poison ivy (nettles, jewelweed, and poison ivy often grow together). Wear long pants and a long-sleeved shirt. If you get stung by the nettles anyway, try crushing jewelweed leaves, stems, or flowers and rubbing the sticky green paste on your skin. The juice should soothe the stinging. Cherokee herbalists prescribe the juice of seven jewelweed flowers for both nettle stinging and ivy poisoning. In spring, hepatica, bloodroot, violets, sweet cicely, wild geranium, and other flowers bloom along the trail. The thin forest of small locust, maple, and tulip-trees indicates that this area was logged within the last 40 or 50 years.

After about 0.5 mi. the trail turns right and climbs steeply to the ridge crest on switchbacks. In wet weather, this part of the trail may be slippery, making going up much easier than coming down. At the crest, the trail turns left, away from the roadbed, and ascends more evenly.

The trail climbs steadily, with some relief on switchbacks, and keeps to the sharp ridge crest with many crystalline rock outcrops. Larger trees, including yellow birch, tulip-tree, and red oak, appear, and some of the larger boulders have crops of rock tripe, a papery lichen that grows from cornflake to Frisbee size. Lift a piece of rock tripe and look at the black-velvet underside with a hand lens. (You'll need some rest stops on this hike, and hand-lens investigations are a great excuse to take off your pack, have a drink, and catch your breath.) Rock tripe is edible and tastes, not surprisingly, like mushrooms.

On foggy or rainy days (all too common here), look for amphibian fellow hikers: bright orange-red efts. These 3- to 6-in. salamanders have poisonous skin and warning colors and rarely try to flee or hide. Pick one up (it's poisonous only if you eat it) and let it walk across your hand. This is an immature, or teenage, stage of the red-spotted newt, an aquatic salamander that populates forest ponds and swamps. Newts hatch from eggs to gilled larvae in a pond and eat worms or mosquito larvae all summer. The larvae metamorphose into red efts, which breathe with lungs and wander on land for 2 to 5 years, eating flies, termites, maggots, or spiders. Then they return to the same pond and change to olive-green air-breathing swimmers for mating and egg laying. Since male newts can't sing as their relatives the frogs and toads do, they dance to attract mates.

At 1.3 mi. a side trail goes 50 yd. right to Beartown Mt., a rock promontory that offers views to the west. On a clear day look for Unaka Mt. to the northwest and the fields of Buladean,

North Carolina, in the valley below your feet. Just 0.1 mi. farther is the summit of Beartown Mt. and a welcome but short descent on easy trail.

At 1.8 mi. reach 5340-ft. Ash Gap, which has a pleasant campsite on a broad ridge crest that is about the only spot on this hike level enough to pitch a tent. A trail leads 0.2 mi. right to a small, unreliable spring; it's best to carry water if camping here.

The dominant tree here is beech (not ash), typical of habitats above 5000 ft. Look for its smooth gray bark, oval leaves with toothed margins, and the prickly garbanzo-bean-sized fruits containing triangular beechnuts. Beeches and oaks are in the same botanical family and share a habit of retaining dried-up leaves all winter and finally dropping them when spring buds open to produce new leaves. Billowy grass, yellow jewelweed, white wood aster, and goldenrod form the groundcover of the gap. Usually (but not always) orange-flowered jewelweed grows at lower elevations, while the jewelweed of higher elevations has yellow flowers.

After Ash Gap the trail starts on the serious climb of this hike, up through boulders, gnarled trees, and twisted root handholds. Notice the deciduous forest of sugar maple, striped maple, yellow birch, beech, and oak trees. Another sign of elevation gain is viburnum, or hobblebush, a shrub with large heart-shaped leaves, velvety-brown buds, and flat clusters of white flowers in May. In the cluster of flowers, only the sterile outside flow-

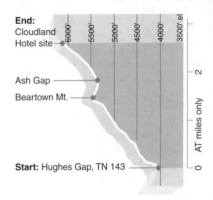

ers have petals, and these attract the pollinators. Viburnum berries turn bright red in fall, and the leaves turn dark red or burgundy.

At about 2.0 mi. spruce and rhododendron appear, and as the trail continues to climb, these evergreens gradually replace deciduous trees, making the woods dark and the handholds harder to see. Trailside flowers at this elevation include filmy angelica, false hellebore, and white snakeroot.

Near the top, young Fraser fir trees mix in with the spruces. Here's how to tell these two needle-bearing trees apart: Grasp a twig gently with your fingers and test the ends of the needles with your thumb. Spruce needles are sharp (almost sharp enough to hurt), while fir needles are blunt. Spruce needles are square in cross section, while fir needles are flat. Both smell good, but fir smells a little

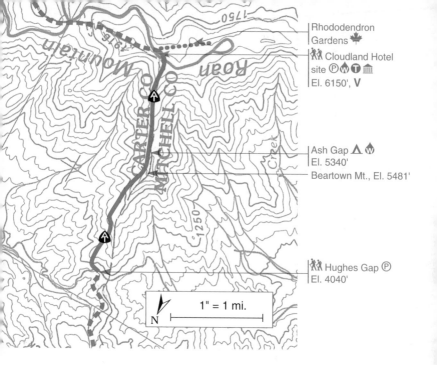

Rhododendron
Gardens 🍁

🚶🚶 Cloudland Hotel
site Ⓟ Ⓦ Ⓣ 🏛
El. 6150', **V**

Ash Gap **Δ** Ⓦ
El. 5340'

Beartown Mt., El. 5481'

🚶🚶 Hughes Gap Ⓟ
El. 4040'

1" = 1 mi.

N

more like Christmas. Many of the mature Fraser firs here have been killed by the accidentally introduced balsam woolly adelgid, an aphidlike insect that burrows into the conductive tissue of the trunk. Along the trail and especially at the top you can see gray tree skeletons above the other trees. However, many fir trees at Roan Mt. remain healthy, and the Forest Service allows seed collection from some of them by researchers and Christmas tree farmers.

At 2.5 mi. turn sharp left and ascend to the grassy summit. If you come to a tangle of fallen trees, check for blazes; you may have missed the turn. Turn right in the open area to the Cloudland Hotel site (see Hike #37), the U.S. Forest Service parking area, and views of the Black Mts. The AT continues straight 0.5 mi. to Roan High Knob Shelter, and there are wonderful side trips ranging from 0.5 mi. to 1.5 mi. to the Rhododendron Gardens and to Roan High Bluff at the other end of the parking area. (See Hike #37 for details.)

Note: Relocations of this section scheduled for 2013 will make it about 2 mi. longer and much less steep.

Miles N	**NORTH**	Elev. (ft./m)	Miles S
2.6	**End:** Cloudland Hotel site; USFS parking lot, toilets, water; jct. **Cloudland Trail** to the **Rhododendron Gardens.**	6150/1875	0.0
1.8	**Ash Gap,** camping; spur trail to unreliable spring (0.2 mi.).	5340/1628	0.8
1.4	Summit **Beartown Mt.**	5481/1671	1.2
1.3	Side trail 50 yd. R to rock promontory, views W.		1.3
0.0	**Start:** Hughes Gap, parking area.	4040/1231	2.6

SOUTH

HIKE #37
Carvers Gap to Roan High Bluff and Rhododendron Gardens

Maps: ATC Map 2, Moreland Gap to Sams Gap

Route: From Carvers Gap to Cloudland Hotel site; Cloudland Trail to Roan High Bluff; backtrack to road and loop through Rhododendron Gardens; return on AT

Recommended direction: N to S

Distance: 4.6 to 5.6 mi. total (2 to 3 mi. in Rhododendron Gardens); 2.6 mi. on AT

Elevation +/-: 5512 to 6285 to 6150 ft.

Effort: Moderate

Day hike: Yes

Overnight backpacking hike: No

Duration: 4 to 5 hr.

Early exit option: Cloudland parking area, at 2.6mi.

Natural history features: Spruce-fir forest; Rhododendron Gardens; grassy bald; rare plants

Social history feature: Cloudland Hotel site

Other features: Cross-country ski trails; scheduled naturalist weekends and arts and crafts festivals

Trailhead access: From US 19E in Roan Mt., TN, go R on TN 143 for 12.8 mi, passing through Roan Mt. State Park to Carvers Gap at the NC state line, Mitchell Co. line, and AT crossing. From NC, Carvers Gap is 13.0 mi. N of Bakersville on NC 261 (the continuation of TN 143). The gravel parking area R has two sections, an information sign, and toilets.

Camping: Roan High Knob Shelter

Roan Mountain is a place of mystery, legend, wild beauty, and superlatives. The largest of the southern Appalachian grassy balds (see "Grazing, Lightning, or What?" in Hike #15), it also boasts one of the most beautiful displays of Catawba rhododendron in the world, more rare or endangered plants than the Smokies, the northernmost AT sections above 6000 ft. elevation until Mt. Washington, the best cross-country ski trails in Tennessee, the highest shelter on the AT, the oldest moun-

tains in the world, and the oldest rock of the entire AT. This moderate hike leads you to two high points, excellent views, and several different mountain habitats. In good weather, you may want to spend all day lying on soft grass or investigating with binoculars or hand lenses. This section of the AT goes from Carvers Gap to the site of the Cloudland Hotel, and two other U.S. Forest Service trails make a nice loop to explore the Roan Highlands south of Carvers Gap.

The AT starts on TN 143 about 30

Rhododendron

Thousands of people go to Roan Mt. every June to see the Rhododendron Gardens. However, you can see rhododendron on any hike in this volume, and we encourage hikers to visit alternate sites to see this flowering bush, especially in early summer. In fact, rhododendron is doing something interesting all year long.

Rhododendron is a member of the heath family (Ericaceae), a huge botanical group that includes mountain laurel, flame azalea, sourwood, doghobble, blueberries and cranberries, wintergreen, and trailing arbutus. Botanists use flower structure to determine relationships, and it is the flower that draws most attention. Rosebay rhododendron, the most common species and the one that grows in tangled masses along creeks, has clusters of white flowers in late June that persist at higher elevations until August. The top petal of each flower looks as if it has been splattered with a fine spray of fresh avocado pulp. Bees zero in on these greenish-yellow spots, brush against the outstretched anthers and stigmas, and pollinate the flowers. Catawba rhododendron, which grows on high-elevation exposed ridges or balds, has rose to lavender blooms. The fantastic Catawba rhododendron flower show of Roan Mt. (usually during the third week of June) exists because loggers took all the trees but left enough rhododendrons to flourish in the sunlight.

Both rhododendron varieties have large and leathery evergreen leaves. Here's the easy way to tell them apart when the flowers are gone. Rosebay rhododendron leaves are 8 to 12 inches long and pointed on the end.

---

yds. into Tennessee from the parking lot. Bear left down the road bank and look for the AT sign and a blue-blazed trail on the right, leading to a good spring. A large patch of green alder grows to the right of the AT. This small tree usually grows only in New England and Canada. It is a glacial relict, and Roan Mt. is the only southern bald still cool enough to support it. The glaciers did not extend this far south. Canadian and arctic plants moved here during the cold times, and when the glaciers receded, high-elevation spots like this served as a refuge for cool-climate plants that could both survive here and repopulate the destroyed land far to the north where mile-high glaciers had been.

The trail passes two boulders and crosses some low bridges over wet areas. At 0.4 mi., turn right onto an old road that is graded and has switchbacks for an easier climb. This road was part of the carriage road that served the Cloudland Hotel in the 1880s and '90s; it was a long,

Catawba rhododendron leaves are shorter and rounded at the end. Rosebay grows at all elevations, while Catawba grows mainly above 4000 feet.

In October, a few rhododendron leaves turn bright yellow and fall off, but most stay on for another year of photosynthetic duties. After the deciduous trees lose their leaves, the somber, dark-green rhododendron leaves, which were shaded by their neighbors in summer, get full sun — what there is of it. However, to pay for the use of fall and winter sun, rhododendron leaves must prevent freezing and water loss from their large surfaces. On cool days they droop down from their twigs like the ribs of a closing umbrella. Near freezing temperature, each leaf curls around its midrib, eventually forming a tube when the edges touch. The tube tightens as the temperature drops into the teens. At around 10 degrees Fahrenheit, rhododendron leaves look like long, thin stringbeans and rattle against each other in the wind. If you can see right through a rhododendron thicket, don't worry — the plants aren't dying. But you'd better have on your hat, mittens, and long underwear.

Look for two kinds of buds at the ends of rhododendron twigs. Leaf buds are thin and pointed, while flower buds look like miniature artichokes. Most rosebay rhododendron growing along creeks have few flower buds, but up on a ridgetop, with more of that valuable sunlight, flower buds may outnumber leaf buds. On winter hikes to remote areas, keep track of where the rhododendron in exposed areas seems to have the most buds. Then at midsummer (or later at a high elevation), repeat that hike to enjoy your private rhododendron garden.

rough ride. The carriages carried guests (who had traveled to Johnson City by train) as well as the supplies, food, and drink needed by a luxury hotel. In good weather the guests would hike up the carriage road, getting an early start on their mountain cure, which might last a month or more. But on raw, windy days, the carriage driver would ferry them up the mountain, supplying plenty of blankets and, in extreme cases, allowing the guests to get an early start on the whiskey keg.

Turtlehead (a summer-blooming pink flower), soft mosses, and ferns line the trail through the spruce-fir forest. Many of the Fraser firs have died from insect damage, and you will see more and more dead trees as you ascend. The insect, an aphidlike adelgid, came from Europe on lumber or nursery stock. It kills trees by destroying the thin layer of transport tissue in the trunk and has invaded the entire range of Fraser firs.

At 1.5 mi. a steep blue-blazed trail leads 0.1 mi. left to Roan High Knob

Random and Low-tech Hiking Tips

- Never step on wet wood, especially debarked water bars. These logs are placed in the trail at an angle and a slope, and slimy algae grow on them. If you step on them instead of over them, they can remove you from the trail as efficiently as they remove water.

- Walk several paces back from the hiker in front of you. It is your responsibility to avoid branches that snap back. Also, some folks are lethal with their walking sticks when they stumble.

- If you are going down or up a steep or rocky section, wait until the area is clear of previous hikers before you start.

- Stuff a few plastic grocery bags in your pack. Use them to sit on, to keep spare clothes dry in your pack, to store wet clothes after a clothes change, and to pack out other peoples' trash.

- Keep all your food in one bag. Put lunch trash back into the same bag —and don't forget to clean it out as soon as you get home.

- Carry lots of water (I know we said that before, but it can't be said too many times) and drink it all. Fill a small bottle that you can carry in a front pocket or on a belt loop, so you don't need to stop to drink. Refill the bottle at rest stops.

- Bring a self-seal bag of chocolate chips and an orange. On your first break, eat the orange, and put the peel in with the chocolate chips; eat the chips later. Remember to compost the orange peel when you get home. Also try spearmint or peppermint.

- If you wear glasses, carry at least two bandannas—one to wipe sweat and oil from your face and the other (in a small plastic bag) to clean the glasses. If your glasses fog, lick the insides of the lenses and rub them dry with the glasses bandanna.

- If you are the leader of a group of children, establish one rule before you start: "Do not pass me on the trail unless I tell you to." With this rule in place, you can enforce any other rules or make up new ones.

Shelter, which, at 6285 ft., is the highest shelter on the AT. A tall fire tower once stood here, and the two-story wooden shelter is the rebuilt fire watcher's house. This shelter has an overused cooking and eating area in front and a second-story sleeping loft with a window at mid-tree level. If you visit the shelter, watch the blazes carefully because hikers have trampled a maze of confusing trails in the area. A piped spring is about 75 ft. down a path to the right of the shelter.

After the shelter, the AT descends gently on good trail past some large rock outcrops and then into an open area with blackberries and filmy angelica. The trail crosses an old parking area at 1.7 mi., now blocked with boulders, and ascends steeply through blackberries and some mud. At 1.8 mi. an elegant rock chimney with an AT blaze blocks the trail; as you squeeze around it, you can see the flat place where the cabin once stood. In a grassy area at 2.0 mi. the trail forks twice. The AT continues right; the first left fork leads to the location of the front veranda of the former Cloudland Hotel. To the east, Mt. Mitchell and the Black Mts. are visible. Directly west of a fire ring is a flat rock between a fir tree and a mountain ash tree, marking the spot of the hotel's front door. Most of the foundation stones have been moved, but enough remain to show a rough outline.

The Cloudland Hotel was built in 1885 by John Wilder, a former Union general. He used local fir, cut and sawed on site, and nails from the Cranberry iron mines that he owned in the valley. Furniture and paneling were made from local cherry and maple trees. The hotel had 250 rooms but only one bathroom; however, every room had a huge copper bathtub. Guests—who included European royalty, politicians, famous botanists, and people who arrived in Johnson City in their own private train cars—could enjoy golf, bowling, tennis, horseback riding, and ballroom dancing. The dining-room table straddled the state line, and guests who wanted to drink alcohol had to remember to sit in Tennessee, since North Carolina was a dry state. The

NORTH Carolina Travel and Tourism

Hikers and rhododendron, Pisgah National Forest

hotel did well for about 20 years but then started losing money. It was abandoned in 1910 and auctioned off by the room. Many houses in the Roan area are built from Cloudland lumber, and some have hotel room doors, complete with numbers. The huge dining-room table with the painted state line was taken home by a farmer and cut down to fit in a small kitchen.

Lumber companies were the next visitors to Roan Mt. They cut everything, caused erosion and great fires, and left a mess. Champion Lumber Company built a board road on stilts halfway round the mountain so they could reach trees on the steepest bluffs. Landscapers came next and dug rhododendrons and azaleas to sell in northern cities and abroad. Roan Mt. looked bad for a while, with no large trees and deeply eroded gullies, but the U.S. Forest Service took over much of the acreage in 1941 and has protected it since. A local group, the Southern Appalachian Highlands Conservancy, raises money to buy land parcels before developers can build on them. What you see on this hike is all regrowth over the past 50 years.

After exploring the area, leave the AT and follow a path to the left of the hotel site down to the paved Cloudland parking lot, visible from the Cloudland site. Water and bathrooms are available here. At the far end of the lot, pick up the Cloudland Trail, which runs through fir woods and pretty open areas. It passes two other parking lots and reaches the end of a gravel loop road in about 0.6 mi. An endangered plant, the mountain avens, lives here, and the Forest Service protects it by clearing away other plants. It has a yellow summer flower like a large buttercup and round crinkly leaves that turn burgundy in the fall.

Cross the road into a picnic area. This is where you can try the "Stomp" —stomp on the ground and see if some spots sound more hollow than others. (But don't stomp on the rare Roan Mt. bluet or the three-leafed cinquefoil.) Though legends have

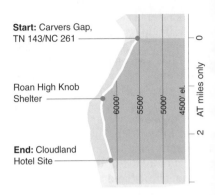

Start: Carvers Gap, TN 143/NC 261

Roan High Knob Shelter

End: Cloudland Hotel Site

6000' 5500' 5000' 4500' el.

AT miles only

0

2

caverns and little people living down there, a park ranger says there might be some deposits of organic material that have rotted away.

Beyond the picnic tables and the grassy area, the Cloudland Trail rises and becomes rockier. It passes through an area where the Fraser fir trees are healthy; the Forest Service supervises commercial fir seed harvest here in September. The seeds are used for Christmas tree farms and for research into ways of saving these insect-threatened trees. At 1.5 mi. from the Cloudland parking lot, the trail comes to a wooden observation deck at Roan High Bluff (6267 ft.). The view here includes Buladean, a small community down to the left that used to be called Magnetic City because of its magnetite ore, Unaka Mt. to the south, Johnson City to the northwest, and the parallel ridges of Iron Mt. and Holston Mt. to the west and north. At least 50 mi. of the AT

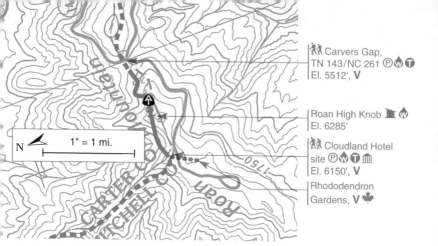

Carvers Gap,
TN 143/NC 261 ⓟⓌ🅣
El. 5512', **V**

Roan High Knob ▮🈂Ⓦ
El. 6285'

Cloudland Hotel
site ⓟⓌ🅣🏛
El. 6150', **V**

Rhododendron
Gardens, **V** 🍁

N   1" = 1 mi.

run through this view, and this over-look is one of the best places to watch Fourth of July fireworks.

Backtrack to the gravel road, and follow it back to another USFS infor-mation sign with maps and inter-pretive displays. Trails here make loops into the Rhododendron Gar-dens and another overlook deck (as well as the bathrooms); one trail is paved for handicap access. These rhododendron plants are not culti-vated or clipped. The removal of so many plants 50 years ago allowed the survivors to grow without com-petition into rounded, symmetrical shapes. They bloom during the last 2 weeks of June and draw crowds

of visitors, many of whom drive to the mountaintop.

To return to Carver's Gap, back-track to the Cloudland parking lot and follow the AT back down.

Other options for this hike include leaving one car at Carver's Gap and another at one of the Forest Service parking lots near the Rhododendron Gardens, or starting the hike at the gardens and hiking down the AT to Carver's Gap. If some members of the group need more exercise, you could drop them off at Hughes Gap (Hike #36) and meet them at the Cloudland Hotel site.

HIKE #37   Itinerary

Miles N	**NORTH**	Elev. (ft./m)	Miles S
	Total: 4.6 to 5.6 mi. with Rhododendron Gardens		
2.2	**Start:** Carvers Gap; TN 143/NC 261, parking, water, toilets.	5512/1680	0.0
1.0	Side trail to **Roan High Knob Shelter,** (0.1 mi.); spring 75 ft. R.	6285/1916	1.5
0.0	**End:** Cloudland Hotel Site; parking, water, toilets, trails to **Roan High Bluff** and **Rhododendron Gardens.**	6150/1875	2.2

SOUTH

HIKE #38
Carvers Gap to US 19E

Maps: ATC Map 2, Moreland Gap to Sams Gap

Route: From Carvers Gap to Yellow Mt. Gap, to Dolls Flats, to US 19E

Recommended direction: S to N

Distance: 14.8 mi.

Elevation +/-: 5512 to 5807 to 2880 ft.

Effort: Strenuous

Day hike: Optional

Overnight backpacking hike: Yes

Duration: 8 to 9 hr.

Early exit option: Yellow Mt. Gap

Natural history feature: High grassy balds

Social history feature: Overmountain Trail from East Tennessee to Battle of Kings Mt.

Caution: This hike can be dangerous in storms. Fog or snow make it difficult to follow the trail.

Trailhead access: *Start:* From US 19E in Roan Mt., TN, follow TN 143 for 12.8 mi. through Roan Mt. State Park. Carvers Gap and the AT are at the state line. Gravel parking area on R has two sections, an information sign, and primitive toilets. *End:* From the junction of US 19E and TN 143, go E for 3.9 mi. From Elk Park, go 2.5 mi. W on US 19E. A small pullout at a break in the guardrail has room for 5 or 6 cars, but vandalism is a continuing problem here. Safer parking (and sometimes a shuttle) available for a fee from nearby businesses.

Camping: Stan Murray Shelter; Overmountain Shelter; Apple House Shelter; several campsites

Wide-open spaces, miles of waving grass, alpine wildflowers . . . Is this the southern Appalachians? Botanist Asa Gray observed in the 1880s that he could ride his horse for 14 mi. on Roan Mt. and not pass a single tree. The Roan Massif, a chain of high peaks in northeastern Tennessee, is almost as high as the Smokies and significantly farther north, so it supports northern species of plants and animals. Jane Bald, Hump and Little Hump mts., and Grassy Ridge make up the largest of the southern Appalachian

grass balds on mountains said to be the world's oldest. Botanists don't understand the origin of balds, which look as if they have a treeline, (see "Grazing, Lightning, or What?" in Hike #15).

This spectacular hike has three shelters, several campsites, panoramic vistas, and an unusual history. The original AT route did not include the Roan Massif. However, the late Stan Murray, the ATC chairman from 1961 to 1975, fell in love with Roan Mt. and worked with the U.S. Forest Service and TEHC to include it in the

AT route. Then Murray became the director of the Southern Appalachian Highlands Conservancy (SAHC), which works to protect the Roan Highlands by land purchase and conservation easements. In sports, this is called following through. Murray's widow, Judy, wrote a doctoral dissertation on AT hikers, and since Stan's death in 1990 (his ashes were scattered on the Roan), Judy continues his conservation work on these beautiful mountains.

Caution: Weather can be extreme on any part of Roan Mt. Wind, rain, snow, ice, dense fog, and lightning can all be dangerous. Check for current conditions by calling the U.S. Forest Service or by asking at the state park visitor center on TN 143. Stay off the balds in thunderstorms. In cold weather, some hikers bring crampons to wear on icy trail.

To start, go north from the parking area, cross TN 143, climb the road bank, and cross a log stile. The AT swings left up the grassy hillside and enters spruce-fir forest at 0.2 mi.

Curving back, the trail emerges on open bald and passes a patch of red spruce planted on the bald in the 1940s by Dr. D. M. Brown of East Tennessee State University. He wanted to solve the mystery of the balds by seeing if trees could live in the treeless area of thick grass. His trees grew well, but they did not reproduce, and now they are dying of old age or insect damage.

Asa Gray described Roan as the most beautiful mountain east of the Rockies, and he explored them all. Three hundred species of plants, seventy-five of them rare, live here, including Gray's and Michaux's lilies, which bloom in July and are favored by hummingbirds. And one hundred species of birds nest or pass through here: warblers, snow buntings, saw-whet owls, and peregrine falcons. Saw-whet owls, smallest and rarest of eastern owls, live in spruce-fir and are named for their call, which is like a saw being sharpened. Listen for it after dark.

The AT continues up past patches of Greenland alder, flame azalea, Catawba rhododendron, mountain ash, and a few scraggly yellow buckeyes. At 1.0 mi., the AT descends to Engine Gap, where a sawmill engine once pulled Tennessee logs up to the top so they could be sent down to North Carolina sawmills (there weren't any sawmills in Tennessee back then). At 1.1 mi. the AT turns left on a grassy path near the summit of Jane Bald, named for a woman who died there of milk sickness. An unmarked trail goes on straight to Grassy Ridge at 1.9 mi. Watch for white blazes on rocks or posts.

Weathered exposed boulders here are Precambrian; that is, formed before there were hard-shelled animals to leave fossils as layers of rock accumulated. This rock was probably formed in what is now South America, but it is so old that geologists cannot determine where it came from. Look for gneiss — rock that has light bands of quartz and feldspar alternating with dark bands of mica or hornblende. With a hand lens, crystals of quartz in the light bands should be visible. This metamorphic rock endured extreme heat and pressure, which caused the compounds in it to melt and flow together before hardening again. Pink feldspar and green epidote are two other rock types on the trail.

You may meet some goats and a goat herder in summer (Switzerland? No, East Tennessee). This is part of SAHC's "baatany" project to keep the bald open and grassy to preserve plant species that are here because of the balds.

The AT swings along the north side of Grassy Ridge through short alder trees and then through beech forest. A flat, grassy campsite is at 2.0 mi., and 100 yd. farther is a good spring.

The trail turns left again and descends on switchbacks through stunted beech trees and twisted yellow birches. This north-facing slope may be covered with ice even when spring flowers are blooming up on the bald.

At 3.6 mi. the AT levels at Low Gap (5050 ft.), and the Stan Murray Shelter (built in 1977) stands on the left, surrounded by fat-trunked yellow buckeye trees, looking like African baobabs, all the same height because of the strong wind in the gap. There's a spring 100 yd. to the right, and the view to the right shows the summit of Grassy Ridge, 1100 ft. higher.

Ascend from the gap through more stunted beech trees. Look for beech drops, parasitic flowering plants that grow under beech trees and suck food from their roots. Beech drops look like brown 8- to 12-in. twigs growing out of the ground.

From the crest, descend by switchbacks and an old road to Buckeye Gap at 4.6 mi. Watch white blazes carefully; trails, roads, and turns of the AT can be misleading. After the next summit turn right and descend along an old fence to Yellow Mt. Gap at 5.6 mi. The historic Overmountain Victory Trail crosses the AT here.

The Overmountain Men were colonists who defied King George's 1763 proclamation that English settlers must stay east of the mountains. Sixteen families settled in Sycamore Shoals, Tennessee, negotiated the Transylvania Purchase—a 20-million-acre real estate deal—with the Cherokee, and established the first democratic government on this continent in 1772. (Not all Cherokees agreed to the deal; Chief Dragging Canoe besieged Fort Watauga, the first of many conflicts that didn't end until the forced removal of the Cherokee in 1838. During the siege, John Sevier—nicknamed Nolichucky Jack—saved a young woman named Bonny Kate by pulling her over the fort wall; they later married.) On September 7, 1780, during the Revolutionary War, a troop of Overmountain Men led by John Sevier passed through this gap on their way from Sycamore Shoals, Tennessee, to King's Mt., South Carolina. They defeated the southern flank of the

British Army under Colonel Ferguson, freeing the South from British domination and allowing General Washington to focus his attention on the North. More details on the Overmountain Men (and women) can be found at Sycamore Shoals State Historic Area in Elizabethton (pronounced with the emphasis on "beth"), Tennessee.

From Yellow Mt. Gap, the Overmountain Victory Trail leads left down to US 19E. To the right, a blue-blazed trail goes 0.3 mi., passing a good spring, to the Overmountain Shelter, with a view of the Roaring Creek Valley. Grants and workers from L.L. Bean, the U.S. Forest Service, Tennessee Eastman Hiking and Canoeing Club, and Appa- lachian State University helped to transform an old barn into the largest shelter described in this volume. Covered cooking and eating areas occupy the ground floor, and twenty-five people can sleep in the hayloft (or maybe more, given the AT adage that "the shelter's not full until the last hiker comes in"). The movie *Winter People*, from a novel by John Ehle, was filmed partly on this site, using the barn and the great valley view to illustrate the harsh but beautiful conditions of pioneer life in the southern mountains.

After Yellow Mt. Gap the AT curves into the woods twice as it climbs Big Yellow Mt. Look for wild strawberries in late spring and blackberries in late summer. The view to the right into Roaring Creek Valley is spectacular

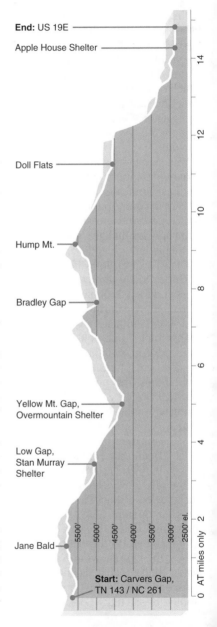

End: US 19E

Apple House Shelter

Doll Flats

Hump Mt.

Bradley Gap

Yellow Mt. Gap, Overmountain Shelter

Low Gap, Stan Murray Shelter

Jane Bald

Start: Carvers Gap, TN 143 / NC 261

5500' 5000' 4500' 4000' 3500' 3000' 2500' el.

AT miles only

🏃🏃 US 19E Ⓟ

Apple House ▬ 🅦

Doll Flats ▲ 🅦

Hump Mt., El. 5587'
🏛

Yellow Mt. Gap,
Overmountain ▬ 🅦
El. 4267', **V** ▲

Stan Murray, ▬ 🅦

▲

Jane Bald, El. 5807', **V**

🏃🏃 Carvers Gap,
TN 143/NC261 Ⓟ 🅣 🅦
El. 5512', **V**

N ◀ 7/8" = 1 mi.

in the fall, with trees of all colors. Watch blazes for a sharp left turn just before the summit, and skirt north.

Skirt to the left of Little Hump past big black rocks with orange and yellow lichens, white blazes on posts, and a view of Grandfather Mt. on the right. Descend to Bradley Gap at 8.5 mi., with tent sites and several springs. Follow the white blazes straight up Hump Mt., past more boulders. Cross a fence and talk with the cows if they are here. Their job is to keep blackberries and small trees from invading the grassy bald. Climb to the Hump Mt. summit (5587 ft.) at 9.4 mi. The vista includes the Doe and Toe River valleys, Beech and Grandfather mts., and Grassy Ridge, where you started this hike. In about 50 yd. is a memorial plaque to Stan Murray.

Descend across the bald and turn right, leaving the cattle fence and now entering thin woods of stunted beeches. If there was ice on the trail higher up, there is probably some here as well because this slope faces north and melts last. Hikers pack the snow, so there is often more ice on the trail than beside it. Hang on to the trees. After several switchbacks, the AT crosses an open field to Doll Flats at 11.7 mi., a good tent site with tall red maples. The AT swings left and then right as it meets another branch of the Shell Creek road. Tent sites at the beginning of Doll Flats are overused and trampled, but nearer this road there are grassy sites. At Doll Flats the AT leaves the

Tennessee/North Carolina state line for good and strikes out through Tennessee, heading north toward Virginia.

Descend from Doll Flats, steeply at first, through thin woods. After several sets of rock steps, a path leads 50 feet left to a rock outcrop and an overlook of Shell Creek Valley and Whiterocks Mt. The AT turns left and under this outcrop and goes along a cliff to a small stream. Descend into cover hardwoods and Wilder Mine Hollow at 13.8 mi. Some of the mines are still open, but it is dangerous to explore them. Union General Wilder (1830–1917) invented a better rifle and helped to hold off the Confederate Army at Chickamauga, near Chattanooga, Tennessee. After the Civil War, Wilder developed iron foundries in Rockwood, Tennessee, and mined ore from here and from other spots around the base of the Roan Massif. He invested some of his profits in the Cloudland Hotel near Roan High Bluff and owned most of the mountain. One of his advertising brochures persuades people to "Come up out of the sultry plains to the land of the sky — magnificent views above the clouds where the rivers are born." However, by 1910 loggers had cut all the trees on Roan Mt., leaving bare earth and erosion gullies, and the hotel was abandoned and sold off by the room (see Hike #37).

At 14.3 mi. pass Apple House Shelter on the left, a small old shelter with a creek for water. If the Overmoun-

Miles N	NORTH	Elev. (ft./m)	Miles S
14.8	**End:** US 19E, limited parking.	2880/878	0.0
14.3	**Apple House Shelter,** creek.		0.5
11.3	**Doll Flats,** campsites, spring 0.1 mi. L.	4560/1390	3.2
9.1	**Hump Mt.;** Stan Murray memorial plaque.	5587/1703	5.4
7.1	**Bradley Gap.**	4960/1512	6.3
4.7	**Yellow Mt. Gap,** trail to **Overmountain Shelter** (0.3 mi.) and spring.	4267/1301	9.2
3.0	**Stan Murray Shelter** at **Low Gap,** spring 100 yd. R.	5050/1539	11.2
1.1	**Jane Bald,** Precambrian boulders.	5807/1770	13.4
0.0	**Start:** Carvers Gap, TN 143/NC 261; parking, toilets, water.	5512/1680	14.8

SOUTH

tain Shelter is too crowded, this is the next best place, but it sits in a dark hollow and isn't nearly as pretty. After Apple House, the AT turns left, then right, and descends to a bridge over a creek and a possibly muddy field below the road bank of US 19E. Climb the road bank to a five- to six-car parking area at 14.8 mi.

There is additional parking across 19E; use extra caution in crossing road here.

The best one-car alternative to this long hike would be to start at Carvers Gap and hike the first 4 or 5 mi. and then backtrack. Another possibility would be to combine a hike to Grassy Ridge on this hike with parts of Hike #37 at the Rhododendron Gardens.

Dennis Cove to US 19E

Maps: ATC 1, Damascus VA to Moreland Gap; ATC 2, Moreland Gap to Sams Gap

Route: From Dennis Cove to White Rocks Mt., to Moreland Gap, to Walnut Mt. Rd., to Bishop Hollow, to US 19E

Recommended direction: N to S

Distance: 24.4 mi.

Elevation +/-: 2500 to 4105 to 2510 ft.

Effort: Strenuous

Day hike: No

Overnight backpacking hike: Yes

Duration: 13 to 14 hr.

Early exit option: Walnut Mt. Rd., at 12.7 mi.

Natural history features: Views of Iron, Holston, Unaka, Beech, Grandfather, and Roan mts.

Social history features: Old homesteads; old White Rocks Mt. fire tower

Other features: Cows

Trailhead access: *Start:* From junction of US 321 and US 19E at Hampton, head 0.8 mi. E on US 321/TN 67. Turn R onto USFS 50 (Dennis Cove Rd.) at Citizens Bank for 4.0 mi. to USFS Dennis Cove parking on L. AT going S climbs road bank across from parking lot. USFS Dennis Cove Campground is 0.6 mi. farther on R. *End:* From junction of US 19E and TN 143 in Roan Mt., TN, continue S on 19E for 3.9 mi. to gravel roadside parking on L. From Elk Park, NC, head N on US 19E for 3.0 mi., passing TN/NC line at 2.1 mi. To find AT going N, look for blazes leading up into the woods.

Camping: Moreland Gap Shelter; several campsites; USFS Dennis Cove Campground

W hen Earl Shaffer made the first recorded AT thru-hike in 1948, he shared shelters with cows and endured many miles of road walking. Bit by bit, the AT has been tucked into protected woodlands; now, 50 years later, only a few short stretches of trail remain on roads. This section of the trail was once the last rural road walk in this volume, but relocations in the last 10 years have moved it into the woods. The cows of Bishop Hollow graze on public land with permission from the

U.S. Forest Service.

Hike #39 is described from north to south because parking is easier on the north end and because the Dennis Cove Campground and USFS side trails offer varied hiking opportunities. Parking at US 19E (the hike's south end) is not safe. Shuttles and parking with permission (sometimes for a fee) are available at businesses on US 19E on either side of the AT crossing.

Shorter day hikes can be arranged on this long section. One 3.6-mi. loop combines part of the AT and Coon Den Falls Trail to Dennis Cove Campground, and the Laurel Fork and Lacy Trap trails can be used for longer loop hikes from the campground to White Rocks Mt. (Check with the Forest Service for maps and current conditions.) For a day hike on the southern end, hike from US 19E to Jones Branch Falls and backtrack to your car (11 mi. round-trip).

The hilly landscape of Hike #39 has supported logging, moonshining, homesteading, cattle grazing, and, more recently, Christmas tree farming. The trail is well graded and well blazed, with a few rocky or muddy places.

Several years ago, some conflicts between hikers and landowners gave this section a bad reputation, with stories of car vandalism, fake blazes, and threats of violence. A shelter was burned here in 1990. One sign of those times is destroyed blazes—look for scars on trees about the size and position of a blaze, some with bits of white paint around the outside. Those tree scars all look old, and problems have not been reported here for some time.

From the Dennis Cove parking lot, cross USFS 50 and climb the road bank. The AT joins an old road past a house and a woodland pond with turtles, bullfrogs, dragonflies, and possibly red-spotted newts. At about 0.4 mi., the trail swings by a log barn on a road lined with walnut trees and Chinese chestnuts. After a field crowded with young hemlocks, fol-low switchbacks and log steps up to a more mature hemlock forest. Cross a creek on stones, and ascend to a rock outcrop and a view of Elizabethton and the surrounding valleys at 1.5 mi. At 1.7 mi. the AT reaches the upper end of Coon Den Falls Trail, which leads left 1.3 mi. to the falls and Dennis Cove Campground. After switchbacks through more hemlock, turn left at one ridgetop, and climb the side of White Rocks Mt.

The AT descends through hemlock woods. Among the trail rocks are chunks of white feldspar, which looks chalky and breaks at right angles, and green epidote, which looks like the mold on Roquefort cheese. Feldspar is the most abundant mineral in the Earth's crust, and weathering breaks it down into clay. The 600-million-year-old Precambrian granite gneiss of White Rocks Mt. contains crystals of feldspar, epidote, and quartz that formed from the metamorphosis of sedimentary rocks.

The AT passes under a power line (with blazes on telephone poles), turns left, and crosses a grassy forest road at 3.6 mi. that leads left 0.1 mi. to Lacy Trap Trail. This trail and the parallel Leonard Branch Trail, just 0.2 mi. farther ahead, lead left to the intriguingly named Frog Level and from there back to Dennis Cove Campground on Laurel Fork Trail. The AT continues to descend gently, crossing a mowed deer browse and an overgrown slope with a view right of Christmas tree farms in the valley.

At 4.0 mi. a blue-blazed trail on the right leads 200 yd. to a small spring. Just past a fence corner, ascend through woods to a rocky summit, the actual crest of White Rocks Mt. and, at 4206 ft., the highest point of Hike #39.

Continue on a ridgeline through stands of Catawba and rosebay rhododendron, and descend to Moreland Gap Shelter, a cinder block box with a wide overhang and a cooking grill, at 6.0 mi. A blue-blazed trail leads 50 yd. left to a spring; if the spring is dry, go farther down the narrow valley to find creek water.

Climb for 0.4 mi. to the next summit (4121 ft.). Look through the trees for views north and south, with the Roan Massif dominating the latter view.

For the remainder of this hike, the AT swings east to stay on USFS land, and the creeks, which run through pastures and ridges above the trail, may be contaminated. Carry water or collect and treat water from the Moreland Gap spring.

At 7.4 mi. the trail passes a lichen-covered outcrop, descends through a rhododendron thicket, and crosses the first of many creeks on bog bridges. In about 0.1 mi. there is a small mossy campsite beside a creek. Moss grows slowly; if you camp here (or anywhere), pick up rocks and sticks from your tent site rather than kicking them out of the way. Before you leave, scatter them back over the site—another technique of leave-no-trace camping.

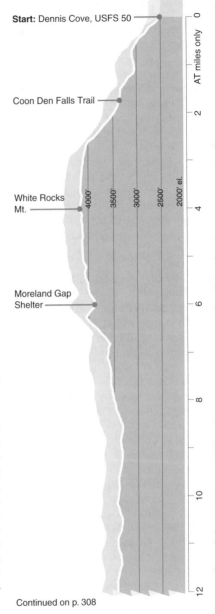

Continued on p. 308

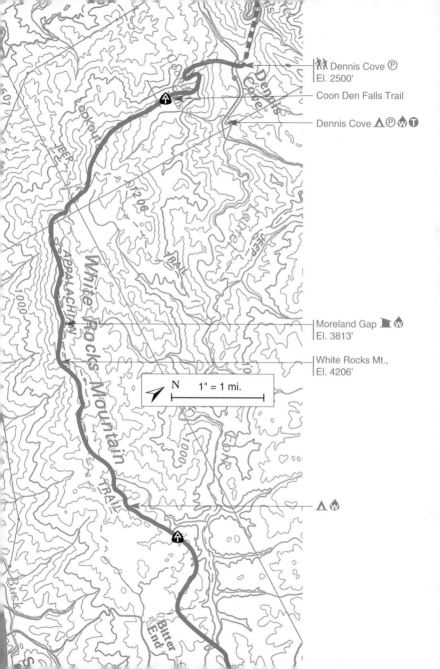

Dennis Cove Ⓟ
El. 2500'

Coon Den Falls Trail

Dennis Cove ▲ Ⓟ 🔥 🚻

Moreland Gap 🔥
El. 3813'

White Rocks Mt.,
El. 4206'

N   1" = 1 mi.

▲ 🔥

The AT continues with gentle ups and downs through oak woods and crosses yet another stream flowing through rhododendron at about 8.0 mi. Many trees along this stretch fell in a recent storm, producing mounds of decaying roots and pits where the roots used to be. Fungi, termites, beetles, and other decomposers will eat the wood fairly quickly, but the pit and mound will remain part of the forest ecology for decades. Some plants and animals grow well on the mound, and others favor the sheltered pit. Treefall increases forest diversity.

The AT crosses several more creeks—some with steep muddy banks, a sign of past forest use. When an area is clearcut or plowed, rainwater rushes down the creeks, cutting deeper channels. A few patches of white pines along here were probably planted after clearcutting.

At 9.8 mi. the AT climbs over a small ridge, then joins an old road and descends on log steps to cross a logging road at 10.2. mi. Look for a dead tree trunk on the left with rectangular pileated woodpecker holes.

Ascend, bearing right, through rhododendron and then another pine plantation. Many old roads wind through here; watch the blazes. At a flat spot, vigorous young tulip-trees and red maples are invading an old field, and smaller oaks and hemlocks will soon catch up. Descend on switchbacks at 11.8 mi. (don't cut across them!) to Laurel Fork, and

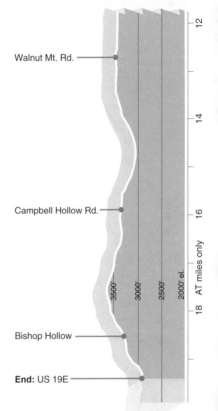

enjoy a creekside stroll for about 0.2 mi. After a log bridge, climb to another small ridge crest at 11.0 mi. The trail goes straight through a patch of sourwoods, then into a field with views to the south of Grandfather, Beech, and Roan Mts. Entering the woods again, the AT crosses several streams and small ridges. Many large multiple-trunked Fraser magnolias grow along here. Look for 1- to

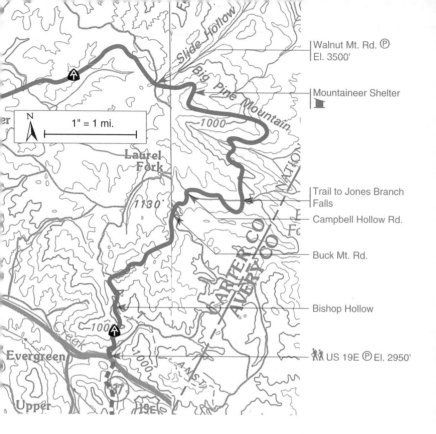

Walnut Mt. Rd. Ⓟ
El. 3500'

Mountaineer Shelter

Trail to Jones Branch Falls

Campbell Hollow Rd.

Buck Mt. Rd.

Bishop Hollow

US 19E Ⓟ El. 2950'

1½-ft.-long leaves with lobes at the base, big creamy, fragrant flowers in April, and magenta 4- to 6-in.-long fruits in late summer.

Cross gravel Walnut Mt. Rd. at 14.0 mi. (Though not a good place to leave a car, this road could serve as an early exit or as place to drop hikers off. To the right, Walnut Mt. Rd. leads about 2.0 mi. to Buck Mt. Rd.; turn right and then immediately left

onto Blue Grass Rd. to US 19E in another 2.0 mi.) Descend through hemlock woods and then thick stands of rhododendron. Two club mosses, princess pine and running ground cedar, grow here. Princess pine looks like a 10-in. spruce tree with a pointed top, while ground cedar has a 2-in. stalk with branches that fan out and curve down. Club mosses grow from underground runners; a large patch may be just one plant.

Ascend along the side of Big Pine Mt. A winter view left (southeast) shows Beech Mt. and, farther away, Grandfather Mt. The trail passes a field, then descends a south-facing ridge carpeted with galax, trailing arbutus, wintergreen, mountain laurel, and blueberry bushes. After another gully and creek crossing, the trail ascends into an area of same-age tulip-trees with an excellent tent site and lots of ground cedar. (This was probably a cornfield 40 years ago, perhaps supplying the nearby stills with mash.) Other trees grow slowly in the shade of the tulip-trees but will reach the same height, making a more diverse forest. Check back in a hundred years.

Descend left at 14.1 mi. across Slide Hollow. At 15.6 mi., look for a blue-blazed side trail to the Mountaineer Shelter, built in 2005 to replace the Don Nelan shelter that was burned by vandals in 1990. The AT reaches the Elk River at 17.2 miles (elevation 2675 ft.) and follows it for 0.7 mi. Good riverside camping is available in grassy spots. Look for a small waterfall above the junction of Sugar Hollow Stream and the Elk River.

At 19.1 mi. come to a 0.1 mi. side trail to Jones Branch Falls, possibly the highest falls of the entire AT, at 100 ft. of free fall and cascade, with giant square boulders along the way. The AT used to go along Campbell Hollow Road, but now, because of land purchase and many days of trail relocation work, the trail stays in the woods and crosses that road at 20.8 mi.

After a small pine-covered crest, descend to another swampy area and cross a small stream. Climb switchbacks to paved Buck Mt. Rd. at the High Point Memorial Baptist Church. Steps on the other side of the road lead up to a cleared pasture with a view left of Beech Mt., looking like a distant shark fin on the horizon.

Enter woods at the top of the field, pass a rusty dump rake—a relic of a bygone farm—and turn left into another field. At 21.5 mi. pass Isaacs Cemetery, and enter pine woods on a dirt road. Then turn right to execute an odd maneuver: Hike parallel to the field for about 60 yd., do a tight U-turn left, hike back toward the dirt road, and emerge a few feet up from the first turn. This could be called a paper clip turn; don't skip it if you want credit for every step of the AT.

Cross the road and continue by switchbacks up the slope to a 3820-ft. summit at 21.9 mi. Blackberries and small tulip-trees are indications of recent clearing, and the trail soon crosses a plank stile into a current pasture. The trail turns right after the stile, but walk left into the pasture for a view, if the resident bull doesn't mind. To the east is Beech Mt. again. Beyond is the craggy outline of Grandfather Mt.; look for an old man's reclining profile, forehead to the left, bearded chin to the right, and his dentures out while he sleeps.

Return to the stile, and descend

through thin woods. At the bottom of the hill, look left for a cinder block house foundation near a good spring — good, that is, in quantity. Houses and pastures lie upstream, and even spring water may be contaminated.

Ascend along a roadbed lined with grasping rose bushes, blackberries, greenbrier, and poison ivy. Dogwood and sassafras trees stand along the road, which soon turns left into a growth of black locust trees and tangled grapevines.

Cross a barbed-wire fence on a pole stile and then again on another, ramp-type stile. After the AT descends through woods, it enters the top of a rocky pasture in Bishop Hollow. Turn left at a rock cairn and follow blazes down the valley, generally keeping right of a small stream. In fog or rain the blazes may be hard to see.

The Forest Service permits grazing in this formerly farmed hollow. Explain to the cattle, if they're here, that you are a tax-paying citizen just passing through. The few trees here are all blazed and allow some identi-fication practice. Tree 1: an old sugar maple at the end of a low stone wall. Tree 2: a white oak. Tree 3: a very old dogwood. Tree 4: another sugar maple with an impressive collection of yellow-bellied-sapsucker holes. These small woodpeckers make holes and then come back to drink the sap and eat the insects that get stuck in it. The next three blazes are on posts. Tree 5: American hornbeam, also called ironwood. Notice the smooth, sinewy bark and the little pagoda-shaped seed clusters in fall.

Bear right from the pasture up through more pine woods. Cross the barbed wire on a pole stile to a hemlock grove. At the ridge crest, turn right and descend on switchbacks. After another valley, ascend along a rock face with an open sandy cave. Descend to a solid bridge over cascading Bear Branch, and climb log steps to Bear Branch Rd. at 24.2 mi. Cross one more small ridge and head down through hemlocks to US 19E at 24.4 mi. Use caution: Traffic is fast and heavy here.

Miles N	NORTH	Elev. (ft./m)	Miles S
24.4	**Start: Dennis Cove,** USFS 50; parking lot.	2510/765	0.0
24.2	Woodland pond.		0.2
22.7	Jct. blue-blazed trail L to **Coon Den Falls** (1.3 mi.).		1.7
20.9	Power line.		3.5
19.5	**White Rocks Mt.** crest.	4206/1281	4.9
18.4	**Moreland Gap Shelter;** blue-blazed trail to spring 50 yd L.	3813/1162	6.0
13.6	Jct. **USFS 293,** leads to Buck Mt. Rd.		10.8
12.6	**Laurel Fork footbridge.**		11.8
10.4	Jct. **Walnut Mt. Rd;** early exit option.	3500/1067	14.0
8.8	Side trail to **Mountaineer Shelter.**		15.6
6.1	**Elk River,** good creekside campsites.		18.3
5.4	Jct. side trail to **Jones Branch Falls** (0.1 mi.).		19.0
3.3	**Cross Buck Mt. Rd.;** High Point Memorial Baptist Church.		21.1
2.9	**Isaacs Cemetery.**		21.5
1.5	**Bishop Hollow.**		22.9
0.0	**End: US 19E,** roadside parking or use shuttle or private parking.	2950/899	24.4

SOUTH

Dennis Cove to Laurel Fork Gorge

Maps: ATC Map 1, Damascus, VA, to Moreland Gap

Route: From Dennis Cove to Laurel Falls, to US 321 at Laurel Fork (Hampton Blueline) trailhead

Recommended direction: S to N

Distance: 3.7 mi. total; 2.7 mi on AT; 5.4 mi. with backtrack to Dennis Cove

Access trail name & length: Laurel Fork Trail (Hampton Blueline Trail), 1.0 mi.

Elevation +/-: 2510 to 1900 ft.

Effort: Moderate, except for 0.5 mi. of rocky, steep trail

Day hike: Yes

Overnight backpacking hike: Optional

Duration: 3 to 4 hr.

Early exit option: None

Natural history features: Gorge and waterfall; Carolina hemlock

Social history feature: Logging history

Other feature: Buckled Rock on Laurel Fork

Trailhead access: *Start:* From junction of US 19E and US 321, turn N for 0.8 mi.; then bear R onto Dennis Cove Rd., marked with a brown USFS sign. Citizen's Bank is in the fork between US 321 and Dennis Cove Rd. (USFS 50 on maps). Go 4.1 mi. on steep, twisting paved road; at about 3.0 mi., pass AT sign. As road levels (large field and some houses R), look for USFS parking area L. *End:* From junction of US 19 E and US 321, turn N as in Start, but continue 0.5 mi. past Dennis Cove Rd. Pass Brown's Store on L, cross a concrete bridge, and look for USFS parking area R for Laurel Fork Creek.

Camping: Laurel Fork Shelter; a few small campsites

A beautiful gorge, a waterfall, a swimming hole, and two short side trails could keep hikers busy all day even though this hike is short. Most of the trail is easy and level, but the sections down to the falls and back up are steep and about as rocky as a trail can be. No need to worry about the intrusion of off-road vehicles here. However, hiking with children or with a heavy pack may require special precautions and plenty of time. We start from Dennis Cove, but it's just as nice the other way—starting from the U.S. Forest Service parking area in Hampton—with a bit more climbing. The option described here requires two cars, but the hike is short enough to use one car and then backtrack. Another two-car option is to combine this hike with the next AT section, Pond Mt. (Hike #41), which would provide an aerobic workout as well as spectacular scenery. The area is popular; on hot summer weekends, both parking lots may be full. Wildlife abounds here, as well.

Checking the trail register

Bears, bobcats, and deer find refuge in the gorge, and snakes and lizards like to sun themselves on the south-facing cliffs and rock piles.

Starting from the Dennis Cove parking area, pass through an opening in a log fence, and proceed along a level trail with Laurel Fork on the right. Most of the trails here are old railroad grades from logging operations in the early 1900s. Some parts of this gorge hold stands of virgin timber that the Pittsburgh Lumber Company couldn't reach, but they are so remote and well protected that even the AT doesn't get near them. An AT mileage sign is nailed to a large tuliptree (named for its orange, yellow, and green flower) on the right, and thick rhododendron grows on both sides of the trail.

At 0.6 mi. the trail passes a Pond Mt. Wilderness sign. This 6195-acre wilderness lies in Carter County and

is protected by the Forest Service from logging, road building, and other development. Several rugged and beautiful areas in the Cherokee National Forest were designated wilderness after hiking and conservation groups proposed lands that they had studied for inclusion in the Wilderness Act of 1964. The volunteers who worked on wilderness studies deserve our thanks, just as trail maintainers do.

Between the wilderness sign and the next landmark, a USFS registry box, doghobble, Fraser sedge, and wild ginger line the trail. Fraser sedge, named for Scottish botanist John Fraser, grows in the Smokies and only a few other protected spots. Sedges are flowering plants related to grasses.

The trail continues level, but to the right, across the creek, high, rocky cliffs signal the beginning of the gorge. Swing left through a railroad cut. (The lumber company really had to pay for wood harvested here —you will pass through several cuts like this.) The quartzite rock breaks into blocks because of its crystalline structure, and the slanted sedimentary lines give evidence of the continental collision that pushed up these mountains 250 million years ago. Quartzite is metamorphosed sandstone. The intense heat and pressure resulting from the continental collision caused the sandstone to crystallize, somewhat like the way sand crystallizes when melted to make glass. Quartzite resists erosion, but the cracks allow roots and water to creep in and slowly break the blocks apart. Look for lichens of all colors on the rock surfaces.

After the railroad cut, the trail turns right and descends at 0.7 mi. to cross Laurel Fork on Koonford Bridge, a neat structure with two cemented rock piers and dovetailed crosspieces to hold the main logs in place. This bridge, built by trail maintainers, won an award for being built of mostly local materials using only hand tools. (Another provision of the Wilderness Act is that power tools are prohibited in the forest; this presents interesting challenges for trail workers.)

A short rocky scramble leads to a small side gorge with jumbled rocks and more good examples of angled sedimentary layers on the rock face. After another rocky side canyon, look down to the left from a ledge at the rapids. The trail bears right through another railroad cut to a great winter view down the length of the gorge. A faint path to the left at 0.9 mi. provides a 0.2-mi. scramble up to Potato Top, a rocky pointed knob, for a fine view any time.

Now the AT starts getting really rocky, and at 1.1 mi. (double blaze and junction with a blue-blazed loop trail to Laurel Fork Shelter) it turns sharply left, gets even rockier, and descends steeply. This is only a 0.2-mi. piece, but it feels longer. At the creek, the falls are upstream to the left, with a large pool at the base. Soak your feet, but don't swim here; the rocks are sharp, and the depth is variable. It is possible to scramble up to the top of Laurel Falls, and when the flow is low, some people climb up the face of the falls. If hiking with children, establish rules before the waterfall noise drowns out your words of caution.

Beyond the falls, the AT continues downstream and approaches a rockface cliff. There's a very small potential campsite at the base of the cliff, but check the rocks teetering on the top. Descend to creekside on stepping stones (the best ones are marked with worn spots), and creep along a very narrow concrete and rock ledge around the overhanging end of the cliff. Look for a prehistoric trail maintainer's handprint in the concrete.

Caution: If the ledge is under water or icy, return to the trail junction and take the blue-blazed bypass trail over the top.

Ascend steeply on more rocky trail to meet the blue-blazed trail from the shelter. Climb higher to an open, rocky ridge with a view back up the gorge. Carolina hemlock and Catawba rhododendron grow here. The relatively rare Carolina hemlock has needles arranged around the twig instead of in flat rows like the more common Eastern hemlock. The needles are also slightly longer, and the tree looks bushier or fuller than Eastern hemlock. Catawba rhododendron is common on ridgetops; it's unusual to find it deep in a gorge like this.

On this ridge, sometime in June, you might see rosebay rhododendron (white), Catawba rhododendron (pink to lavender), mountain laurel (pink), and flame azalea (pale yellow to dark orange) blooming at the same time. These four shrubs are all in the heath family, but only the flame azalea sheds its leaves in fall. Piedmont rhododendron, another evergreen rhododendron, also grows on this ridge. Its leaves look like mountain laurel leaves; it has rose-colored flowers in May or June; and the capsule-shaped seedpods persist most of the year. (Mountain laurel seedpods are round, like brown peas.) To confirm the difference between mountain laurel and Piedmont rhododendron, look at the undersides of the leaves with a hand lens. Mountain laurel is plain green, while Piedmont rhododendron is covered with rusty spots. During winter hikes, the swollen flower buds of all five of these members of the heath family allow predictions of how abundant the bloom will be in June.

Descend through pine woods to creek level, and join an old road at 2.0 mi. (Coming from the north, this junction is marked with a double blaze, but if you miss the AT and continue on the road, it reaches a creek crossing you probably won't want to make. Backtrack 0.1 mi. and look for the blazes.) At 2.2 mi. from Dennis Cove, pass Waycaster Spring, named for settlers of this area. A little creek cascades down and goes under the road, and the spring joins the cascade from the right. Camping is possible here, and if you plan to go on over Pond Mt., be sure to get water here.

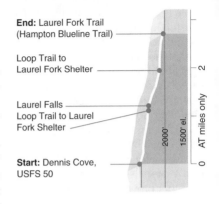

End: Laurel Fork Trail (Hampton Blueline Trail)

Loop Trail to Laurel Fork Shelter

Laurel Falls
Loop Trail to Laurel Fork Shelter

Start: Dennis Cove, USFS 50

At 2.3 mi. cross Laurel Fork on a plank bridge that required more than just hand tools; materials for this bridge were carried from outside the wilderness area. Upstream is a forested creek island. Cross back again on another plank bridge with a smaller creek island, and continue downstream to a junction and a double blaze.

At the junction with the Laurel Fork Trail (Hampton Blueline Trail) at 2.7 mi., the AT makes a sharp right to ascend Pond Mt. (Hike #41). To complete this hike and reach US 321 at the Laurel Fork trailhead, leave the AT now, and continue straight on blue-blazed trail for 1.0 mi. The trail follows the creek with two short climbs over ridges and one rocky section right above the water that could be tricky on snow or ice. About halfway to the trailhead, look across Laurel Fork at Buckled Rock,

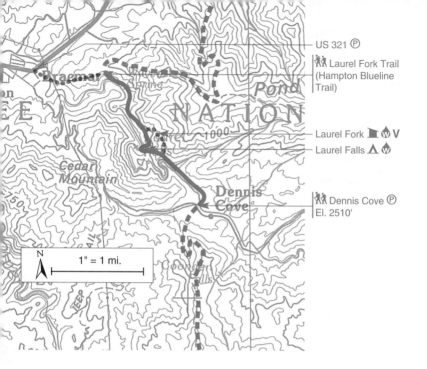

Map labels: US 321 Ⓟ / Laurel Fork Trail (Hampton Blueline Trail) / Laurel Fork ▮ ⓦ V / Laurel Falls ▲ ⓦ / Dennis Cove Ⓟ El. 2510' / Braemar / Pond / NATION / 1000 / Cedar Mountain / Dennis Cove / N 1" = 1 mi.

a sheer rock face made of quartzite blocks curved up in an arch, or buckled. A few hemlocks and rhododendrons are growing valiantly in fissures. Flat places for campsites can be found along the creek, but they may be heavily used in summer.

Laurel Fork Shelter is not directly on the AT; it lies far above the main trail and can be reached on the blue-blazed bypass trail. Coming from Dennis Cove, take the blue-blazed trail that leaves the AT at 1.1 mi., and ascend (partly by scrambling) to a pretty knoll overlooking the gorge.

The rock shelter, built in 1977 on the only flat land in sight, looks south-west with good views up the gorge and great sunsets. It holds six people, has a good overhang for shelter in rain, and is 50 yd. from a small stream water source. To rejoin the AT, follow blue blazes from the right front of the shelter, and descend about 0.4 mi. If you plan to backtrack to Dennis Cove, a nice way to do this hike is to go to the falls first, then hike down to Buckled Rock and return by the bypass trail.

HIKE #40   Itinerary

Miles N	NORTH	Elev. (ft./m)	Miles S
Total: 3.7 mi. with access trail			
1.0	**Access: Laurel Fork Trail (Hampton Blueline Trail)** to US 321, USFS parking.		1.0
2.7	**End AT miles:** Jct. Laurel Fork Trail (Hampton Blueline Trail).	1900/579	0.0
2.2	**Waycaster Spring,** campsite, water.	1900/579	0.5
1.9	Blue-blazed loop trail to **Laurel Fork Shelter** (0.5 mi.); water, views.		0.8
1.3	**Laurel Falls,** campsite, swimming with caution.		1.4
1.1	Blue-blazed loop trail to **Laurel Fork Shelter** (0.5 mi.); water, views.		1.6
0.0	**Start:** Dennis Cove; USFS 50, parking.	2510/765	2.7

SOUTH

HIKE #41
Laurel Falls to Pond Mt.

Maps: ATC Map 1, Damascus, VA, to Moreland Gap

Route: From USFS Laurel Falls parking area, to Pond Mt. summit and Pond Flats, to US 321

Recommended direction: S to N

Distance: 7.2 mi. total; 6.2 mi. on AT

Access trail name & length: Laurel Fork Trail (Hampton Blueline Trail), 1.0 mi.

Elevation +/-: 2000 to 3700 to 2000 ft.

Effort: Moderate

Day hike: Yes

Overnight backpacking hike: Optional

Duration: 5 to 6 hr.

Early exit option: None

Natural history feature: Mountaintop seasonal pond

Trailhead access: *Start:* From junction of US19E and US 321 at Hampton, drive 1.4 mi. E on US 321. Cross two bridges; after the second, look for USFS sign and parking area on R. Access trail is blue blazed; start beside creek, behind parking area. *End:* From junction of US 19E and US 321 at Hampton, drive 3.3 mi. E on US 321 to large USFS sign and parking area on L.

Camping: Pond Flats campsite

P ond Mt. looks like a western butte on the profile map, but it's covered with rich and varied forest. The steep climbs up and down have many switchbacks with glimpses of surrounding mountains and Watauga Lake, and the summit is unusual for the southern Appalachians: a level stretch with no ridges to scramble over or edge around. The AT goes through federal Pond Mt. Wilderness, and hiking groups must have fewer than ten people to minimize impact.

From the parking area, follow the blue blazes of the Laurel Fork Trail (Hampton Blueline Trail), a heavily used access to Laurel Falls. Look for excavations and rock piles, evidence of old iron mines, on the right as the trail climbs over a sandy, eroded ridge. After descending the ridge, sign in to the Pond Mt. Wilderness Area, designated by Congress in 1986. Pass Buckled Rock, a sheer cliff across the creek that shows how sedimentary layers buckled from the collision of the continental plates that pushed up the Appalachian Mts. The trail goes through a steep section of gorge where you must scramble along slanted rocks on the creek bank; this can be very slippery in snow or if ice has formed.

After 1.0 mi. the blue-blazed access trail meets the white-blazed AT (our mileage count begins here). The AT going north to Pond Mt. makes a sharp left here and starts up a steep, rocky hillside. The turn is well marked with double blazes of both colors, but if you are still at creek level after passing a few white AT blazes, turn around and backtrack to the trail junction to go north on the AT.

This narrow and rocky AT section clearly receives less use than the Laurel Fork Trail below. In about 50 yd. it reaches the first of many switchbacks and zigzags up the steep hill. Planned relocations here will make the trail about 0.5 mi. longer and somewhat easier. Bleeding heart, a relative of squirrel corn and Dutchman's-breeches, grows on the trail bank; it has heart-shaped flowers with a petal at the bottom like a drop of blood coming out. Two ferns with black stalks, maidenhair and ebony spleenwort, also grow here.

Many familiar wildflowers use the spring strategy: Grow and bloom before the trees shade the ground with their leaves. A few on this sunny slope use the fall strategy: Produce photosynthetic leaves after the trees have lost theirs. Putty root (Adam-and-Eve orchid) and cranefly orchids are two such examples. Each plant produces one leaf in late fall and puts its life savings into a bulb that sends up a flower the following summer. By the time the flower comes up, the leaf has died, and the two never appear together. Cranefly orchid leaves are dark green on top and bright purple underneath.

The AT uses old railroad grades for about 0.5 mi. and turns left to continue the ascent. At 1.3 mi. the trail emerges from a patch of rhododen-

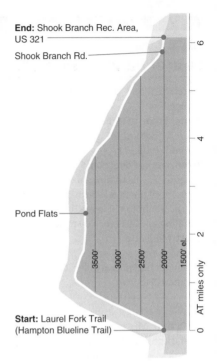

End: Shook Branch Rec. Area, US 321

Shook Branch Rd.

Pond Flats

Start: Laurel Fork Trail (Hampton Blueline Trail)

dron and turns left. A rocky promontory a few yards to the right gives a view up Laurel Creek Gorge, with the lumpy peak of Potato Top in the middle of the gorge and the Roan Massif majestic to the left. The town of Hampton can be seen to the right.

The AT climbs straight up the ridge for 0.3 mi. to a level area at 3300 ft. elevation. Four kinds of pine trees grow here: white (five bluish-green needles in a bundle, cucumber-sized cones hanging down and longer than wide); shortleaf (two or three needles in a bundle, rounded golfball-sized cones upright on the branch); Virginia (two

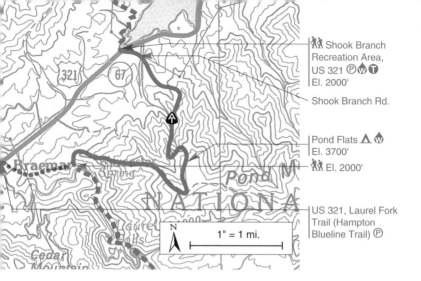

Shook Branch Recreation Area, US 321 Ⓟ Ⓦ Ⓣ El. 2000'

Shook Branch Rd.

Pond Flats ▲ Ⓦ El. 3700'

El. 2000'

US 321, Laurel Fork Trail (Hampton Blueline Trail) Ⓟ

N
1" = 1 mi.

yellowish-green twisted needles in a bundle, rounded golfball-sized cones upright on the branch); and Table Mt. (two dark-green twisted needles in a bundle, large baseball-sized upright cones with fierce spines). White-pine cones fall off the trees, sometimes with the help of squirrels; the other three pine trees retain their cones for years, often until the branches holding them break.

The trail ascends steeply again to the real ridgetop at 2.0 mi. and goes between thick cushions of moss. Look for dark-green rounded wintergreen leaves among the moss plants. The leaves and red berries of this plant taste like teaberry gum. On the left is a stand of bigtooth aspen — common on northern sections of the AT but rare in the southern Appalachians. Look for trees with smooth greenish bark and nearly round leaves with toothed margins.

From the level trail, you can see higher up Laurel Creek Gorge; the Roan Massif is again visible in the distance. The trail crosses a mountain-laurel-covered ridge and curves left toward Pond Flats. On this sheltered side of the ridge, there is more rhododendron than mountain laurel as well as red maple, white oak, and sourwood. The trail moves through an area of thin woods to a flat area with hemlocks above a many-branched creek. The creek rocks are blocks of quartzite, sedimentary sandstone that has been metamorphosed by extreme heat and pressure into a crystalline form. Some of the quartzite blocks along here have been found to contain fossilized worm burrows called Skolithus, about the size and shape of a soda straw. This rock is Precambrian — that is, formed before there were shelled animals to leave more distinctive fossils.

The AT swings left into Pond Flats and crosses a rocky creek. At 2.7 mi. a pleasant campsite sits to the right, and a spring can be found a few yards left, near the creek. Just beyond the campsite is a small pond in a depression. Though it dries in summer, it holds enough spring rain to support tree frogs, wood frogs, and American toad tadpoles — and probably a good number of mosquito, gnat, and dragonfly larvae. Woodland ponds are rare in the southern Appalachians, and most of the animals that depend on them for reproduction can't survive in running water or in bodies of water big enough to support predatory fish. Biologists theorize that some of these pond species evolved along with beavers and bred in temporary ponds. But you still must wonder: How did the frogs find this mountaintop puddle?

At 2.9 mi. the trail swings left at the start of a 1993 trail relocation that avoids a rough descent on Rat Branch and a road walk on US 321. The new trail is well graded and descends by switchbacks through alternating rhododendron and oak forest. In winter views to the north and east, Watauga Lake looks like a complicated jigsaw puzzle piece. Each glimpse of the lake shows a bit more of it.

At 4.9 mi. a blue-blazed trail leads 50 yd. right for an all-season view of Watauga Lake and the dam responsible for it. The long ridge of Iron Mt. (Hike #43) stretches to the northeast beyond the lake, and Holston Mt. and other parallel ridges of the Ridge and Valley geological province may be visible in the distant haze.

Descend through white pines and hemlocks, which give way to large smooth-barked beeches. A pretty farm valley with open hay fields is visible to the right. At 5.0 mi. log steps lead down to gravel Shook Branch Rd. Turn right and follow the road 0.2 mi. down to US 321. Cross the road with caution — fast traffic — and follow blazes an additional 0.2 mi. left to the U.S. Forest Service Shook Branch parking area.

Miles N	NORTH	Elev. (ft./m)	Miles S
	Total: 7.2 mi. with access trail		
6.2	**End:** Shook Branch Recreation Area; US 321, picnic area, toilets, parking.	2000/610	0.0
6.0	Cross US 321.		0.2
5.8	**Shook Branch Rd;** turn R onto road, 0.2mi. to US 321.	2000/610	0.4
4.9	Blue-blazed trail 50 yd. R to view.		1.3
2.7	**Pond Flats;** campsite, spring, seasonal woodland pond.	3700/1128	3.5
2.0	Top of ridge, views.		4.2
1.3	Rocky promontory, view.		4.9
0.0	**Start AT miles:** At jct. sharp L turn onto AT heading N; trail is double-blazed blue and white; steep climb.	2000/610	6.2
1.0	Access: From **Laurel Falls parking area** (US 321), follow blue-blazed **Laurel Fork Trail (Hampton Blueline Trail)** into **Pond Mt. Wilderness Area.**		1.0

SOUTH

Watauga Dam Rd. to
Shook Branch Recreation Area

Maps: ATC Map 1, Damascus, VA, to Moreland Gap

Route: From Watauga Dam Rd. to Watauga Dam to US 321

Recommended direction: N to S

Distance: 4.1 mi.

Elevation +/-: 2240 to 2480 to 2000 ft.

Effort: Easy

Day Hike: Yes

Overnight backpacking hike: Optional

Duration: 2 hr.

Early exit option: None

Natural history features: Iron Mt. Fault; June mountain laurel and rhododendron displays

Social history feature: Watauga Dam

Other features: Lake swimming

Trailhead access: *Start:* From Elizabethton, drive about 2.0 mi. S on US 19E/321. At Siam Rd., go L about 5.0 mi. to the river, following TVA Watauga Dam signs. Turn R onto Wilbur Dam Rd., cross Wilbur Lake, turn L at fork, and look for AT white blazes at the crest. Small parking lot is on L; larger parking lot is 0.9 mi. farther at Watauga Dam Visitor Center. *End:* From junction of US 19E & 321 at Hampton, drive 3.3 mi. E on US 321 to large USFS sign and parking area on L.

Camping: Watauga Lake Shelter; 1 campsite

T his short hike has rocky sections and a variety of low-elevation habitats. Kids will enjoy it, and geologists can spend hours explaining thrust faults and quartz veins. AT hikers may cross the dam; other visitors must be content with a view from the visitor center overlook. But before crossing the dam, you have to pay an admission price: ridge scrambling.

The Watauga River drains a large area, including Roan Mt. on the south and a valley that extends up into Virginia. Then it slips past the end of Iron Mt. to head northwest, as do all the rivers across the southern Appalachians. It meets the Holston and, later, the waters of the Nolichucky, French Broad, and Pigeon rivers to form the great Tennessee River at Knoxville. The river did a good job of keeping its channel open between the solid rock walls of Iron and Jenkins mts. during millions of years of continental upheavals. However, in 1948 the Tennessee Valley Authority (TVA) plugged the narrowest part of that channel with megatons of crushed rock, forming 15-mi.-long Watauga Lake. Watauga Dam was built primarily for flood control, but it also generates electricity. The lake, which provides opportunities for boating, fishing, and swimming, covers the former town of Butler and some Woodland Indian archeological sites.

The AT ascends from Wilbur Dam Rd. on stone steps to an AT mileage sign. It continues up a sidehill trail through a luxurious rhododendron stand, switches back left, and then swings right onto a small ridge crest. Watauga Lake is visible to the left, and a jumble of rocks, including pink quartzite, line and fill the trail. At the 2480-ft. summit (0.6 mi.), rock fern grows on the rock slabs. From here, the trail descends steeply on a rocky surface and twists around, so you probably won't be able to tell which direction the lake is anymore. This area burned in 1970, and the new growth, which includes mountain laurel, blueberries, and small pines, is tangled and thick. There are few blazes, but the trail is easy to follow.

At 0.8 mi., come out of the woods to an unused paved road. (To the left, in 0.2 mi., is a gate and the Watauga Dam Rd. To avoid the rocky ridge walk described above, you could walk down from the trailhead parking area to this gated road, but that would be cheating because only true AT hikers are permitted to cross Watauga Dam. But if the trail is icy . . . well, consider cheating.) Turn right, descend steeply on the road as it swings around a rock face, and reach the north end of Watauga Dam.

The dam was started in 1941, abandoned during World War II, and finished in late 1948. At that time it was the largest earth-and-rock dam in the world. The Aswan Dam in Egypt and other big dams have since been built with the same method. Ahead, you can see rock that was blasted to get the fill. The powerhouse is half a mile downstream, which allows it to take advantage of a longer fall and thus generate more electricity. Water is piped down in a tunnel blasted through the rock, the rate of flow controlled from two concrete platforms standing in the lake just above the dam.

This dam is the highest TVA dam on this drainage, and in winter, water is usually released to enable the lake to catch spring floods. So the winter views of the lake include a wide bathtub ring, but in the summer, the lake fills up.

Downstream from the dam there is no water—just a grassy field, service roads, and some white pines. This creates an odd impression that the dam is holding *all* the water that falls over the years. But the water flows through underneath. And in less than a mile, the same water goes through the Wilbur Dam, making electricity again.

From Watauga Dam, look for the round concrete emergency spillway, like some enormous shower room drain, on the left shore as you face the lake. Then look on the rock face behind the spillway, near the railed visitor overlook, for the Iron Mt. Fault, a diagonal line between dark and light stone. The line, or fault, shows the boundary between the lower, younger ridge and the older ridge that was thrust up over the younger one during continental collision. Iron Mt. and the parallel ridges to the west moved across this fault and many others like it, but most of the faults are hidden deep in the earth. The best way to understand these mysteries is to invite a geologist to come along on the hike.

Across the dam, the service road swings left. Blocky boulders have fallen and cracked the pavement—a good demonstration of the freeze-and-thaw erosion that formed the boulder fields of higher elevations. The road provides access to the flow-control platform, and the AT continues straight on an overgrown road-bed into the woods. Dripping rock face on the right provides cracks for mosses, ferns, and wildflowers, including several in the saxifrage family, whose name in Latin means "rock breaker."

The trail descends into a gully, rises to a flat area with a potential tent site, and drops into another gully filled with boulders. Across the gully at the base of a blazed tree is a patch of walking fern. This fern usually grows where the bedrock is limestone, so it is somewhat rare along the southern AT. It's here because the Watauga River has eroded through the sandstone/quartzite rock to the level of the underlying limestone. Walking fern "walks" by extending stringy tendrils from the ends of its arrow-shaped

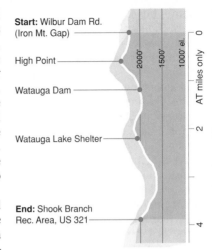

Start: Wilbur Dam Rd. (Iron Mt. Gap)

High Point

Watauga Dam

Watauga Lake Shelter

End: Shook Branch Rec. Area, US 321

leaves. If the tip of the tendril finds a suitable spot for a fern to grow, it starts a new plant and the tendril dries up.

After the walking-fern tree, the trail climbs a steep ridge on switchbacks. Hepatica (one of the earliest spring flowers) and putty root (a summer-blooming orchid) grow here. Ascend through tulip-tree and hemlock woods, turn right at the top of a small ridge, ascend a bit more, and then descend to an old road beside a small creek. Turn right, upstream, with the creek on the left. Look for the Watauga Lake Shelter at 2.4 mi. on a rise to the right, pass it, and then take the blue-blazed trail back to the shelter. The wooden shelter has a picnic table, grill, fire ring, small swap box for maps or notes, a mouse trap, a huge beech tree near the front, water and pleasant gurgling

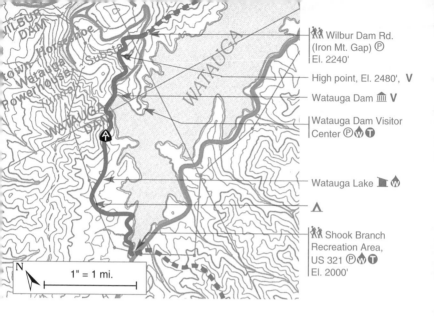

Wilbur Dam Rd.
(Iron Mt. Gap) Ⓟ
El. 2240'

High point, El. 2480', V

Watauga Dam 🏛 V

Watauga Dam Visitor
Center Ⓟ🚻🚽

Watauga Lake 🏖 🚻

⛺

Shook Branch
Recreation Area,
US 321 Ⓟ🚻🚽
El. 2000'

N
1" = 1 mi.

from the creek, and one special feature: knotholes in all walls. These are handy for ventilation, watching wildlife, or entertainment if it's raining too hard to hike: Give each person ten hemlock cones, and see how many throws it takes to toss them all out through a specified knothole.

After the shelter, the AT crosses the creek, ascends to a small ridge, joins a grassy road, crosses another creek, and ascends to an intersection of two more grassy roads at 2.7 mi. Just past the intersection, the AT turns left and winds through a stand of tall white pines with possible places to camp (heavily used in summer) or swim in the lake. The campsites are about 50 yd. from the shoreline, which is sandy with rough layers of crumbly rock (water shoes might be

advisable). The protected cove provides peaceful deep-water swimming without much boat traffic — a good place to lounge on an air mattress or play water tag.

The trail then leaves the pine forest, joins an old dirt road, and crosses wet areas and small streams. It swings around the end of Watauga Lake and goes between the lake and US 321, passing two old highway markers probably from a road that was inundated when the dam was closed. The trail enters the Shook Branch Recreation Area and passes below the bank of the Forest Service parking lot, the end point of this hike. You can either scramble up to the parking lot or continue through the recreation area, which has picnic tables, toilets, and a swimming area.

HIKE #42   Itinerary

Miles N	NORTH	Elev. (ft./m)	Miles S
4.2	**Start:** Wilbur Dam Rd. (**Iron Mt. Gap**) parking lot.	2240/683	0.0
3.6	High point of hike.	2480/756	0.6
3.2	Jct. gated paved road; to Wilbur Dam Rd. (0.2 mi.).		1.0
3.0	**Watauga Dam.**	2000/610	1.3
1.8	**Watauga Lake Shelter,** creek for water, picnic table.	2020/616	2.4
0.8	Campsites, swimming.		3.6
0.0	**End:** Shook Branch Recreation Area, US 321; parking lot, toilets, water, swimming, picnic tables.	2000/610	4.2

SOUTH

328   HIKE #42: Watauga Dam Rd. to Shook Branch Recreation Area

TN 91 to Wilbur Dam Rd.

Maps: ATC Map 1, Damascus, VA , to Moreland Gap

Route: From TN 91 to Iron Mt. to Watauga Dam Rd.

Recommended direction: N to S

Distance: 16.4 mi.

Elevation +/-: 3470 to 4190 to 2240 ft.

Effort: Moderate to strenuous

Day hike: Optional

Overnight backpacking hike: Yes

Duration: 8 to 10 hr.

Early exit option: None

Natural history features: Profusion of rhododendron blooms in June; Big Laurel Branch Wilderness

Other feature: Nick Grindstaff Monument

Trailhead access: *Start:* From junction of US 321/19E and TN 91 in Elizabethton, go N on TN 91 for 19 mi. Look for large USFS parking area with an AT kiosk on the R. *End:* From Elizabethton, go about 2.0 mi. S on US 19E/321. Turn L at Siam Rd. for about 5.0 mi. to river, following TVA Watauga Dam signs. Turn R onto Wilbur Dam Rd., cross Wilbur Lake, turn L at a fork, and look for AT white blazes at crest. Small parking lot is to R; larger parking lot is 0.9 mi. farther at Watauga Dam Visitor Center.

Camping: Iron Mt. Shelter; Vandeventer Shelter; several campsites (water is scarce).

This is ridgetop hiking at its best — 14 mi. on remote, beautiful Iron Mt. From north to south, as described here, the ridge has many easy ups and downs and one long, steep plunge at the end. The trail, sometimes on old logging roads and sometimes a narrow graded path, is excellent. Hikers will need two cars or a shuttle, and water may be hard to find. In fall and winter, the ridge provides great views, but the best hiking time might be in June when the rhododendron, mountain laurel, and flame azalea are in bloom. Rhododendron grows everywhere — all the hikes in this volume offer this wonderful broadleaf evergreen — but in open areas with plenty of sun, like ridgetops, the blooms can be spectacular. You can go to the Rhododendron Gardens of Roan Mt. (near the end of Hike #37) and join the crowds, or you can hike Iron Mt. for a private show.

This hike's narrative and mileages start at the AT kiosk on TN 91, where a driver could drop hikers off. A one-car hike to Iron Mt. Shelter and back (9.2 mi. round-trip) would include some of the best rhododendron displays.

Enter the AT on the south side of TN 91, where the trail begins a gentle ascent through oak, beech, and rhododendron woods. At 0.5 mi. it crosses a grassy old road leading from the Forest Service parking area on Cross Mt. Rd., which is visible through the trees for a while on the left. The trail swings right, away from the road, and descends through thick hemlock and then thick rhododendron. Swampy spots here could be a problem, but wire-covered planks do a great job of getting hikers across with dry feet. Wintergreen, galax, and princess pine club moss line the trail. Short ups and downs, with tiny creeks or standing water (and perhaps tadpoles, frogs, and salamanders), signal the end of Cross Mt.

Ascend to a ridgetop of Iron Mt. at 1.4 mi. and turn right, or southwest —the direction this hike takes for 14.0 more miles. Fraser magnolia and sourwood trees mix with the luxurious clumps of rosebay rhododendron that, in some June displays, will be covered with masses of white blooms. Like most plants, rhododendrons run their business on a fiscal year from July 1 to June 30, and the decisions about bloom investment for spring are made the summer before, based on general health, "savings accounts" in roots, loss to leaf eaters, water, temperature, and sunlight — so some years are better than others for bloom.

The AT crosses or uses many old roads during this hike. They are easiest to see in the fall or winter, but be careful to stay with the white blazes. If you don't see a white blaze for a while, look back. If you still don't see one, backtrack for a while until you do. Short backtracks once in a while can keep you "found."

The ridgetop narrows to about 20 ft. in width, and you can get the first glimpses of a valley view to the left (southeast). Sounds of woodpeckers, other birds, and distant human activities rise to this ridge, and it may also get very windy. The trail veers left from the crest to bypass beautiful rocks with rock tripe and rock fern, then provides a good warm-up ascent (whether you need it or not). Along this ascent, look for a thick crop of oak seedlings that appear to be all the same age. They probably are. Oaks have a good strategy to keep acorn eaters from eating all their seeds. The trees produce some acorns, or mast, every year—enough to keep a moderate population of squirrels, chipmunks, and turkeys alive, but every few years they produce a bumper crop, more than the animals can possibly eat. These seedlings came from one of those big crops, and the relatively clear area along the trail gives them a good chance to get started. As they get bigger, they will compete with each other for light and soil nutrients.

At 1.9 mi. the trail veers left and descends, then switches back right to regain the ridgetop. At 2.7 mi. it reaches a 4120-ft. summit, descends on a rocky section, then resumes an easy grade on an old road. A wide area in the trail next to an old gnarled sugar maple tree could serve well as a campsite.

At 3.2 mi., in a large patch of shagbark hickories, a blue-blazed trail leads right 100 yd. to a spring. The first blue blaze and the little metal water sign are on one of the hickories, and thick hickory husks and nuts may be scattered along the trail. Just 0.1 mi. farther on, look for the Nick Grindstaff monument on the right. Uncle Nick, an orphan, became a hermit in his twenties and lived on Iron Mt. for 45 years. He died in 1923, and his epitaph on the back of the monument reads, "Lived alone, suffered alone, died alone." Though maybe not completely alone: Uncle Nick is said to have had a pet rattlesnake. The Grindstaff family was among the early European settlers to this area. A car dealership in Elizabethton and other local businesses are run by Grindstaffs. On January 1, 1997, I hiked this trail and saw a fresh green Christmas ribbon tied to an iron ring on the monument.

The trail continues with gentle ups and downs through more banks of rhododendron and occasional winter views to the southeast. It passes through a cut chestnut log that, at least 60 years after the chestnut blight, is finally being nibbled by a few fungi. At 4.6 mi., the AT reaches the Iron Mt. Shelter. Facing southeast, the cinder-block shelter has an overhang for cooking and eating under when it's raining, a picnic table, and a fire ring. Water is available at a

Dale Gelland

Bloodroot

good spring 0.2 mi. farther on the AT; this may be the most reliable water source of the trail, so if you plan to camp or stay at Vandeventer Shelter, stock up now.

After the shelter, the AT descends 0.2 mi. to a gap, a creek, and the spring. In dry weather, water can be found by going farther down on either side of the gap. With more easy ups and downs and short stretches on old jeep roads, at 5.3 mi. the trail reaches a power line and the first good view to the right: Holston Mt., which runs parallel to Iron Mt., and farms dotting the Stony Ck. Valley in between. The communities in this valley are Sadie, Buladeen, Winner, and Siam. These parallel mountain ridges, along with the next range of Bays Mt., look like huge wrinkles in a giant rug and form the Ridge and Valley province of the southern Appalachians. The ridges, or wrinkles, were created during the continental collision between African and North American tectonic plates about 250 million years ago. The Precambrian rock of these mountains was formed from ocean sediment 30 to 40 mi. east of here and got shoved right across the Tennessee border. It resists erosion better than the softer, younger rock of the valleys.

At 5.6 mi. the trail reaches another summit of Iron Mt. (4190 ft.). For the next 2.0 mi. along the AT, several old roads or tracks go right, and off-road vehicles may appear. In general, the AT keeps left at the junctions, but watch the blazes.

The trail descends to Turkeypen Gap at 6.2 mi. (3970 ft.) and then ascends through white pines. Flat areas good for camping appear on the left and right on the ridge crest, but there is no reliable water source. At 7.3 mi. a spring to the left of a swampy area may provide water, but probably not in summer. Beyond the spring are several more tent sites.

The trail ascends through tuliptrees, hickories, and oaks. As the trail gets narrower, the trees get bigger, indicating that you're reaching the wilder, less accessible parts of this mountain. Then at 8.0 mi. the trail descends left on switchbacks to the drier, south-facing side of the ridge crest. Mountain laurel arches overhead, and its dry-adapted companions—trailing arbutus, wintergreen,

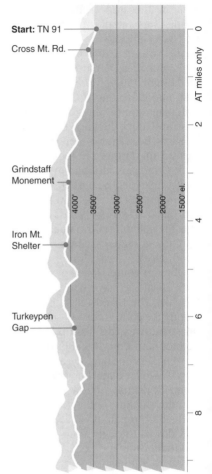

Continued on p. 334

and galax—line the trail. Rocky trail and more switchbacks lead across the ridge again to the north-facing slope, where many moisture-loving spring flowers, such as toothwort, hepatica, and violets, grow.

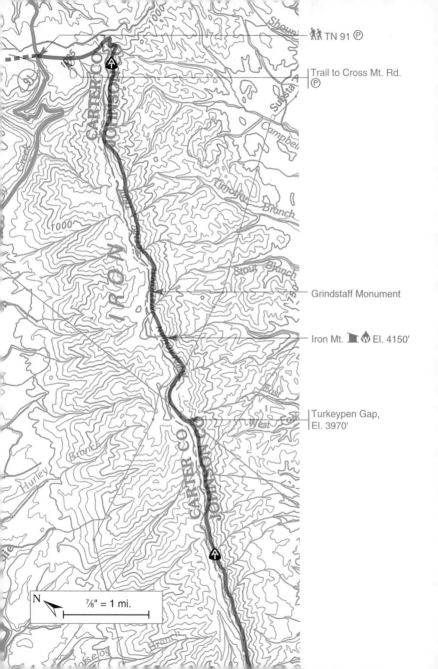

🥾 TN 91 Ⓟ

Trail to Cross Mt. Rd.
Ⓟ

Grindstaff Monument

Iron Mt. ■ Ⓦ El. 4150'

Turkeypen Gap,
El. 3970'

CARTER CO.
JOHNSON CO.

IRON

N
⅞" = 1 mi.

Back on the ridge crest, a spur trail at about 9.4 mi. leads left to a good view over rocks covered with vigorous lichens. You can see a lumberyard in the valley below and microcars creeping along US 321. Beech Mt. is to the southeast, and Roan Mt. is directly south.

The AT turns right, follows the ridge through thick patches of rhododendron, and enters Big Laurel Branch Wilderness at 10.1 mi. This 6251-acre tract, which covers the southwestern end of Iron Mt., was designated by Congress in 1986 after conservation and hiking groups proposed it for inclusion in the 1964 Wilderness Act. The sheer cliff that forms the northern "bank" of Wilbur Lake is part of the wilderness area, and its south-facing rock faces must be heaven for rattlesnakes, copperheads, fence lizards, blue-tailed skinks, garter snakes, and other professional sunbathers. If you have time at the end of your hike, you could swim across Wilbur Lake and check.

The trail regains the crest, passes more good views to the left, descends through a wide valley, and follows switchbacks back up to the ridge crest. There's an especially good lookout at 11.2 mi. Yellow birches block much of the view, but you can climb a small rock slab to see over them.

The Vandeventer Shelter appears at 11.5 mi.: another basic cinder-block building with a fire ring and a grill. This shelter faces Holston Mt., but behind it are some rock slabs that give the best view so far of Watauga Lake

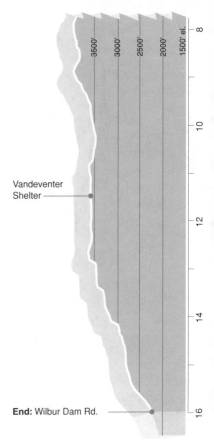

and the mountains to the south. The nearest spring is a long way down and may be dry when you get there, so bring water if you plan to stay here.

Beyond the shelter the trail joins an old road and descends into a saddle with a creeklet and occasional water source. A blue-blazed trail

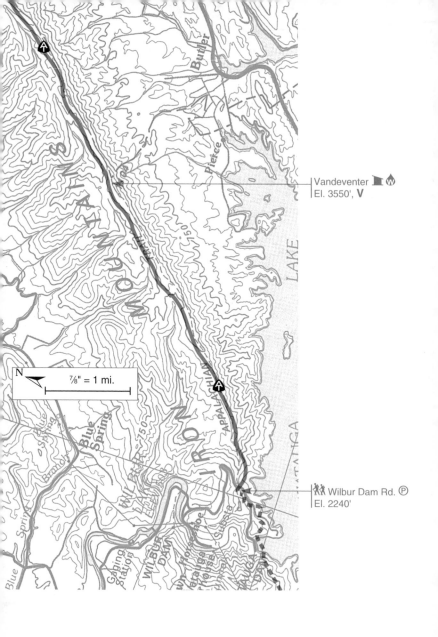

Butler

Pierce

Vandeventer ⬛🪵 **W**
El. 3550', **V**

LAKE

N ⬊   ⅞" = 1 mi.

Blue Spring

Blue Spring

Branch

Blue Spring

APPALACHIAN

IRON MOUNTAINS

750

Gauging Station

Wilbur Dam

🚶🚶 Wilbur Dam Rd. Ⓟ
El. 2240'

leads right to a seasonal spring about 0.3 mi. down. Ascend on the road to an open ridge with blackberries, grapevines, and tall yellow sunflowers in fall. Huge rock slabs and occasional views continue on the left. Turn left into a hemlock grove, and at about 13.0 mi. start down the end of Iron Mt. toward Watauga Lake. Many of the hemlocks here are Carolina hemlocks, which are somewhat rare in Tennessee. The hemlock woolly adelgid attacks and kills both Carolina hemlock and the more common eastern hemlock. Watauga Lake seems to be rising to meet you as you descend without much relief for the knees for nearly 3.0 mi. The AT finally reaches a gap (2240 ft.) at Wilbur Dam Rd., with a Wilderness Area sign, a trail registry box, and an AT mileage sign.

HIKE #43 Itinerary

Miles N	NORTH	Elev. (ft./m)	Miles S
16.4	**Start:** TN 91; parking to R on USFS 53 in 0.4 mi.	3470/1057	0.0
16.1	Trail to USFS parking lot, Cross Mt. Rd.		0.3
14.3	Blue-blazed spur trail to spring (100 yd.).		3.2
13.2	**Nick Grindstaff Monument.**		3.3
11.9	**Iron Mt. Shelter,** good spring 0.2 mi. farther on AT.	4150/1265	4.6
10.2	**Turkeypen Gap,** campsites.	3970/1210	6.3
9.1	Seasonal spring to L.		7.4
7.4	Spur trail L to good view.		9.1
6.3	Enter **Big Laurel Branch Wilderness.**		10.2
4.9	**Vandeventer Shelter,** views.	3550/1082	11.6
3.4	Start steep 3.0-mi. descent.		13.4
0.0	**End:** **Wilbur Dam Rd.,** parking; Watauga Dam Visitor Center 0.9 mi. farther, toilets, water.	2240/683	16.4

SOUTH

TN 91 to Low Gap

Maps: ATC Map 1, Damascus, VA, to Moreland Gap

Route: From TN 91 to Double Springs Shelter to Low Gap

Recommended direction: S to N

Distance: 6.5 mi.

Elevation +/-: 3450 to 4080 to 3384 ft.

Effort: Moderate

Day hike: Yes

Overnight backpacking hike: Optional

Duration: 4 to 5 hr.

Early exit option: None

Natural history feature: Squirrel nut middens, Osborne Farm

Social history feature: Daniel Boone's Wilderness Road

Other feature: Shady Valley Community

Trailhead access: *Start:* From junction of US 321/19E and TN 91 in Elizabethton, drive N on TN 91. At 19 mi., look for USFS parking area on R. From junction of US 321/19E and TN 67, go about 12.0 mi. to Doe Valley Methodist Church and turn L onto paved USFS 53. Pass a microwave antenna station at 4.7 mi. and reach US 91. Park in USFS lot on L. *End:* From junction of TN 91 and US 421 in Shady Valley, go 2.8 mi. W on US 421. At crest of Low Gap, look on L for parking at a picnic area and AT signs and blazes. Low Gap is 18.0 mi. E of Bristol, TN, and I-81.

Camping: Double Springs Shelter; some campsites

In the 1700s, the Appalachian Mts. formed a great blue wall that held back the flood of European settlers, trappers, farmers, and traders. Daniel Boone (1734–1820) was one of the first white explorers to penetrate the wall in upper East Tennessee. He is said to have passed through Low Gap in 1767 on a hunting and trapping trip, and in 1775 he was hired to lead settlers into Kentucky on the Wilderness Road through Cumberland Gap, to establish a fourteenth colony there. Plans changed; Kentucky became a county of Virginia, and Boone was kidnapped and adopted (at age 44) by

Indians. He escaped in time to save Boonesborough, Kentucky, from a siege by English and Indians in 1778 and became an international folk hero, inspiring seven stanzas of *Don Juan*, a narrative poem by George Gordon, Lord Byron (1788–1824) about an aristocrat who seduces a beautiful girl and kills her father. (Don Juan seduces several thousand women and suffers various sorts of revenge; it's a pretty long poem.) On this hike you can trace Boone's steps, and you might want to take a 50-mi. side trip to Cumberland Gap, which has been restored as an historic site.

This is a moderate hike on 6.5 mi.

of graded trail along the northern ridge of Holston Mt. with occasional views of Holston Lake on the right and Shady Valley on the left. Iron Mt. and Holston Mt. form the western rim of the Appalachians, blending into the Ridge and Valley province between the Blue Ridge and Cumberland mts. This section of the AT crosses between Iron and Holston Mts. on Cross Mt., a ridge of resistant sandstone deposited sideways by the shifting of a geological fault. After Cross Mt. the AT turns north onto Holston Mt. and heads toward Damascus.

The AT through Hikes #43, #44, and #45, plus side trails maintained by the U.S. Forest Service, form a huge **H** of hiking trails. Excellent campsites, good views, and easy hiking warrant spending extra time in this area, especially in fall color season. Don't expect crowds on the trails.

After crossing TN 91, the AT passes through an accessible stile and enters the Osborne Farm, which the Appalachian Trail Conservancy bought to protect it from development. The trail here is constructed with minimal grade and sideslope and meets federal accessibility standards. Pass apple trees and the barns of the old farm. Reach a bench at 0.5 mi. with the best views of Shady Valley, a scenic valley which hosts the only cranberry festival in the Southeast.

Continue through fields and enter woods at 0.8 mi. Hepatica and bloodroot bloom here in early spring; white wood asters, goldenrod, and spiderwort appear in late summer.

At 1.7 mi. the AT joins dirt Double Springs Rd. and follows it for 0.4 mi. to a fork. The AT continues on the left fork, while the right fork leads 50 yd. to a grassy campsite sheltered by large white pines. An old metal wheel rim has been recycled into a convenient fire ring. Between the campsite and the AT is a good but somewhat muddy spring.

The AT crosses another open area with a large patch of running ground cedar, a club moss that sends up fronds from extensive underground roots. Some of the fronds produce light brown spikes that release spores. Over a slight rise, another club moss, princess pine, becomes more common. Club mosses are related to ferns and were the first plants to develop a system of vascular tissue to transport water upward, allowing for taller growth than the real mosses. For a while, club mosses and ferns ruled the plant world, but during the Age of Dinosaurs, seed-producing plants developed better vascular systems and took over, and today only ground-creeping club mosses remain.

The AT ascends along a heavily eroded section of the road with high, rocky banks. A view to the northeast shows the long, even ridge of Holston Mt. Witch hazel, a shrub with smooth bark and asymmetrical leaves, grows along the trail. Crushed witch hazel leaves smell somewhat like fresh sweet corn. Small white ash trees and patches of woodfern also grow here.

At the crest of a ridge at 2.7 mi., look for pileated woodpecker holes in dead trees. The holes are roughly rectangular, and if the woodpecker has been working recently, there may be an impressive pile of shredded wood on the ground. If you hear its distinctive cackle, look for a red-crested dark bird larger than a crow flying through the woods. Like all woodpeckers, pileated woodpeckers have an undulating flight pattern as they move from trunk to trunk. They are also zygodactyl: they have two toes facing forward and two back—the better to stand on tree trunks. Another woodpecker adaptation is special brain padding (which would be useful for human boxers or soccer players) to prevent damage from constant pounding.

The trail descends to a gap at 2.8 mi. and reaches Double Springs Shelter on the left at 3.0 mi. This shelter receives a lot of use; campfires and tents have damaged the area around the shelter. Water is available at a piped spring about 100 yd. down beyond the shelter on a blue-blazed trail; in summer, you may have to go farther down the steep draw to get to water with enough flow.

The AT continues in front of the shelter with a steep, short climb (0.1 mi.) to a gap on Holston Mt., with a campsite and a trail junction. The blue-blazed Holston Mt. Trail turns left and goes about 10.0 mi. to a Forest Service backcountry parking and camping area on USFS 56.

Turning right, the AT descends

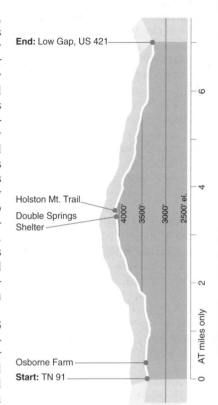

gradually along the ridge crest of Holston Mt. Oak and hickory trees dominate on this ridge, and stumps and snags (standing broken trunks) of American chestnut show that this was once a great chestnut ridge before the chestnut blight of the 1920s and '30s. Squirrels, wild turkeys, chipmunks, blue jays, and black bears depend on masting (nut-producing)

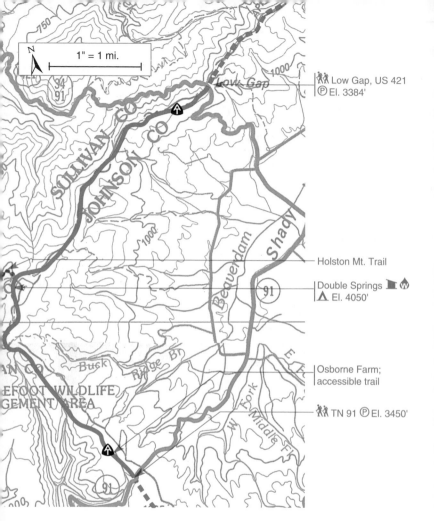

Low Gap, US 421
El. 3384'

Holston Mt. Trail

Double Springs
El. 4050'

Osborne Farm;
accessible trail

TN 91 El. 3450'

1" = 1 mi.

trees for winter survival. Chipmunks collect nuts in underground store-houses; look for their round holes on the sides of the trail, especially under roots. Red and gray squirrels stay above ground all winter and carry nuts to logs and stumps so they can watch for foxes or wildcats while they eat. Acorn caps, bits of acorn and hickory shell, and wings of ash seeds and tulip-tree seeds collect on these logs as little waste piles called middens. Look for squirrel middens along this trail, especially in fall and winter, to find out what menu items are in season.

The trail continues down the ridge with occasional views to the left of South Holston Lake and the low ridges and farmed valleys beyond it. Sections of barbed wire and rail fences remain from when this area was used for grazing. As the AT descends on the left side of the ridge, thin woods to the right show signs of recent wind and ice storms. Red maples and tulip-trees have been snapped off, and the more flexible hickories and oaks have been bent into twisted shapes.

At 5.1 mi. the AT crosses an old roadbed, recognizable by its high banks. To the right, posts with blue blazes indicate a side trail through old fields that leads about 0.2 mi. to a campsite and spring. After the side trail the AT skirts right of the ridge across the top of an open field with views of Shady Valley and Mt. Rogers in the distance.

The AT swings right through a scraggly growth of young red maples, crosses the ridge to the left side, and descends to a flat campsite at 6.4 mi. This used to be a homesite; daffodils bloom in spring, and boxwoods indicate where a walkway or front door once stood. Appalachian settlers planted boxwoods for their chickens to roost in; the thick evergreen foliage sheltered the birds, and proximity to the front door may have discouraged foxes.

Follow a woods road through a field of tangled sumac trunks, and descend to Low Gap at US 421. There you'll find a picnic area and a piped spring.

Miles N	NORTH	Elev. (ft./m)	Miles S
6.5	**End: Low Gap,** US 421; parking, picnic area, piped spring.	3384/1031	0.0
6.4	Campsite.		0.1
5.1	Jct. blue-blazed side trail R (0.2 mi.) to campsite, spring.		1.4
3.0	Jct. **Holston Mt. Trail;** campsite; **Double Springs Shelter;** piped spring 100 yd. beyond shelter on blue-blazed trail.	4080/1243	3.5
2.1	Campsite 50 yd. R., spring.		4.4
1.7	AT joins Double Springs Rd.		4.8
0.5	Osborne farm; overlook; accessible trail.		6.0
0.0	**Start:** TN 91.	3450/1052	6.5

SOUTH

HIKE #45

Low Gap to Damascus

Maps: ATC Map 1, Damascus, VA, to More-land Gap

Route: From Low Gap to McQueens Knob, to Abingdon Gap, to Backbone Rock Trail, to Damascus, VA

Recommended direction: S to N

Distance: 15.0 mi.

Elevation +/-: 3384 to 3885 to 1950 ft.

Effort: Moderate

Day hike: Optional

Overnight backpacking hike: Yes

Duration: 10 to 11 hr.

Early exit option: McQueens Gap, at 3.7 mi.; Backbone Rock Trail, at 10.2 mi.

Natural history feature: Shinleaf, a rare flower

Social history feature: Trail Days in Damascus

Other features: Smallest AT shelter

Trailhead access: *Start:* From junction of TN 91 and US 421 in Shady Valley, go 2.8 mi. W on US 421. At crest of Low Gap, park on L at a picnic area marked with AT signs and blazes. *End:* Go 14.0 mi. E of Abingdon (I-81), VA, on US 58, or 12.0 mi. N of Mt. City, TN, on TN 91. Look for AT white blazes on Laurel Ave. (US 58); park behind United Methodist Church (The Place, hiker hostel).

Camping: Abingdon Gap Shelter; some campsites

T he trail to Damascus is a long ridgetop hike with very little elevation change through second-growth forest and old fields, quiet, pretty woods, and then a long descent from the Tennessee state line to the main street of a small, trail-friendly community. The best camp-site is past Abingdon Gap Shelter at 5.0 mi. In summer the spring at Abingdon Gap Shelter dries up, and water can be a problem; plan to carry it.

The AT crosses US 421 just west of Low Gap at a large parking area with a picnic table and a piped spring. Fill your water bottles here. Going north, the trail descends a few yards into the woods, then climbs on dry trail with gravel and roots. After a right turn, it reaches the ridgetop at 0.2 mi. and joins an old road with a well-built stone wall on the left. Poison ivy is abundant here in summer, but in spring, may-apple, Jack-in-the-pulpit, and yellow mandarin bloom. By late July, nettles and blackberries swarm from one side of the trail to the other, unless you are lucky enough to hike right after trail maintainers do their weed-whacking run. (Most hiking clubs would be glad to have new vol-unteers for this job, and weed whack-ing will develop upper-body strength to balance those great lower-body hiking muscles.) A summer hike on this trail will give you plenty of time to reflect on the values of annual trail clearing.

At 0.5 mi. a white-pine and hemlock grove shades the ground and gives some relief from the weeds. The trail forks; stay to the left while the road goes straight ahead. Old roads and trails cross or parallel the AT in several places on this section; watch the blazes carefully.

Mountain mint, yellow star grass, and swamp milkweed grow among the nettles as the trail continues on the almost level ridge crest. At 1.5 mi. a campsite on the left is flanked by a large rock pile, probably pushed there by the same road builders who used other rocks to build the stone walls that now line both sides of the trail. Witch hazel trees and blueberry bushes surround the campsite.

The AT descends to Double Spring Gap (1.9 mi.), an overgrown saddle where a road once crossed. Tall bracken ferns grow beside the trail, and down in wetter areas, waist-high cinnamon ferns are abundant. At 2.3 mi. the trail ascends past a few white pines to a boxed spring on the right. This spring may be the best water supply of the trail, but it may dry up in summer.

A small pool below the spring produces a seep that supports huge circles of cinnamon fern with 5- to 6-ft.-tall fronds. In late May, a cinnamon-brown reproductive frond sprouts up in the center. The large tree growing almost on top of the spring is a white ash, the only common large tree with

Doris Gove

Fraser magnolia bloom with beetles

opposite compound leaves. This member of the olive family provides strong, flexible wood, and pioneers used it for tools, butter paddles, and wagon tongues; more recently its strength has contributed to baseball bats, snow skis, and water skis.

From the spring, ascend easily along good trail in thin woods. The presence of many small black locust trees indicates that this area was logged recently. As this ridgetop matures (protected by the AT corridor), oaks, hickories, and maples will grow higher than the locusts and shade them out. Sassafras saplings also grow on cleared areas; they are edge species, and the majority will disappear when the big trees take over. Sassafras trees grow slowly, and most of the giant specimens were harvested by early settlers for export to Europe and use in health tonics. (This was before Sir Walter Raleigh promoted the health claims of that other American crop, tobacco.) A

small campsite is on the right under hemlock trees.

At 3.3 mi. the trail reaches McQueens Knob, an open, weedy area and the highest point of this section. There is a U.S. Geological Survey benchmark and a sign to the right of the trail. The benchmark, a disk slightly larger than an Olympic gold medal, was set in a concrete block in 1934. It looks as if the geologist who installed the benchmark stamped in the *4* of 1934 with a hammer after the disk was in place. Check back in the weeds for concrete foundations of the former McQueens Knob fire tower. Red bee balm, daisy fleabane, blackberries, and tall grasses join the nettles. (If it's raining, you'll notice that wet skin greatly intensifies the sting of nettles.) A tangled mass of virgin's bower, or wild clematis, climbs trees on the left, producing a cloud of white flowers in July. The fruits appear in September, each with a silvery 2-in. strand attached. Clematis is another light-dependent species and grows at the edge of clearings and along fence rows.

The AT joins the tower access road and descends from McQueens Knob to the smallest shelter on the southern AT—a three-sided log cabin around a sleeping platform about the size of a double bed. The big logs have been chinked with little logs, and a new gutter drains rain from the tiny roof (providing the only water supply). The log over the door says "Holiday Inn," but it could just as well be called a honeymoon suite.

Continued on p. 348

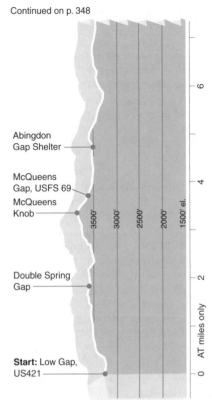

The AT continues down the dirt road. Look for toppled telephone poles and the remains of a stone wall along the road. After a rusty bar gate at 3.7 mi. in McQueens Gap, the AT crosses USFS 69, a rough but usually passable road from Shady Valley 3.0 mi. away.

Ascend to another nettle-covered ridge and swing right on good trail that descends, and then thankfully

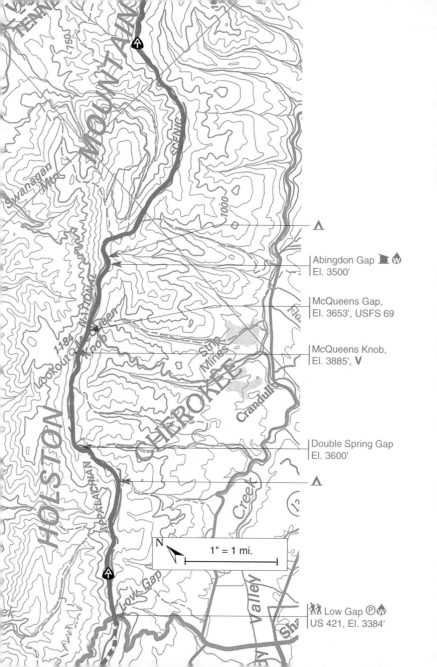

Abingdon Gap ◼ W
El. 3500'

McQueens Gap,
El. 3653', USFS 69

McQueens Knob,
El. 3885', **V**

Double Spring Gap
El. 3600'

Low Gap Ⓟ W
US 421, El. 3384'

N
1" = 1 mi.

becomes too wide for nettles, in older woods. The small Abingdon Gap Shelter, a standard cinder-block cabin with metal roof overhang, accommodating only five people, appears on the right at 4.8 mi. A blue-blazed trail leads 0.2 mi. behind the shelter down to an unreliable spring. In January 1997, a tree fell onto the shelter and threatened to crush it. USFS rangers and Tennessee Eastman Hiking Club members managed to lift it off with ropes and pulleys, repair the damage to the roof and gutter, and recycle the tree into a log bench.

The theme of the shelter register here was: "What do you plan to eat when you get to Damascus?" Answers ranged from Ben & Jerry's Chunky Monkey to champagne and strawberries. One practical hiker wrote that there was no need to go as far as Damascus for good food and thoughtfully provided a recipe for boiled nettles: serve with skewered mice (see Hike #11 for recipe).

A few yards after the shelter, the trail forks. The left fork off the AT goes to pretty, grassy campsites, and the right fork continues the AT with a curve to the left beyond the campsites. Fraser magnolias are abundant along the curve. Look for papery leaves more than 1 ft. long with a lobe on either side of the petiole, or leaf stalk. Botanist William Bartram named this tree *Magnolia auriculata* because the leaves had big earlobes, but the name *Magnolia fraseri* was published earlier and honors the Scottish botanist John Fraser. Fraser

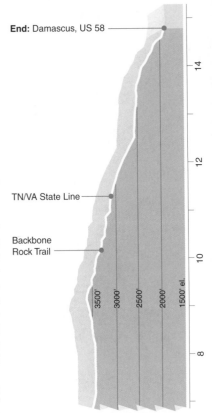

magnolia is deciduous, while its close relative, the southern magnolia with the waxy leaves, is an evergreen. The flowers, the largest flowers of the Appalachians, show the relationship better than the leaves do.

The AT descends through tangled mountain laurel, and galax lines the trail. Keep an eye out for the leaves or flowers of pink lady's-slipper.

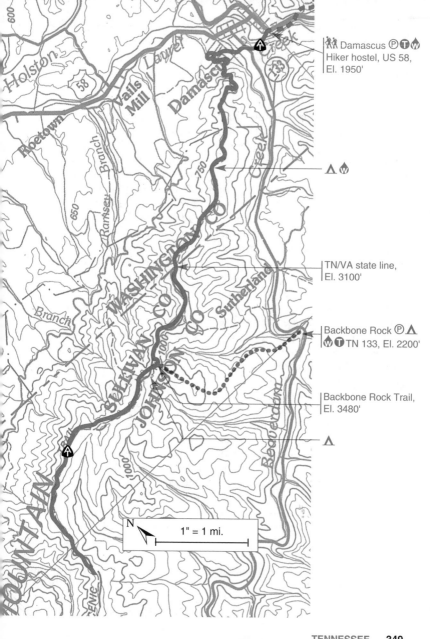

Damascus ℗ 🚽 🚰
Hiker hostel, US 58,
El. 1950'

△ 🚰

TN/VA state line,
El. 3100'

Backbone Rock ℗ △
🚰 🚽 TN 133, El. 2200'

Backbone Rock Trail,
El. 3480'

△

N

1" = 1 mi.

Openings in the trees to the right give views of Doe and Iron mts. Within the next mile there are three small campsites. The trail slips to the right side of the ridge at about 6.0 mi. but regains the crest in 100 yd. During a short climb, look for rounded waxy wintergreen leaves on the trail bank. They smell and taste like teaberry gum. American chestnut sprouts also grow along the trail, and some may become large enough to flower, but others show the swollen cankers and cracked bark from chestnut blight.

The trail shifts to the northern side of the ridge and passes a moist bank with still more nettles as well as jewelweed. The juice of jewelweed is said to prevent and relieve itching from poison ivy, and it definitely helps to soothe nettle stings. The Cherokee used it for this purpose and also as a tea for pregnant women to speed delivery. Cinnamon ferns grow tall here, and mushrooms of many colors pop up during rainy periods.

The trail wanders back and forth as it descends the ridgeline. Two summer wildflowers now appear. Whorled loosestrife has whorls of leaves growing from one node on the stem, like the ribs of an umbrella (most plants have either opposite or alternate leaves; only a few are whorled). The small yellow flowers of this loosestrife are also whorled, and there are usually two or three tiers with four flowers each. This plant is also called liberty-tea because it was used by the American revolutionaries as a substitute for the taxed British tea. Another wildflower here is shinleaf, a member of the wintergreen family and a relative of pipsissewa. This rare plant has small, rounded, waxy basal leaves and a central stalk with eight to ten white, perfumed flowers. Members of this plant family have small leaves and live in shady places on acidic soil; their secret to success is an association with underground fungi that provide them with food, perhaps stolen from other, taller plants.

At 10.1 mi. the trail passes a good, level campsite, and 0.1 mi. farther the AT makes a sharp left turn while blue-blazed Backbone Rock Trail swings right and descends 2.3 mi. to Backbone Rock, a narrow ridge that arches over TN 133, one of the roads to Damascus. Backbone Rock Trail is steep but well maintained and easy to follow down to a USFS campground that also provides water and toilets.

From the trail junction, the AT descends steadily, skirting left around a steep knob and then returning to the ridgetop. A mixture of mountain laurel, flame azalea, rhododendron, and hemlock keeps the trail both shaded and beautiful.

At 11.3 mi. the AT crosses from Tennessee into Virginia and from the Cherokee National Forest to the Jefferson National Forest. The trail continues down a broad ridge of white pines and reaches a pleasant campsite at 12.9 mi. Water may be available at an old homesite spring about 0.2 mi. right on a steep blue-blazed trail. Follow an old road, and then turn left into pine woods. At 14.0 mi. cross an overgrown field, and turn right into woods again. Follow the switchbacks with occasional views of the valleys. Leave the woods at 14.5 mi.

Descend into the residential streets of Damascus, and follow white blazes along Water St., past AT Drive. Turn left and go through an arch into a creekside park with a model AT shelter (not for sleeping in) and picnic tables. Continue along Beaver Dam St., past a narrow-gauge railroad and caboose on the right, and turn right onto Laurel Ave. (US 58), the main street of Damascus. The Virginia Creeper Trail crosses both the AT at the corner of US 58 and the creek on a railroad trestle bridge. Continue along Laurel Ave. (there's an outdoor outfitter store in case you need the next guidebook in this series), and turn right just before the United Methodist Church for parking and The Place, a hiker hostel run by the church. Other parking for hikers may be available in town with permission.

For several years, Damascus has hosted Trail Days, a celebration of the AT in May. Thru-hikers hitchhike in from whatever AT section they happen to be on, then hitch back afterware, and AT alumni come from all over the world for the three-day party. In the last year or two, however, Trail Days has gotten too big for this little town, and there are plans to spawn an alternative Trail Days in the other town the AT runs through, Hot Springs, North Carolina.

HIKE #45 Itinerary

Miles N	NORTH	Elev. (ft./m)	Miles S
15.0	**End:** Damascus, VA, United Methodist Church; US 58; parking, hiker hostel.	1950/594	0.0
13.1	Campsite; unreliable spring 0.2 mi. down steep blue-blazed trail.		2.1
11.5	TN/VA state line.	3100/945	3.7
10.4	Jct. **Backbone Rock Trail** to **Backbone Rock,** USFS campground; water, toilets, parking (2.3 mi.).	3480/1061	4.8
5.0	**Abingdon Gap Shelter,** blue-blazed trail 0.2 mi. to unreliable spring.	3773/1120	10.2
3.9	**McQueens Gap;** jct. USFS 69 to Shady Valley (3.0 mi.).	3653/1113	11.3
3.5	**McQueens Knob,** USGS benchmark, tiny log shelter down trail.	3885/1184	11.7
2.5	Boxed spring.		12.7
2.1	**Double Spring Gap.**	3600/1097	13.1
0.0	**Start:** Low Gap, US 421, parking, picnic area, piped spring.	3384/1031	15.0

SOUTH

Useful Information

US Geological Survey Topographical Maps

USGS maps used in this series are scaled at 1:100,000 (1 cm = 1 km), but in this book we have converted the scale generally to 1 in. = 1 mi. or a close fraction thereof. The contour interval is 50 m (161.04 ft.).The maps listed below, which cover all the AT miles in this volume, are quadrangles covering the area surrounding the named town (approximately 50 mi. E-W and 35 mi. N-S).

> Johnson City
> Asheville
> Knoxville
> Fontana Lake
> Toccoa
> Dalton

To order USGS maps, see "Web Sites" and the Bibliography.

Appalachian Trail Conservancy Maps

ATC sells its own 4-color topo hiking maps and some maps published by regional hiking clubs. Together these maps cover the entire AT. Generally AT maps are scaled at 1:62,500 (1 in. = 1 mi.). Maps referred to in this volume are listed here.

ATC Map 1, Damascus, Virginia, to Moreland Gap

ATC Map 2, Moreland Gap to Sams Gap

ATC Map 3, Sams Gap to Davenport Gap

Trails Illustrated Map for Great Smoky Mtns. National Park

ATC Map for North Carolina — Bly Gap to Fontana Dam

ATC Map for Georgia — Springer Mountain to Bly Gap

Many ATC maps are double maps on one sheet (a map on each side); for example, ATC Maps 2 & 3 appear on one sheet.

To order ATC maps, see "Address & Telephone" and "Web Sites."

Definitions

Easy: gentle ups and downs, fairly smooth path, few obstacles

Moderate: elevation gain or loss of up to 1000 ft.; narrower, rocky path; some obstacles (for example, brook crossings with no bridge)

Strenuous: elevation gain or loss of more than 1000 ft.; steep ups and downs; difficult, challenging path; numerous obstacles; possibly unsuitable for young children or the infirm.

Hikes

EASY

#42, Watauga Dam Rd. to Shook Branch Recreation Area

MODERATE

#4, Neels Gap to Hogpen Gap

#9, Deep Gap to Timber Ridge Trail

#11, Albert Mt. Bypass to Winding Stair Gap

#16, Stecoah Gap to Yellow Creek Gap

#17, Yellow Creek Gap to Fontana Dam

#21, Newfound Gap to Clingmans Dome

#26, Lemon Gap to Max Patch

#28, Hot Springs to Tanyard Gap

#29, Tanyard Gap to Allen Gap

#35, Iron Mt. Gap to Hughes Gap

#37, Carvers Gap to Roan High Bluff and Rhododendron Gardens

#41, Laurel Falls to Pond Mt.

#44, TN 91 to Low Gap

#45, Low Gap to Damascus

MODERATE TO STRENUOUS

#1, Springer Mt. to Hightower Gap

#3, Woody Gap to Neels Gap

#13, Wayah Bald to Tellico Gap

#40, Laurel Fork Gorge

#43, TN 91 to Watauga Dam Rd.

STRENUOUS

#2, Hightower Gap to Woody Gap

#5, Hogpen Gap to Unicoi Gap

#6, Unicoi Gap to Tray Gap

#8, Dicks Creek Gap to Deep Gap

#10, Timber Ridge Trail to Albert Mt.

#12, Winding Stair Gap to Wayah Bald

#14, Tellico Gap to Wesser

#15, Stecoah Gap to Wesser

#18, Fontana Dam to Shuckstack and Doe Knob

#19, Doe Knob to Spence Field

#20, Clingmans Dome to Spence Field

#22, Newfound Gap to Charlies Bunion to Cosby Campground

#23, Cosby Campground to Low Gap

#24, Cosby Campground to Davenport Gap

#25, Davenport Gap to Max Patch

#27, Lemon Gap to Hot Springs

#30, Allen Gap to Devil Fork Gap

#31, Devil Fork Gap to Sams Gap

#32, Sams Gap to Spivey Gap

#33, Spivey Gap to Nolichucky River

#36, Hughes Gap to Roan Mt. Cloudland Hotel Site

#38, Carvers Gap to US 19E

#39, Dennis Cove to US 19E

VERY STRENUOUS

#7, Tray Gap to Dicks Creek Gap

#34, Nolichucky River to Iron Mt. Gap

SHELTERS & CAMPSITES

See page 14 for general notes about shelters and campsites on or close to the AT. We list here the shelters, the U.S. Forest Service and National Park Service campgrounds, and some of the campsites (a.k.a. tent sites) described in this book. When shelters have tent sites nearby (within 0.4 mi.), we indicate "campsite" below. Consult the narrative of each hike for information on unofficial tent sites at some shelters and on shelters that are farther off the AT.

Hike #	Shelter	Campsite	Lodge/Cabin	Name
1	x	x		Springer Mt.
	x			Stover Creek Shelter
	x			Hawk Mt.
		x		Three Forks
2	x			Gooch Mt.
3	x			Blood Mt.
		x		Byron Reece Memorial
4	x			Whitley Gap
5	x			Low Gap
	x			Blue Mt.
6		x		Several campsites
7	x	x		Deep Gap
	x	x		Tray Mt.
8	x			Plumorchard Gap
	x	x		Muskrat Creek
9	x	x		Standing Indian
10	x	x		Carter Gap
		x		Betty Creek Gap
		x		Mooney Gap

Continued on next page

Hike #	Shelter	Campsite	Lodge/Cabin	Name
11	x	x		Big Spring
12	x	x		Siler Bald
13	x	x		Cold Spring
14	x			Wesser Bald
	x			A. Rufus Morgan
			x	Nantahala Outdoor Center
15	x			Sassafras Gap
			x	Nantahala Outdoor Center
16	x			Brown Fork
17	x	x		Cable Cove
	x			Fontana Dam (thru-hikers only)
18		x		Birch Spring
	x			Fontana Dam (thru-hikers only)
19	x			Mollies Ridge
	x			Russell Field
			x	Gregory Ridge
20			x	Double Spring Gap
			x	Silers Bald
			x	Spence Field
22	x			Icewater Spring
	x			Pecks Corner
	x			Tricorner Knob
		x		Cosby Campground
23	x			Cosby Knob
		x		Cosby Campground
24		x		Cosby Campground
	x			Davenport Gap
		x		Big Creek Campground
25		x		Big Creek Campground
		x		USFS Round Mt. Campground
	x	x		Groundhog Creek
26	x			Roaring Fork
		x		Round Mt. Campground car camping
27	x			Walnut Mt.
	x	x		Deer Park Mt.
		x		Round Mt. Campground car camping
		x	x	Hot Springs car camping

Hike #	Shelter	Campsite	Lodge/Cabin	Name
28		X		USFS Group Camp
29	X	X		Spring Mt.
30	X			Little Laurel
	X	X		Jerry Cabin
	X			Flint Mt.
31	X			Hogback Ridge
32		X		Spivey Gap Recreation Area (car camping)
	X			Big Bald
33		X		Spivey Gap Recreation Area (car camping)
	X			No Business Knob
34		X	X	Nolichucky Gorge Campground
		X		USFS Rock Creek Campground
	X			Curley Maple
	X			Cherry Gap
35	X			Clyde Smith
36		X		Ash Gap
37	X			Roan High Knob
38	X			Stan Murray
	X			Overmountain
	X			Apple House
39	X			Moreland Gap
	X			Mountaineer
		X		USFS Dennis Cove Campgound
40	X			Laurel Fork
41		X		Pond Flat
42	X	X		Watauga Lake
43	X			Iron Mt.
	X			Vanderventer
44	X	X		Double Spring
45	X	X		Abingdon Gap

Day Hikes

Depending on your starting time, physical condition, ambition, and the weather, the following hikes can be manageable day hikes. Check "Duration" and "Distance" in the information block at the beginning of the hike before starting. Many of these hikes work well as sections of longer backpacking hikes, and most appear in the "Overnight Hikes" list as well.

- #1, Springer Mt. to Hightower Gap
- #2, Hightower Gap to Woody Gap
- #3, Woody Gap to Neels Gap
- #4, Neels Gap to Hogpen Gap
- #5, Hogpen Gap to Unicoi Gap
- #6, Unicoi Gap to Tray Gap
- #7, Tray Gap to Dicks Creek Gap
- #9, Deep Gap to Timber Ridge Trail
- #10, Timber Ridge Trail to Albert Mt.
- #11, Albert Mt. Bypass to Winding Stair Gap
- #12, Winding Stair Gap to Wayah Bald
- #13, Wayah Bald to Tellico Gap
- #14, Tellico Gap to Wesser
- #16, Stecoah Gap to Yellow Creek Gap
- #17, Yellow Creek Gap to Fontana Dam
- #18, Fontana Dam to Shuckstack and Doe Knob
- #21, Newfound Gap to Clingmans Dome

- #22, Newfound Gap to Charlies Bunion to Cosby Campground
- #23, Cosby Campground to Low Gap
- #24, Cosby Campground to Davenport Gap
- #26, Lemon Gap to Max Patch
- #28, Hot Springs to Tanyard Gap
- #29, Tanyard Gap to Allen Gap
- #31, Devil Fork Gap to Sams Gap
- #33, Spivey Gap to Nolichucky River
- #35, Iron Mt. Gap to Hughes Gap
- #36, Hughes Gap to Roan Mt. Cloudland Hotel Site
- #37, Carvers Gap to Roan High Bluff and Rhododendron Gardens
- #38, Carvers Gap to US 19E
- #40, Laurel Fork Gorge
- #41, Laurel Falls to Pond Mt.
- #42, Watauga Dam Rd. to Shook Branch Recreation Area
- #43, TN 91 to Wautauga Dam Rd.
- #44, TN 91 to Low Gap
- #45, Low Gap to Damascus

Overnight Hikes

These are overnight backpacking trips. Segments of most overnight hikes can also be manageable day hikes.

- #1, Springer Mt. to Hightower Gap
- #2, Hightower Gap to Woody Gap
- #3, Woody Gap to Neels Gap

#4, Neels Gap to Hogpen Gap

#5, Hogpen Gap to Unicoi Gap

#7, Tray Gap to Dicks Creek Gap

#8, Dicks Creek Gap to Deep Gap

#9, Deep Gap to Timber Ridge Trail

#10, Timber Ridge Trail to Albert Mt.

#11, Albert Mt. Bypass to Winding Stair Gap

#12, Winding Stair Gap to Wayah Bald

#13, Wayah Bald to Tellico Gap

#14, Tellico Gap to Wesser

#15, Stecoah Gap to Wesser

#16, Stecoah Gap to Yellow Creek Gap

#17, Yellow Creek Gap to Fontana Dam

#18, Fontana Dam to Shuckstack and Doe Knob

#19, Doe Knob to Spence Field

#20, Clingmans Dome to Spence Field

#22, Newfound Gap to Charlies Bunion to Cosby Campground

#23, Cosby Campground to Low Gap

#24, Cosby Campground to Davenport Gap

#25, Davenport Gap to Max Patch

#26, Lemon Gap to Max Patch

#27, Lemon Gap to Hot Springs

#29, Tanyard Gap to Allen Gap

#30, Allen Gap to Devil Fork Gap

#31, Devil Fork Gap to Sams Gap

#32, Sams Gap to Spivey Gap

#33, Spivey Gap to Nolichucky River

#34, Nolichucky River to Iron Mt. Gap

#35, Iron Mt. Gap to Hughes Gap

#36, Hughes Gap to Roan Mt. Cloudland Hotel Site

#38, Carvers Gap to US 19E

#39, Dennis Cove to US 19E

#40, Laurel Fork Gorge

#41, Laurel Falls to Pond Mt.

#42, Watauga Dam Rd. to Shook Branch Recreation Area

#43, TN 91 to Wautauga Dam Rd.

#44, TN 91 to Low Gap

#45, Low Gap to Damascus

OTHER TRAIL SYSTEMS

Scores of trails connect to the southern AT, many of them offering vistas and facilities similar to those on the AT itself. A number of short connecting side trails are noted in the AT hike narratives in this book. Avid hikers and those wanting to avoid crowded conditions on popular sections of the AT may enjoy exploring some of these more extended trail systems.

Georgia

The Duncan Ridge National Recreational Trail (DRT), blazed with blue rectangles, runs from Three Forks (Hike #1) to Slaughter Gap (Hike #3) in 31.7 mi. and can be combined with the AT for a loop of 55 mi. For more information write to USFS, Chattahoochee National Forest, 508 Oak St., Gainesville, GA 30501.

The white-diamond-blazed Benton MacKaye Trail (BMT) starts at Springer Mt., swings west of the AT, and runs for 79 mi. in the Cohutta Mts. It extends into Tennessee and will, after more trail construction, rejoin the AT in the Smokies, providing an alternate route for long-distance hikers. For information, maps, and opportunities to help with maintenance and trail extension, contact the BMTA, P.O. Box 53271, Atlanta, GA 30355-1271. http://www.bmta.org.

North Carolina

The Bartram Trail runs northwest through western North Carolina, joining the AT at Wine Spring Bald (Hike #12) and leaving it just beyond Wayah Bald (Hike #13). It extends more than 30 mi. into Georgia and is being lengthened. When the northern part of the trail is completed, it will join the John Muir Trail in Tennessee. Where possible, the trail follows the route of William Bartram's travels of the 1770s; it is blazed with yellow rectangles. One section of the Bartram Trail near Franklin is a canoe trail. For more information and maps, contact the NC Bartram Trail Society, Route 3, Box 406, Sylva, NC 28779. http://www.bartramtrail.org.

The Mountains-to-the-Sea Trail starts at Clingmans Dome and runs with the AT for 4 mi. before heading east to go 900+ mi. to the Outer Banks. http://www.ncmst.org.

Tennessee

The Cumberland Trail, under construction, will run 220 mi. from Chattanooga to Cumberland Gap when completed. Though it does not cross the AT, it may provide an alternative route on a mountain range that is parallel to the Smokies but very different in ecology, geology, and social history. Several sections are already open, and a Breakaway Program run by Vanderbilt University recruits college students to spend their spring breaks on trail construction. For more information, contact Cumberland Trail Conference, Route 1, Box 219A, Pikeville, TN 37367. http://www .cumberlandtrail.org.

Major Organizations

American Hiking Society, 1422 Fenwick La., Silver Spring, MD 20910;
301-565-6704; http://www.americanhiking.org

Appalachian Trail Conservancy, P.O. Box 807, Harpers Ferry, WV 25425-0807;
304-535-6331; http://www.appalachiantrail.org

Southern Appalachian Hiking Clubs

Georgia Appalachian Trail Club, P.O. Box 654, Atlanta, GA 30301;
404-634-6495; http://www.georgia-atclub.org

Nantahala Hiking Club, 31 Carl Slagle Rd., Franklin, NC 28734;
http://www.nantahalahikingclub.org

Smoky Mountains Hiking Club, P.O. Box 1454, Knoxville, TN 37901;
423-558-1341; http://www.smhclub.org

Carolina Mountain Club, P.O. Box 68, Asheville, NC 28802;
http://www.carolinamountainclub.org

Tennessee Eastman Hiking Club, Bldg. 89, Eastman Rd., Kingsport, TN
37662; http://www.tehcc.org

Piedmont Appalachian Trail Hikers, P.O. Box 4423, Greensboro, NC
27404-4423; http://www.path-at.org

Note: Hikers in the southern Appalachains and others hiking in northern
states may be interested in the activities of the Appalachian Mountain Club,
5 Joy St., Boston, MA 02108; 617-523-0636. For their hiking guides: Box 298,
Gorham, NH 03581; 800-262-4455; http://www.outdoors.org

NOTE: Most websites are updated periodically. Some listed here were still in development when we visited them.

Major Organizations

American Hiking Society   http://www.americanhiking.org

Dedicated to promoting hiking and to protecting and maintaining America's trails, AHS offers programs, publications (magazine), legislative updates, volunteer vacations, and links to many clubs and resources.

Appalachian Long Distance Hikers Association   http://www.aldha.org

Aimed primarily at thru-hikers. Savvy advice, networking, forums, volunteering opportunities.

Appalachian Mountain Club   http://www.outdoors.org

Granddaddy of the eastern hiking clubs, AMC covers not only the northeastern AT but activities and trail reports on many other trails. AMC books, AMC *Outdoors* (magazine), adult and kids' activities (trips and workshops year-round), conservation initiatives, hiking trip planning, AMC hut reservations, and much more.

Appalachian Trail Conservancy   http://www.appalachiantrail.org

This site is comprehensive, with many lists of and links to regional trail clubs. ATC's "Ultimate Trail Store" has arguably the biggest selection of AT books and maps anywhere (member discounts). Updated trail conditions, permit regulations, and other helpful subjects.

AT Regional Trail Maintaining Clubs

Many regional hiking clubs have their own websites, and most of them can be found easily by way of links from the Appalachian Trail Conference website listed above. Here are some websites concerned with the AT in the states covered by this book.

Georgia AT Club Home Page   http://www.georgia-atclub.org

Nantahala Hiking Club   http://www.nantahalahikingclub.org

Tennessee Eastman Hiking Club   http://www.tehcc.org

Piedmont Appalachian Trail Hikers   http://www.path-at.org

Other AT Websites

Appalachian Trail Place   http://www.trailplace.com

Center for Appalachian Trail Studies. Hosted by Dan "Wingfoot" Bruce, a thru-hiker who lives in Hot Springs, North Carolina, near the AT. A spin-off from Wingfoot's *Thru-Hiker's Handbook*. Dozens of searchable databases on AT subjects, many especially helpful to long-distance hikers or those with natural history interests. "Mailing lists" of former and would-be thru-hikers, women hikers, teenage hikers, others. Chat rooms. Bibliography. One of the better sites.

Commercial and Government Web Sites

GENERAL

GORP   http://www.gorp.com

Great Outdoor Recreation Pages. From various purveyors of travel and outdoor adventure information, services, and supplies. The AT is one small part of this huge, diverse site. Rewarding for those with time to fill.

Magazines

Backpacker   http://www.backpacker.com

Extensive, well researched information about hiking worldwide. Many articles on either the AT specifically or on hiking skills and equipment useful to AT trekkers. "Trail Talk Forums" bring hikers together on-line. An "Encyclopedia" includes a section on "Backcountry Jargon." "Gearfinder" is a searchable database of hiking/camping products. The site is fueled by links to *Backpacker*'s advertisers, a convenience or a distraction depending on your disposition.

Outside   http://www.outsideonline.com

Most of the magazine, online. Hiking per se and the AT specifically are only occasionally featured in *Outside* (whose travel beat is worldwide), but the treatment is usually in depth and colorful. Generally aimed at the underforty crowd. Good articles on fitness and training. Excellent book reviews.

Bookstores

Amazon   http://www.amazon.com

The leader in online bookstores. Search the database for the words "Appalachian Trail" for a long list of titles.

Barnes & Noble   http://www.barnesandnoble.com

They're everywhere and they carry almost everything. If the local store doesn't have it, search online for "Appalachian Trail."

Maps

Delorme Map Co.   http://www.delorme.com

Detailed atlases for the following AT states: North Carolina, Tennessee, Virginia, Maryland, Pennsylvania, New York, Vermont, New Hampshire, Maine.

Perry-Castaneda Library Map Collection   http://www.lib.utexas.edu/maps

An extensive collection of links to on-line map resources around the world. Including not only topographic maps but also historical and weather maps.

United States Geologic Survey (USGS)
http://www.usgs.gov/pubprod/maps.html

A giant site for both the general public and scientists. This address is for ordering maps. A database facilitates finding the correct map, at the desired scale, for the area you're hiking.

Weather

The Weather Underground   http://www.wunderground.com

Up-to-the-hour weather reports and forecasts for many cities in the U.S., including numerous smaller cities near the Appalachian Trail.

National Oceanic & Atmospheric Administration   http://www.noaa.gov

NOAA offers continuously updated weather reports and forecasts all across the country on dedicated radio channels (a lightweight weather-only radio is worth carrying on extended backpacking trips). Weather forecasts are also available online.

Bibliography

Hiking Guides

Albright, Rodney, and Priscilla. *Hiking Great Smoky Mountains.* Globe Pequot Press, 1994.

Chase, Jim. *Backpacker Magazine's Guide to the Appalachian Trail.* Stackpole Books, 1989.

Chew, Collins, ed. *Appalachian Trail Guide to Tennessee–North Carolina.* Appalachian Trail Conservancy, 2009.

De Hart, Allen. *North Carolina Hiking Trails.* Appalachian Mountain Club, 1996.

Great Smoky Mountains Natural History Association. *Hiking Trails of the Smokies.* Great Smoky Mountains Association, 2004.

Hoffland, Rusty. *Mountain Getaways in Georgia, North Carolina, and Tennessee.* On the Road Publishing, 1994.

Homan, Tim. *Hiking Trails of Joyce Kilmer and Citico Creek Wilderness Areas.* Peachtree Publishers, 1990.

Homan, Tim. *The Hiking Trails of North Georgia.* Peachtree Publishers, 1997.

Johnson, Randy. *Hiking North Carolina.* Falcon Press, 1996.

Ketelle, Richard, Don O'Neal, and Lisa Williams, eds. *Appalachian Trail Guide to North Carolina–Georgia.* Appalachian Trail Conservancy, 2008.

Manning, Russ, and Sondra Jamieson. *The Best of the Great Smoky Mountains National Park.* Mountain Laurel Place, 1991.

Molloy, Johnny. *The Best in Tent Camping: Smoky Mountains.* Menasha Ridge Press, 1997.

Murray, Kenneth. *Highland Trails: A Guide to Scenic Walking and Riding Trails.* Overmountain Press, 1992.

Skelton, William H., ed. *Wilderness Trails of Tennessee's Cherokee National Forest.* University of Tennessee Press, 1992.

Wise, Kenneth. *Hiking Trails of the Great Smoky Mountains.* University of Tennessee Press, 2005.

Maps & Atlases

DeLorme. *North Carolina Atlas and Gazetteer.* DeLorme, 1993.

DeLorme. *Tennessee Atlas and Gazetteer.* DeLorme, 1992.

National Geographic Maps. *Trails Illustrated* maps. National Geographic Maps, 2011.

U.S. Geological Survey. *US Topo* maps. USGS, 2012.

Field Guides & Natural History

Alden, Peter. *Peterson First Guide to Mammals of North America.* Houghton Mifflin, 1987.

Alsop, Fred J. *Birds of the Smokies.* Great Smoky Mountains Natural History Association, 1991.

Chew, V. Collins. *Underfoot: A Geologic Guide to the Appalachian Trail.*

Appalachian Trail Conference, 1993.

Hutson, Robert W., William F. Hutson, & Aaron J. Sharp. *Great Smoky Mountain Wildflowers.* Windy Pines Publishing, 1995.

Kemp, Steve. *Trees of the Smokies.* Great Smoky Mountains Natural History Association, 1993.

Lawrence, Eleanor, and Cecilia Fitzsimons. *An Instant Guide to Trees.* Longmeadow Press, 1991.

Moore, Harry L. *A Roadside Guide to the Geology of the Great Smoky Mountains National Park.* University of Tennessee Press, 1988.

Newcomb, Lawrence. *Newcomb's Wildflower Guide.* Little, Brown, 1977.

Peterson, Lee Allen. *A Field Guide to Edible Wild Plants of Eastern and Central North America.* Houghton Mifflin, 1977.

Peterson, Roger Tory. *Peterson First Guide to Birds of North America.* Houghton Mifflin, 1986.

Peterson, Roger Tory. *Peterson First Guide to Wildflowers of Northeastern and North-central North America.* Houghton Mifflin, 1986.

Sutton, Ann, and Myron Sutton. *Eastern Forests* (Audubon Field Guide). Alfred A. Knopf, 1993.

Watts, May Theilgaard. *Tree Finder.* Nature Study Guild, 1986.

White, Peter. *Wildflowers of the Smokies.* Great Smoky Mountains Natural History Association, 1996.

General Books: Appalachian Trail

Appalachian Trail Conference. *Walking the Appalachian Trail Step by Step,* Appalachian Trail Conference, 1993.

Brill, David. *As Far As the Eye Can See.* Rutledge Hill Press, 1990.

Bruce, Dan "Wingfoot." *The Thru-Hiker's Handbook.* Center for Appalachian Trail Studies, 1997. (Updated annually)

Chazin, Daniel D. *Appalachian Trail Data Book 1996.* Appalachian Trail Conservancy, 1997. (Updated annually)

Emblidge, David, ed. *The Appalachian Trail Reader.* Oxford University Press, 1997.

Fisher, Ronald M. *The Appalachian Trail.* National Geographic Society, 1972.

Mueser, Roland. *Long Distance Hiking: Lessons from the Appalachian Trail.* Ragged Mt. Press, 1998.

O'Brien, Bill, ed. *Appalachian Trail Thru-Hikers' Companion.* Appalachian Trail Conference, 1997. (Updated annually)

Whalen, Christopher. *The Appalachian Trail Workbook for Planning Thru-Hikes,* Appalachian Trail Conference, 1995.

Practical Advice: Hiking & Camping

Berger, Karen. *Hiking & Backpacking: A Complete Guide.* W. W. Norton, 1995.

Cary, Alice. *Parents' Guide to Hiking & Camping.* W. W. Norton, 1997.

Fletcher, Colin. *The Complete Walker.* Alfred A. Knopf, 1984.

McManners, Hugh. *The Backpacker's Handbook.* Dorling Kindersley, 1995.

Meyer, Kathleen. *How to Shit in the Woods: An Environmentally Sound Approach to a Lost Art.* Ten Speed Press, 1994.

Viehman, John, ed. *Trailside's Hints & Tips for Outdoor Adventures.* Rodale Press, 1993.

Wood, Robert S. *The 2 Oz. Backpacker.* Ten Speed Press, 1982.

Background Reading

Campbell, Carlos. *Birth of a National Park*. University of Tennessee Press, 1969.

Dykeman, Wilma. *The French Broad*. Rhinehart, 1955.

Hudson, Patricia L., and Sandra L. Ballard, *The Smithsonian Guide to Historic America: The Carolinas and the Appalachian States.* Stewart, Tabori and Chang, 1989.

Mooney, James. *Myths of the Cherokee & Sacred Formulas of the Cherokee.* Cherokee Heritage Books, 1982.

Murray, Kenneth. *Footsteps of the Mountain Spirits . . . Appalachia.* Overmountain Press, 1992.

Schlesinger, Arthur M., Jr., ed. *The Almanac of American History.* Perigee Books, 1983.

Waterman, Laura and Guy. *Forest and Crag: A History of Hiking, Trail Blazing, and Adventure in the Northeast Mountains.* Appalachian Mountain Club, 1989.

Index

Page numbers in *italic* refer to topographic maps and itineraries.

ABOUT THE AUTHOR

DORIS GOVE has a lifelong interest in biology and natural history. Her writing includes five books for children; trail narratives, nature trail brochures, and science journal articles for the Great Smoky Mountains Natural History Association; and magazine articles. She has directed two environmental education centers and taught high school, college, and adult programs such as ElderHostel. Gove grew up in Massachusetts, studied at Barnard College, earned a Ph.D. in biology at the University of Tennessee, and taught with the U.S. Peace Corps in Africa. She lives in Tennessee with her husband and daughter and prefers writing jobs that require hiking.

The Exploring the Appalachian Trail™ series

Hikes in the Southern Appalachians: Georgia, North Carolina, Tennessee
by Doris Gove $21.95   400 pages

Hikes in the Virginias: Virginia, West Virginia
by David Lillard and Gwyn Hicks $19.95   432 pages

Hikes in the Mid-Atlantic States: Maryland, Pennsylvania, New Jersey, New York
by Glenn Scherer and Don Hopey $21.95   384 pages

Hikes in Southern New England: Connecticut, Massachusetts, Vermont
by David Emblidge $21.95   304 pages

Hikes in Northern New England: New Hampshire, Maine
by Michael Kodas, Andrew Weegar, Mark Condon, Glenn Scherer $19.95   400 pages

Available from your favorite bookseller or outdoor retailer, or from the publisher.

STACKPOLE
BOOKS
5067 Ritter Road
Mechanicsburg, PA 17055
1-800-732-3669
www.stackpolebooks.com